AF587534

CONVERSATIONS 3

For Maria-Karina and Marpessa,
again and always.

RÉMI COIGNET
CONVERSATIONS 3

LAURENCE AËGERTER

Laurence Aëgerter was born in Marseilles in 1972. She lives and works between Amsterdam and Marseilles. Her practice includes photography, in situ *installations, participatory projects, textile work and artist's books. Her work is included in many private and public collections, including the J. Paul Getty Centre, Los Angeles; the New York Public Library; the Metropolitan Museum of Art, New York; the Dolhuys Museum of the Mind, Haarlem; the Fries Museum, Leeuwarden; the Museum Van Loon, Amsterdam; the MAMAC, Nice; and the Bibliothèque Nationale de France, Paris. She is the recipient of the Nestlé International Prize for Photography awarded at the 2015 Images Vevey Festival, and the Rencontres d'Arles Book of the Year Award in 2018 for* Photographic Treatment©. *She is the author of 11 books to date.*

Congruence is probably the term that could best define the work of Laurence Aëgerter, an amazing artist, both in her appropriation practice and her collaborative research. She also has an inclination for re-enactment, which goes as far as to re-interpret photographs taken by Claude Lévi-Strauss in Brazil in the 1950s, by the inhabitants of a village in … the northern Netherlands! While the book is one of her favourite playing fields, intervention in the public space is also part of her explorations. Appropriation has arguably become an established artistic genre, and Laurence Aëgerter offers a singular approach to the principle, often taking hold of dated publications, dictionaries or museum guides, twisting them around in uncanny ways. Meaning that the selected publications always carry an emotional charge for her, which may not be directly brought forward but is nonetheless underlying her work. With *Photographic Treatment©*, recipient of the Author Book Award at the Rencontres d'Arles in 2018, Laurence Aëgerter closely brings together three of her major interests: appropriation, collaboration (even as a social practice) and the work of art. Conversation in my library. In a cordial yet humorous gesture, which I didn't immediately perceive, Laurence offered me two pots of heather, a subtle echo to her book *Meer Vreugde Met Kamerplanten* [More joy with house plants].

She also brought some of the very limited editions of her artist's books, so that we could explore the various levels of meaning she develops.

Rémi Coignet: *Appropriation is a large part of your work, even if you often deliver hybrid versions of it, away from the practice of the great predecessors of the 1980s – I'm thinking of Sherrie Levine, among others. A special feature of your work is not only that you appropriate images but also already existing book forms. What does this mean?*

Laurence Aëgerter: Why do I make facsimiles? If we look at *180° Encyclopaedia*; *Tristes Tropiques: illustrations hors texte*; *Catalogue des chefs-d'oeuvre du musée du Louvre*; and *Meer Vreugde Met Kamerplanten*, this will help me to answer. I will try to reply book by book. Because it's hard for me to do a global analysis, but I'll try.

RC: So, the four books you just mentioned are: an encyclopaedia; a dictionary; a catalogue from the Louvre; and a gardening manual. It's a double appropriation.

LA: Yes, and there is also *Cathédrales*, a book about France's cathedrals and churches. What does that allow for? Well, in *180° Encyclopaedia* and *Catalogue des chefs-d'oeuvre du musée du Louvre*, for example, this was absolutely necessary, since the point was to infiltrate the book itself. The form of the work had to be accurately similar to that of its source. It had to be a double that takes you elsewhere. There is a slightly subversive side to this. But for me at least, it's always more of a tribute than irony or derision. Of course, I select books that I like very much. I wouldn't be so crazy as to work with books that bother me. It's always a tribute in the beginning, because they are books that interest me for what they represent or what they are. For example, I love the lyricism of the text and the graphics in the Louvre catalogue. For the encyclopaedia, it was a love-hate relationship because I was annoyed that a book could describe the world as it is. How could I express this, because it shrinks everything … Of course, it's convenient, but somehow, it's unacceptable to describe the world like that! [Laughs] So consistently, so rigorously, when for each proposal, there are endless underlying perceptions, which is why I worked on the reverse of the depicted landscapes.

RC: We're going to talk about that, yes.

LA: The images in the encyclopaedia are deceptively objective and definitive. In this case, I really needed to start from the source object, very clearly, to achieve this infiltration that allows a reversal of the situation, of the gaze. A gesture that leads the reader who is holding the book in hand to adopt a reflective attitude in relation to the usual use of an encyclopaedia, a dictionary or a museum catalogue. The readers find themselves placed in a surprising, slightly uncomfortable situation that can sometimes be humorous while somewhat disturbing, since we all have reflexes, habits in our use of these referential objects.

RC: Let's look back for a moment on your first book from 2005, A Meeting on Paper, *the appropriation of a Dutch encyclopaedia. And, in fact, you only kept the lemma, a word I didn't know.*[1]

LA: Me neither, I only found out when I did this project. [Laughs] It's a nice word.

RC: Very beautiful! So, you kept the lemma at the top of the page and the image that coincidentally was underneath, and deleted the rest of the page.

LA: Yes. You see, for example, we have an Osaka pagoda, and above, it reads "Osborne".
The attitude is the same as in the two books we previously mentioned. It's about blurring the lines. And perhaps, behind it, there is a will to loosen up the meaning and open the field

[1] A lemma is the word printed in bold and placed at the top of the first column of a dictionary page. It shows the first entry of the page, allowing you to quickly find a precise word in the alphabetical order.

of possibilities ... As a way to leave more freedom in the approach of the world, perhaps. In any case, I grant myself that freedom by doing this work, and I wish to share it with those who might be sensitive to it, who might enjoy it by watching this work.

RC: On another page of the book, you selected the lemma "Dictator", and underneath, there was a photo of a potted plant ...

LA: Yes, because anything is possible. Once again, it raises many possible reflections, free associations of ideas ... Can a plant be a dictator? Can a dictator be a green plant? If so, under what circumstances? And what stories can develop from this starting point? So, in fact, these are proposals to generate an infinite number of scenarios.

RC: We'll talk about green plants later with your book that has a Dutch title that's ... well, unpronounceable and incomprehensible. [Laughs] Fortunately, Google helped me translate it.

LA: Yes, *Meer Vreugde Met Kamerplanten* [More joy with houseplants].

RC: You often associate images and texts. This is the case in A Meeting on Paper, *but also in your second book, in 2006,* LA LA LA LA, *which we have here, with video stills of karaoke. I see it as a Dadaist poem, or* cadavre exquis. *What was your purpose with this book?*

LA: Well, there were a lot of possible combinations of images and texts, but these are just pre-existing combinations. I simply extracted them from reality, they are "24ths of a second".

RC: Yes, film stills.

LA: That's it. I first collected a large number of images and image-texts that I found of interest. And for one reason or another, they contradicted or complemented each other. In any case, the two elements interacted with each other, which surprised me in a way. Then I restricted my selection, because I had gathered, if I remember correctly, almost 200 of them. I kept 16 that coincided with my state of mind at the time. Ideas and feelings that inhabited me. So, even if it's completely invisible, I made it into a kind of self-portrait of my concerns of the moment, not at all in a literal way. So, *cadavre exquis*, perhaps the expression of the unconscious. Though this literary game was played collectively.

RC: Yes, the surrealists each wrote a word to form a sentence.

LA: Let's say that in this case, the cameraman was certainly not very professional – well, mostly the producer wasn't. The cameraman actually looks pretty good. But, between us, it looks like it was done with friends. As for the people who pasted the texts under the images, it's clear that they have given no thought to it. So perhaps they too were surrealists. Seen from this angle, they were around the table with me to write this poem, this "exquisite corpse". [Laughs] Let's say that I extracted from these video stills the few elements that I could associate with the most.

RC: In 2007 you introduced a new and important aspect in your practice: collaborative work. 180° Encyclopaedia *is a facsimile of the 1972* Petit Larousse. *You replaced 167 images of places and monuments presented in the dictionary with images showing the exact reverse of the place depicted. For example, instead of the representation of Notre-Dame de Paris, you show a bus passing by and the police headquarters right across the forecourt. In addition, you invited friends and artists to participate, to contribute to the project according to a very strict protocol. I have several questions. Where does your obsession with dictionaries, catalogues, etc. come from? And why show what, according to the editorial "institution", is of no interest?*

LA: So now you're asking me a question that I need to take time to think about. Where does that come from? I can tell you that the dictionary I used for *180°* was mine when I was 15 or 16 years old. I used it for school, but I also used it to dream.

It allowed me to discover the world through the vignettes of landscapes. It offered me an escape from my daily life, in fact. And I couldn't wait to be 18 to be able to do what I wanted and go on an adventure. To literally jump into the vignettes. But, as I said earlier, at the same time it also annoyed me a lot because it was too restrictive in a sense. I still have that dictionary, on which I had written in large letters and red pencil: "A dictionary is sacred", followed with something like three or four question marks, on the flyleaf. So, for me, this was a statement. [Laughs] And in fact, it was ironic, because it was both the case and not so. Yes, it is sacred, because we need these references and they fascinated me.

RC: A dictionary is a bible.

LA: You're right. But it is not so, because it says a lot and at the same time nothing. Many things are wrong or could be said much better or differently. In any case, it would be good not to claim to be right when everything is always changing.

RC: Nor to be complete, because each year there is a new edition of the dictionary.

LA: Exactly. And with each edition, the authors present themselves in the prefaces as very modest and doing their best. But when you look at the object critically, this person is very important and is going to have so many lines, and that one, perhaps less considered, is still on the page but only with two or three lines.

RC: And they will vanish a few years from now.

LA: Yes. So, in the section of the proper names, we have monuments, famous people, artworks, mainly; and countries, an interesting field as well. But the question also generally arises for catalogues. There's something magical about classification because it openly gives you the opportunity to deregulate the mechanics of it. It's an invitation to play the game: since rules are already laid, we can fiddle with them, upset them. Yes, maybe that's what I like doing.

RC: And is playing important for you?

LA: Oh, very important! It's the main thing, because I think it's through play that we best express the most serious and deepest things. And that we can achieve the most profound transformation. In yourself and in others. I strongly believe this.

RC: Starting with 180°, *you developed a very important collaborative practice. And for this specific project, you invited other artists or friends, according to a relatively strict protocol.*

LA: Yes, very strict. And in total contradiction of course. [Laughs] But it was necessary that the protocol be strict because otherwise it would have been a mess. It was therefore necessary to determine a precise approach, not exhaustive either, but properly developed all the same. If I remember correctly, at the time I had calculated that I had replaced about half of everything that was photographed outdoors, monuments and landscapes, in this *Larousse*. I covered a few countries myself – France, Italy, Belgium too. And for the rest of the world, I asked my friends for help by sending them the original little vignettes and asking them to use them as control photos, to find the right place, and be very accurate in re-photographing them: if this meant going up three flights of stairs, well it was absolutely necessary to climb them. The exact position had to be determined, which is not at all obvious at times. And then simply turn around to take the picture you see in my book.

RC: Yes, and the protocol suggested to your friends can be found on your internet site.

LA: Oh really? I can't even remember having put it online! [Laughs]

RC: It's very interesting to read.

LA: Yes, it helps to understand. I was pretty strict about it because otherwise, as I said, the work would have lost its value and purpose. This kind of work requires a German-style upstream precision. [Laughs] It had to be correct.

RC: Apart from the practicality of having correspondents all over the world for this specific project, what is the greater interest of collaborative work?

LA: The interest of collaboration is to bring air. To reach beyond my own limits, my own eyes, my own choices, my aspirations ... Furthermore, an encyclopaedia aims to reach out to the largest audience. It's really for everyone. In this case, of course, there was a very practical aspect: I couldn't run around the world on my own. And it did take me a year and a half, or even two years, to complete the project. But above all, it was very enjoyable to share this adventure with many friends and friends of friends. To see what they collected during their strolls or in their resorts, to recover the elements, receive their messages and the stories that sometimes came with them. This is a personal wealth that I didn't explore, that I didn't put in the book, because I didn't want the project to become documentary. I wanted it to stay pretty dry. And finally, the protocol I was imposing was so precise, it shows that I'm absolutely interchangeable [in the process].

RC: In 2009 you initiated a project on a 1976 book, a catalogue of masterpieces from the Louvre Museum. The book is a facsimile of the original, kind of kitsch today with its 1970s aesthetic and graphic design. But you replaced 48 of the original images with others you took yourself for 3 days "as a tourist" in the Louvre. You photographed with an amateur camera and you can see the visitors in front of the artworks. Obviously, it reminds me of Thomas Struth's Museum Photographs *series in the late 1980s. Was it a reference for you? Or did you want to take the flipside of it? Or was it to disrupt the reading of a catalogue designed for a general audience?*

LA: It's not a reference to Struth's series, because I didn't know it when I started the project. Quickly, friends showed it to me. But it didn't bother me at all, because I thought he had an extremely different approach than what I was looking to design.

RC: Yes, between 3x2-metres prints on a wall and small vignettes in a book, there's a difference.

LA: True enough. And moreover, I reduced the framing of the images to the surface of the painting, so the environment and even the frame are excluded. The starting points are really different. I really feel his approach to the museum is more of a sociological, ethnographic or documentary study, an aspect that is not primary in my work. Obviously, considering the context, there are commonalities, because people wear the clothes they wear, have the hair or the hairstyles they have. But I didn't feel it was a valid reason not to do this project, because for me, they are completely different spheres. What was the second part of your question?

RC: Was it to disrupt the reading of a catalogue designed for a larger audience?

LA: I don't really think my intent was to disrupt. Let's take an example: here I have *Saint Joseph the Carpenter* by Georges de La Tour with its Caravaggio light, and in front of it, the blond hair of an elderly lady. The point is not to disturb; it's a story of collisions, of total chance. I didn't spend hours waiting for the right "match", so to speak. I wasn't interested in that kind of approach either. Things were there in front of me, offered to me. I was able to wait sometimes two or three minutes, but if nothing happened, well, I would take what was coming and then I would go to the next painting. So, my point was not necessarily to disturb. What I really wanted to see was what chance could offer you in the perception of an existing work of art and perhaps also in the deepening of its understanding. There is certainly a disturbance, but mostly the notion of reopening, re-suggesting, and therefore even deepening. Indeed sometimes, and even quite regularly and surprisingly, situations seem to have been staged but that is not the case. When you look with that eye, amazing little miracles often happen without having to produce much of an effort. [Laughs]

RC: A hanging is a staging.

LA: The hanging is the setting, yes, but tourists or visitors passing while you are there, that's chance. So, the work is like a double staging, if you will. There is a fixed aspect and a moving one. And that movement brings this project closer to that of the karaoke images. The difference being that the painting does not move. In a way, I place myself in a position to come across images that make sense in spite of themselves. Which are sometimes metaphors. And sometimes, they lead nowhere. It's a bit like you're a ball in a small pipe ... and there were many possible openings on the way.

RC: You mean like a pinball machine?

LA: No. But you have many small openings that offer exit doors. Though not all of them come through at the end of the day. Not everything is interesting. The question that I ask myself, and that I ask others, is to look at what is interesting or not. And to come to terms with the fact that, all the same, many situations are so. Without making much effort, they offer you unexpected exit doors that will enrich your experience.

RC: Maybe this can bring us to your next book: 10 Days, 22 Months. *It seems to me that this is your most personal or autobiographical book: the connection with the crash of a plane from El Al in a suburb of Amsterdam; the reproduction of newspaper headlines and photos published in the 10 days following the disaster; and the accidental death of your cousin, whose portrait you re-photographed over a period of 22 months, the size of the original photograph decreasing over time like a* mise en abyme. *So, it seems to me that time and space, through appropriation and collaboration, are two major aspects of your work. What is your relationship to these two notions of time and space?*

LA: Time and space sum up in merely two words the great adventure of being alive. They therefore touch on the essence of the human condition. And obviously, I do, again and again, ask myself these existential questions via multiple forms with various and varied emotions. They're exciting, they're fascinating. They affect us a thousand times more than an accumulation of anecdotes that can be interesting, but time and space, however, are the highlight of the story.

RC: I feel like this is the project in which you are the most involved in, meaning that it's the one in which you have clearly highlighted the relationship between public and private.

LA: True, you're right. Well, in a very visible and clear way. But you know, the Louvre catalogue was given to me by my father, when we visited the museum together when I was a teenager. So for me, there is also a private-public relationship. It was in my library. The same goes for the dictionary that we were talking about earlier, *180°*. There is, not always though often, a very personal dimension in the selection of the book, of the reference text. And in these cases, it's no easy task.

RC: I guess it can be very painful.

LA: It's painful because I wouldn't want to be, how to say ...

RC: Dramatic?

LA: You need to be fair. Both in the emotion and in the distance from it. You know what I mean? To not make a deep and personal sadness impermeable and cold. I'd be really sorry if I did that, you know. But I find these to be complex issues, very complex even. And you need to take a fair distance. Otherwise I wouldn't be interested, it doesn't match with my character to act otherwise. So, finding the proportion in the distance established with the emotion is important in this work. Then, the result comes out of an intuition. I'm not going to probe the elements for years on end. It's still pretty straightforward. You test things, and it's yes or no.

RC: Moving on to something somewhat lighter. In 2010 you published An Alphabetical Index of Some of the Stories, *which takes the shape of a Chinese restaurant menu on which each dish is usually pictured. What you did was to photograph the hands of diners and you replaced the images of the dishes with these. You say it's a tribute to Perec, why so? Is this an attempt at exhaustion? [Laugh]*

LA: These are people who say, "I want this, I want that." They're the diners. And the dishes are really those in front of them. I bothered them and photographed them while they were eating. What made this possible is that the restaurant had this long bench. I was sitting at a table that allowed me to talk easily to all my neighbours and integrate their story. The title is *An Alphabetical Index of SOME of the Stories* because the restaurant offered a very large number of dishes. I think there were 100 of them. I limited myself to the number of dishes on the menu. [Laughs] The restaurant is located in an underprivileged area of Amsterdam called the Bijlmer. They serve Chinese-inspired Suriname cuisine. The reference to Perec comes from the fact that at the end of his book *La Vie mode d'emploi* [*Life: A User's Manual*], there's an index titled, if I remember correctly, "Index of Some of the Stories"[2]. That's where the title comes from. And my favourite part in his book is the notion of the index. Naturally, mine is different from his. I don't remember his so well as to tell you the exact difference or the why and the how, because this work goes back quite some time. But I was completely fascinated by the book. All of Perec's work influenced me a lot at one time because he did all this work of classification, play, chance, and the staging of chance.

RC: It's also connected to the dictionary.

LA: Absolutely. And then to establish this protocol of sitting always at the same table for several days over the course of a month or two, until collecting enough stories to match

[2] *The exact title of the summary of* La vie mode d'emploi *is « Reminder of Some of the Stories Told in this Book ».*

the menu, combined with people's chance sitting beside me and listening to what they had to tell me, keeping only one sentence in the end. The one that most impressed me and which was in itself an invitation to an additional stroll. Or a movie to be made. [Laughs] Beyond this, the social aspect is much more direct than in Perec's book, because in his case, it is constructed fiction. Whereas here, I'm working on the real ... You have the hands of different people who exist, eating what's in front of them. This is one of the most prosaic things in life, and at the same time, the most spiritual. [Laughs] So there are several layers of reading. In the end, it was about encounters, and I keep the overall memory that it was quite cheerful to get in touch with so many different people and listen to their stories, even when they were disturbing. I felt like a little mouse in someone's life for a while, and took something out of it that I would subsequently put back into play.

RC: Let's get to Triste Tropiques: illustrations hors texte. *For me, this is one of your most fascinating books. It comprises two notebooks: the first is a facsimile of the photos taken in Brazil by Claude Lévi-Strauss and reproduced in a separate folio in the first edition of* Tristes Tropiques*; the second is a re-enactment, 80 years later, of the scenes presented in this separate section, which you asked people in northern Holland to reinterpret.*

LA: In a small village.

RC: In a small village indeed. Again, the question of time and space arises. But also working in public, collaborating with people who are not necessarily artists, which is another strong aspect in your work, from 180° *to* Photographic Treatment©. *What was your aim in making Dutch people replay situations perceived by Lévi-Strauss as part of an ethos?*

LA: I didn't have a clearly defined or sole purpose. Rather, I felt it was obvious to do it. But today, I would say that it was rather several aims. My first and major question was, "Is this possible?" With the help of my friend Ronald van Tienhoven, who collaborated with me for this work, I had put myself in the position of being “exotic” to them. I had landed in this very wild “Far North” that is Friesland with my typically familiar behaviour: coming from the south, Marseilles, I can sometimes be quite warm in the way I relate with people, something that does not always agree with their ways …

RC: Even if you don't look so much like you are from Marseilles when we look at or listen to you. But I can understand that for Dutch people … [Laughs]

LA: In any case, not that they are stiff people at all, but I thought we would have some cultural differences to overcome, which I was going to experience again. I already knew the Netherlands for a long time, but I thought I'd reach a higher level of knowledge. [Laughs] Because I was going up north, and furthermore, it's commonplace to say that they have a wild side and are not very accommodating. So I thought, “Well, we'll see.” In fact, it was a challenge; was it possible to reconstitute these photos? It was also a challenge in terms of my integration in the Netherlands, because although I'm fluent in Dutch, my accent and my errors are such that I'm clearly not “one of them”. And it was a huge challenge because a lot of the photos were nudes. Can you imagine? The main question was how close one can approach the other with very different cultural identities, how human…

RC: Different, you mean between Lévi-Strauss and Brazil or the Netherlands and you?

LA: Both, in parallel. This raises the issue of intimacy, in fact. And how one can share the intimate and the trust without always having the operating codes of a group. How much trust can you gain? Can the integrity of the process be enough to spark the generosity of strangers? How far can we understand each other, and freely exchange? In Lévi-Strauss's book, the folio is titled “Illustration insert”. It is placed at the end of the book. This is important because in fact, he didn't use any of the 63 photos to illustrate his theories; they were a pleasure for him.

I opted to work with the very first edition because in later editions, the photos were scattered throughout the book. In this first edition, it's a separate folio and it's clear to me that it's personal. That he thinks it's important, but that he also enjoys sharing with the rest of the world his view of the relationship, the intimacy that was established with the dwellers of the three villages in which he stayed.
These are extremely intimate pictures where you see couples tickling each other, rolling on the floor, laughing. Happy girlfriends, others, more or less so. There is a child with a monkey on his head, a pregnant woman asleep on the ground ... In short, their everyday life.
I've never considered Lévi-Strauss as a voyeur, because I feel too much interest, too much humanity in his photos. In any case, this is my interpretation of his work; I feel the love told for a human community rather than any form of voyeurism. It's my approach and my personal conviction anyway.
I wanted to propose to the villagers from Beetserzwaag to repeat the experience. It's a very small village, there are one or two main streets and two perpendicular others. I also wanted to see if it was possible to recreate the photos within a perimeter of 3 kilometres around the small village, both in terms of landscapes and of human interactions. I thought about the concept before I even set foot there. It was quite a challenge. [Laughs] Thank God, with Ronald's combined work, the miracle was total and the experience wonderful and amazing. So much so that, at times, the villagers involved took hold of the project. They interpreted it in ways that no longer suited me. [Laughs] But somehow, it was also good because I didn't want us to get stuck in a hermetically strict protocol. Seeing what is liberated, confident in what is human, what works and what doesn't, is an important aspect of this counter-exploration, a process by which I don't seek at all to do the same as Lévi-Strauss. It's quite different. It's even the opposite of what he's done, since he's studied people in their daily lives, when I suggested to other people to get completely out of their own daily life.

RC: Yes, you have them replay existing images by taking them out of their daily lives.

LA: Indeed, since I created the images made with the village dwellers from Lévi-Strauss's images. But I understand as being at once distressing and interesting, both ethnologically or sociologically, that some of his images could still correspond to their own lives and others, not anymore. For example, a dreamy teenage girl with her head tilted is timeless. While a naked pregnant woman lying in the middle of the landscape probably still exists, but not frequently, in the Netherlands at least. In fact, more than a purpose, it was an experience that I was looking for. You're asking me, "What was your goal?" My answer: it was an open experience. The point was to see whether it could work out, what was going to happen and what it could mean. It was a proposal.

RC: Cathédrales, *published in 2014, is an intimate meditation and, once again, a book appropriation. You chose to re-photograph in your studio a double-page spread of a 1950s book featuring the Bourges Cathedral, with the light moving on the spread as the hours go by. Of course, we think of Claude Monet. As with him, it is a reflection about light; but I also see, again, a reflection about time and its representation through photography. The time that photography is supposed to freeze. The famous "it has been". Is there a desire in this work to reach beyond that point of view that has become a form of dogma?*

LA: I'm not sure I understand what you mean ...

RC: I'm referring to Roland Barthes, who, in Camera Lucida, *basically stated – simplifying it to the extreme – that the only thing you can say with certainty about a photo is that "it has been". So when you made* Cathédrales, *I wonder if there isn't in the work a desire to reach beyond that notion, which has become a bit cliché for me, somewhat dated, that a photograph boils down to "it has been" – it belongs to the past, necessarily to the past.*

LA: Right. In this book, it is indeed quite the opposite. I think the work stems from the idea that everything has always been. And that everything will always be. The cycle of time is the most important. And I would add that if it's not really an end in itself, there's still a little narrative side to the book. *Cathédrales* is perhaps a metaphor through the image, where one could tell time like with a rosary. You always return to the beginning. Even if basically there is no beginning or end. You're going around in circles. These are stratifications of time. It's a sandwich of several eras: you have a medieval cathedral, you have a book from the 1950s, you have a shadow that was that of a few years ago in my studio but that can perhaps be considered timeless. So, this work is mostly about movement, perpetual movement. More than about the end of anything. And also about the desire for a time perpetually on the move, of an image perpetually in motion. Because I didn't want the cathedral to disappear completely at the end. I was especially happy that it was always present, even in the last pictures. Even when it is completely absorbed by the shadow.

RC: In 2015 you published Healing Plants for Hurt Landscapes. *With local people from Leeuwarden in the Netherlands. You took part in the reconstruction of the medicinal garden of the Abbey of St Gall. And at the same time, you searched the internet for images of disasters, either natural or man-induced, and you invited the residents or the inhabitants to "cure" the images with medicinal plants ...*

LA: That's right. That's exactly right. [Laughs]

RC: Thank you! An approach that is obviously as symbolic as it is aesthetic. First, what does the participation of the inhabitants bring to this second phase, where it is a matter of curing images? And what is your discourse about the past, the present, the possibility of rebuilding, the destruction of the environment, and of images?

LA: Sorry, the first question again please?

RC: What does the participation of the inhabitants bring?

LA: Why wouldn't I do it on my own? Because what I wanted was to share the experience. And also because the project had a social vocation. Artistic and social. The city of Leeuwarden commissioned me to carry out an artistic project that would help bring more cohesion to a disadvantaged neighbourhood with high unemployment, a lot of loneliness, etc. That was really my starting point. And I feel that in order to feel better, what can greatly contribute to this is to help others. It's a simple starting point. Voltaire writes in *Candide*, "We must cultivate our garden." But we could turn the proposal around and say, "Our garden must cultivate us."

The project works both ways. It's a back-and-forth between taking care of oneself, taking care of others, taking care of a garden, of objects ... To be caring is a way of looking at things. It's a completely symbolic act. That also deals with the pleasure of tinkering with the material.

For example, plants smell extremely good when grounded in the mortar: this relates to genuine physical enjoyment. Then comes the fragrance, the touch and the visual in this small kitchen of benevolence. But there is also, clearly, an absurd aspect, in the sense that, of course, no one is going to retrospectively cure anyone or anything by placing a cataplasm on the image of a tsunami. And that's when the process becomes very complex. [Laughs] Indeed, anything symbolic is tricky to express. I sincerely believe that it is possible to set in motion profound transformations in people, perhaps to arouse their empathy or very profound but dormant processes. I didn't do it by playing the psychologist or the therapist. I didn't mean it that way at all. But looking back at it with hindsight, I think to myself, "Here, you still tried to encourage empathy, contact with others, self-awareness." The very material and very sensory aspect of the work is super-important to participate in this process. Most of all, it was about expressing an intention. That of repair, of well-being delivered to someone else, to a distant, inaccessible other. By that, I mean that we worked on landscapes from all over the world, but also on images far back in time since there were also images of the Second World War, for example, landscapes that have changed a lot since then. I think I was suggesting them to express a positive intention. It seems to me that this is a pretty nice step to take together. My role was to propose it, then to realize it with them. I did some of these landscapes myself, with great joy.

RC: Healing Plants for Hurt Landscapes is a book but it also exists in another aspect of your work: your interventions in the public space.

LA: Yes. I put all my heart into that garden, and it's a very accurate reconstitution of St Gall's medicinal plant garden. It continues to exist, at least for a few years still, until the city repurposes the place, probably with buildings. But it exists, it is alive, it is fully part of the daily life of the inhabitants of the surrounding area.

RC: You mentioned it, but it was also about going back to the destruction of the images. You chose images of destruction and tried to "cure" them.

LA: Yes. These are devastated landscapes that would be "cured" by the symbolic gesture, and this is a completely hypothetical assumption, as in a fairy tale. [Laughs] It sounds like the Dutch children's game called *heksensoep* [witches' brew]. You mix a lot of ingredients and then you make this or that with it. But the greatest pleasure is in the making of it. [Laughs] We can't go back to what happened. There will always be disasters, but we can, in reverse, wish the best for the victims, even if they are very rarely present in the landscapes I have selected. But the landscape that has suffered is itself very present. And it is well understood that all the living beings who inhabited that landscape suffered with it.

RC: It's in part what you deal with in 10 Days, 22 Months, *right?*

LA: Yes, it's true. Because these are photos that have a public purpose. The images were used by the press for information during these disasters. But it's a treatment ...

RC: Different ...

LA: Yes, it's a very personal search applied to public images. Since each participant was able to choose their photographs of devastated landscapes and their medicinal plants, their way of applying them ...

RC: In fact, you are a witch!

LA: That's it! [Laughs] Damn ...

RC: In 2015 you published Meer Vreugde Met Kamerplanten, *which can be translated as "More joy with houseplants."*

LA: Yes. [Laugh]

RC: This book marks both your continued interest in botany and your first foray into the psychiatric world.
You had patients and caregivers pose indiscriminately with a flowerpot ...

LA: With houseplants. Sometimes flowery, sometimes not.

RC: What was the purpose of this work?

LA: Let me think ... again, the goal was not unique. To begin with, what I wanted with the work, in a rather humorous way, was to stretch a mirror in the context of a closed psychiatric environment ... I worked on isolation cells. In this given context, I transformed an isolation cell of 9 square metres into a nursery for one day.
This work is part of a larger project called "Leviathan".
This book is therefore only part of this larger project that now exists in the form of a video installation at the Museum of Psychiatry in Haarlem, which commissioned the project.
Going back to that week spent in this institution, every day I would transform an isolation cell. One day, it was a museum of Orientalism, with a guide who organized tours; another, it was a terrarium with five giant pythons that stretched out on branches and we observed them from a distance; another day, it was a re-enactment of a Kabakov piece, *Punishment of Household Objects*: behind a large black curtain, I suggested that patients punish a domestic object that bothered them for one reason or another. And if they didn't have the object they had in mind, they could make it out of clay. On another day, it was a meditation centre with directed group mediation.
Finally on Sunday, the room was transformed into a concert hall

with a grand piano on which Simeon ten Holt's *Canto Ostinato* was played, a music that makes you lose the sense of time; it is now included in the soundtrack of the video installation. Every day, it was like a distorting mirror of the reality on the spot. And one day, it was indoor plants. It's very difficult to look after indoor plants and everyone ... well, not everyone, but I at least, feel horribly guilty when I kill a plant. [Laughs] I'm not always able to take good care of them. So I don't have any, because I don't have green fingers.

RC: Oh, is that why you brought me one? [Laughs] Thank you for that.

LA: That's it, I thought, "I'm going to shift the problem." But with heathers, everything will be fine. That's what's wonderful about this plant. You'll see, you won't have any complications. Back to our topic: the purpose of a day dedicated to plants was related to this problem. An indoor plant is totally dependent on the care it is given. And each one needs very specific attention, because they are all unique, just like a human being is not another. In the hospital setting, everyone needs very specific care, both in terms of chemical and psychological support. The dosage must be absolutely accurate. It's complex because it's always evolving, and the consequences and responsibilities are heavy. When an indoor plant dies, it's annoying, but it's of little importance. There, we're talking about people, and their situation is tragic for themselves and for their loved ones. There is also hope for recovery, of course. So, the stakes are high for every patient. And for the caregivers as well, who suffer from possible failures in the healthcare programme for each patient and other painful experiences they can face at work. I thus suggested to the patients and to the caregivers to choose a plant in my one-day plant nursery. Posing with the plant they had chosen was a bit like posing with themselves on their knees. They could then take it with them if they wanted to. And in fact, the book is again a very accurate facsimile of...

RC: Yes, there is an orange sidebar in the photo, and text under the images, but I don't understand a word of Dutch...

LA: That's how the plant has to be taken care of. It's nothing more than that. The text says precisely how to deal with it. And the small orange sidebar indicates the flowering period. You see, there are indications that could also relate to people. [Laughs] For example, from October to December, do this or that. It's a kind of metaphor. The aim was to suggest, with lightness but in all seriousness, an awareness of their own state.

RC: You pursued the psychiatric vein in a geriatric centre with your latest book, Photographic Treatment©. *It includes five volumes, and the project was designed under scientific supervision, but the process is totally different than in* Meer Vreugde Met Kamerplanten.

LA: Yes, it is. For *Photographic Treatment©*, I really clearly gave myself a goal for once – you're always asking "What was your goal?" And for each of these questions, I have to think about what my goal was – but here, my goal is very clear. The aim was to develop a therapeutic tool from photographs, to help bring a positive element in the management of an extremely agonizing and destructive disease: senile dementia.

RC: Well, I know you have another appointment and you must soon leave. So, I'll drop the details, but here, you're returning to appropriation, by pairing photos. Can you explain to me shortly what was the work about and for what result (apart from winning this year's Book Award in Arles)?

LA: What were the results? Well, there are currently about 15, maybe 20 institutions that work therapeutically with my boxes of photographs, the multiple, and a few hundred people who are using the books.

RC: Yes, your idea has been validated, if I may say, by the scientific or psychiatric community in the Netherlands.

LA: Well, it has nothing to do with a curative device, because the disease is currently irreversible. But the aim is to help curb the effects of the illness by offering a tool based on the use of photographs that provoke imagination in people with senile dementia by stimulating their brains through the free association of images. In line with the basic "use it or lose it" principle. The second goal, just as important, is to be a tool for interaction, fuelling discussion about the diptychs of images, or even isolated images, because they can also be appreciated one by one, especially for patients who are at advanced stages of the illness. Selecting this or that image or a combination of images generates communication and language use that contribute to mental exercising and reduce the risk of depression suffered by about one-third of the people with senile dementia.

RC: Tell me, you selected old images, and you showed them to patients, right?

LA: Yes, but only after a fairly long research process in the hospital setting. The project lasted two years, and I also took part in a pilot scientific research project. There was a medical protocol. It was pretty tough. It was time-consuming and also emotionally quite exhausting, but super-important because it allowed me to understand which images were clearly readable by people with senile dementia. Indeed, the sicker you are, the more your eyesight changes and decreases. It becomes very difficult to read images. I had to isolate certain types of images and I created a database of about 1,300 to 1,500 images that I uploaded for free use on the website Photographic Treatment©[3], arranged by themes – which has nothing to do with my personal work, but simplifies the search. The work swung throughout the process between its artistic side and its scientific aspect. And for me, this was an initiation: for the first time in my life, I was venturing into that field. It was really complex obviously, but I had the chance to meet open-minded scientists, including Professor Dick Swaab, an eminent neurobiologist in the Netherlands. He has been very supportive of my research, by his open intelligence and interest in my work. You know, everyone tends to think according to the codes of their discipline. But he was able to look beyond, expand his conception of things and advise me when I needed it. It's been a wonderful adventure and I wish

[3] *http://photographictreatment.com*

it could grow now, but without me, because I'd like to move on. I would be so happy if someone picked this work up. We know that it works well, that it makes these people with senile dementia more present, lighter; and in some cases, it makes them very joyful, as you can see in the video *The Living Image*, visible on my website.[4] It shows a person with senile dementia expressing himself through the photos. You just hear the voice and you see the hand strolling over the surface of the images. This allows you to realize the effect that images can have on people with Alzheimer at a very advanced stage.

RC: This will be my very last question: Photographic Treatment© *is made up of five books. Are these pairs of images that patients associated themselves, or have you reworked them?*

LA: Oh no! That's all me. I composed all the diptychs. But I encourage patients, and anyone else for that matter – children, autistic people or even healthy people – to make their own diptychs. I edited a multiple for this. In the form of a box. It includes the 5 books and 99 blocks of photos issued from the books and from my database, which can be spread out on a table to work with at will and combine with one's own diptychs.

RC: A form of appropriation 3.0?

LA: Exactly! I give back to the public what I took. [Laugh] You're right.

13 September 2018

[4] *http://laurenceaegerter.com/portfolio-item/the-living-image/*

JULIÁN BARÓN

Julián Barón was born in 1978. He lives and works in Valencia, Spain. He is a member of the Madrid-based collective and photography school Blank Paper. In 2011, he published his first book, C.E.N.S.U.R.A.*, which received the honorary mention of the Paris Photo-Aperture Foundation First Photography Book Award. In 2015, he was nominated and exhibited by Fannie Escoulen for the Discovery Prize at Rencontres d'Arles. In 2016, he received a Magnum Photography Award. In recent years, he has devoted much of his time to participatory educational workshops, notably working in Peru. He is the author of seven books, some of which were created as part of his educational projects.*

While Julián Barón produces work of high quality, deliberately provocative and undeniably political, he has over the years, from his first book *C.E.N.S.U.R.A.*, gradually established himself as a theorist in the ecology of the image, its social function, its retinal inscription in the collective unconscious and its use by power. True to himself, he does not merely explore these issues on his own. In recent years, he has initiated collaborative practices in Peru, Nepal, Great Britain and even Spain, trying to help us unlearn images to better understand the issues at stake. Skype conversation between Valencia and Paris.

> Rémi Coignet: *You are a member of Blank Paper, both a collective and a photography school based in Madrid. Can you tell me a few words about this body?*

Julián Barón: The founders of Blank Paper are Fosi Vogue, Óscar Monzón, Antonio Xoubanova and Mario Rey. They founded the collective in 2003 to develop and show their works while creating a common space for intellectual debate. Finally, this catalyst and the founding of the school offered the opportunity to share a specific thinking with more people from our generation. Today, we have an independent structure for the production, exhibition and distribution of our works. This momentum happened at a very specific time of crisis

on the rise, when the institutions no longer believed that the exhibition format offered opportunities to share and think through photography.
That was the main idea. In 2006 Ricardo Cases joined the collective, which then adopted a new way of thinking about photography because Ricardo is truly a very intense guy.
A year later, I met Ricardo and Fosi Vogue at Arco[1] in Madrid as we were working to produce what we could call documentary photos of the fair. And they offered me to join the collective as well as Alejandro Marote. I knew them since 2003 and even before that, because we met at festivals and other photography gatherings.
Until then, I felt really lonely in Valencia, where I live. There were few people who shared my interest in images. So, joining a Madrid-based collective was quite interesting to get out of my loneliness and learn more. Where I live, there are no libraries, especially not a photography one, there's nothing. Everything I learned about photography was self-taught, because I studied industrial engineering.
I fell in love with photography at the age of 16 or 17, and at 18 I made my first photographs. From 2000 to 2007 I worked alone. Meeting Blank Paper truly broadened my vision of and my thinking about photography. I believe it's the ethos of Blank Paper to create a space where all the forces come together to head for a place that doesn't yet exist, and we don't know where it is. So, it's an action, or reaction – I'm not sure about the right term because I think all the members of the collective are people in action rather than in reaction. I guess the initiative was important for us and, it seems, for the students and all those involved in different ways in thinking about photography in Spain.

RC: That brings me to the following question: About the purpose of your work, beyond its political aspect, is it not to give the reader, but also the people with whom you collaborate at school or in participatory workshops, an awareness of images, their meaning and their purpose?

[1] *Madrid's international art fair.*

JB: [Sighs] Yes, I think it's all political, social, economic and cultural. If I mention an image and you can't read all the layers necessary to understanding it, I then need to bring in other disciplines – anthropology, ethnography, sociology, economics, culture, architecture, or simply the audience. I'm learning a lot from the political space in which an image is located. The most important notion of political concept or definition of politics comes from Hannah Arendt in *The Promise of Politics*: "Politics is the space where you create a relationship between two people."[2]
So, the image is political, and you can talk about ideology or other stuff, but I'm sorry, I have to confess to a kidnapping. There is a kidnapping of words in the specific cases where politics does not use those words. So, using the image is the idea for *C.E.N.S.U.R.A.*. To show how this whole political world lives in one same closed space. While we live in other dimensions and levels ...
When I think about images, I think that we must work on visual education. We are children if we don't know how the image works, with all the fake news, the new information, etc., where the image is deeply important.
I don't know that we can create this education, but I think we need to start developing the discourse and the knowledge about the production of photographs, their distribution, their reception and their sharing. We need to create transgenerational conversations, from 10 to 80 years of age. We need to understand the cosmos of the image today, which is I think where politics manifests itself today.

RC: This brings us to your first book, C.E.N.S.U.R.A.*, which deals with Spanish politics and its representation in the media. What was your goal with this project in which politicians and venues of power vanish under a violent flash?*

JB: A really interesting question, because everything started in 2009. In 1999 I started taking photos influenced by documentary photographers from all over the world

[2] *Published posthumously in 2005 by Schocken Books and partly based on her 1993 book* Was ist Politik?.

but mainly from Europe and North America. Then, I felt the need to unlearn. As I do today with my students. It's a very interesting journey.
So, everything took shape in 2009 in Paris at Véronique Bourgoin's Atelier Reflexe studio and a workshop with Boris Mikhailov. His wife Vita was always present with him, and they really changed the way I understand photography. I actually experienced catharsis during this workshop. [Laughs] In a way, Blank Paper has also changed in 10 years. And the group also changed the way I thought about and saw photography five years ago. But truly, that workshop, what a catharsis! It was then that the idea of the *C.E.N.S.U.R.A.* series came to me, and the subsequent regeneration projects in the following years like *Los últimos días vistos del rey*. It's about having an attitude through photography. I think that over the last 10 years, I've developed a different, more personal attitude, another way of thinking about photography. *C.E.N.S.U.R.A.* really presents a work about a mistake. In this case, with the images being overexposed by the flash – a common photojournalism flash but used at full power. Something you're not theoretically supposed to do in this case.
The first feeling I had when showing these images was crazy, because the mistake is not welcomed by the system as it devalues the very values of the system. So, I realized that what I had in my hands was a tool that, via a simple action, made it possible to create a situation in these venues of power by producing an image that embarrassed everyone. They were totally countercurrent to the images that politicians want to show for their communication.

RC: In some images, you also show journalists with cameras filming politicians.

JB: Yes.

RC: So it's a double look at the system.

JB: Yes. The process that ultimately underpins the success of *C.E.N.S.U.R.A.* is rather interesting because the system doesn't admit errors and I know how it works. This process was interesting for me because it was unpredictable. But if you can produce this kind of photograph, then you can show that it's not easy to make a "good" photo at that very moment where politicians and the media only want to deliver the best image. And I was trying to make all that imagery disappear to create another space in which to think inside the proper system.

RC: A kind of Hollywood show...

JB: Yes. I did not participate, but I didn't have control over the success of my mistakes! [Laughs] It's really a contradiction, but I had to make the right mistake. Otherwise all the images would either be all black or all white, and they wouldn't serve me. So, some element in my images are balanced and others not, and that's what makes the work really clear. All I had to do was to adopt the position of the photojournalist and distort the camera's parameters with the flash to the fullest. So perhaps we can talk about a political manifesto, but I don't often think of *C.E.N.S.U.R.A.* that way.

RC: Let's move on to Dossier Humint[3]. *Maybe, at first sight and even if I do understand the subject, this book might seem a little boring, sorry to say so. But we must say a few words about it. You were saying earlier that you worked as an engineer. And the book deals with tiles and the Chinese market. Can you explain the origin of this project?*

JB: The link between *Dossier Humint* and *C.E.N.S.U.R.A.* is the fiery reactions the latter sparked in the photobook industry, in the market and in the system towards me. My response to this crisis was *Dossier Humint*. For me, it's a very interesting book because it has also fuelled many reactions. Many people loved it, others hated it or just found it boring, like you did. For me, these contrasts and tensions are a leitmotif. Also, it was an excuse to work and experience with designer Eloi Gimeno in order to develop news ideas. Between 2005 and 2008 I was working as a quality manager and engineering director at a road signage company. In those days, I experimented with industrial

[3] *"Humint" is an abbreviation for « human intelligence ».*

policy. Towards the end of the experiment, I travelled to China several times, to Shanghai, Guangzhou and Zhengzhou, to carry out a series of quality checks on site of the materials we had developed with a Chinese company.
One of the major problems working with these Chinese companies was checking the customs documents as well as our compliance with European standards. And many times, I was confronted with falsifications on measurements or various parameters. It's a way of working that can drive you crazy, but this is absolutely standard with China.
So after we came back, we maintained a working relationship and contacts with one of these businessmen. Years later, this person wrote to me and offered me a commission to spy photographically on the industry at an international tile trade show, Cevisama in Valencia. I had to take pictures of various items so they would know what to copy: designs, models ... I did it, but I only took unusable photos. From the 6,000 photos I took, I worked with Eloi Gimeno and other people. The result is the 500 copies of the publication of this file.

RC: And did you continue your spying till the end and give the Chinese man a copy?

JB: Yes, but a PDF copy. [Laughs]

RC: So, you printed it out and distributed it. Was it a mere denunciation of economic espionage or also a game, like Sophie Calle when she followed someone on the street?

JB: I love Sophie Calle! [see p. 48]

RC: About Los últimos días vistos del rey. *You know this better than I do – this book is a response to two propaganda books released after Franco's death and the establishment of King Juan Carlos*[4].
Today, we may think it's comical that these two books were published by the Ministry of Information and Tourism of the time. I have several questions about these three books.

[4] Los últimos días de Franco vistos en TVE, Los primeros días del Rey vistos en TVE, *1975*.

First of all, why do you think the propagandists of the time chose to photograph a television screen when they could have sent 10 photographers out to document these moments? And do you think that at the time, the etiquette seen on television served as some kind of proof in their mind?

JB: Yes. *Los últimos días vistos del rey* is a book that examines the construction of history through television. The theme is the abdication of King Juan Carlos and the proclamation of the new King Felipe VI.

RC: Yes.

JB: It was in June 2014; the abdication took place on 2 June and the proclamation on the 19th. I remember it perfectly. Within two or three weeks, we had a new king in Spain. On the 19th, all the TV broadcasters and especially TVE, the national television, went on live for eight hours. During these hours, I spent my whole time linking the creation of this book to the two books on Franco and Juan Carlos. And I like the idea that Fernando Nuño created these two books that are like living documents of these 1975 events.
The interesting thing is that at that time, they were in great haste. They were in a hurry to create an event to keep history and the regime going.
It seems to me that they chose not to integrate all the photographers because they could have disrupted the rhetoric they wanted to assert. So, they asked Fernando Nuño to make books... [Laughs]

RC: And they thought it was easier to capture the images from the state television?

JB: I guess. I'm not sure, but he must have spent weeks in TVE's editing room photographing the screens.
And that's how they designed these books. For *Los últimos días vistos del rey*, I chose to use the same method to create an illusory trilogy.
Even if I had no illusions myself. And then, I worked with Eloi Gimeno on the design, and he created all the possibilities

to relate to these two historical publications while at the same time dealing with the present time; to discuss our desire for or against monarchy; to be the witnesses or the actors, questioning my personal perspective since I was born in 1978.

RC: Yes, it was ...

JB: The beginning of the transition. I was a child but I was educated in this system and so I worked on it and I know how it works. Finally, this book is a response to the duplicity of all these people.

RC: You mean, in the propaganda books or in yours?

JB: I think it's the same in mine as it is in the others. You can find many levels of meaning. You can find a lot of information about what was going on then, because working in the context of these previous books, every page, every image of mine had to relate to the past. For example, they used the same car as for Franco ...

RC: Really?

JB: The same car, yes! And many other symbols related to that past.

RC: Don't you need to be Spanish to make these connections?

JB: Yes.

RC: These propaganda books were widely distributed with I don't know how many hundreds of thousands of copies in Spain, so I guess they have marked the collective memory. And when you say that you wanted to produce a third volume like a trilogy, is this a way of recalling the propaganda that accompanied the transition to democracy? Or are you more deeply republican? And we know what that word means in Spain.

JB: Yes, we certainly do know the meaning of that word.
But what I can say is that with the current situation in the north,[5] we must give up this idea.
Maybe the idea of the republic was an option, but it's history now. I'm not sure that we can push the masses in that direction. But I think the system, whatever it is, makes it difficult to continue working in this world. I have the idea of a republic, but it seems to me that we should be talking more about "republication". [Laughs]

RC: What do you mean by that?

JB: The very idea of a republic, and not establishing something that would only be a reproduction of what we have in mind. Perhaps we can redefine all this and not replicate the existing one, because the system is really locked. Can we talk not only about the republic, but also about democracy?
We have the same notion of the republic, of representative democracy, as the Greek philosophers. Not that it should be rejected today. I don't know that it's the best model, but we don't have any other unless we turn to self-management.

RC: Sorry to be very political, but do you see monarchy as a continuation of fascism?

JB: Yes, it's an involution, I think. Yes, of course.

RC: Even abroad, we have heard about the various scandals surrounding the royal family. [Laughs]

JB: It's an involution.

*RC: Joan Fontcuberta [*see Conversations 2, p. 64*] told me that he had lived the first 20 years of his life under the dictatorship. You were born in 1978, so you didn't. Why come back to it?*

JB: Well, I was raised by my parents in the educational, social and cultural system of those transition years. And why not look

[5] *Julián Barón most probably refers to the separatist tensions in Catalonia.*

back? My story, my life, are the product of my education. And for someone who works and uses photography, I ask myself a question: how can I not use the images that were put in my head? It's really a question I ask myself every day. And I'm now working on creating a library of schoolbooks from 1920 to 2020. A century of Spanish schoolbooks.

RC: Fantastic!

JB: I am now looking into other ways to read the images. I no longer need to take pictures on the street.

RC: Yes.

JB: The idea is to create this library in order to work with other disciplines, other teachers and photographers, artists or anyone else ... I started with a personal notion of photography and then learned to think in more collaborative ways. Now I think we need an ecology of the image. So maybe we don't have to create any more images and we should start talking about and discussing the images we have in our mind. Those of the last century, for example. The goal being to better understand the core of the visual idea that builds us, just like our parents and grandparents built us. It's my sense of appropriation and of connection to the past, and how to think about it.

RC: I feel like after Los últimos días vistos del rey, *taking pictures yourself became less and less interesting for you ...*

JB: Yes, I think so now. But with *Tauromaquia* also, my ability to work with photography has expanded even further. I'm starting to think of it as a free code. Why not think and share with other people another way to think about photography? Why not think of it as a free code?

RC: Sure, your work is political, but I have the feeling that after Los últimos días vistos del rey, *you started to analyse history in the frame of the contemporary political process. What do you think?*

JB: You need to understand the political process according to Hannah Arendt. To create a space that generates relationships between people ...

RC: But C.E.N.S.U.R.A. *was an immediate response to the media and to politicians. Whereas I feel that from* Los últimos días vistos del rey *on, you integrate history into an understanding of contemporary politics.*

JB: Yes, I think *Tauromaquia* is a good example of connection between the present and the past. In this work, the history of Spain relates to what you can see today: the police use a bullfighting arena to give lectures to children, schoolchildren. So yes, I'm interested in contemporary consciousness and situations related to our entire history. Remember, I think that the best proof of that system is this library I was talking about.

RC: Yes, the library you're creating.

JB: Yes. I don't know why I got involved, but I think the process or the leitmotif is that notion of unlearning. I think that through our education, we have of course a lot of information. But education is not only your schooling, it's also your family, your neighbourhood, your friends, the people you know or those you meet.
I think this way of working with images is interesting for everyone. Not only for the photographers who are interested in art, but also for the galleries and all that market and all that fucking system that works with photography.
Today it's a free code that we have at our disposition, that creates and develops our identity structures and uses them to move the masses towards consumption and everything that goes with it. It seems to me that creating new spaces to talk about photography and the images that surround us is fundamental to creating an intergenerational dialogue.
That's why I think that through a political space for photography or for the image, we can take another path; otherwise, we have the choice of continuing to talk about and repeat the same ideas and mistakes.

RC: Let's talk about Tauromaquia. *Before buying your book, I'd never heard about the Spanish police showing their know-how – the presentations, say, for school kids in the country's bullfighting arenas. There is, of course, a dual symbol there, the police and the arenas. First, what was your purpose in showing this?*

JB: The images in *Tauromaquia* are, as you said, documents of the presentations that the police organize in the bullfighting arenas for school audiences. I discovered the story in 2009. Between 2009 and 2010, I suffered from a truly incredible catharsis [Laughs] thanks to the many conceptions about seeing through photography. That year, for the first time, I saw these scenes in several Spanish newspapers. I collected hundreds of images and video screenshots on the internet. The resulting folder contained many different images and points of view. It was rather difficult for me at first to control and put all this material in order, the different viewpoints we have through all the images of presentations that are somehow like movies played by the police in the arenas ...
The local media and the teachers are there with the kids. They take pictures and videos and then share them. And really, the set of images shows the incredible fervour generated by these presentations from multiple perspectives, including from the school children coming into the arenas and the representation of the "execution" of a delinquent individual. My purpose, my goal with this project, was really to bring it all together. To show what's happening quite naturally on TV at 2 o'clock in the afternoon while you're having lunch. My reaction was to create an object. To tell myself that's not normal. I felt like I was living 200 years ago. [Laughs] In the time of Goya and his bullfighting engravings. My goal was to focus on and draw attention to this point: you can feel really happy watching this on TV at home. But actually, you're swallowing and digesting all these images. My idea was therefore to create a different digestion to draw attention to the police and media actions. And to do it in a book, using a format that works.
These files were my only source of research. I tried to attend these shows but it was "mission impossible" for me.

So, I set out to gather even more material. Then I created a PDF containing, I don't remember now, maybe 100 images, and I went to the copy shop down my street. And when I saw the result, all I could think of were Goya's engravings, *La Tauromaquia*. That's how I started to consciously work with the photocopy machine instead of with my reflex camera. Right now, through photocopying, I think of all this visual junk and I feel the opportunity to talk about these images my way. As I told you, with all the images that were put in my mind, I can work on the issue.

RC: Sorry, but you didn't really answer my question regarding your position on bullfighting?

JB: That's right. For me, the link is related to these police shows because the brutality is the same when you end the ceremony with the death of the animal or when you "act" out the killing of a man. It's always the animal that's killed, isn't it?
So I think that in light of the educational system set up in Spain today, the comparison stands with this type of staging by the police. There lies the link.
Then, we can talk about the notion of what's at play when a man and a bull are performing the ceremony of the *corrida* in the arena. It must be clear that the audience is necessary. Just like in *Los últimos días vistos del rey*. It's always the same: the system needs an audience. And it fully understands that not only will spectators watch the event, they will also assimilate the content. This not only allows a form of control but also positively shapes public opinion.
The brutality is the same because it resides in the act, in its repetition. For me, it's really amazing. For example, I am now testing this concept in the last series that I've been working on, "El Laberinto Màgico" [The magic labyrinth], on re-enactments of the Spanish Civil War.

RC: Yes, I've seen that.

JB: It's comparable. It's always a question of thinking about simulation, the representation and the function of the image in this context.

RC: Even if for Los últimos días vistos del rey, *you've re-photographed images from the TV,* Tauromaquia *is the first time you've used images found on the internet, on police films, etc., and much of your work since could then be considered appropriation. Is this term one that you could agree with?*

JB: Yes, but I'm not really interested in the definitions of appropriation delivered by art institutions. There're others. For example, as I said before, why would I be an appropriation artist individually and not all of us, collectively? I always have in mind the example of the seed, the source of life. If we eat tomatoes or carrots today, it is because our parents or grandparents collected a seed, planted it, preserved it and passed it on.
History itself is an appropriation. But if we can't work with it to produce through the image an evolution or an involution, the scope of which I can't yet measure, of this technique or of this notion of appropriation, I disagree. That's why I think that it's important to work on this notion for the image but also with the idea of the assemblage that would not merely boil down to a book. The assemblage must really be brutal.
I find this to be very interesting, and we need to develop this conception of the assemblage to create through it a new way of understanding, reading and sharing images.

RC: Starting in 2017 and throughout 2018, you've carried out only collective projects, leaving aside all your strictly personal work. You've worked on three continents, in Peru, Nepal and Great Britain. Why is that?

JB. I'm interested in thinking and working with photography collaboratively to get it out of the autonomy it has been driven to today. We can understand it through its history, but I felt there's a potential not to think about it in itself. This involves other ways of accounting for or sharing the distribution and circulation of images. Everything is changing and we need to be careful.
Perhaps we need to create alternatives to all this rational and logical history that we learn through schooling, parents, books, etc.

It seems to me really important to pay attention to images to make people understand the visual aspect they hide. Thus, living a collective experience allows me to create new approximations to understand how images work in our society. That's why, for the last three years, I've been working on collective projects in different places around the world. And the connection between all these experiences is made, I feel, around my person, my opinions. People need, it seems, to embrace the image in a different way because they're incorporated, willingly or unwillingly, into an individual, auto-referential process. But if you share this feeling with others, you can tell yourself, "Damn, my problem is the same as that of many others!" And this work that I do broadens the horizon and opens the perception to the different layers of meaning that the image provokes in us.

RC: So, you're looking to reach out to a much larger audience than the small world of the photobook, where 500 or 1,000 copies sold is a success ...

JB: Yes, it's a process just like life. You can get different tools that you're going to use properly or not. For me, the book is one tool among others.

RC: So if you want to reach out to a larger audience, perhaps you need to find other media, whether it's workshops, photocopies or videos?

JB: Yes. I think there's an audience out there that entertains an incredible relationship with consumption and from whom a possible reaction can be expected. For me, from an educational standpoint, young people between the ages of 3 and 18 are the big losers in our contemporary society, because we'll never be able to experience and understand what they desire and feel. We need to work with that audience, and through teaching, change the way we all see or learn about the image and photography.

RC: So you're working on a new project, El Laberinto Màgico. *I know it deals with the Spanish Civil War.*

After two or three years without taking pictures, you've picked up the camera again.

JB: Yes. The idea, much like before, is to understand the past, my story and our history. I don't know if it was in 2015 or 2016 that I saw these re-enactments of the Spanish Civil War. To me, it seemed really amazing because it was a simulation of war. In a way, it was quite crazy. I try to place this in another context, another flow, another way of thinking with images.

RC: They play Republicans and Fascists, is that right?

JB: Yes, they're trying to do really interesting re-enactments, because governments don't want to get to the bottom of the problem: mass graves dug where the Nationalists killed the Republicans.
Many people carved a grave in the mountain, a memorial ...
It's comparable to the Holocaust. Many families have lost their grandparents and don't know where they are ...
But governments do nothing, and the people organize themselves to create these places of remembrance of the history of the war, because at school it's not taught that way. It's quite crazy to know about this part of history only through these simulations. Furthermore, there's an important tourism of war. Many small villages use the idea to promote their economy. These events are therefore perfect for this.
The re-enactments and all these ideas seemed crazy to me. So, I went to the site of one of the battles near Zaragoza. I took pictures, and I plan to return next year. But I have a lot more research material. From Asturias to Córdoba in southern Spain, from north to west, in all parts of Spain, we may have 10 or 12 battle re-enactments. And since 2016, I've taken pictures of these events. But why take pictures? To create an archive, to have an experience of it. Last year, the work was unveiled at the Getxophoto Festival; and this year, I'm working on a book as part of the celebrations for the 80th anniversary of the end of the war. I think it's interesting to contribute with images of these really crazy and contemporary scenes.
I'm trying to break taboos, and because of that, I can hardly exhibit anything in Spain. [Laughs] I generally understand it,

and that's why I try to turn to other forms of expression, to share experiences with others. However, the real taboo is video.

RC: Are you telling me you can't exhibit in Spain?

JB: Yes. I experienced that in Barcelona, the first time when someone wanted to show *C.E.N.S.U.R.A.* in Spain. That was five years ago. And shit, politicians got involved and *C.E.N.S.U.R.A.* was censored! With the curator, we had the idea to use instead *Los últimos días vistos del rey* – but same problem. We didn't even try to show *Tauromaquia* – "mission impossible".
So we created another form of participation to the exhibition by organizing a workshop with students: "Lesson Plan: European Experimentation" – the video of which you can see on my website.
So this is my experience in Spain, curators are not interested in *C.E.N.S.U.R.A.*, *Los últimos días vistos del rey* or *Tauromaquia*. That's the way it is.

RC: You're not politically correct…

JB: No! [Laughs] And that's one more thing we could talk about. I'm also interested in the politically correct, because we all now live in that kind of world. We have left too many new things go by without understanding them. But we'll continue the fight to move on to the next level! [Laughs]

RC: That's probably a perfect conclusion.

19 February 2019

Since our conversation, Julián Barón released two new books: *No hay nada que celebrar, mi casa está vacía*, a collective publication made during the Ser Libro workshop in Mexico, Gato negro Ediciones, 2019; and *El Laberinto Mágico*, Max Aub Foundation, 2019.

SOPHIE CALLE

Sophie Calle was born in Paris in 1953. She lives and works in Malakoff, France. Her work is included in the most prestigious public collections and was presented at the Centre Georges Pompidou in the exhibition "M'as-tu vue" [Have you seen me] in 2004. In 2007 she represented France at the Venice Biennale with "Prenez soin de vous" [Take care of yourself], "hiring" Daniel Buren as curator. In 2010 the Palais de Tokyo presented the exhibition "Rachel Monique" and she received the Hasselblad Award.
Excluding exhibition catalogues, she is the author of more than 50 books published mainly by Éditions Xavier Barral and Actes Sud.

Sophie Calle is a contemporary art superstar, thus drawing large crowds at her exhibitions and performances. Her books come in large print runs and some of them are regularly reprinted – a popularity that unarguably speaks to the quality of the work and probably also to the fact that she holds a mirror up to us: everyone sees what they want to see.
Her recognition comes with a few misunderstandings: she supposedly spends her time following people on the street. Something she hasn't done in over 30 years! And she exposes her private life ...
The reality is clearly infinitely more complex and subtle. While Sophie Calle does use biographical elements to create her art pieces, about half of her work doesn't refer to her personal life, notably *L'Absence* (2000) and *Blind* (2011). In the end, the focus of her practice is the gaze and its ability to grasp, or not, the real. For this reason, the book, with images and texts, is a major vehicle for her.
Conversation during the Rencontres d'Arles in the coolness of the lounge of her publisher, Actes Sud.

Rémi Coignet: *In the first of the two articles he wrote about you in* Le Monde[1] *in 1984, which you mention in* Exquisite Pain, *Hervé Guibert claims: "Sophie Calle is one of the few* *artists who use photography with no kid gloves to tell a story." Would you agree? You tell stories?*

Sophie Calle: Yes. Not always, but yes, I tell stories.

RC: You said in Exquisite Pain *that you are a character in Hervé Guibert's* À l'ami qui ne m'a pas sauvé la vie *[To the friend who did not save my life], and we know from* Double Game *that you are also a character in Paul Auster's* Leviathan. *Are you a fictional character? Or would you like to be?*

SC: I wanted it so badly that I asked Paul Auster to become one. And then I realized that he had used my life in a chapter in *Leviathan*. His heroine follows people on the street and is a maid... in short, there were many elements borrowed from my work. I also saw that there were two rules of the game invented by Paul Auster in that chapter – namely, living according to the chromatic range, and living under the domination of three alphabet letters: B, C and W. So I decided to play the game so that the chapter would be completely true, and I "entered" the fiction. My wish was to become the heroine of a novel, so I asked Paul Auster to turn things around. Since he had chosen me and my work and turned me into a novel character, I asked him to write a novel about a woman of my age who would be called Sophie, who would be French, and I offered him a year of my life to do everything that the novel would command me to. The project never saw the light of day because Paul didn't want to feel responsible if, for example, by obeying to the script written for me, anything bad happened to me. Then I asked the same thing from other writers, including Enrique Vila-Matas, who talks about it in his book *Explorers of the Abyss*, but for many different reasons it never came to fruition.

RC: You've named Double Game *the box set inspired by* Leviathan. *I'm not going to quibble about the possible double entendre in French:* je/jeu *meaning either "I" or "game". But more simply, is double-play inherent in your work?*

[1] Le Monde, *9 August 1984 and 16 August 1984.*

SC: No, a title is a title. When I realize my projects, I don't wonder whether I fit into this or that category. When I'm lucky enough to have an idea that seems to suit me, either because it has potential on the wall or on the pages of a book, I don't ask myself that kind of question. These are questions for critics or journalists. I don't have the distance needed from my work.

RC: Is one of the aims of your work to get out of your life, as Paul Auster writes in Leviathan*?*

SC: Get out of my life? No, I don't go out of my life. On the contrary, my mother dies, I talk about her. In *Exquisite Pain*, a man leaves me and, even if it brings me to nausea, I don't get out of my life. On the contrary, I go...

RC: Head-on?

SC: Yes, even if "head-on" is not a word that belongs to my vocabulary.

RC: I'm sorry.

SC: No, you're right, it's consistent with what I think, but I just don't know what word to use... In short, I take hold of things that happen to me and I tell them. Speaking about my mother all the time is a way to keep her alive. She's not estranged, she's there. When I talk about the break-up letter, the man too is there, in a more playful, less sad, less painful way, less related to the failure. He is always there, but with a distance. It's a distant way to look at this break-up.

RC: Most people's lives are very mundane. I have the feeling that you often slip a grain of sand into the mundane to see if anything interesting will happen. I'm referring to "Where and When?", for example, or the act of following a man all the way to Venice...

SC: Yes, but at the same time, I'm telling mundane things. A man leaving, a mother who dies, break-ups. And there's also all the work that doesn't deal with me: a stolen painting, a blind person. Everyone in this room was left once, has received a break-up letter or a phone call or text message today...

RC: Which must be even more violent, I guess.

SC: Words are violent! But the fact that it's an email is no more violent than when it's a handwritten letter. The fact that he left was more violent than the medium.

RC: What I meant is that in some of your work, whether it's "Where and When?" or following a man to Venice, your intervention changes the banality of everyday life.

SC: I've always loved to play. Already when I was five, I loved to invent my own rituals. Rituals are wonderful and relaxing. For example, to decide that I will follow this man no matter where he goes. And no further questions, I just do it.

RC: Talking about rituals, I do understand how they can be reassuring in everyday life; I would like to know what they allow in artistic creation?

SC: You are again asking me to autopsy my work... The day before yesterday, while I was looking at a work of art, I was introduced to a person, and suddenly the guy started to photograph me as if I were a flowerpot, without asking me anything. He was there taking a picture of me as if I were a still life. I said to him, "I am alive, here, in front of you! You could at least ask me if it doesn't bother me!" Why am I telling you this? What does it have to do with your question?

RC: We were talking about rituals and the rules of the game.

SC: Oh, yes. So, I don't dare photograph someone like that. On the other hand, if I decide that this person enters my scenario, then, all of a sudden, I will be able to ask questions that I would not otherwise dare to ask, I will be able to take pictures that I would not dare to take. The ritual allows for this.

RC: Which brings an anecdote to mind. Two or three years ago, Daidō Moriyama [see Conversations, p. 200*] was exhibiting here at the Rencontres d'Arles. A tour with the public was organized and the translator was missing. Moriyama and the whole audience were waiting. And many people were photographing him in a rather wild, rude way. He remained impassive, and after a while he pulled out his little Ricoh camera and took a picture of the audience and said, "You photographed me, now it is my turn to photograph you."*

SC: The funny thing is that the guy who was photographing me without asking my opinion said: "OK, OK, I'm destroying the image." Which he did before my eyes. And in the second that followed, he asked me: "And now, can I photograph you?" And I said yes.

RC: Do you ever, as writer W. G. Sebald sometimes did, place an image as an attempt to convince the viewer of the veracity of what is claimed in the text?

SC: Not in this way. For example, when I was following someone on the street or when I was a maid, the image served as an observation, regardless of its quality. Not really to prove that it had happened but as a simple observation. I don't need to prove it.

RC: You affirm?

SC: That's not what matters. Even if I say it happened, it might not have happened. Anyways, the mere fact of selecting a small portion of text, an instance in a whole story, implies that this is not the truth of the story. It's happened, it's gone, but it's not the truth. When I made the film *No Sex Last Night,* we lived together for a year, we filmed 60 hours and we released a 1-hour movie[2]. We could have made 30 films that would have said one thing or the opposite. In this case, we had decided to focus on me and my frustration and him and his addiction. We could have made a film only about landscapes, or silence. It would

[2] *With Greg Shephard.*

have been another movie, but it would have happened as well. I'm not trying to prove, because there's nothing to prove.

RC: Looking again at "Where Could You Take Me?" in And So Forth[3], *I wondered whether the text was not primary in your work, and photography a means to make it plastic.*

SC: It depends on the projects. Curiously, it was so in the beginning. But, for example, in *En finir*, I found the images and I had no text. And it was very new for me to have only the images, and to find them beautiful. But I was desperate, because I didn't know what to do with them since the text had always been a priority for me. And it took me 16 years to figure out what might work with these images.

RC: It's a very important aspect about your work: projects can run over 15 or 20 years.

SC: Or sometimes go very fast...

RC: And sometimes be taken up in different forms. I'm thinking about Blind. *How important is it to you to take the time?*

SC: It is how it comes. For example, for *En finir* I searched for 16 years and couldn't find anything. Baudrillard had written the text for me, but I thought, 'I didn't make the images myself, and I wouldn't have written the text either.' Sometimes I would have an idea, but it didn't need the company of these images. After 16 years I thought that the story had to be this actual failure. And since I'm used to working on what is missing, it became clear that the lack of ideas was to be the spine of the project. In *Take Care of Yourself* I had delegated the text to the women who were interpreting the break-up letter. But then I wondered, "What are you doing?" So, I focused on the images. Then I realized that they were better quality than usual. I was never a great photographer. And then, suddenly, these images were holding up. And I think they did because, unconsciously, I thought

[3] Editions Xavier Barral for the French edition; Prestel Publishing for the English edition, both released in 2016. The series was presented within the group show "S'il y a lieu je pars avec vous" at Le Bal, in Paris, from 11 September to 26 October 2014.

that having lost the text, I had to make up for it somehow. I had to find my place. I received the Hasselblad Award[4] soon after this project and I thought to myself that things were in their right place. I don't know that the award was deserved, but it certainly would have been even less so before this project.

RC: So how important is the book to you in presenting your work in relation to the exhibition?

SC: The wall has always been my first inclination because, as I've said many times, I wanted to seduce my father who had art hanging on his walls. So, producing something he might put on his wall was my real driving force. The fact is that both always worked simultaneously. I can't imagine an exhibition without a book or a book without an exhibition. I always thought they were complementary. Sometimes the two forms, exhibition and book, can be similar. But for *Take Care of Yourself*, the book allowed me to achieve more freedom on the wall. Some of these women wrote 20 pages of analysis covering my break-up letter. I couldn't hang such massive writings. So I sought in their statements the word, the phrase that would allow me to create the pieces that hang on the wall. But, considering that someone had just worked hard and provided me with a 20-page analysis, I also couldn't simply choose one word. The book allowed me to fully respect their words and, on the walls, I had the right to play with them, to use them as material. In this case, the exhibition could not have existed without the book.

RC: When you represented France at the Venice Biennale in 2007 with the piece "Take Care of Yourself" and you "recruited" Daniel Buren via an advert in Libération*, he basically told you "display it on the wall as if it was a book page".*

SC: He was right. I was so right to have listened to him. It could have been empty words, but for one, it was Daniel Buren, and second, I listened to him. That's why I tried to do something on the wall that was different from the pages of the book.

[4] *Sophie Calle was the recipient of the prestigious Hasselblad Award in 2010.*

RC: I'd like to understand how a Sophie Calle book is born. Do you make dummies on your own and then see your publisher, whether it is Actes Sud or Xavier Barral? Or do you meet with the publisher and tell them you have a subject and discuss how it can be shaped in an interesting form?

SC: Generally, one of them asks me, "Do you have a new project?" So, no, I don't go and ring their doorbell! Then, I tell the story of the project, and generally it gets started. Either Raphaëlle Pinoncély at Actes Sud or Xavier Barral starts making a dummy, we discuss it ... I don't work alone, but I'm very involved.

RC: That was my next question. Your recent books are very refined with, for example, a selection of different types of papers according to the progression of the narrative, of coatings, etc.

SC: These choices are made together each time, between the artistic director and me.

RC: In the books you publish with Actes Sud, why do you often choose to adapt to the characteristic format of their textual collection?

SC: I haven't used this format for a long time. *Blind* is not in that format; *Take Care of Yourself* and *Voir la mer* neither. The exception is *True Stories*,[5] which is regularly reprinted and therefore kept in its original format.

RC: That was not a criticism.

SC: I don't take it as such. But when I look at the books from Actes Sud today, the latest ones are not in the classic format, apart from *True Stories* ...

RC: Does the title True Stories *mean that others are not?*

SC: No, it was a joke. Everyone always asked me, "Is that true?" So I thought to myself: "I'm going to write that it's true,

[5] *In 2018* True Stories *was in its sixth edition.*

and they'll stop asking me whether it is." Except now, I'm being asked, "Is that really true?" [Laughs] But in the beginning the idea came from my weariness of being asked that question.

RC: In the bibliography that concludes And So Forth, *you distinguish "artist's books" from "exhibition catalogues", which is altogether logical. But you don't qualify your other books, notably all the ones published by Actes Sud or Xavier Barral. What is their status?*

SC: Well, they're books! Artist's books – I didn't choose this description – are books produced in limited copies, handmade and not distributed in bookstores. I set catalogues apart because most often, I did not conceive them, though sometimes I manage to control the process, like the one from the Centre Pompidou, for example, made with Xavier Barral. But for others, it's less the case. The one from Hasselblad, I barely saw it. In the end, a catalogue is a more rigid object; it must deal with what is displayed on the walls. It doesn't offer the same freedom.

RC: And So Forth *ends with a portrait of you with the following caption: "M'as-tu vue, Ainsi de suite ... Mais encore?"*[6] ["Did you see me, And so forth... Yet again?"] *Is it to say that there might be a third volume?*

SC: That doesn't mean that there will be one, but that there could be one. That was the idea. I'm perhaps not quite finished with my career as an artist. As a matter of fact, I'm also working on a new exhibition in October at the Musée de la Chasse in Paris, with pieces that are not included in *And So Forth*. It will be called "Beau doublé, Monsieur le marquis!", because I invited a friend, my artist friend Serena Carone, whom I like a lot, to share this exhibition with me. She will show her work there, but we've also tried to have a dialogue about certain subjects. For example, I do a piece about my father's gaze, and she bounces back with another piece on the gaze.

[6] *Sophie Calle combined two exhibition/publication titles ("Ainsi de Suite" and "M'as-tu vue?") in a final pun to Ainsi de Suite, perhaps to announce a third project/ volume to come.*

I also made a very short film about not having any ideas anymore. I went to film my fishmonger in Malakoff because I remembered an old advertisement: "Catch your ideas at your fishmonger's." So I explained to him that since the death of my father, I felt paralysed, I had no more ideas and I asked him for help. And he tells me about salmon, that there are a lot of things you can do with salmon skin. Serena responded to that little film with a wall covered with salmon skin…
I will therefore present these new projects, including one on *Le Chasseur français*[7], made from the marriage adverts published in the magazine since 1895, trying to spot by decades the main qualities that the men who published their adverts sought in women. It begins with "not poor" from 1895 to 1905; then from 1905 to 1914 it becomes "with or without blemishes" – which means whether or not a virgin, etc.
I tried to do new stuff for this exhibition… So there may be a *Yet again*. But if I stop tomorrow it will be a very small book.

> *RC: In preparing for this meeting, I watched the video produced by the ICP on occasion of the award you received.*[8] *And you were saying then that you no longer wanted to talk about* Suite Vénitienne *or* L' hôtel…

SC: It's not that I don't want to talk about it anymore. But sometimes people still ask me, "So, when do you follow people?" When I haven't followed anyone since 1980! I realized a while ago that you are tattooed for life with a project; it's impossible to get rid of it. I've done other stuff since then. When I'm interviewed and I only have an hour, I tend to want to talk about more recent stuff. And then, the question is rarely asked in these terms: "In 1979, when you were making *Suite Vénitienne*…" – now it's just summed up to: "When you follow people…" That's why I always need to restore the facts, the chronology. Apart from that, I have no problem talking about it. I loved these projects, I still love them, and I'm showing *Suite Vénitienne* at the Musée de la Chasse.

[7] Le Chasseur français *is a French magazine on hunting and fishing, once well known for its matrimonial ads.*
[8] *Sophie Calle received the Infinity Award from the International Center for Photography (ICP) in New York in the "Art" category in 2017.*

RC: Yes, that's why I was finally asking you.

SC: I'm showing it because it seems fair to me to contrast it with the hunt for women. I had fun at the Musée de la Chasse; I tried to conceive new things while incorporating older projects, and this is always exciting.

RC: Rachel, Monique...*'s long title in the French edition ends with: "My mother liked to be talked about." We could say that about you, right?*

SC: Yes. But not as much as my mother! I like to talk about my work, which is quite different. At the same time, I don't know of many artists who would appreciate that their projects remained completely mysterious, secretive and not seen by anyone.
I don't know if you've noticed, but you haven't read many articles about me where I talk about the places I love, the books I read, the music I listen to. You only rarely see pictures of my home. I usually refuse to answer those kinds of questions because I feel that my tastes in literature would bring nothing new. I'm not enough on the lookout for the novelties, I don't have much to teach others. So I don't see why I should speak about these issues when there are others better suited than me to do so. But if we talk about my work, then yes.
My mother liked it when people talked about her. There's a variation.
Sometimes, some people think they know my life. I don't believe so. It doesn't feel to me that I'm talking about my life. I feel that I'm telling a specific moment, according to a very specific ritual or rule of the game. Even in *No Sex Last Night*, a piece that would most fit my day-to-day life, I was not under the impression that I was telling it. If you make a 1-hour-long film out of 60 hours of rushes, it becomes a fiction.
I have now lived for 13 years with the same man, and I have never talked about him in my work...

RC: I don't think that we're discovering your life in your work. It's either staging, scenography or storytelling.

SC: Except that people have the opposite feeling... Very often, they come to me and tell me, "I know all about you." It's always said in a kind and friendly way. Yes, they know I was left in 2006. It's a part of my life, a part that I deal with, that I use, but it's not my life! Or they know that my mother died, but this happens to everyone. That's not private life...
I say this with no aggression. I just think that there is sometimes a mix between work and life. But it's no more annoying than that. And then viewers tend to forget that half of my projects are not about me: *Blind, Seeing the Sea, Le Chasseur français*...

RC: Such is the dual nature of your work – on one hand the pieces about you, and then the others dealing with very different issues.

SC: Yes, and I'm not sure how I go from one to the other. It's not at all thought through. I told you, I don't have 10 million ideas. When I have one in the year, and I can see where it can take me, I take hold of it without asking myself whether this is a good year to talk about myself or others. I don't have enough ideas to be able to put them on a table and wonder which one to pick.

RC: And often, your ideas will go on for years and years.

SC: Yes, it's true. Though not always. For *Take Care of Yourself*, it took me three days to find the idea and have it clear in my mind. I was meeting my best friend and telling her how my lover had left me. I asked her, totally ingenuously and certainly not with any notion of a project in mind, "What's behind that letter? What does it mean? Is it a final break-up or not?" She replied, and boom! There came the idea. Three days after receiving the letter, I already knew what I was going to photograph and how to proceed. I didn't know yet what the format and the rest would be. It took me three years to do that. But I already knew I was going to ask women to interpret the letter.
For *Exquisite Pain*, I interviewed people, I got better, I was coping. And then I dropped the project in a drawer for 16 years, at first because I was afraid of falling back into my sadness, and afterwards because I didn't quite know how to show the idea. After 16 years, the story was far behind me and I came up

with the embroidery idea… 16 years to find the way! So, there isn't a single scenario. For *Pour en finir*, I had the images and no idea; for *Exquisite Pain*, I had the idea but I didn't know how to actualize it; and for *Take Care of Yourself*, it was settled in three days.

RC: Very last question. Is it important to have a feminine – even feminist – point of view on events and situations?

SC: I don't know that it's important. But when I followed people on the street in 1979, if I had been a man following a woman, it would have taken on a different meaning. The project wouldn't have been the same.
And maybe if a man had asked women to come and sleep in his bed, they would have had the jitters?
So, it wasn't deliberately conceived from a feminist standpoint. Though it's true that being a woman brings another perspective to the project.
For example, for *Take Care of Yourself* I thought that the letter was typically a letter from a man to a woman. That's why I asked women to analyse it. Later, I wondered whether I wasn't going to ask men to do the same. And I got wary that in this case, the interpretations by women might be compared to those of the men, and the project would have become sociological. It may become a feminist piece, because it is a woman who chooses to distance herself from a break-up letter sent by a man. I remember an article, though not in which newspaper, that said: "Even if you don't like art or photography, but if you're a man in your thirties looking to meet a girl, go to the Bibliothèque Nationale de France, because all the thirty-year-old girls are there right now for Sophie Calle's exhibition." They referred to the show as a place to meet girls! [Laughs]

RC: This is very Chasseur français*!*

SC: It's true that the public was mostly female. But for me, this piece wasn't a female revenge. I was first trying to understand the letter, and only after did I see the artistic potential of the project. If there was revenge, it was not conscious… Let's just say that it wasn't clearly my intention. I tried to express that with the sentence written on the very last page of the book *Take Care of Yourself*: “It was a letter, not a man…” And in the end, even his letter was not so terrible… It’s not easy to leave.

4 July 2017

EDMUND CLARK

Edmund Clark was born in 1963. He lives and works in London.
After studying History and French at the University of Sussex and at the Sorbonne in Paris, he worked as a researcher in London and in Brussels before earning a postgraduate degree in Photojournalism from the London College of Communication, where he now teaches.
His work is present in many collections, including the Winterthur Fotomuseum, the George Eastman House in Rochester, and the Imperial War Museum and the National Portrait Gallery in London. Edmund Clark was the recipient of an ICP Infinity Award in the documentary category in 2017, was nominated for the Prix Pictet in 2012, and was the recipient of a W. Eugene Smith Memorial Fund award in 2017. Negative Publicity: Artefacts of Extraordinary Rendition *won the Photo-Text Book Award at the Rencontres d'Arles in 2016. He has authored seven books over the past decade.*

Constancy, perseverance, obstinacy even, are qualities that Edmund Clark can't deny. All his published work deals with confinement and the use of coercion by powers, be it in judicial or extra-legal contexts – from British prisons to the Guantanamo base. This working context leads him to develop strategies that reveal what is generally hidden from citizens' sight, thus crossing real or bureaucratic walls and acknowledging in the process the limits of photography and its difficulty in showing the reality of power and strength. Conversation in my library on the occasion of Paris Photo.

Rémi Coignet: *A question I often ask is whether the work is political. I think this topic is a good starting point to help the reader understand what you do and why. For you, however, I will put the question in a different way, as it's clear to me that your work is political, if only going by the subjects you select. So, my question is: Do you see yourself as an activist, or as a cold, demanding documentary artist?*

Edmund Clark: You do start with the most difficult question! Well, my usual reply to this question is that this decision, this categorization, is something I leave to the people who are reading my books or looking at my exhibitions. That's a choice, a decision, that they must make as to what my intentions are. So yes, my work is clearly political, but for political work to be successful it has to leave the audience, the reader, with space and time to engage with the subjects you're exploring as an artist, as a photographer, as a writer. What works for me is work that engages my imagination, engages my attention and wants me to spend time with it, to reflect on the questions it is asking me, the complexities of its forms; and that process is what will bring me to reconfigure my own beliefs and thoughts about the subjects. So yes: I want my work to engage an audience, I want my work to make an audience think again about the subject that I'm dealing with. But it is for them and only them to decide whether that work is activist, documentary, art or all of those.

RC: Let's consider now your books in chronological order. For the first one, Still Life: Killing Time, *published in 2007, you spent three years photographing E Wing at HMP Kingston, Portsmouth – an institution dedicated to elderly people sentenced to life in prison.*

EC: My initial instinct to go and work there was quite journalistic. Previously, I had done a body of work about teenage fatherhood – talking to, working with, photographing very young fathers with their children, discussing their motivations for having children. One thing leading to another, I did some work in an institution for young offenders, where I was able to talk to a person about the prison service of Great Britain and issues that were important to them. That person described the E Wing unit at Kingston Prison and how the prison service of Great Britain was having to confront the fact that people over the age of 60 are the fastest-growing population segment in prison. So that caught my imagination. I knew all about prisons in America, about the geriatric prison system, about people who are on a life sentence and who will never get out. So, my initial instinct was to see how that issue was playing out in the United Kingdom.

RC: Right.

EC: It took a long time, six to seven months, to get access. Thereafter, the work transformed quite quickly into being a study looking at time and space. I spent two to three years working there, long enough to realize that every prison is but a microcosm of the society that produced it.
It was about observing the inmates' experience of time and space – their engagement with the passing of time, their relationship with the space ... and it was about issues of control and power – for some, it was about empowerment, and for others it was a complete lack of agency at all. You could see that playing out in the environment around them. That's what really fascinated me.

RC: Indeed, the reader can perceive the notion of time passing. For example, with this conversion table of the ancient pound sterling into the new decimal system.[1] *And the book format for this one is very classic, something that will gradually change in time with* Guantánamo *[2010]. It seems to me that the very strong and rigorous editing is meant to mark the passing of time, and simultaneously the suspended time of detention. I did mention the currency chart, but how important was it for you that this notion of time be not only translated through the images but also through their editing and sequencing?*

EC: Well, two things led to that. For one – and this is quite important –, this body of work marked a change in the way I saw myself as a photographer. Spending time in that environment took me back to my university studies. Reconsidering the history of art actually made me stop working as a documentarian, technically, and I started to use my own understanding of art and imagery, of iconography, to say something with photographs that I felt went beyond the documentary. And since this is about time passing, it relates to the notion of vanitas, still life, painting, and how you can actually read those meanings

[1] *In 1971 Great Britain decided that the pound sterling would be divided into 100 pence. Previously, the pound was one of the oldest currencies still in use, and the system was, it is fair to say, somewhat baroque ...*

that relate to time, the passing of time, through the everyday objects that surround people in this specific environment. As for the second point, sequencing ... it takes the viewer inside the prison through the communal spaces into the cells, the shared spaces, the places where these men live. But the ending was a problem for me.

RC: But the end is brilliant ...

EC: Do you think so?

RC: I do.

EC: Well, it involves a compromise. My original idea was to have no views of the outside. I didn't want that. And ... [Edmund Clark shows the penultimate picture] that was the picture I wanted to end with, a timeless one, softly out of focus, looking through a window, with shallow depth of field.
My publisher[2] felt it needed something more definitive. So the compromise we came up with was that the images that I wanted would take their place in the middle of the book, in the central part, and the two images from the outside would come before the introduction and after the postface. They represent the starting point and the conclusion to the book. And with distance and hindsight, I believe he was right.

RC: Your second book, Guantanamo: If the Light Goes Out, *came out in 2010. And my question is purely related to form: What is the meaning of the embossing on the back cover?*

EC: Oh, yes. I really regret not having included the text that explains what that is. It's a motif that comes from an Islamic tomb, I think in Cairo. I can't remember exactly now, but I think it's the number 14, which is known to be the prophet's number. In the Lunar calendar, it's the point when the moon is the brightest, when it delivers the most light. And the book's subtitle is *"If the Light Goes Out"*, which comes from an ex-detainee in Guantanamo who was talking about the light in his cell.

[2] *Dewi Lewis.*

If the light went out in his room, he felt he was back in his cell in Guantanamo. The book is all about that notion of light, so I wanted to reference that notion from the Islamic view of light. That's why this is on the back cover. I didn't include the text that explained it because I just wanted it to be something mysterious.

RC: I thought it might be something Islamic, but I wasn't sure exactly what.

EC: Retrospectively, I wish I had given some explanation, because it's relevant, and I made it too obscure.

RC: This is always an issue with the work of artists and their books – do you need to explain or not?

EC: This is true.

RC: As you write in your foreword, the work deals with the notion of home through three spaces: the American base where soldiers live; the camp itself; and the houses of released prisoners around the world. How do these various places fit the notion of "home"?

EC: This is hard to answer, because I saw that notion from so many different perspectives. Through the eyes of the men I was photographing, where they lived after Guantanamo Bay, working with them in terms of their experience of home. That first idea of home for me was to create a contrast in people's mind with the representation of people in Guantanamo Bay: people in orange jumpsuits whose face you're not allowed to show. An imagery meant to confirm the message that these are the worst of the worst, not even human, this is what was coming out of Guantanamo Bay, and I wanted that first iteration of home to be something that surprised and shocked people. Particularly in the United Kingdom, where the audience would see these pictures of homes as incredibly ordinary British homes and places, typically British. Yet these were places where these exotic, dehumanized forms were based. I wanted to shock and surprise people with that representation of home. But then

I realized that these men I was working with had an incredibly problematic view of these homes. They were living there, yet as they spoke to me they were mentally back in those spaces in Guantanamo Bay that had been their home for three, five, six years. How could you conceive of those detention spaces as a home, a personal space? So I went to Guantanamo Bay, eventually getting access to work there. And as you know, I wanted to view the American base. I didn't really know what that was going to be like, and when I got there, it was fascinating, because I realized that the US naval base at Guantanamo Bay had been there since 1898 – which is a long time in the history of the United States. It existed as an incarceration facility since the Cuban Revolution, so we were looking at a microcosm of American life, of American domesticity, of the American way of life, at a time of extreme tension due to the "War on Terror" and what was happening with the people in there. In short, all the motifs of refinement, militarism, religiosity – all these elements of the American experience of the War on Terror that we all kind of see on the wider international level, I could see them all there, condensed through the domestic spaces, through the ordinary spaces of the American community in Guantanamo Bay.

Naturally, these three visions of homes intertwined, and ultimately I wanted the viewer to be confused by these different sorts of home. What do I mean when I say that this is a home? But at the same time, I don't tell you what you're looking at. I don't tell you which type of home it is. That's a deliberate omission, because on the one hand I'm trying to make you uncomfortable in terms of your notion of home through what I'm exploring and presenting. The point was thus to create a sense of disorientation. I wasn't only trying to show images that were related to the spaces and the people who worked there or were being held there. And on the other hand, I also wanted to say something about the experience of being there, which was made to be disorientating, to make you paranoid and dependent on your interrogator, through the use of light, heat or movement. So I tried to create a disorienting experience for the viewers, to make them feel uncomfortable, in a sense to undermine the message that this is about home.

RC: And this disorientation also comes from the way you edit your images and captions. Unlike in Still Life: Killing Time, *which followed a geographical and temporal logic, here three spaces are mixed in the editing without any visible logic. And the captions only mention "Plate 1", "Plate 2", etc. We have to refer to the index at the end of the book to find out for sure what place, what "home", it is about. Of course, you know you're in the naval base when you see the Ronald McDonald clown; or that you're in the camp when you see coercion tools. But for other images, it's not so easy to say. You might have possibly partly replied to the question, but is this only meant to disorientate the reader?*

EC: It is. But also, I think that I'm now starting to understand, on a personal level, that it's about disorientation on a more global level as well. You know, having worked on these subjects for the last 10 years, having been in some very strange places, I've now realized that this has been a very disorientating experience. And not just for me personally, because it has also disturbed my relationship with the world that I thought I knew and understood before all this happened. You know, looking back at this book with its disordered narrative, and, as you said, illogical editing compared to the previous book, I find that it's reaching another level of meaning for me as well.

RC: And in this book, you introduce documents, which will be the case in all your subsequent work. Here, they are letters in the form of photocopies[3] received by a former prisoner, Omar Deghayes, and his own story he wrote of his detention and his changing reaction in the view of these letters from relatives but also from strangers around the world. They are reproduced on thin, mat paper, unlike your photographs. How important for you was it to include these documents at this time?

EC: The documents are really important. For me, they are far stronger than the photographs. For two reasons: the documentation already started appearing in *Still Life: Killing*

[3] The redacted original documents were retained by the American censors.

Time, but I was showing it as photographs. I was photographing bureaucracy. I'm really interested in bureaucracy and how it appears in the visual form, because when you're dealing with issues of control, particularly the exercise of power and control by a government or an organization over an individual, the way in which that control manifests itself is usually via a piece of paper. The words that are used and the way they appear on that paper speak volumes about that form of control and the power implicit in that control. And about these letters to Omar, what I really think is interesting about them is that they are copies – there is nothing original, because the man was never given anything original. These are new images.

RC: The censors kept the originals.

EC: He was at the highest level of control because he was a non-compliant prisoner. Every detail of his life was controlled by his interrogator, including when and in what form he got any correspondence. The absence of the actual card or letter of support was very cruel. He was deprived of the messages of support people sent to him – he would only get them in this modified form...

RC: And at one point – sorry to interrupt you – he writes that he is going crazy thinking that perhaps the letters have been written by his interrogator...

EC: Exactly. And that's why these documents are interesting – because visually they are new images and not merely historical documents. They show the choices people made through the kind of image and message they wanted to send to someone. They are related to a historical context, but are indeed new images, abstract forms specifically created by the bureaucratic process at Guantanamo Bay, which I find visually fascinating and rather beautiful in form. This is quite troubling. However, the visual realization of the censorship also betrays carelessness. Some of the documents are upside down; most are in black and white and not in colour. And everything was photocopied – envelopes, blank pieces of paper ... everything went through this absurd process of the exercise of power over an individual.

Then you're right, Omar received so much of the material. On one hand, he said he was grateful people were aware of his situation, and some gave him information he was not aware of. But on the other hand, some of that information was obsolete. It was made complicit of the controlling authority over him that determined when and in what form the letters came, and this ended up adding to his sense of paranoia. So the documents, the letters reproduced in that series, were produced by Guantanamo Bay. They are witness to the changing and degrading custody. And they are deeply implicated in the actual experience of the individual. So you see, they do something more visceral than the photographic series.

RC: But your images of Guantanamo are anti-spectacular, very quiet, and yet very carefully constructed and meaningful. What allows such detachment?

EC: I think that way of seeing has grown out of how I photographed in *Still Life: Killing Time*, with a large format camera. In the book about Guantanamo, I photographed people's homes with a large format camera, which is a slow, very deliberate, composed process. But I couldn't photograph like that on the base of Guantanamo Bay, because there you could only use a digital camera. I knew, however, that this was an aesthetic, a way of seeing that I wanted to continue. It was a reaction against the news agency imagery I had seen about Guantanamo Bay. Their perfectly good photographers were going in there, but they were creating images that were feeding the media machine, fuelling, even unconsciously, the message of dehumanization. I wanted to make images that were as far away from that as possible. In the end, I included a few images that widened the spectrum of the edit a little; I did include a few images that relate to that format, a little bit. I basically just wanted to make images that were as detached from the media representation as possible. So I used a camera that allowed me to do that, using a tripod. And that idea continues in the way the book is put together, using plates rather than numbered images, giving no captions. This is all about giving you detachment from the spectacle that was playing out on our screens.

RC: And so, of course, photographing in Guantanamo, there was the risk of being manipulated. Is this way of working a way to circumvent that problem?

EC: To a certain extent. I think I actually welcomed that form of manipulation in some ways, because, as you know, working as a photographer, as an artist, the control, manipulation and censorship that the organizations of power have over my work is a direct, adult way of illustrating that very form of control that I seek to represent in my subjects. In Guantanamo, you're meant to photograph in a certain way; you're told things you can or cannot represent. In the prison camp, you sit down at the end of the day with a security consultant who will make you delete some of your pictures. In some ways, I actually wanted to experience that to see how it shaped my work. I wanted to feel that power over my images as a way of illustrating much larger and more important aspects of power.

RC: And now moving on to Control Order House *[2012], in which, to a certain extent, your photographs are the opposite of those published in the previous book, even if here you also amplify what you initiated with* Guantanamo. *You reproduce many documents, and the very first one is unbelievable. It looks like a typical rental lease specifying the rights and duties of each party, though this is about administrative detention. Do you feel that this bureaucracy is a way to protect power itself, and at the same time a sign of its weakness?*

EC: This is a very interesting question, and it relates to notions of secrecy. With *Control Order House,* I kind of put myself in the place of a government lawyer having to create, write and codify a form of control over an individual who has been made to live in this house. That lawyer almost has to create a network around that individual, like a web within which the person has to live. If they go down the wrong path, they can even be criminalized. But you know, because the authorities cannot hold, arrest and imprison this person, because they cannot provide a proper legal process, they create this bureaucratic web around them. For me, that situation works as a metaphor for the position that a government finds itself in when faced with the potential fear of terrorist activity: How do we create something that can protect us? Hence this sort of codification, which is the control order in that document. It's thus a very minor Home Office lawyer having to write words that are going to protect us by keeping this person stuck in a web, trapped in this house. I find this interesting because there is something absurd in this legal arrangement. They say that this is a tenancy agreement because the government got a property company to find these properties and rent them from the landlord. It's absurd that on the grounds of national security, someone has to live in this house. But the details of the control that is to be exercised, if only for the legal protection of the government, must include a tenancy agreement that specifies whether they have a pet, or a satellite dish. This is crazy.

RC: You yourself have had to sign documents and work under censorship. Can an artist agree to this, and what is the right response?

EC: I've spoken already about how engaging in that form of censorship is an important creative part of what I'm doing. But at the starting point of this, it's necessary if you want to do work on these subjects and get as close to them as possible. You must deal with that. In Guantanamo, I had to agree to work in certain ways; there, I had to say to the government that they could see everything I was making. If you want to get close, you must comply with these constraints. Maybe, in a sense, I've done things a bit differently than the many other artists who have done work on these issues but from a distance – and their work is seen from that distance. If you want to get up close, you must deal with what you need to do to get through those gates, get that access.

RC: So, regarding Control Order House, *let's talk about your images, the editing.*

EC: Right.

RC: You were given permission to photograph there for six days. But in the end you were only there for three and half days because the inmate was transferred ...

EC: Yes.

RC: You photographed without framing, with the automatic flash on. And in the book, you decided to reproduce without editing – with thumbnails of all the images you took in chronological order. Why this choice?

EC: When I was making those images I didn't know that this was what I was going to do. I thought I was actually going to make a film-based digital installation, but I didn't get to make the films because the guy was moved before I got to do that. The idea for the book grew out of having to submit every image I made to the government to be seen. So, I just sent them a file with all the JPEGS, with just the JPEG numbers in the order they were taken. And on reflection, I realized that reproducing the images that way in the book spoke about order and control as a photographer, because in this particular case, as an artist, I didn't exercise any control over what I made. So, I show the result in chronological order, with no hierarchy in that sense. And this reflects the situation of that man in the house: he's had to give up any agency, forced to live in this very strange form of control and detention. This is what I meant to translate visually. You see the whole of the house, every centimetre, because initially I thought I was going to make panoramas of each room and I wanted to get that information and stitch pictures together. However, showing them as a series of photographs is a claustrophobic experience and also an act of surveillance. I went around the house twice. You also see every decision that I made, which, again, reflects the experience of the individual who he is being surveyed, even if someone's not looking at him in the room. The house was bugged; he had to report to a police station every day. He was wearing an electronic tag and had a curfew.

So, just through the photographs, you see the mistakes I made, where I looked at something close up, where I pulled back, where I moved. It's a form of visual exposure and powerlessness that somehow reflects the individual's experience in that space.

RC: Yes, but you have also chosen to select some of the images and to reproduce them a second time, each spread over half a page. Are they more meaningful than others? Do they hold any details that are somehow not visible in the thumbnails?

EC: No – it is a decision I regret in hindsight.

RC: Why?

EC: Because conceptually there is no hierarchy of images, and the visual experience is of all these small thumbnails. But at that stage of designing the book, perhaps we felt it was too extreme an experience. We felt that it had to offer something more photographic to the viewer. Which is why we did bring out some images, and that immediately introduces the notion of why the images were chosen, when there is no real reason. With hindsight, I wish I hadn't done that.

RC: Very honest to say so.

EC: When I show it in museums, galleries, exhibitions, that's what happens: these images all just get reproduced exactly in the same size, there is no hierarchy in the installation. But in the book, it was a design decision, and I don't think it was the right one.

RC: Again, very honest. And now I understand the process that led you to take such a decision, because – and even if it is conceptually different – I meet publishers and photographers very often confronted with these editing issues, asking themselves whether or not to spread an image over a double page to give pace to the book. And since we're talking about this, I'd like to know how important the book form is in the presentation of your work?

EC: Often, the book is the starting point for how I think about my work. I feel that thinking about books brings a sense of structure to the subject I'm dealing with. It helps me to actually understand the material I'm collecting from a formal perspective, and what I'm doing with it ...

RC: So, while you're working, you're already thinking in terms of the book form.

EC: Yes and no. I'm thinking about how I can make the book, but not about how it can look. With *My Shadow's Reflection* (2017), I was more engaged with how the book was going to look. But normally, no. Knowing that I want to make a book makes me structure my thinking, but the actual form in which it is going to come out when published is a process of reflection. Often, because of the nature of my work, the subjects are difficult to access, or I have limited access and I'm working with different sorts of material. It's not a linear experience – the material I gather is not a narrative in its own right. You have to work out the structure of the form to try and say something else with that material. So yes, the book is the starting point for my thought process. But you know, I've been fortunate in the last three years to have had a series of big exhibitions in which I had the opportunity to deconstruct those books into installations that try to offer an overall experience, bringing in *Control Order House*, *Guantanamo* and "Secret Prison Programme", to say something at a more global level. And that has been a really interesting experience, taking book projects and then deconstructing those, bringing in new material, making new bodies of work to go specifically into installations that have nothing to do with the books. That was creatively very interesting, very rewarding.

RC: As we said, since Guantanamo, *the design of your books has become more and more complex; and since* Control Order House, *all your books have been designed by Ben Weaver.*[4] *What is your involvement in the book design? Do you have a clear idea of what you want before working with the designer?*

[4] *Graphic designer, co-founder of Here Press and artistic director of* The Wire.

EC: No, no ... Every book I've done has been a collaborative process, and that's how I see it: we talk, get down a lot of details about the format. Sometimes, it goes right down to font type, font size ... we go right into those details sometimes. I've worked with Ben on a number of books, and that's partly because of my relationship with Crofton Black, the co-author of *Negative Publicity*, who already knew Ben. Now I know Ben's design approach rather well and I trust his choices. But if I'm not happy with it, we go back and rethink the project. And yes, I want to be involved in every element of the design. What I like about working with good book designers, good curators or good multimedia editors, is that their ideas, their experience, bring a perspective to what I'm trying to explore that actually strengthens my work and takes my ideas in another direction, enriching the overall concept I'm trying to come up with. So yes, I really enjoy working very closely with a designer.

> *RC: Coming back to* Control Order House*, the diary you asked "CE" (the prisoner) to write is very trite and repetitive. Do you see it as an echo of your photographs for this project?*

EC: I don't see it as an echo of the photographs – I see it more as a contrast, because the photographs are so impersonal. I decided to reproduce his diary in the handwritten form because that's the only presence of the individual you see, though it is certainly very limited. I originally asked him to write for two weeks. He was depressed when I went back to see him the second time. He said he had written for three days, and those three days represented his every day. So yes, I see in his handwriting the trace of a presence relating to and in contrast with the detached and repetitive quality of my photographs. But his handwritten words are also a sort of exercise of power. The book is conceived in blocks: the first, the largest part of it, is a sequence of 500 photos; and then the handwritten pages of his diary, printed on very thin paper; and at the end, you have the High Court judgement, which is also a very significant part of the book. And he, through his handwriting, is squeezed in between these two blocks.

RC: The photographic part of the book, right after the diary, ends with close-ups of walls.

EC: Yes, it does ...

RC: And I wonder if these are not from other pictures, reframed?

EC: No, those were taken with a large format camera. But you see similar things in the thumbnails.
As I said, I didn't know initially what I was doing in that space. I had the idea of making films that show 24 hours in this person's life, but then I also did all the thumbnails because I thought it was the thing to do. And I also did this large format work because I thought it was going to have some purpose. I didn't know what I was going to use – all I knew was that I had access to this space, so I wanted to record it as much as possible.
The other reason for that indecision came from one of the forms of control exercised over me. My work must not identify the individual and must also not locate the house. Anyone who knows him or knows the house must not be able to look at my work and make that connection. So, someone who may have visited that house could not look at my images and say, "Oh! Well I know where that is, that's in that town." It's conceptually almost impossible for a visual artist to work with such constraints, so I did those really close up, large format details of wallpaper with the view camera. It's just so close up, it's abstract, and every house of a certain type in Britain has that kind of wallpaper. It becomes universal; it's incredibly typical of a certain type of British house. It's Britain. And I was trying to show that through these wallpaper details. And as I looked at the large format negatives, I was also interested in the fact that you can see every detail, every brushstroke, every spot or mark. They become very topographical; some patterns are incredibly ordered, regular and repetitive, others are more like chaotic swirls. For me, they became a sort of topography of the controlled person's mind. Living with this form of control, trying to create some sense out of his life mired in this web, his own mind was unravelling, becoming chaotic in that experience. So those close-ups metaphorically sketch out topographical mental maps.

RC: I understand. And if I remember well, in the lease agreement it is stipulated that the "tenant" cannot hang anything on the wall.

EC: Exactly. And the closer you get to those surfaces, the more you see the marks, the scratches, the traces. It becomes claustrophobic.

RC: The Mountains of Majeed*, which you published in 2014, is again about walls and settings. On the US Bagram Air Base in Afghanistan, you discovered Majeed's paintings representing the country's idealized mountains. You also photographed the landscape seen from the base. And there are images of the base that you also included in the next book. Can this work be considered a "side project" of* Negative Publicity*?*

EC: Yes, yes. I went to Bagram Air Base to basically take one photograph, but I couldn't tell people that such was my purpose. So, the rationale to go to Bagram was to ask to look at the base as a living space, a home space, in the same way I had looked at the base in Guantanamo. Which was true. But when I was there during and after operations, Bagram was the biggest base in Afghanistan. And as I understood it, America has a similar legal contract for Bagram in Afghanistan as it did with Cuba over Guantanamo, which creates a sort of local semi-autonomous American region. And that was interesting. I didn't want to look at it as a base, I wanted to look at it as a place where people lived, and I wanted to look at the infrastructures of power, sewage, water treatment, etc. It was almost like town planning, organizing all the aspects of normal life. I did that with the backing of a German magazine, and yes, it was an offshoot of *Negative Publicity*. And then, once I had come back from Afghanistan, looking at the imagery I had and the experience I had, notably of the mountains at night and the insurgency, of rockets firing, *The Mountains of Majeed* came about. Through these photographs and through these paintings, I photographed an experience of occupation from the viewpoint of the occupier as well as the occupied. So, this is not about Bagram. Basically, it is about the experience of the occupation of Afghanistan, the technology on one side and a relative lack of it on the other. The inside and the outside.

RC: But in Bagram, you found these paintings by Majeed that offer an idealized view of the mountains, when your images represent these mountains seen through the walls of the base. Would you agree that the book deals with the ideal versus the reality?

EC: Well yes, these paintings are a dream, as well as propaganda. Representing the mountains inside the base is partly propaganda. I think that Majeed's painted views are an idealized form of propaganda for the Western aesthetic. Those are all questions that are implicit in the images: Why are they there, on the walls of a dining facility? Who made them? What do the people who have served on that base actually see? Have they looked at them? Why has the painter made them that way? Those are various aspects of the exercise of occupation and power, and the experience of the individual living under that form of power and control. It is also about technology and about the new landscapes created. You know that the history of occupation – and I'm not referring specifically to the War on Terror, but history shows that occupying powers establish their base in enclaves of high technology because their presence is made possible by their technology, which is superior to that of the countries they are occupying. In Bagram, there were incredibly sophisticated killing machines, and I'm there working with a very sophisticated digital camera, and my view is carried out through that technology. And then there's Majeed working with acrylics (I don't think it's oil painting) on small canvases with wooden frames. That technological gap speaks about the distance between the person on the inside and the person on the outside, and thus about occupation as a detached experience. I realized that most of the people who served in Afghanistan never actually went to Afghanistan. They went from places like Kabul International Airport directly to a base like Bagram. And if they were a town planner, an administrator or a bureaucrat – in other words, a cog in the massive military machine that operates behind the soldiers – they never left those places. Their experience of those countries is what they see over those walls, or what they see represented inside the base. That's the country they're occupying. So, my views of the outside are a sort of representation of the occupation. In fact, you almost don't even set foot on Afghanistan soil because the ground is covered with tarmac, gravel or stone – as if a new landscape had been laid out over the surface of Afghanistan for them to walk on.

RC: And you know the irony: even with very sophisticated technology, they weren't able to win the war.

EC: Exactly, exactly.

RC: Perhaps, as you said, because they don't know the country, since they stayed behind their own walls… they could not understand what was happening beyond these walls, despite their technology.

EC: Exactly; there's a gulf in understanding. Inside the base, their understanding relates to what is being projected back in the American and Western media. Again, this is very typical of these forms of occupation. You have the occupied around the outside, being an irritant, doing things that are sapping the power, sapping the energy, sapping the patience of the occupying force, waiting for them to finally be disrupted and leave. It's almost like an inverted siege situation, where the insurgents around the outside, the occupied, are just waiting and disrupting, and eventually the occupier will go. It's a matter of time and patience. You can see that in history. Philosopher Howard Caygill wrote a book called *On Resistance*[5] that deals with this notion of occupation and resistance. I read that book when I came back from Afghanistan, so it got me thinking about these interesting questions as I was deciding to make that book in the way I did.

RC: So, let's get to the big piece, Negative Publicity. *The title comes from a declaration by the president of Richmor Aviation, complaining in court that the use of their planes*

[5] *Howard Caygill,* On Resistance: A Philosophy of Defiance, *Bloomsbury, 2013.*

by the CIA was negative publicity. Choosing this title, was it a way for Crofton Black and yourself to explain your own purpose?

EC: Yes of course, it is about that. And the subtitle is *Artefacts of Extraordinary Rendition*[6]. But yes, *Negative Publicity*[7] is the key to the court case, and that court case was a key part of Crofton's research because it revealed this documentation – the invoices, the reconciliations, the flight schedules. The court case was a flash of light in his research process. It revealed the secrecy, the obfuscation and the denial. It's about the opposite of publicity, it's about negative publicity – which is, I suppose, another way of expressing secrecy and denial. It also relates to the relationship between publicity and evidence. And the book, in its visual form, is about the black triangle of information; it's about the strikeout. It reveals the inability of photography to actually show anything. But the act of showing nothing reveals the network. This is essentially what I was doing photographing those places. The form of the book can address this notion of negative evidence, by which the act of revealing nothing reveals something. So you see, this is kind of what the book is about, and the title reveals these various ideas.

RC: This is not an easy book. I would even say it is complex. Consider the binding, to mention a trivial and simple detail: while it's perfectly coherent with the subject, you cannot flick through the pages. You must set it on a table and turn the pages one after the other, taking the necessary time. Is this format-related difficulty in accessing the content intentionally meant to confront the reader with the complexity of the subject?

EC: Yes, it's exactly that. The starting point for me was the subject, but also that Crofton Black had done this enormous research

[6] *"Extraordinary rendition" refers to a reality that has no international legal basis and designates the* de facto *extra-judiciary transfer of an individual from one country to another, or from one jurisdiction to another.*

[7] *Publicity should be understood in its double meaning: what is made public and advertising.*

process, which led to finding that something that occurred here was related to a plane and an airfield over there. That kind of criss-crossing, he explains, is related to medieval philosophy. Maimonides, who talks about knowledge as flashes of light. Crofton's research process was like that: a flash of light over here reveals something somewhere else. So, the work cannot be delivered in a linear book. The reader's initial engagement with a document or a photograph is not one that reveals anything more than what they can see or read on the page. But they are given the option to cross-reference, to go to other places, physically going through this awkwardly veiled book, to go through this process of criss-crossed investigation through which it is possible to make connections about planes, about individuals, about certain pieces of testimony. The reader is literally carrying out a process of investigation by which they are recreating a global network.

> *RC: Indeed. And as you said, the book presents many documents in a non-linear way, and at first glance the reader can fear getting lost. But in fact, the structure is really clear, with six chapters, each one conceived in the same way with an introduction by Crofton Black, reproductions of documents, photographs and finally, explanations and a picture of the home of a former inmate. The structure is thus really strong. And as you said, there are all the cross-references that would logically make it impossible to transcribe a network into linear form.*

EC: Right. The linear form doesn't work because this is a global situation, and when you're dealing with secrecy and denial, you don't have a linear experience. You're being denied that understanding while accountability is not happening. That idea of a linear progression of events, revelations and accountability does not happen, and our comprehension of this is not linear either. It is piecemeal and also a process of imagination, because one of the points about negative publicity is that you try to fill in the gaps and filling in the gaps in your own mind then touches on something else. Because then, you're starting to look at how terror works, and terror is about the imagination more than it is about the actuality;

terror is about the fear of the potential threat, the potential violence. That is what we've been dealing with throughout the War on Terror. We've been dealing with our government's responses to that threat, that fear, and what these responses actually entail regarding the forms of control that are exercised over us. This happens through absence, through imagination, through potential.
So, on another level, the book deals with the black triangle, with effacement, with the facade behind which torture happens and which you never see. It also puts us in touch with a more basic primeval fear within ourselves: the fear of the unknown, of the potential threat, and how that moderates our own behaviour and allows countries to bring in forms of control that moderate all of us.

RC: Yes, this runs through all the book. But what can architecture teach us about strategies of confinement?

EC: Two things. On the one hand, bureaucracy, the words inscribed on a page, can teach us about the exercise of control over the individual. The architecture in which that takes place also expresses something about the nature of that control. It also touches on the imagination and how we would feel in those spaces of control. And as I said, photographing architectures of control is photographing absence. Because the one thing that is absent is the raddled body of the individual. That goes full circle. It goes back to the problems I have with access, to the problem of control over the work I make, to devising strategies in which the absence of the individual is something I use as part of something in which I try to engage people. It is about the limits of photography, about the limits of what we can see. Very often, what we cannot see is more important than what we are given to see. In other words, it is about what we are not being shown, and how that relates to what is commonly seen on our screens, the spectacle on our screens: the quietness, the absence of the violent message, of the violent representation. What is going on behind the screen is what is important. It is what my work is about. And it is all linked together.

RC: In his text for the book, Eyal Weizman compares your work to a mask: you can see the mask but not the face behind it. So, you may have already answered in part, but does your practice question what photography can do?

EC: Yes, absolutely.

RC: Let's now consider My Shadow's Reflection. *Is this book a form of closure of the loop initiated by* Still Life: Killing Time, *since you're again dealing with detention experiments within the democratic frame after exploring much more controversial ways of confinement? And in a way, you're returning home with this book, would you agree? Are you done with that subject or do you plan to continue?*

EC: Very good question. I was reluctant to go back to working in a prison because I had done *Still Life: Killing Time* ... I didn't want to revisit that subject. But this is such an extraordinary process ... this is Europe's only wholly therapeutic prison, where a small number of men who have committed extremely violent crimes or extremely sexually violent crimes must deal directly with that in an extraordinarily democratic, consensual, shared responsibility situation. They have to talk about what they've done and must listen to what the others have done. And they have to reveal what was done to them. It's unlike any other prison I've ever been to. So, that very new experience led me to agree to work there. What I think is significant in this project is that I came away with pictures of the participants, the protagonists, that are not in focus because ...

RC: You used a pinhole camera.

EC: Yes. I wasn't allowed to bring them into focus. The people are there, but they're blurred. These are people in pain. But unlike my other subjects, these are people who have also inflicted tremendous pain. A legal process has taken place, and these are people who have created chaos and violence in other people's lives and who are now having to confront that.

RC: So, with this book, you have radically changed your photographic approach in a way, with the use of three processes: black-and-white photographs taken with a view camera of the outdoors; portraits of the inmates with a pinhole camera; and very nice colour photographs of wild flowers growing in the prison outdoors. Why this choice, and how, in your mind, do these three elements combine?

EC: First, another reason I agreed to work in this prison is that I could do whatever I wanted. I said to myself, as well as to the people who commissioned me, that I was not going to work the same way I had before. I was going to experiment. Secondly, the work was made primarily for an exhibition. So, this was the first time ...

RC: Indeed, there is also a small volume produced for the exhibition.

EC: Yes. The end result was an installation, and the will to experiment and the exhibition were the starting point for this work. *My Shadow's Reflection* was something that grew out of an idea of how I was going to install these three types of images together. This was quite a process of reflection, because those are three types of images that were made for very different reasons at three very different stages of the residency.
The architectural images are what I started with and my response to this extremely intense place. They are architectural as well as sculptural. They are black and white. They are about form, though very strange forms. They are about how they affected me on an emotional as well documentary level. The flower images actually grew out of a conversation with my partner, who is a writer. She visited the prison, and while we were discussing what goes on there, she asked if I had considered looking at what is growing there – very simply, what grows in this place. Yes, a very simple idea, but meaning that you need to look at what is planted and what grows wild, what is cultivated and what is chaotic: what is meant to be there and what is not meant to be there, what is accepted and what is not accepted. The way in which these plants, whether sown or wild, are collected doesn't really matter. Nor does it matter that I learned to press

them on my own, because I had never done it before. But the idea of looking at the various processes of restriction, refinement, transition and transformation, and re-photographing these in light boxes, came from the exhibition itself. There was an installation of light boxes arranged in a square that you could walk into. The internal dimensions of that space were those of the cell. The first space you walked into was thus a space of confinement, but surrounded by all the beauty of these pressed flowers and weeds. Looking at them attentively, you could see their translucency, the veins, the creases, every bit of decay, every tear... you could see the physical manifestation of every detail of life, and how the flowers were affected by the extended pressing. The photographs are the manifestation of that, in the second part of the installation.

RC: Then this is a kind of a metaphor...

EC: Yes, exactly, but then it relates to the third part, with the pinhole images of the men themselves. The decision to work with a pinhole camera was made for several formal and conceptual reasons. One, it has no lens and it's a long exposure; it's unlikely to create focus or create images that are identifiable. And on another level, the absence of the lens means that there's nothing mediating the view of our criminal, of the "monster". There's no medium, no message, nothing. No binary vision of good and evil. We're just seeing the image the person has created of themselves. The word "camera" comes from the Latin for "vault" or "dark chamber". The pinhole camera has the smallest possible aperture letting the light in, which, in this particular context, is in contrast with the light boxes and translucency. Obviously, the double device approach has also got to do with the idea of the panopticon and the prisons built according to that principle, where theoretically you could see everyone at a glance. The prisoners knew that they were being watched at all times, though in fact they probably weren't. If you look at a panopticon prison, it has windows at the back, so what is probably seen is a shadow, a silhouette, a presence. That's the kind of image that a pinhole camera reveals. The prison I was working in, however, was not architecturally a panopticon one. To be admitted there meant for an inmate to reveal what he had done, and to understand what had happened to him in order to understand what led to the event, to the crime. The way in which this is carried out is that everyone is on show the whole time. From the moment they leave their cells in the morning, their behaviour is being held to account by the people with whom they live, and all are encouraged to hold their peers' behaviour to account. Thus, they need to learn to deal with things they don't like: everything you say or do when you're out of the cell can get you in trouble. The inmate will be called to account to his group or to his community, so it becomes like a psychological, psychotherapeutic panopticon in which you're seen the whole time. That's how the model works. That relationship between that prison system, the architecture and the pinhole camera is a formal, conceptual one. But it relates my images – in the way I've done them in black and white, the way they were framed – to the history of the representation of the criminal going back to Bertillon [see Stéphanie Solinas, *Conversations 2*, p. 186]; how we have viewed the "other", the "monster", the criminal through photography. My images are made in a group context, which means that the men took turns to stand in front of the camera. The exposures are six to seven minutes long and we did two portraits per person. Meanwhile, I and other people in the group would ask the subjects questions, or they would talk about what they had done, why they were there and their experience of living there. It was sometimes very serious, sometimes not so much… but these are images created that record a conversation with someone talking about why they are there. I wasn't allowed to record those conversations, so they're records of a conversation. The images are troubling. I didn't like them when I first saw them; I was worried I was perpetuating the image of the "monster", of the prisoner. And when I took them back to the men, to the groups, to the community they live in, each spoke about the way they saw themselves, what they saw of themselves. These are men dealing with what they have done. They see themselves as monsters. Some see themselves in a process of transformation, some of them don't; some of them feel disembodied, trapped, oppressed. And they spoke again about the process they were put through and the effects. It is their words, reproduced in the middle of the book, that make

the pictures work for me. Words that are a literal, visual manifestation of them as an uncertain, fluid and sometimes monstrous presence. The way in which these men take ownership of that relationship with the image reflects the process they're going through.
The three types of image work together to give sense to that space, but it's a troubling space. The architectural images for me are more sculptural and more of an emotional response, but then you do have a dialogue between the revelation, the translucency, the detail of things that we commonly find beautiful but that we destroy as weeds. I'm not actually comparing men with beautiful flowers; in a sense, that would be too obvious. I mean that my subject is seeing... it is light... it is about viewing. It is also about not being able to visualize an individual. It is about what is inside them, but also about what is inside us: it's not about a duality of good and evil, because were it not for the opportunities and privileges I've had, I could definitely be where these men are. It's about what we accept as beautiful, about deciding whether to consider them as a plant or a weed. Looking at the men through a tiny pinhole, you just see a presence, a silhouette, an impression... and that's how they see themselves. However, I also see my shadow's reflection, because these feelings exist within me as well. These notions are intertwined.

> *RC: This reminds me of what you wrote in* Negative Publicity. *At one point, you had the opportunity to photograph the houses of two pilots who flew planes for the CIA, and you voiced your own doubts: "Should I take this photograph? Should I not? And If I do, what will it reveal about me?" In the end, you decided to take the photographs and displayed them pixelated, for legal reasons. What does this reveal about you?*

EC: Are you asking me what it reveals about me?

> *RC: Yes, because you took the photographs, but then you put a veil over them.*

EC: On one hand, as you said, there was a legal aspect because the people living in those houses have a legal right to expect privacy and security in their own home. I would never reveal where they are or who they are. Obviously, though, that's not something that the passengers in their planes were afforded. Which is why the narrative includes these images, even redacted, because again, they reveal the absence of these individuals before the law and their accountability. On another level, it's about disorientation again. And I mean, I hate talking about myself, but in some ways it's about defining your own ethical place in front of these subjects: Where do you stand? What do you believe?
And again, to make this work, I've been to strange places and have had pretexts for going there. I've said one thing and done something else. I've created my own web, which has not been linear, and not always entirely transparent. I think it's an impossible aim for any photographer who isn't ultimately dealing only with themselves but has to consider their relationship with their subjects. I'm defined by the subjects I've chosen and by the strategies I've had to put in place to that end. So, that says something about me. Now, why I want to do this work, why I spend time in these places, I'm not sure exactly…

RC: You could have chosen to photograph the beach instead. It would have been much simpler!

EC: I could have… [Laughs].

9 November 2018

ANTOINE D'AGATA

Antoine d'Agata was born in Marseilles in 1961. Since the early 1980s, he has lived and worked wherever he happens to be in the world. He took his first pictures in Nicaragua in 1987. In the early 1990s, he studied at the International Center of Photography in New York and published his first books, Mala Noche *and* De Mala Muerte, *in 1998. From 1999 to 2004, he was represented by Agence Vu in Paris. In 2001 he was awarded the Niépce Prize and joined Magnum Photos in 2004. In 2013 the important exhibition "Anticorps" was presented in Paris at Le Bal. The accompanying eponymous book, published by Éditions Xavier Barral, won the book of the year award at the Rencontres d'Arles. Antoine d'Agata is to date the author of over 50 books.*

For a long time, I didn't understand a whole part of Antoine d'Agata's work. Or to be more exact, the necessary articulation between its different parts. I humbly admit. However, I felt and still feel uneasiness at the reception by an aesthete audience of a practice whose necessity is a thousand miles away from a desire to please. I knew, however, that he was a major artist and an incomparable book maker. Food for thought. Moreover, at each of our meetings, I was amazed by his incredible kindness and availability. In contrast to the power, force and violence of his images or the disdain of certain artists. The kind encouragement of a few friends, including Fannie Escoulen, a great specialist in Antoine's work, with whom I conducted this conversation, led me to work to understand Antoine's singularly coherent logic, necessity and position, beyond the clichés. Having a conversation with him then became imperative. The meeting took place in Marseilles, a few steps from the Noailles market, around Fannie's kitchen table.

Rémi Coignet: *Anyone interested in your work knows the "legend" or "mythology" of your youth: your attraction to punk and anarchy, to drugs and brothels before your 20th birthday. And also, the 10 years you spent abroad from 1983. I would like to clarify two points that will take us to* Mala Noche. *This is rarely mentioned in your biographies, but I ended up finding out in* Mala Noche *that you had started photographing in Nicaragua in 1987. What prompted you to pick up the camera then?*

Antoine d'Agata: In 1987 I was travelling with two friends: Bruno Le Dantec and Raphaël Chirchietti. Raphaël, at the time, was a press photographer in Marseilles. The three of us travelled from Mexico to Central America. Raphaël was ill with AIDS. It was his last trip. He knew it and he was compulsively photographing. I took my first pictures on this trip. But it took me a long time to understand why he was photographing so much, knowing that he didn't have much time left to live. And I believe that the way he was photographing to hold on to life profoundly influenced my way of thinking about other possible photography practices. When Raphaël photographed, he had no professional perspective, nothing related to the desire to preserve a memory. It was a free effort, on the spur of the moment, an act of presence, a way to stay alive, to stay in the world. You know, a desperate relationship to life and the world. And a few years later, when I was in New York, I finally agreed to use photography as a tool to get out of a similar spiral.

RC: This was when you were studying at the ICP?

AdA: That's right. To get out of drugs, I began to photograph instinctively, viscerally, desperately, with the few rolls of film I had brought back from Central America. In 1987, before the trip ended, I was taken by the army in Chalatenango, El Salvador. You know it was the civil war at the time. They jailed me, took me to the capital, San Salvador, and handed me over to the police. Well, it's a long story, but I ended up in the hands of the death squads, and they were the ones who processed my first films. The photos are very bad, but I still have some of the images they processed.

RC: Oh well, that's a good start! And after New York and the ICP, between 1993 and 1996, you gave up photography for the first time. Why?

AdA: After the ICP, I did a long internship at Magnum Photos, and little by little, I started to assist photographers, to get paid, and I think that cooled my photographic fervour. [Laughs] That time at Magnum's confronted me with the reality of a certain trade, a profession, practices opposed to mine. I came back to France, I gave up photography, I had children and worked for several years as a bricklayer and bartender ... the break was long.

RC: What made you decide to pick it up again and to publish Mala Noche *and* De Mala Muerte *in 1998?*

AdA: The end of a story, the end of a relationship. I separated from the mother of my first two daughters and went back on the road. At the time, a trip to Haiti, and Mexico again, with the Zapatista movement then very recent. And Morten Andersen [see *Conversations*, p. 10], whom I believe you know well, used to come visit me from time to time in Marseilles. One evening, we sat at a table, took out all my contact sheets, and in one night we edited the inextricable chaos that had resisted any selection process for years. We selected 70 images, I think. He took the negatives to Oslo, where he made reading prints. From there, I was able to show my work and I started photographing again.

RC: All right. Considering this context, can Mala Noche *be considered a journal of the 1990s as you experienced them? Or part of those years, at least?*

AdA: The images in *Mala Noch*e are significant of the 10 years before my arrival in New York, but it's more complicated. It was painful for me to agree to fit into logics that for years I had completely rejected. And becoming a photographer meant regaining a place in society, in the community. For weeks I was unable to photograph. I was drinking and trying to accept having this strange object in my hands. The camera became the symbol of renunciation, or betrayal. It was a rather complicated relationship to reality, a form of social rehabilitation. Returning to Mexico with the camera, after the first two months of this classic photography training, was an antidote, a way to make sure I was going back to where I belonged. It was a way, I feel, to protect myself from a certain logic, cultural

and professional, which remained foreign to me. And so *Mala Noche* only documents that one moment of psychological and emotional violence: ephemeral relationships, the nights spent there, in this social vacuum. After two years or more in New York, I found a certain truth, a certain intensity. I found the territories that had been mine during those 10 years.
It's hard to go back to those past perspectives. I sometimes talk about these years before photography as a deep black hole.
I fell into the violence of the world and I gained, I believe, an ability to absorb the experiences, the stories, the humanity that faced me but without ever being able, before photography, to spit out, regurgitate all the intensity of this life or non-life.
In fact, from those first weeks in Mexico, these images retrace ... [Silence]

RC: Are you catching up?

AdA: I recover the places to which I belong.

RC: In the opening text of Insomnia[1] *[2003], Christian Caujolle points out your "refusal to be a voyeur". He adds, and I quote: "Necessity, practice, reflection and choice, successively. Thus, commitment." You yourself would then greatly develop this notion of refusal to be voyeuristic and think extensively about what you consider a valid artistic practice. Can you sum up in a few words what you define as a valid practice?*

AdA: I am in line with the situationist theories of the late 1950s that insisted that life prevails over art, always. And on the other hand, with the two responsibilities that each human being, each social being has. The first being to look around, to criticize, to analyse, to understand the context in which they evolve. Something that the photograph or the photographer generally often does effectively and relevantly.
Our second responsibility – which few artists in general, and photographers in particular, assume but that I strive to put into practice – is, when one is lucid about a context, to generate within it an autonomous position through acts, actions, gestures.

[1] *Antoine d'Agata,* Insomnia, *Images en Manœvre, 2003.*

This is the basis of my practice. In other words, beyond speech, thought, intelligence, relevance, gaze, I strive every day to return to this need to act, to define my existence by deeds. For this, photography is a privileged tool since it is the only language that allows, requires and demands a physical presence in the world, in the expression, in the very elaboration of its discourse. At the moment of creation, at the heart of the photographic process, one has a responsibility towards the photographed context. And I try to assume this position by any possible means.

RC: It seems to me that you wrote somewhere that you live what you are photographing, and you photograph what you are living.

AdA: Yes. This is a complex, impure relationship. There is no possible balance. At no time can we achieve a balance, harmony. Life or photography always takes over. I am constantly struggling to find that balance, which is impossible. But this very attempt is worth living. I think it makes the experience more intense because the photographic distance allows an intelligence of the lived moment that makes it deeper, more ambiguous. And of course, living these situations instead of just observing them, in my opinion, gives relevance to the photographic language that exempts it from any possible voyeurism. This allows me to go beyond the illustrative function of photography, to deny the function to which it is reduced, which is to illustrate concepts, ideas and discourses, and allows me to bring it back to a physical experience of the world.

Fannie Escoulen: *That relationship to the world is present from the beginning in you work. You managed to translate it very early on ...*

AdA: No, I wasn't conceptualizing it then. But, instinctively, from *Mala Noche*, I wanted to make the presence of the photographer obvious. Whether it is through a hand that comes to rest on the subject's outfit or by the relationship to these women photographed in brothel rooms, there is, in fact, it seems, a claim to the presence and assumed role of the photographer in a life situation.

RC: In one of the texts in Manifeste[2], *reprinted on the back cover, you write: "No particular tenderness for photography but the need to make the camera spit out what has not been told." Does this mean that photography is always a means and never an end? Or, as you said, is this practice like an unstable balance between end and means?*

AdA: I think that forging my own photographic analysis over years of life experience frees me from any complex or responsibility in relation to the acknowledged history of the medium. From the beginning, I felt alien to these logics or traditions, which, more often than not, have made photography an art of excellence and of the relevance of the gaze, and according to which photography is considered only from the perspective of the ability to watch and keep a trace.
I forgot your question.

RC: Is photography a means or an end? Or is it an unstable balance between the two?

AdA: For me, it is a means, and the tool is incredibly efficient when you get caught into it. We start a sentence that we must finish. Few photographers go through the full process and agree to put their life on the line or even in question. Having to go through with my choices, to shape and invent a form to these life experiences, to these positions that are as political as they are existential, has become vital. I need to go to the end of this need to say, both to impose my own logics or to contaminate the most comfortable academic perspectives. It is an almost insidious – at least invisible – way of taking part in the debate. And at the same time, it reinforces my beliefs or ideologies of life. Photography, which I had seen for a very long time as an impediment, had then become, on the contrary, a tool that allowed me to go even further in the search for excess or intensity.

RC: I'd like to say a couple of words about Insomnia. *Looking at it, I feel an influence from Anders Petersen.*

[2] *Antoine D'Agata,* Manifeste, *Le Point du Jour, 2005; not to be confused with* Antoine D'Agata: Manifesto *(often abbreviated to* Manifesto*), Studio Vortex, 2017.*

[see Conversations, *p. 218] Not only because you photographed in Hamburg's Sankt Pauli district, but really in the mood, in the approach.*

AdA: I first read *Café Lehmitz*[3] in 1990 or 1991 in New York. Then, I had no access to the book for quite some time, only the memory remained. I think it had some influence on my way of understanding how the photographic subject can be physically addressed. But yes, in the same way that Daidō Moriyama [see *Conversations*, p. 200] and Nan Goldin were strong influences ... but my system was always to protect myself from them. Very quickly, I wanted to destroy everything that could lock me into any tie to a given tradition or history, in a loss of autonomy. I was able to draw strength from these photographic experiences, different and pre-existing to mine, but it also allowed me to part from them, to free myself from all the assumed filiation. There is a sacrificial aspect to the process. [Antoine smiles] It's tantamount to killing something essential in order to draw the strength to invent one's own path from this act. And so, all the influences were ...

RC: Digested and spat out?

AdA: Yes.

FE: Quite simply, you also need to consider the notion of the father figure. You had to exist without them. And to not be too contaminated by the other practices. You're still like this today: you'll feed on literature in particular, and not so much on contemporary creation. You protect yourself a lot from it.

AdA: Regarding photography, I feel that my questioning about what it is today or what it has been is quite radical. To be fully in line with my logic, I can't be affiliated with any group, with any accepted idea of what photography is. Otherwise, it would become a possible allegiance, friendship or fidelity, which would constantly prevent me from taking positions as extreme as mine. So, I've been in permanent refusal and

[3] *Anders Petersen,* Café Lehmitz, *Schirmer-Mosel, 1978.*

in a lonely fight, until today. Often, my most violent relationships are with those close to me, who support me, because such possible dependency is the most dangerous. Again, these insidious logics.

FE: Since you're very detached from any movement and any filiation, neither the photography and art markets or institutions and environments have the capacity to give you some space. Indeed, there are some influences, but ultimately, you're not in the lineage of Nan Goldin or Larry Clark, as some have claimed. Neither Moriyama's or anyone else's. In the end, you're very autonomous, very singular and unique. This also makes your practice a parallel and …

AdA: Chaotic.

FE: Well, not necessarily chaotic.

AdA: If not chaotic, then how should we say? A road …

RC: With twists and turns? But regarding what you're saying, Fannie … I think, Antoine, that the fact that you can't be put in a box is also because you have very different works and levels of work: Psychogéographie *has nothing to do with* Ice, *for example.*

AdA: Actually, it has everything to do with it. But I never made the effort to make it intelligible, to submit to these cultural logics that imply providing immediately readable pieces …

FE: I think it's all about that: the inability of the art world to digest Antoine's work and equate it with something existing. Since he's out of the frame of reference, it's impossible to categorize him. And the institutions that show his work are also on the edge of the frame. You don't belong to anything even if you're undeniably, in the history of photography, one of the great contemporary artists. But nevertheless, not being associated to any filiation, history, predetermined movement … it is extremely difficult for art authorities to "fit" Antoine anywhere. And since, furthermore, he is a free mind …

AdA: The environment is corrupt, mediocre and cynical. Part of the responsibility is mine, and I assume that, which is to worry more about finding the strength to continue and to go through with ...

FE: Your sentence?

AdA: Yes, my sentence too. [Antoine smiles] It's essential for me, but it's true that I never made the effort to explain myself as much as the system would have liked.

FE: But you did make that effort.

AdA: I did it at times, when it was vital, when I had to.

FE: At some point, the question is: who wants to understand, who wants to reach out to the work? You've explained your work a thousand times. Manifeste *was an important focus moment. So it's too easy to say, "We're missing out because we don't have the explanations."*

AdA: I think there is true laziness and blatant cowardice on the part of the cultural bodies. If we're talking about institutions, or the various agents involved in the photography scene, or, more precisely, the hierarchies in the artistic milieu, then yes. There is the laziness and cowardice of the people who mostly care about their cultural comfort. For my part, I have no desire to submit my logics to the ideological timorousness of values that are not my own.

RC: Since we're talking about Manifeste, *texts are more important than images in this book, even in terms of layout. Was this an attempt to make yourself understood?*

AdA: No. It was essential for me at that very moment to mark my territory, to cut the ties. After a few years in Paris, and having made no compromises, I was in a simple, obvious radicalism. I wanted to state things. For me, wording has always been a strategy, a way to then have to live up to my own words. Which is to say that even theoretically, the writings are there to then force me to assume that position and live it. Similarly, I often write fictional scenarios and then live up to them. Therefore, writing was intended to set the bar very high, and then not be able to escape the inevitable consequences that I impose on myself. [Laughs]

FE: In Manifeste, *for the first time, you state things in such an explicit way.*

AdA: Yes, but sometimes I do it through images. *Vortex*, a very small book, was also a way to enforce a logic at work through images, via the image, and to impose on myself a scenario of life and work that I'm then obliged to apply strictly.

RC: Let me go back a little bit. If we consider Insomnia, *the images are not captioned, but at the end there is a text by Bruno Le Dantec in the form of a diary and a list of the places where the images were shot. There are 34 locations on 3 continents. But, for the viewer, it's almost impossible to determine which image or journey Bruno Le Dantec's text is referring to or to connect the names of the places to the images. Why do you often choose to separate the two?*

AdA: To make it harder for the viewer ... I believe that work or images (I'm not sure which term to use and I'm not going to use "oeuvre" about myself) ... but these images have various functions, various natures, various ambitions ... It's already quite difficult to inject the existential, political and aesthetic dimensions in one same photo. And I've always held back from including too much information into my images. As if I wanted to protect myself from anything exotic or anecdotal.
For this, I need a certain neutrality, the absence of details, of context, of time or geographical details. It's a way to reach to the core of things, not even taking into account the character of the subjects. They have no defined psychology. I'm trying to free myself from anything that might not be essential. As a means to reach out to the essence.

RC: This might be a little bit provocative, but it seems that this text-image disconnection reaches its climax with Ice *– where,* *similarly, the photos are taken in completely different places. The question is: what is the point of travelling if you find the same situation in Latin America or in Asia?*

AdA: Movement allows for perpetual reset, the constant renewal of risk and effort. For me, it has always been essential to remain fragile, to maintain a capacity of absorption but also to be at the mercy of those I photograph, to prevent comfort, to never settle down, build or capitalize on the places, the habits, the relationships, friendships. A way to always allow me to start again from scratch. To find in each interaction – and there are many – a certain tension in the relationship to someone else, a stranger, in order to recover the urgency and intensity of the encounter. For a long time, the purpose of travelling was simply to abandon a certain comfort and a certain status, to return to a brutal relationship to the "other". We can see it in the film *White Noise*[4], which gives more room for the "other" to exist in their own right, if only through the words. I've always tried, from nothing, to confront the outside world; to provoke the brutality, the complexity and the fullness of the relationship by which we give everything to the "other" and demand everything in return: their image, body, words, love. And each time, not to play on previous experiences but to start afresh.

RC: I understand ... Since we're in Marseilles, let's move on to Psychogéographie.

FE: OK, but there's a book you didn't mention, Rémi, which is also important in the construction of Antoine's approach ...

RC: Which one?

FE: Home Town[5]*, which came out just after* Mala Noche*, Antoine, right? These are images made in Marseilles, because, in fact, you were then back. How was it when you got back?*

AdA: For me, yes, it was an intense period.

[4] *Antoine d'Agata,* White Noise, *2016.*

[5] *Antoine d'Agata,* Home Town, *Le Point du Jour & Galerie du Théâtre, 2002.*

FE: Rémi, you were talking about the notion of diary about Mala Noche, *which in fact isn't one; but couldn't* Home Town *be closer to this notion of diary? If only because it is a series around your home town?*

AdA: Many things are essential in this book ... But for me, all books, however fragile and innocuous they may seem, are meaningful and irreplaceable. Each is one step closer to a possible final coherence.

FE: I would say one more brick.

AdA: Yes ...

FE: But what does this brick mean to you, Antoine? Because all the images are taken in Marseilles.

AdA: Yes. At the time, I was coming out of four years without photography. It was a rather dark, rather complicated period and I was trying to draw from this frustrating reality the strength to leave again.

FE: That's also when the self-portrait came in, right?

AdA: Perhaps in a more deliberate way. At least more conscious. You're right, there are flagrant self-portraits. A flagrant presence of life [Laughs]. Many images where I appear are made by others. Sometimes I'm completely out of it. The images are made accidentally or not by others.

FE: Many of them made by Morten Andersen, right?

AdA: No, not in *Home Town*, but in *Vortex*, yes. I can't remember all the people who had the camera in hand, but this book is loaded with the need to reinvent my position. Many of these people have died. But yes, I think I had to face all the challenges pointed out earlier. Again, I had to make life choices, give up the comfort of stillness. The overriding aspect of this strategy of life is that in the path I have chosen for myself, nothing is ever taken for granted. The effort is permanent. Forced every day to reconsider, to fail, to waste, to go on, to repeat these dramatic and essential choices. It is always a matter of putting yourself back in a position of absolute fragility. And at that point, the process was complicated and painful.

RC: Maybe we can consider Psychogéographie *from a different perspective. The book opens with a warning*[6] *and I think that there, you're very good. The work is a commission to document the Euroméditerranée project,*[7] *and in fact, you pervert it ...*

AdA: As soon as this commission was given to me and I accepted it, it was clear to me that I could only work against my commissioners. Then, I simply developed a narrative strategy, found a possible angle to say what I had to say and at the same time make sure I wouldn't fall into the trap of being held hostage by opposing logics. So, from the beginning, the idea was to hold a discourse, to accomplish an act that felt unacceptable to the commissioners. It was a significant moment because for the first time, I was working on my "day photography" – if one considers that my work is shaped in two dimensions, day and night, that generate and nourish both sides of the same violence – and I designed a book that shows this more overtly political part of my photographic perspective. It's true that many didn't understand it. They didn't catch the relationships, the coherence of it ...

RC: Compared to your previous work?

AdA: Compared to my night work. This book was decisive in marking the dichotomy of my photography, to insinuate a possible relationship between politics and the dark romanticism of self-destruction.

[6] "Psychogéographie *is not a scholarly, neutral and exhaustive publication but an artistic work shaping certain elements of the real to deliver a necessarily subjective vision of them. By asserting this freedom, the authors claim a political act in favour of an open city, respect for the other and social equality."*

[7] *Euroméditerranée is a vast urban redevelopment project covering more than 3,000 hectares, launched in 1995 by Marseilles's city council.*

RC: Since we're talking about this, one of the last times we met, you were explaining to me the difference between day images and night images.

AdA: The difference is illusory. Finally, the two antagonistic violent forces merge into one that destroys the world. The day images show a violence that I live but that I suffer. It is political, and above all, economic. It goes from top to bottom. It destroys those who have nothing. When I work with migrants, workers, refugees, people in certain urban areas, it is a responsibility that I force myself to take into account, a violence that is foreign to me. I first set out the stakes and then try to confront the violence and take it on. My photography then is lucid, conscious, intelligent, distant and cold. I show violence in the most relevant and responsible possible way.
The night violence, on the other hand, is mine. I belong to it, body and soul, and I photograph it in an opposite, absolute and animal way. In other words, by preserving myself from any control, any intelligence. By provoking the most extreme states of sexual or narcotic unconsciousness, by delegating the photographic act to others. Using all possible strategies to be able to experience that violence in the first degree, in my flesh. And incidentally document it ... but first, to live it.

RC: And in Psychogéographie ...

AdA: My approach was deliberate.

RC: Yes, and you made photomontages ...

AdA: Yes, like in a piece of propaganda ... But for me, the essence of this book is the words. I did some research for many months, starting with the internet, about this long tradition of xenophobia and racism against Marseilles, both in the intellectual and cultural circles of society. This is the main thing. Then, given the magnitude of the work, I asked Bruno Le Dantec for help, and we continued the research together. Very quickly, I felt the need to invent a new type of propaganda images to support a hidden statement. It was in the early stages of digital photomontage. We worked without a net, it was a very experimental and very clumsy technique, but we used its systems. The general idea was to bring the expelled inhabitants back into the deserted urban landscapes of the neighbourhoods where they had once lived, through the digital. How can you photograph a gentrification process that is moving hypocritically under the pretext of renovation and modernization? How to render a physical dimension to the magnitude of hidden or invisible architectural gestures? Finally, how to play with reality, and deconstruct the political lie, elaborating another poetic, troubling lie? Some images in the book are real and others are montages. I also photographed the new inhabitants, the (barely) privileged class in their dark suits, who replaced the excluded. Of course, it was a perversion of reality, but it was also a minimalist way, even without montage, to press where it hurt. To show in a caricatural way, as any propaganda is, the reality of this process of exclusion.

> *RC: In fact, the series of the new inhabitants reminds me – even if it was not an issue yet in 2005 – of the reversed representation of "the great replacement" fantasy manipulated by the far right to stir up fears.*

AdA: Yes, because in this particular case, there has really been a change of population. Deliberate and brutal.

> *RC: You were just talking about the importance of the texts you have accumulated for* Psychogéographie. *And to stick to that, most of your books are peppered with quotes. The list isn't exhaustive but you notably refer to Pessoa, Bataille, Italo Calvino, Dino Buzzati, Artaud, Breton, Burroughs, Camus, Céline, Robert Conrad, Guy Debord, Deleuze (*Francis Bacon: The Logic of sensation*), Genet, Godard, Henry Miller, Nietzsche, Pasolini, Sade, Julio Cortazár… or even the band Crass and Lou Reed. This constitutes a very coherent intellectual world in itself and in relation to your work. I wanted to know, where does literature stand in your life and in your practice?*

AdA: The truth is that literature has always played an essential role in my thinking and the way I face my existence. [Antoine smiles] It's so hard to live, so complicated to invent a destiny for oneself, that I have always drawn other options, other possible strategies, however foolish they may be, from literature. In fiction, they are limitless. Reading has always allowed me to generate or look into other life scenarios that can be considered despite the inherent realism or pragmatism of everyday life. Thus, to be able to draw from fiction a desire for the impossible, an impossibility, which I must then strive to live. My interest in literature is linked to the possibility that it offers me to seek to live the impossible. That's how I work.

FE: This need to feed from literature to invent a life is quite paradoxical when nothing is more real and tangible than photography.

AdA: Yes, but this allows me to set out possible strategies to extend the field of reality, not just to document the state of things but to challenge it, to be intransigent and ambitious. I can question my own existence and put my reasoning to the test. This allows me, once again, not to be reasonable, to consider lifestyles, experiences and logics that are *a priori* impossible to experience, and then strive to live them... or to endure them.

RC: To rise?

AdA: That's it: living up to the words, living up to fiction, living in a senseless way.

RC: You've heard the expression "bigger than life"?

AdA: And I don't know what it means, actually.

RC: It usually refers to an extraordinary character. Along the lines of Citizen Kane, for example.

AdA: We're all able to consider the possibility of pushing the boundaries of impossibility. And if I believe that comfort is the most pernicious and dangerous thing, it's because we all want to take refuge in an ease that protects us from the risk, from the very possibility of going too far. Today, if the expression "too much is not enough" comes up in different forms in my books, it's indeed because it sums up the need to go too far. Going too far is the only way to live with dignity.

*RC: Since we're talking about literature and texts, you've published over 50 books. If we consider only the select bibliography in*Manifesto*, there are 44. And if we take into account the titles you've published since, we must exceed 50. How important is the book to you in relation to the exhibition or the screening?*

AdA: Two things are important. First, this book production does not meet any quality logic. By that, I mean that I'm never in the position to show a completed work in the most elegant possible way. I only make books to find the strength to go to the end of the logic of the current work. The book forces me [Antoine smiles] to take another step, to go through with it, to complete a stage. They are all designed in pain. Mine and the editors'! [Laughs] It's painful because I'm constantly in some imperfection, frustration, clumsiness ...

FE: That's because they're produced with a true sense of urgency.

AdA: That's it. Urgency is the basic principle. I provoke it, I don't control it, but such is the goal. [Antoine smiles] So, all my books are designed according to this logic. Which is very different from the practice of most photographers, who publish works only to give them a final format.

FE: Yes, with most photographers, there is a time of maturation of the format, the selection of the images, the conceptualization of the object, which is not exactly your approach. Let's just say you work very fast to make a book. It's pretty amazing, actually. You're very quick, but the object is very thoughtful. You have it in you to try to find a form for what you're trying to express even if, quite often afterwards, you deny it by saying that it wasn't exactly what you wanted to do. I can testify to the number of times I've seen you dissatisfied with the object you had just produced. But it seems to me that this is a way for you to move forward, to move on to the next thing. In fact, I feel that the books are steps in your production.

AdA: Yes, but the books mark upcoming deadlines. They mark the need to go much further.

FE: Actually, it's a passage. I feel that without the books, you wouldn't be coming home. These are production steps.

AdA: Today, for the month of November, I have about 10 books in the works. With 10 different publishers. [Laughs]

FE: Well, this is turning into bulimia!

AdA: No, no. It's still a way of freeing myself from all logic, from all reason. It's a means to function in a way that is intimately mine, and not to meet other criteria or logics from the cultural circles from which I do everything I can to detach myself.

FE: But why 10 books? Does this mean that 10 publishers came and offered you to publish a book, because you're in great demand? Or is it you needing to formalize 10 objects because there is available material?

AdA: Sometimes, they come to me and then I try to elaborate or impose an idea that will lead me to something essential. Or I have a real need to go to the end of a story, and I contact the publishers.

FE: You exhaust your material in books. You summon your images a lot ...

AdA: No. Today, I'm the one exhausting myself. I no longer have the physical strength; I no longer have the resistance. In Marseilles, on the street, when I was young, I was given the nickname "Double Dose". It's necessary for me today to document this will or need for exhaustion, and the inescapable ensuing failure.

FE: How do you document this exhaustion?

AdA: Again, I'm in the dynamics of an impossible effort, doomed to failure, an impulse, a repetition, the inability to satisfy an excessive desire, to go to the end of a gesture, a story. A duration and pain too: I'm caught in such a chaotic economy ... I teach around the world without interruption, and I'm riddled with debt. I photograph in a desperate and fragmentary way. There is shortness of breath, physical and mental wear and tear. The writing process has dried up, you see, I can't think, I can't write, I can't say or organize things. This forces me into a position in the world where, without having to renounce any of the principles that are mine, I can finally only but deliver, one way or another, the frustration of that position.

FE: And this finally leads you to overproduce ...

AdA: No.

FE: Yes, because 10 books in a year is huge!

AdA: Yes, but each book has its own humble, tiny logic. And each one matters.

FE: But by this gesture, aren't you bearing witness to this exhaustion?

AdA: Yes, but I don't accept having to merely look at the consequences of my failure to jeopardize a system.

RC: You wrote in Ice*: "It will be the collapse that will allow for the writing of the book, another book."*

AdA: There's lucidity or pessimism in that. Regarding the frantic publication of these books, I must take into account the only criterion that counts: an image or a book is only worth existing if the gesture that generated it was worth living. The relevance of the final purpose is only due to the fairness of the intention, to the relevance of the risk taken.

All of my words and my background respond to complex rules and balances. The very fact of being a photographer is a kind of compromise, if not betrayal. I have no choice. And each of these books fits into this logic and this necessity ...

RC: It is a brick, as Fannie said earlier.

FE: But isn't it a little futile to think that there could be an object that would sum up everything?

AdA: No, it's not in vain. But that route has already been done. Today, I believe I've acquired or reached a form of serenity in the sense that, whatever the journey accomplished, I know that I've done what I could. I know that I was out of breath, that I went to the end, that I made every required effort. I have made every human gesture possible to live this life in the most honest and courageous possible way. So, it's not in vain. However, is it possible to conclude, to draw a consequence, to deliver an answer? Can I, at some point, find the strength to build this ideal object?

FE: But in the end, isn't the object the accumulation of everything you've already published?

AdA: Sure. But the overall object would be a monument to the void. [Antoine smiles] A monument to the futility of an immense effort.

FE: But you still have the strength to make books. This means that you're still in an attempt to produce ...

AdA: Well yes, why not? I'm still looking, without the illusion of finding anything, but I won't give up looking ... [Smiles]

FE: You're exhausted, but you still find a little energy to move on ...

AdA: Exhaustion is primarily physical, but it's also emotional and mental ...

FE: It could prevent you from producing, working, giving birth to books. I mean, 10 books, it seems so crazy and requires such energy.

AdA: No, because I'm acting quite minimalist. The physical efforts are minimal, and I accept the inevitable lack of quality of the object. Objects are what they are. I believe that being desperate and in conflict with a global cultural logic gives me the rage and strength to work. As well as the freedom to experiment. I think I've preserved a potential desire, a capacity for empathy, that allows me to live whole. The latest book project came about a fortnight ago, together with Tania Bohorquez, we carried out a project for several weeks in a prison in Mexico. This encounter with men on the brink, this intensity, which is certainly not mine but theirs, gave rise to a book. But I believe it was possible because in this particular context, I gave up existing as a photographer ... I always go there with a desire to take it in the face. That position allows me to feel and react. It actually allows me to see.

RC: I'd like us to talk about Ice *now, because it seems that we can join two themes that you have already mentioned. The book opens with a chronology that, for someone who has never put themselves in this kind of situation, has everything to do with a descent to hell. And you were just talking about your physical exhaustion today. This book is both terrible and at the same time, extremely lucid. You were talking earlier about the desire to preserve your lucidity. How do you see this apparent paradox between losing control ...*

AdA: I guess there are two possible answers. The first is that "crystal", methamphetamine, the drug I was operating on at the time, is terrible. It's undeniably the most brutal, the most destructive, the cruellest of the recent molecules. But paradoxically, this drug makes you extremely lucid. [Chuckles] This has allowed me to work for years in these extreme states of perception, absorption and interaction with the world. You're not in a state of unconsciousness, you don't escape reality, you don't anaesthetize yourself. You're ultra-aware of the depth and complexity of the moment, on all levels: physical, physiological, sensory, emotional, mental. It's therefore an extremely effective chemistry that allows you to go to the end of the physical possibilities of the body while keeping in mind a number of essential things. Secondly, there's another chemistry specific to this book. All the images were made under the effect of methamphetamine, but the whole book was made under the effect of morphine, as a way to regain an impure form of balance. I had to come back down. Or risk staying up there. So, it was a pretty complex chemical process. Besides, I was working at the time with Rafael Garrido, with whom I had previously designed *Agonie*[8]. He was quite instrumental in the book, in the sense that he allowed me to go to the end of a certain madness, assuming the role of centre of gravity as I was blowing up. He was acting as a catalyst. I was in orbit while he kept a certain sense of reason and balance. He allowed me to consider a form that could comply with more or less logical montages and detours. This collaboration allowed me to pretend to give shape to narcotic madness. Finally, the book is quite simple in the sense that the images have their own logic, which is not that of the texts. And yes, there was a kind of descent into hell, because in those years the point for me was to penetrate the violence of the world in an unlikely way. Nevertheless, the book looks very classic to me today. It's sometimes difficult for me to paint the horror of the world with its excesses, and perhaps I can only make an account of it ...

RC: A chronological one?

AdA: Yes, and this constant confrontation – between a given context, identified places on the one hand; and events and gestures that go beyond what reason can accept on the other – offers the possibility of mixing fiction and excessive life.

RC: So, it's not unique to Ice. *About the blurring of your images, which I believe is more often due to long exposure than to movement, is it a consequence of your condition or its representation?*

[8] *Actes Sud, 2009.*

AdA: Long exposure, what do you mean?

RC: I mean that you're perhaps on a two- or three-second-long exposure ...

AdA: I might be mistaken, but no. My way of working is simple. In *Ice* in particular, many images are taken by other people and my camera is constantly on automatic. There is no technical decision per se.

RC: OK, but if there isn't enough light, the shutter will stay open for a longer time?

AdA: Yes, but it depends on the position and stability of the device, the light, the physical movement of the bodies. There's no deliberate will to go into the dark. In fact, *Ice* is one of the last books where blurring is present. At that time, there was a total rejection on my part of the aesthetic in which I was being locked in. The book has gone too far in the search for another level of reality. And at the same time, readers were constantly pointing to the aesthetic aspect of the images – for the sake of protecting themselves from their content, I guess. And to not lock myself into some form of aesthetic logic, I've since strived to return to a sharpness of forms.

FE: You mean the blurring wasn't deliberate. It was simply generated from the shooting conditions ...

AdA: Exactly. The blur was born in my photographic writing in the 1990s. I was talking earlier about my inability to assume the position, new to me, of being inside the system when for 10 years I had lived totally outside of it. I had to learn how to cope. It was very complicated for me to agree to move forward with a camera. For months, I was only able to make images under the influence of alcohol. Hundreds of contact sheets bear witness to this social ineptitude with an unlikely visual porridge. Then, little by little, images began to appear from this magma, this shapeless mass. From the outset, the blurring came inevitably from my inability to assume the position of photographer and, in these states of extreme unconsciousness, to give tangible form to the world. The first blurry images come from there. But from the day that my position, my language or my speech were reduced to a formal issue, to a style, I did everything to escape that definition, to try to equate the same degree of excess, intensity, unreality and fiction through sharp images.

RC: This may explain why the only image of Henri Cartier Bresson you picked for Manifeste *is the brothel in Mexico, which runs against the decisive moment.*

AdA: Yes. Because his photography is always perfect, and there was a failure. [Chuckles] As if he had given up. At that moment, it was impossible for him to shape the geometry of the world. When he told the story of this image, he said that he had opened a door, had the vision of the chaos of the bodies, and immediately closed the door. I find this gesture of closing the door beautiful but frustrating. That way of saying "I give up!" was beautiful [Chuckles] As if these moving bodies, the violence of the bodies, went beyond his will to reveal the geometry of the world. I thought it was very beautiful. I have a lot of affection for the photography of Cartier-Bresson. I find this ambition to put the world in order futile and superb at the same time. After that, the laziness of generations of photographers, for nearly 30 years, resulted in the stagnation of the photographic language. [Laughs] Photography has been reduced to despairing mimetic practices that until today trap its language in false values. But yes, I think it was a beautiful instance of renunciation. A nice defeat.

RC: You've already said all the evil you thought of the art world, and even about Psychogéographie, *your willingness to go against your commissioners. So, we understand your position in relation to money and capitalism ...*

AdA: I'm only trying to use the system without being used by it. I have no choice and I have no qualms. I'm forced to use the means at my disposal. My freedom of movement depends on it. My convictions and my existence run counter to the cultural logics of art today. And I protect myself to the extent of my physical, financial and intellectual capacity. For me, this is not a compromise, but an inescapable context, and I'm ready to pay the price for my convictions and commitments.

RC: About Ice *again, because I feel that drugs and prostitution represent the wildest capitalism… if we place ourselves in the position of the proletarian, to use a Marxist term, it is still the most unbridled capitalism…*

AdA: The forces that govern the legal economy, of which we are all complicit, are far more cruel, hypocritical and insidious than those that govern the world of crime. On the other hand, I don't put myself in the position of the proletarian. I've always been aware of the difference between my position and that of my subjects. I'm here by choice; for them, it is out of necessity. At 17, I made choices that were primarily political, and still are: to live the violence of the world in my own flesh, to develop a political position that is more brutish than media-friendly, to opt for delinquency over intelligence. At the time, I belonged to the autonomous movement under situationist influences. There was a precise, deliberate logic of violence. I was not there aimlessly, but to experience that violence in the most absolute possible way. It has always been a choice to be where the pain takes precedence over the rest, and I still haven't given up. Comfort is temptation and the ultimate danger. But in front of me, no one had a choice. Each tiny story is a tragic and immense fate. Misery is never chosen; it is always suffered. This being said, the position of these subjects allows them to generate or develop lifestyles that exceed those of the communities of the norm. And I chose to live by their side …

RC: You're there by choice.

AdA: Yes, my position isn't the same. And I'm aware, more than anyone, of the tragic dimension of these exploitation processes, but my position is neither humanistic nor humanitarian. And I refuse to give anyone who doesn't experience the criminal misery from the inside the right to judge, because above all, they are blind accomplices. My priority isn't to live in the comfort of certainties but to develop survival and resistance strategies.

RC: Which ones?

AdA: Well, to develop a tangible form that accounts for this narcotic and sexual violence, which is sprawling but invisible, and which is deliberately denied by the rest of the community. And to the extent of my means, to live the world in the excess of its insanity. But your question also points to the moral aspects of things. The nature of my relationships with those I photograph is one of the reasons I made a four-hour film, *White Noise*. To deliver another voice from these women, one that doesn't comply with any journalistic or humanitarian model, one that is authentic and dignified, worthy of their pain and infamous beauty, so to speak. I report directly to them, and to no one else.

RC: To the day world, you mean?

AdA: Yes, logics that are not mine. As for the drugs, there's no such thing as a pure or clean economy. All the dominant economies are equal, and the drug economy is neither better nor worse than any other. I don't establish any moral hierarchy between these economies that govern the world. They are the different facets of the same cruelty. During my last trips to Mexico, I journeyed through a society plunged into widespread violence that blended both liberal and criminal violence. This destroys any desire for humanity. And I chose to go as close to it as possible to confront my position with this violence. But there is no obvious answer, there is no possible resolution to the dilemma of everyone's responsibility: this violence reaches such a degree of insanity, its destructive capacity, not only on human beings but on social relations, is such that there is no way out. People are no longer just exploited but raped, massacred, tortured ... So, the only thing I can do as an autonomous individual is to be as close as possible to it, closer to the crime scenes, to the morgues. The point is not to testify; it is to avoid seeking refuge in ignorance, to refuse to let my consciousness be numbed by it. And in fact,

it's complicated. You must be careful with words.
I experienced these two types of violence in my flesh during a stay that turned out to be a nightmare. At night, I was under the influence of extreme chemistry with paranoia and the ensuing madness, and during the day, I was with the cops and coroners in the morgues and at crime scenes. And then, you become aware of the world we're living in [Antoine smiles], especially in this type of society that gradually contaminates the rest of the world and is responsible for all this and refuses to admit so. This is basically unliveable. Today in Mexico, I'm forced to operate differently because the context leaves me no other choice, and I work in prisons. There is no life, no possible rationale. Nothing makes sense. What else is there to say?
About prostitution again, whose principle governs our world, one of the books I'm working on this year with Éditions de l'Œil is an adaptation of the monologues in *White Noise*. It is imageless and consists of 2,788 phrases said by these women.
Twenty-three women speak in 14 different languages about the reality of their existence and our exchanges. My decision is to allow for these words to be heard. They tell what they tell, and I give shape to their words. So again, we're never in a relationship of pureness. But these women tell the senseless nature of these relationships in which everyone asks everything from others. I'm asking for everything from human beings who are experts in violent relations with others [Smiles], who extort from men what they can and what they need to survive. Bringing it any further would mean having to tell each one of these stories. Take it or leave it. At your own risk.

RC: Well, perhaps I'm the one with a moral stance. One thing has bothered me for a long time in your work: its reception by the audience. Let me explain. I know, I can see that part of your audience is young, enthusiastic and revolted.
But at the same time, we also know that an educated, relatively wealthy, let's say bourgeois audience – since I was talking about proletarians earlier – come to museums, galleries, art centres, even bookstores to contemplate what you've recorded, what you've been through, and who may draw some aesthetic pleasure from it. Doesn't this overhanging position bother you?

AdA: That's the price to pay for my freedom of movement. I have no accountability to anyone, and even less to the viewer, to the public. I don't have an audience. I don't have much respect, as I said, for the agents of the cultural logic and I don't have much respect for those who consume my images. Every time I find myself confronted with a viewer, I put them in front of their own responsibilities, their basic laziness. The consumer position is unacceptable as such. The purpose of my photography is to help me, myself, escape the role or function of the consumer, the organized fatality of the spectacle. So I don't take spectators or consumers into account. I seek to impose on myself and impose on others a position that I hope contaminates the logics of the prevailing laziness. I state a position, vaguely hoping that it will allow others to develop their own. But even if my financial autonomy, assuming I have financial autonomy [Smiles], but this is incidental ... even if my ability to be self-reliant comes from a system, I draw from it the resources to optimally "use" the world and this certainly doesn't mean that I must respond to or be responsible for logics that are, again, not my own.On the other hand, when I teach, the context is different. It's not systematic, but many young photographers come to me filled with illusions and desires. I feel the need to put them back in their place, to force them to take responsibility, to assume their real position. I put all my energy into "bringing them into the world", to the extent of each one's ability t o question themselves. I try to show them the blandness of their fantasies, to make them aware of the indulgence with which they contemplate their own fate.

FE: But at the same time, it seems to me that you have a relatively broad willingness to receive. You are able, unlike many artists, to exhibit anywhere, from the smallest bar to the largest museum. You also have an ability to give a lot and to ignore the codes of exhibition and display. You said, Rémi, that you felt embarrassed by the public receiving Antoine's images, because, indeed, viewers have this overhanging position, but I believe that Antoine has this ability to give.

AdA: Yes, my detachment from the cultural economic system allows me extreme freedom of action, for better or for worse.

My last exhibition took place in Mexico and the unique, original pieces cost only a few tens of dollars. What I mean by that is that having no calculated agenda, business logic or planned career, because I constantly meet the imperatives of survival, I am in a position where the possibility of denouncing cultural corruption is a necessity, since it allows me to delineate my own field of action. At the same time, no hierarchies or obscure logic determine my artistic gesture. There is a need to do and to tell.

FE: What's bothering you, Rémi? The fact that viewers delight at Antoine's work or the fact that Antoine shows his images to these viewers in those venues?

RC: No, no, it's the audience, who adopts an overreaching position, boasting, for example, "Oh look at that brown!" or "Look at the light on the flesh!", etc., when I can see that Antoine is in a truthful relationship.

AdA: Recently, at Les Filles du Calvaire Gallery in Paris, I said to the audience: "If you understand my work, get out of here and go build your own life!" If someone buys an image, yes, it will help me to move forward, to continue, but everything is done to state the possibility available to anyone to live outside of the imposed consumer-spectator position.

RC: You wrote somewhere, I quote from memory, that "while it is illusory to think that art can change the world, one can try to undermine the system from the ground up".

AdA: Yes, which is why the word "contamination" often comes up in my remarks. I must live accordingly, knowing the limits of my capacity for nuisance and at the same time, I do not give up that capacity, which is mine.

RC: We said a word about it earlier, Fannie, before Antoine arrived, but after Ice, *you conceived* Anticorps[9] *together – well,*

[9] *"Anticorps", exhibition, curators: Fannie Escoulen and Bernard Marcadé, Paris, Le Bal, 24 January – 14 April 2013;* Anticorps, *publication, Éditions Xavier Barral, 2013.*

not only the two of you. Was it then a way to bring the pendulum back to the centre, and not to let you, Antoine, fall into the caricature of the photographer of drugs and brothels?

AdA: Exactly. How to remain "audible" without giving up the most extreme images and experiences. It was important that *Anticorps* – and we talked often and extensively about it with Fannie – included these images from *Ice*, these unacceptable images. In one corner of the exhibition were these unwatchable images. Images that everyone, until then, had refused to see. But in the context of *Anticorps*, and because we had managed to impose a certain balance to my purpose, a perspective on the violence of the day and that of the night, these extreme images found a context. It was not a process, but a precision added to an ideological position led by a junkie praxis. The day images had existed since 2002, even before. My first images figured Haitian strikers in New York in 1991. There was Bosnia, the images made in Jerusalem in 2000 and in the West Bank in 2002, and so on. But it was actually the first time I tried – we tried – to show this duality.

RC: This goes beyond duality, because there's a common logic, right?

AdA: I know that in the end, the various types of violence blend into one ...

FE: But this was perceived as a duality.

RC: In the exhibition, and you surely each have your own opinion about it, but superimposing the images on the wall showed me the thickness, the various levels of meaning and production of meaning in your work.

FE: That was exactly what it was.

AdA: In a way, yes. There are as many logics as there are situations and actors in these situations. The will is not to list, but to reveal that violence.

FE: It was only by superimposing the images, by making them coexist, that one could give meaning to the various types of violence that form one. We tried everything. Opposing them or putting them face to face clearly didn't allow them to meet. Only by adjoining them could we make it clear that they all came from the same approach.

AdA: Yes. I've always tried to give new, original forms to the display of violence. Especially for the series made during the day, because I have no system or pre-established working protocol. There are as many improvised narrative strategies as there are situations. And if there was one system, it would be, in every situation, to wait for a moment of panic where I must force myself to the point of having to react physically, instinctively, photographically, to a given violence. And then I must generate, invent a form that is born directly from the reality of a given situation. There is no systematic style or practice. The point is to touch closely upon the economic cruelty, in order to find myself in a situation of weakness or powerlessness and in the obligation to develop a position or strategy of resistance. To then be able to utter it in spontaneous form.

FE: You're talking about forms, but what are they? Is the book a form?

AdA: No, I'm talking about actions to be developed at the heart of situations, to be at the origin of tiny but significant events. For example, when I go to Jerusalem and try to show the perspective of two opposing sides in a street battle. Or when I go to Calais and show the migrants only from behind, in dehumanized, uniform anonymity. When I go in search of clandestine migrant camps in the mountains of North Africa and sleep with them in a forest or in a cave, the images are born from lived situations, assumed actions. There is no pre-established concept.

FE: Yes. And no prior device either ...

AdA: Exactly.

RC: But then you conceive the devices after the fact? The grid, for example?

AdA: Yes, by rejection, or weariness of the effective or iconic image. I look for new perspectives and types of storytelling to account for the violence. It doesn't matter that the viewer may reject them. I feel that the grid is yet another way to account for a given course or experience. Gradually, it became a way of displaying, of showing the excess of an initiative doomed to failure. The sentence is not beautiful, but this violence is unheard of, and I had to come up with a language that would live up to the stakes. It was no longer a question of trying, or not, to toy with psychology and emotion, but simply, how to say?

RC: To account for the enormity of the thing?

AdA: Yes. The grid is an endless enumeration ...

RC: But then, does the grid join the lists? I'm not only talking about the lists of sites. You also like to make lists of words around a theme ...

AdA: I like boxes too. [Smiles] Lists, boxes, grids ...

RC: Do these approaches come together?

AdA: The grids have imposed themselves early in my photographic practice. Parallel to the attempt to undo the accepted forms, the bodies, the flesh, to reach for another essence of humanity in invented figures ... From the beginning already, I photographed the day in a systematic orderly manner – facades of buildings, faces, bodies, reduced to their social or economic function, symptoms of a cold, determined violence ... Grids that locked the gaze into the genocidal logics of the system. They allowed me to create structures in which I could myself get lost. Perhaps I was lost to the point of feeling the need for some kind of framework.

RC: So, this brings us back to the earlier work. Perhaps to Stigma *[2002], where you have interior scenes punctuated by buildings.*

AdA: Exactly. And even before *Stigma*, the first grids are there. The Haitian strikers in Brooklyn, the facades of Alexandria, the ruins in Bosnia, the mining landscape of the Vosges, the dilapidated landscape of Marseilles, the migrants from Calais, the besieged cities of the West Bank, all these series carried out before 2002 ...
It's all there in *Désordres*[10]. In *Manifeste*, they take on other forms, but in *Désordres*, we can clearly see the importance of these first grids. I've always been aware of my inability to account for the extent of the disaster. Sometimes, it was these rigid urban or human forms that also allowed me to give some kind of framework to the shapeless. I need to hold on to something more tangible than the deliquescence of bodies.

FE: But the grid is also a way to enclose, right?

AdA: To enclose, to protect, to annihilate ...

FE: But isn't that perhaps also a way to react to the confinement in which you live?

AdA: I don't have an answer. I don't think anyone is able to escape the feeling of confinement, in one form or another. We can read Sartre, Beckett or Kafka again, or, like Artaud or Bacon, sketch a sign, a line, a frame with chalk to then get lost, destroyed or blended into the madness of men. I feel this is linked to a healthy necessity.

RC: Fannie told me earlier that you're a ... I don't think "collector" is the right word ... but let's say that you bring back from your travels a significant number of books devoted to Francis Bacon.

AdA: Yes, but this has to do with a ritual, a magic gesture. Most of them are still wrapped in their blister. [Laughs] I'm not

[10] *Antoine d'Agata,* Désordres, *Editions Voies Off, 2015.*

a collector; I treat myself with photography. There is a connection.

FE: Sacred...

AdA: No, sincerely, these books give me an invisible strength. It's a habit, a pagan ritual ...

RC: I'd like to ask you two or three questions about appropriation. We can start from Position(s), *the book you did with Giuliana Prucca*[11]*, where a selection of your images are treated in a particular way. Not only are they all black and white, but they only preserved the black flat tint and the white paper. Relatively often, you entrust your work to others or you leave it..*

AdA: To be precise, I went to see Giuliana with a book by Jean-Luc Godard. It wasn't *Histoire(s) du cinéma* but an old book found at some book dealer, in which the images were treated exactly the same way. So, it wasn't by chance. That said, it's true that I always have the will to put my images to the test of someone else's gaze. Recently, it was with silkscreen prints made by Pakito Bolino and Éditions du Dernier Cri; or with *Oscurana*, a work entrusted simultaneously to six different publishers to see what they would do with it. In general, I know exactly what the final form of my images should be, but my patience is limited, and that's not what matters most ...

RC: You've put your images to the test with Baudelaire's Les Fleurs du mal[12]*, which you're currently preparing with Vincent Marcilhacy*[13]*.*

AdA: Again, I worked with the publisher and the technician. I exercised the necessary control because there was an aesthetic

[11] *Giuliana Prucca, founder of the artist's book publishing house Avarie, released* Position(s) *in 2012.*

[12] *The book is a facsimile of the first edition of* Les Fleurs du mal, *published in 1857 by Auguste Poulet-Malassis, "illustrated" with Antoine's images treated as engravings.*

[13] *Vincent Marcilhacy is the editor of The Eyes Publishing and therefore of the present volume.*

"risk" to it. And I'm aware of the fact that the process can escape me and damage what is understood as the photographic integrity of the images. But it's a real pleasure for me to mistreat my own images and test them with random techniques, perhaps to prove to myself that my purpose doesn't lie there, that meaning must withstand form. These new, fragile, foreign forms, these alterations and various interpretations, allow for the images to circulate, to penetrate unknown spaces the rules of which escape me, and that's fine for me. In Mexico's prisons, groups of prisoners are currently making woodcuts from dozens of my photographs, and I'm curious about the mysterious or sacrilegious meaning these images will take in a context the parameters of which I know nothing about.

RC: The images take on different forms, but what do these changes bring you personally?

AdA: The shape doesn't matter to me even though, to a certain extent, I depend on it as well. I try to preserve the meaning and put the form back in its place. Form is a means. I like this impurity of forms; I take stock of the contemporary fatality of the contamination that threatens forms ...

FE: But your images are also raw material. An object you don't have complete control over. You generate that material. You produce it, but then it belongs to everyone.

AdA: Exactly. It's like that old habit of mine of giving the camera to others to make the images, while creating the conditions for their images to incorporate some narrative or visual logic that is mine. At the same time, there is renunciation of the notion of artist or of the status of author, because the stakes are different and more important than the production of a purely iconographic work. Technical advances and the incestuous global culture have rendered any aspiration to excellence futile. Photography is no more than a fool's game. The stakes are others.

RC: Inversely, it makes sense to me that if you entrust your images to others - even if you keep an eye on them - you also

take hold of others' objects. And I mean Fractal *and [*Antoine d'Agata:*]*Manifesto.
Fractal *seems to push the logic of the grid to the extreme, with a zoom-like editing. It starts from this huge mosaic of thousands of mugshots of prostitutes, which gradually dissolve into an abstraction of pixels. However, I find odd the explanation I read here or there, claiming that the pixel destroys identity and makes it impossible to see the detail of an expression. I say this because for me, the same process is at work in Antonioni's* Blow-Up. *What led you to make this motionless journey? Was it an outrage at the power that reveals the identity of these individuals? A critique of what the internet has become, when it initially started as a libertarian space?*

AdA: I'll first reply about *Fractal* and then more broadly about appropriation. *Fractal* is the observation not of failure but of powerlessness. As disproportionate as my efforts may have been to develop a valid, honest and decent position, and as far as I can go in my exploration of the darkness of the world and of the violence and madness of those who inhabit it, there is, in these images found on the internet, something that reaches beyond anything I could ever accomplish. These girls are represented at a moment when they are destroyed, abused, humiliated, in the hands of an institutional power and being scrutinized by the cruel and barbaric eye of pitiful police officers, at the very moment when the abuse takes place, and despite the vulgarity of the tortured gaze, because of this barbaric brutality, they touch to the depth of the sublime, like the portraits of Auschwitz or S-21[14] touch to an intolerable degree of the humanity of those who face the apparatus of the camps. I saw these images and was left silent in front of this endless sequence of tragedies. I felt I had to give up any photographic effort. A multitude of anonymous and pathetic cops had stuck their nose into the misery of the world, and, by their very position at the heart of the law enforcement apparatus, they had direct access to the violence of the world.

[14] *S-21 was the detention, torture and killing centre of the Khmer Rouge regime in Cambodia.*

Their immoral posture did not change that, and I had to account for it. The poetry of the pixel is a detail. All that remains is the truth of those stolen moments. At the time, I was building the exhibition at Le Bal in Paris, and there was no other possible starting or ending point than these images. I needed to return to that pure violence, that brutality that went beyond anything I had experienced or observed. The fascination is each day repeated in the face of the proliferation of raw images grinded by mass communication. It is enough to spend a few minutes in front of a screen to feel submerged by an amazing mass of senseless images that bear witness to the consistency and meticulousness displayed by human beings when they are determined to destroy other human beings. Today, I have given up searching the rubbish bins of our common genocidal memory to continue to feel, desire and act. The photographic gesture becomes increasingly useless. We live in a world writhing in pain that is dying before my eyes. But we have no choice but to continue to live, hallucinated by a constant stream of cursed images.

RC: Yes, including automatic images ...

AdA: Everything! The horror is filmed from every angle. There are billions of auto-generated images each day.

RC: You said that you started appropriation "handcraftedly" around 1999, and now we come to these billions of images ...

AdA: I claim to be a photographer, I try to determine a mode of responsibility and a way of life. It's not feasible for me to continue pretending to impose a perspective, but the temptation is there: it would be enough to tap into this mass of images that capture the horror. Which many do, and the process is endless. These images overwhelm any possibility of resistance, any pretention to intelligence or rationale. Barbarism is without possible measure. I try to resist the temptation of prostration. Joan Fontcuberta [see *Conversations 2*, p. 64], with whom I was talking a while ago, talks about the image that remains to be invented. But what image? I doubt this possibility, though I respect the optimism of the statement. My conviction is that

it is not an image that has yet to be invented, it is about gestures, events that we must provoke to put an end to the immobility that crushes us, to the fatality of impotence and comfort.
The words don't matter. The only way out is to generate new life positions, not images. The images irreparably condemn us to be complicit in our own damnation.

RC: I was talking about that with Mishka Henner [see p. 150]. Four or five years ago, he did a book you may have seen, No Man's Land, *with images of girls on roadsides in southern Spain retrieved from Google Street View. And at the same time, Txema Salvans was publishing a very similar book,* The Waiting Game, *with photos taken with a view camera, for which he travelled hundreds and hundreds of kilometres. I quote this anecdote only to concur with you: everything has been photographed, and now even Google photographs.*

AdA: Yes, but there are others. Doug Rickard was among the first. But what worries me about this process is that is a sign of renunciation. It brings the photographer back to a position of curator, spectator, consumer. It comforts them in a passive and alienated position, while once again, photography has the ability to be the only artistic language developed within the moment that can generate it. Photography allows and requires above all experience, presence to the world, the unique perspective of each individual, induced by the responsibility of a physical position that they assume, alone in the face of reality. Renunciation is not an option ...

RC: You mean there are still positions to be found?

AdA: I find that the paralysis of time and mutant technology impose their logic on our degenerate societies. But I believe that in the meagre interstices of the paralyzed human history and of cruel systems of production and performance, within the economic order of things, in the recesses of existence and human consciousness, there remain flaws to be explored, attitudes and deviations to be invented, destinies to be written and lived. I have condemned myself to live the tiny scenario that I forged out of my fears and desires; and photography, as corrupted a medium as it may be, remains a possible strategy in the face of the almighty digital power.

RC: Yes, with deep learning computers are already able to recognize a dog, for example. Even if there is first a black dog, then a white dog or even a chequered dog, the machine will recognize it as such ... Finally, this is just the beginning.

AdA: The outlook is frightening, but language remains the place of all the aberrations, deviations, all the possible subversions. It is enough to get rid of the logics and habits of the past, to protect ourselves from the beauties, the poems, the intelligence that enclose us all in our passivity. The only remedy for this endless fascination with the image is dissent. Turning the eyes away from the screen, facing the world and living. It is a vital necessity to refuse to give in to the hypnotic capabilities of the system. There is no conspiracy logic in this finding; the system feeds on itself and we are reduced to the condition of ...

RC: Consumers ...

AdA: More than that, to animal life ...

FE: Yes, a very passive position.

AdA: Giorgio Agamben says that there is no substantial difference between the organization of concentration camps and that of modern capitalism, and I live this violence day after day. My radicalism or my rage comes from what I see on every street corner. Environmental violence is unthinkable, and unacceptable. And my effort is tiny, it is ...

RC: It's a grain of sand in the cog ...

AdA: I don't think so, we have to be more pessimistic. The process is still in the making, but the economic logics are now crushing the possibilities of life.

RC: I'd like to end with Manifesto. *In 2017,* Magnum Manifesto[15] *was released. And a year later, you published* Antoine d'Agata: Manifesto[16]. *I was talking about appropriation ...*

AdA: Six months later.

RC: Six months later, sorry. So, the same number of pages, similar cover, similar layout, similar typography. What happened? To quote our president, it must have cost you crazy money[17]. *You couldn't ignore that you were going to get in trouble for copyright issues.*

AdA: Sure enough.

RC: Plus, you were attacking your own agency, Magnum Photos. I think it' a great idea, but why take such risks?

AdA: Once again, there is the imperative for me to act freely, including within the structures that carry or support me. Without going into detail, I felt a real need for autonomy, for freedom of speech. The reactions were many and very violent, but I do what I have to do, and I say what I have to say. Nothing else comes into play.
I told Clément Chéroux, the author of the [Magnum] book, that I didn't agree with his perspective on what Magnum is ... that I would reply to him, and I'd do so publicly. I did, without taking the possible consequences into account. I accepted them and Clément Chéroux understood it.

FE: He did?

AdA: Yes. In any case, he bought my book and enjoyed it, I believe. Regarding the book, I don't know what I can or can't say. When there's a non-disclosure agreement, can we say that there is a non-disclosure agreement or not? [Laughs]

[15] *Clément Chéroux, Clara Bouveresse,* Magnum Manifesto, *Thames and Hudson, 2017.*

[16] *Antoine d'Agata,* D'Agata Manifesto, *Studio Vortex, 2017.*

[17] *This refers to a comment made by France's President Macron about social welfare costs.*

There's a protocol. I don't know what I can legally say. I'm not allowed to talk about the book.

FE: Ah, downright to talk about it?

AdA: No, I mean, I'm not allowed to give the details of the agreement. So, I don't know what I can say. In any case, today I'm not allowed to sell the book.

FE: But Rémi has the right to talk about it? [Laughs]

AdA: I don't know! [Laughs]

RC: So, you signed a form of a peace agreement or a truce ...

AdA: No, no, it's an agreement ... but no peace. [Laughs] Not even a truce. In fact, it's not even an agreement; a protocol has been established that provides an opportunity to prosecute the offender.

FE: In other words, a framework for the use of the book had to be defined.

AdA: Yes, it's simple: I have the right not to destroy it, but I don't have the right to sell it.

FE: You have the right to display it, to show it, to broadcast it, but not the right to sell it.

AdA: Yes.

RC: This agreement, the terms of which I don't know, seems to me, in all proportion, comparable to the trial of Les Fleurs du mal *or to Sade's prosecution. By that I mean that public or private censors create a desire for what they aim to remove from sight. People have always read Sade, or tried to read it. And so, in fact,* Manifesto *has become a collector's item. How do you feel, and I mean it in a broad sense, about the counterproductive effects that censorship, and therefore power, can have?*

AdA: Again, to think that way forces me to consider logics that are not mine... In a very general way, if I consider the obscene, or pornography, or what is showable or not, I'm forced to turn to rationales that should not be mine. I think that when we talk about the violence of images, the obscenity of images, of my images, in fact, my perspective is different. I look for excess, the impossible, the intensity. I want to get close to death in the most effective way possible, but death in life. Therefore, it's dangerous and counterproductive for me to consider futile reasoning, whether cultural, commercial or artistic.
It's a trap, a danger that lurks constantly. Hence the importance for me to take what is to be taken, to remain as lucid as possible about my purpose, my logic and the possibilities that are mine.
The risk of diversion is permanent. I realize that in the end, the system – if by system, we mean the global relationships, the power relations, the interests and lies that preside over the functioning of a given community – is terribly effective and logical with itself.
In the end, it's difficult for me to resist, to continue, day after day, despite their soft yet persistent attempts to mitigate or silence any alternative speech. And I'm not even paranoid.
On the contrary, I feel quite serene about my isolation.
I constantly renew the stakes tied to my practice. I try to hold on physically. I try to ignore the wear and tear.

22 April 2019

AMAURY DA CUNHA

Amaury da Cunha was born in 1976 in Paris, where he works and lives. He graduated from the École Nationale Supérieure de la Photographie in Arles. He has written many reviews on photography and literature, including for Le Monde des Livres. *Since 2005, his photographic work has been exhibited in France, especially at the Rencontres d'Arles or in Paris in the context of the Month of Photography, and internationally in Spain, Italy and Belgium. Today, he is the author and co-author of eight books.*

Amaury and I have been communicating via email for a long time. The 4 or 5 kilometres between our homes is too much of a distance for Parisians to meet without a good reason. This happened in 2012, when he asked me to curate his first exhibition in Paris, "Après tout", as part of the Month of Photography. At the same time, Fabrice Wagner published *Après tout* at Éditions Le Caillou Bleu. An unfailing friendly trio was then formed.

Amaury's practice stands out in contemporary production for many reasons. First, the texts he authors are as important as his images. In the beginning, they were only fragments included in his photography books. Then, they became a story as well as various essays published in a literary collection. Second, he is outstanding in his photographic approach: avoiding protocols and series, he indulges himself in a being-in-the-world attitude, capturing weird, small distortions of the day-to-day. Whereas his eye was quite amazed at the beginning, it became darker over time. The coherence of this work lies in the themes he addresses: disappearance, loss, the cumbersome body and eluding identity.

For a long time, we had promised to have a face-to-face conversation. The opportunity came when Patrizia Brandellero and Fabrice Wagner organized a long festive weekend in the castle of a hamlet in Condroz in Belgium. Perched on a hill, it overlooks a valley and a pond facing the forest. This conversation took place on a spring morning in the castle courtyard under an immaculate sky, birds chirping in the background.

Rémi Coignet: *In your first book,* Saccades, *you write: "At times, believing that the writing and the image may perhaps help to assert his singularity, which, otherwise, would suddenly become mundane." So, is it all about narcissism?*

Amaury da Cunha: Let me first be a little silent. Your question is somewhat abrupt, but let's not confuse everything. If one photographs and writes to forge oneself as a subject, that does not mean that one falls into narcissism. To live without writing or rummaging the surface of the world by photographing it, can make me very unhappy: I do not feel alive anymore. I remember the words of critic and writer Bernard Lamarche-Vadel that terrified me and that I read as a terrible warning: "I was never made alive." As soon as I feel a drive to write or a desire to see, I'm in the world again, in my place. Otherwise, everything goes down the drain.

RC: From your first book, you blend in texts and images. What relationship do you establish between these two modes of expression?

AdC: Brevity first, and variety. What interested me in *Saccades* was to gather images without any hierarchy of subjects or themes. The skull of a man photographed in an airplane, foliage, a female silhouette in a car park ... To quote René Char, whom I was reading a lot at the time, it was about photographing "the infinite variety of the faces of the living". In a rather wild and anarchic manner. And when I could no longer photograph, I would write short sentences, aphorisms, descriptions of things, micro-fictions. I was perhaps looking for a way to equate images through writing. In any case, I wanted these texts to be read as quickly as photographs are looked at.

RC: Throughout your books, you have explored various ways to create a dialogue between the texts and the images: texts intersecting the images in the second part of Saccades, *at the end of the book in* Après tout *and* Incidences, *and in two separate chapters and in two separate volumes in* Histoire souterraine *and in* HS. *With hindsight, is there a form that is best suited?*

AdC: Each book is an adventure, and I hope not to repeat myself, but it's true that with each new project, even if I plan, for example, to make a book of images only, I end up including some texts. They are often separate from the pictures.
But as a book is also a mental space, I don't think it's difficult for the reader to make up associations between photos and texts. This need to write, on the margin of the images, is irrepressible. As a friend who wrote the preface to *Saccades* said, the problem is that I cannot help but talk...

RC: Jean-Baptiste.

AdC: Yes, Jean-Baptiste de Froment in the preface entitled "The Last Sock". Photography is silent, obscure... it often leaves me disappointed and always causes me a feeling of lack. Perhaps at the core of my work is that notion of lack. The poet Stéphane Bouquet, with whom I worked, speaks of the "missing third" that he has noticed in some of my photographs. Which may explain the need to write. The use of the text as a desire to dispel silence. It is also a matter of utterance. In the images I shoot, one could say that there is an "I" that is a little shy, and a distant, possibly cold "he". In the photos of Denis Roche, with their assumed lyricism, the omnipotence of the "I" is put to the test of time. I may be more on the side of indeterminacy. There is self-effacement in photography that is both salutary and a bit tragic. Writing is a way of regaining the power to speak after being deprived of it.

RC: What I understand from what you've just said is that your work, to paraphrase Michel Foucault, is words and things.

AdC: Yes, it's probably a poetic search for dialogue between words and things, also assuming their differences.
I'm acknowledging today that my work increasingly summons primitive memories. I didn't photograph when I was seven or eight, but I spent days during the summer in a small garden in Brittany, in Saint-Malo, gazing at flowers. In the evening,

my delight was to open a loosely scientific book where I could find images of things I had seen (plants, flowers, trees). Thanks to this book, I could finally, in a state of total exaltation, put words to the things I had seen. Was that enough for me to enter the secret of the world? Probably not. As writer Roger Laporte says: "The duty to name is unspeakable." This echoes another sentence from a photographer who has meant a lot to me, Arnaud Claass, a double-edged sentence compared to what I just told you. He wrote, as far as I remember: "Photographing things is naming them without words." It's undoubtedly a liberating statement, but at the same time it can only mean much frustration to anyone who wants to write. Writing may perhaps release the speech that is taken hostage by an image.

RC: Photography books are most often conceived as series according to a theme or geographical place, for example. This isn't the case with you. I have a feeling that your books are like progress reports and that you follow the same story. What is your feeling?

AdC: Yes, I follow the same story, and I think that each book does not correspond to a series, but rather to a period of life. Nor is it an autobiographical work in the strict sense of the term: everything I photograph is often borrowed from immediate life – by chance, by accident. I play a game, which is to deflect the most intimate things and closest to my life, to put them into a certain opacity. The images mask the identity of the human beings and suspend time. We don't quite know where we are, or in what time of life. This shift has always interested me. A psychoanalyst, J.-B. Pontalis, calls "autography" the art of digging into one's life arbitrarily rather than viewing it as an absolute material. Life is a material like any other, more object than it is subject. The purpose is to set up a form of displacement and transformation, as in any artistic project.

RC: How important is the book in the presentation of your work? What does it allow?

AdC: I guess this passion first derives from my veneration of literature books. The first book I published at Yellow Now was a small format, comparable to literature paperbacks. To put it in an obvious, almost banal way: the book is what remains. The life of images can be displayed on walls, but what do they become at the end of an exhibition? That's not what thrills me most, and what interests me with books is the sequencing process. I have plenty of images and everyone can shoot singular images. But you need to know what to do with them.

RC: In 2012 you published Après tout *with Fabrice Wagner. The same year you did me the honour of asking me to be the curator of the eponymous exhibition. We displayed a pretty dark hanging…*

AdC: Why dark?

RC: Well, we highlighted the threatening, disturbing side of this work. The book is more poetic, even if I don't like this word. Is your work plastic? Can the perception of your images be modified according to the way they are displayed?

AdC: Definitely! I can't remember the name of the philosopher who talks about the concept of the bird-image. What I find interesting is to be able to transform the images according to where they are displayed. There are photographers who display their images always in the same manner on the wall and their books echo their spatial installation. To me, the life of an image is not congealed. From one exhibition to the next, from one book to the next, I must be able to hang it differently, to mix it with others, as in a deck of cards.

RC: What you say refers to Evidence *by Mandel and Sultan, for example.*

AdC: Yes, absolutely. But I also want to say that in my photography books I find it interesting to collaborate with others. I like the idea that someone can use my images, get them out of myself, a publisher for example, because they are moved by my way of doing things. I don't give them full free rein, but I feverishly look forward to their proposals. Sharing images makes them richer.

RC: This book, Après tout, *is the first you published after your brother Charles committed suicide. Has this tragedy changed your photography?*

AdC: Yes, I guess so. I made this book at a time of mourning. And while mourning, one is deprived of comforting images. My brother committed suicide in July 2009. I didn't have any pictures of him, I never saw his body again. There was this absolutely terrifying lack. There was also a lack of dreams, in the almost neurological or biological sense of the term: I was no longer dreaming at night. My nights were completely deprived of images. So, this had to be offset by a kind of frantic photographic quest in which unconsciousness was having a field day. Suddenly, the issue of absence could be embodied in things without apparent tragic dimensions. Like a dog locked in a car, or a woman stranded on a rock.

RC: From that point on, sexuality became explicit in your work…

AdC: What is explicit sexuality?

RC: Your girlfriends naked, things like that. What was only metaphorical or alluded to before. Why is it important to show it?

AdC: I think it's already the metaphor of unveiling through the notion of nudity. Let me think a little because the question you're asking is not obvious… [Long silence]

RC: We can go on if you want.

AdC: Yes, perhaps.

RC: In 2013 you published a beautiful little book, Reste le rouge. *In this poem, you write: "The image is a beautiful slut." What do you mean? [Chuckles]*

AdC: The association between the image and the slut comes from a specific context, a poem. The sluts are sometimes liars, right? They can deceive, seduce, betray too. It is perhaps this very ambiguous relationship that I have with photography. I'm easily captivated by its form, but I'm wary of what it gives me to see. A slut promises things she doesn't necessarily deliver. And photography kind of goes in that direction. I wrote in a book that it is both about promise and regret. The image is also about that. That is to say, the promise of something that we can perhaps recover, that we can perhaps grasp, that we can embrace. In fact, I would say that the image is more a tease than a slut, to be a somewhat more precise; a reality show-off.

> *RC: Your father is and has been a photographer, producing both shots for the press and SAS[1] book covers. As a child, he shot you (not for an SAS cover, of course). Has this influenced your calling?*

AdC: I don't think so ... but without a doubt, photography had a crucial place in my life. My childhood memories are full of images of my family, of my sister, of my brother and of myself. My father kept photographing us on holidays, on beaches. He was making a family album, but at the same time he was using these images for magazines such as *Bien-être et santé* given out free of charge in chemist shops, with topics such as "beware of excessive sun for children". So I thought he was celebrating the child, the son I was to him ... which he was doing, but at the same time he reused the images to illustrate articles. I have a recollection that I have written in *Fond de l'œil*: being photographed by my father to illustrate the book by a judge in charge of cases involving children murderers. I remember precisely shooting in his studio on Rue Pigalle at the time; I was handcuffed, face down, wearing a Mickey Mouse T-shirt. I felt like I was facing a firing squad, and at the same time I didn't want to disappoint my father. I often found myself in his studio, proud to be his model, but at the same time I felt I was stuck in a quite deadly stillness. Being there, not moving, waiting for it to happen ... I couldn't see my father clearly, I was

[1] SAS is a a series of French erotic spy novels.

dazzled by the two flashes in front of me, I saw him gesticulate while I was handcuffed ... That image left a lasting impression, and that's perhaps why I wanted to get behind the camera, to carry on.
No doubt it's also for the mythology of what photography represented in those years: a cool and heroic medium. My father went on to report for travel agencies, photographed models and great writers like Julien Green. He photographed people like Pierre Soulages too. The first images I shot, which don't look much like what I'm doing today, were focused on the face. My father lent me his studio; I was imitating him, I was moving around, acting as though I were him.

RC: In 2014 you published Les Oiseaux favorables, *where your images interact with short stories by Stéphane Bouquet ...*

AdC: Narratives more than short stories.

RC: How did you work together?

AdC: This is the purpose of a publishing company called Les Inaperçus, where the publisher, Frédérique Breuil, chooses a photographer or a plastic artist whom she associates with a writer. She first asks both of them if they want to work together, and they do. Stéphane Bouquet is a magnificent poet.
I discovered him when we started to talk about our project.
I was interested in him because he had been a literary critic at *Libération*, which I also did in *Le Monde des livres*. Criticism can quite possibly also lead to creation, in spite of what people sometimes say. He collaborated with Sébastien Lifshitz as a screenwriter for his films, he was a dancer and now he's a writer. He's interested in photography, even though he's suspicious of it when it's paired with a text. He'd never wanted to mix the two media before. When he discovered my images that the publisher showed him, what interested him was the question of the fragmented body. For him, there was something about lack, as I've said earlier. And for a writer such as him, these partial images become reservoirs of possible narratives.
We have worked in a simple manner: he looked at the images, and not to fall into a form of illustrative text, he decided not

to look at them again while writing the story. He was inspired by them; he relied on some of the photos in very concrete ways and created a character close to these images: a woman wandering, kind of in suspension in her own life. She's about 40, and after a break-up she tries to fill her life again with the images she describes. What's amusing is the fictional part he adds to my photos. For example, she visits the exhibition of a photographer whose name sounds Portuguese. She visits an exhibition, my own exhibition, which Stéphane Bouquet recreates by including real images from several of my series but also by making up others. I was very moved that he used my images to create others. It was an inspiring dialogue, because once the text was written, I had the freedom to insert my images where I wanted in the text.

RC: In this book, there's a picture you took one day when we were both in Amsterdam. You can see a man half-naked by a window. I remember perfectly that we walked along a canal talking when suddenly you said, "Wait, stop!" I hadn't at all noticed the scene. Is that your work? To spot the small, discordant element in the real?

AdC: Yes, because the setting was a pretty, picturesque building, nothing more. What captivates me is to see oddity popping up into normality. That's what has always interested me in photography. The oddity was that barely outlined body at the window, incomplete, standing behind the window. I often photograph these bodies in awkward positions in their living environment. I was very impressed by Antonioni's cinema, who keeps questioning the difficult relationship between men's and women's bodies. It's not related to psychological problems, but to the apprehension of space, often cumbersome, so that we're ceaselessly playing hide-and-seek with the world, with the "other". Through what is most normal, we get to access the strangest things. That's why I've never been interested in works that are a bit surreal. Moreover, I believe that when one pronounces the same word and repeats it several times, it gradually empties itself of its meaning. You say the word window: "window, window, window" and soon, it doesn't mean anything, you can start imagining other meanings – like "win dough" – if you want to have fun and be extravagant.

RC: Does this also correspond to what you say about the metro pickpocket in Saccades?

AdC: Maybe! The photographer is close to the pickpocket, when he photographs the world without people knowing. I sometimes have the feeling, you see, when I photograph a passer-by or a tree without them knowing [Chuckles], that I'm adopting the posture of a voyeur. Even if the tree doesn't look at me, I still feel like I'm intruding on its privacy and committing a robbery. Photographing is violating what Pasolini called "the sanctity of reality". What is untouchable, impregnable, impossible. So, yes, pickpocket – but cop, too. On the street, a cop sees something wrong, and he gives a fine. The writer-photographer also: faced with irregularity, they verbalize, they make sentences to make a mark, to sanction the beauty.

RC: In 2015 you published Fond de l'œil, *your first text-only book. What I find interesting is that you never talk about photography from a theoretical point of view but from real images…*

AdC: From experiences.

RC: …Or things lived (like the scene about the choice of the portrait of Modiano in Le Monde*). What does this empirical approach allow?*

AdC: To write or photograph, I need existing material. I don't make up anything in my texts, I have no interest in fiction – except for films or series. The novel, for example, is something I reject, because of my idea of reality, which I find far superior to the rest. It's always accompanied by imagination. I need to step back after experiencing something intense, after a picture taken hastily. A photograph always provokes stories, not to say problems. In a newspaper meeting room, because of that, you can be in disagreement with an editor-in-chief who necessarily has the last word because it is he or she who will be signing the final proof before it goes to press. I like it when the images sow some discord. And this book, *Fond de l'œil*, is made up of these kinds of small stories: when photography arouses tension. Like when you pick out a portrait of a new Nobel Prize for Literature one morning, and you're told that in black and white, the reader may think he's dead. I think that says a lot about these gruelling prejudices that continue to interfere with photography. This forces us constantly to remain vigilant. People often have an equivocal relationship to images: between fear and idiocy. It's true that it's a book of experiences, of memories. And of how these memories of images summonand provoke language.

> *RC: You were talking about it – does working in the photographic department at* Le Monde *somehow influence your own photos?*

AdC: No, on the contrary, it reassures me as a photographer, because I'm absolutely not in the journalistic document. Well, maybe I'm in another kind of document, documenting my psychic life. Photographs, even the most intuitive ones, always result from an act of thinking. At the newspaper, I'm dealing with the contemporary world. In my personal work, I try to swerve from it. From this time anyway ...

> *RC: Yes, but what I wanted to say is: does it affect your work, even conversely? Because you spend your days looking at pictures.*

AdC: Yes, it could totally have cut my wings and any desire. But on the contrary, all these images that I see every day are a form of test. Thanks to them, to their invasion, I tell myself that if I still do want to photograph, it is because there is an internal and absolutely implacable necessity. I also feed on these images. When you look at images of Iraq from an excellent photojournalist like Laurent van der Stockt, unconcerned with the real, though still documentary, you may very well find a similar feeling when you photograph a tree, or anything else. A friend told me one day that I was shooting like a reporter who has gone mad. Photojournalism captures the symptoms of a world in crisis; I cannot feel foreign to it. Actually, a photographer, the one who made the *Travelog* book...

RC: Charles Harbutt.

AdC: Yes, Charles Harbutt really interested me for that reason. It has to be checked, but I think he was a member of Magnum Photos at some point.

RC: I believe so too.

AdC: Then, he turned away from real facts. In the end, we always question what the visible is, whatever forms it takes.

RC: One of the central issues in the book Fond de l'œil *is whether photography is on the side of life or death. For the most part, you seem to relate photography to death. Yet you also write: "When I photograph, I have the feeling of being reconciled with life in what is most precious and most immediate: the present." But as soon as it is taken, the photo becomes past or death.*

AdC: Roland Barthes conveyed, in a quite annoying way, the notion that photography is on the side of melancholy, of the crackling of time. It is the famous, though disastrous and painful "it has been", for those who stay and contemplate images (not to mention those who shot them, whom Barthes has always utterly ignored). I feel much closer to Robbe-Grillet [see sophie Ristelhueber p.248]when he says that in the image, verbs are always in the present tense. In front of a photograph that moves me, I have the feeling that it is still happening before my eyes. I have never felt nostalgic about an image I took 10 years prior. We gaze at a frozen thing, but which offers a wealth of future projections. There is an immense capacity for the mobility of the photograph through its psychic assimilation. And it's true that writing afterwards about photos is giving them a second life. Photography allows me to reunite with things I already know; it updates them, because I'm alive. I need the image to make a mark, preserve the beauty of a presence without the delirium of wanting to immortalize it. Perhaps it's a matter of immediate connection to the world, the famous photographic act. There are days when I could almost photograph without a memory card.

RC: The same year you published Incidences *with Patrick Le Bescont*[2]*. This is not specific to this book but is found often in your photos: faces shy away. Why is that? And yesterday, you told me that you're currently interested in faces.*

AdC: My first experience with images was mostly in films, watching faces in Bergman's films. I was captivated by their cold, autonomous beauty, desperately waiting for something. I remember a film called *The Passion of Anna*, where a photographer is showing pictures he's taken of his wife and there's one depicting the face of a radiant woman. And the photographer shows these images to one of his friends. Dazzled, he says, "What a beauty, what serenity," and the photographer replies, "That day, she was exhausted after three nights of insomnia and an absolutely appalling headache, she was depressed." It's this equivocation that interests me: how something, in image, rarely conforms to its origin. Photographing a face, what a challenge! How to escape the person's individuation? I would like to photograph heads, to consider first the issue of the body, even through a face, and not have to fall into the psychology or the fantasy of interiority.

RC: In 2015 you also started the project "Being Beauteous" with Anne-Lise Broyer, Nicolas Comment and Marie Maurel de Maillé, a book and a series of exhibitions. What is the meaning of this collective project?

AdC: We all had a different relationship to our own practices, but we all empathize with some aspects of the history of photography. We all liked the relationship between photography and text. This so-called literary photography that had been defended by pioneers, in *Les Cahiers de la Photographie* in particular, by people such as Gilles Mora, Denis Roche or Bernard Plossu. And we had this feeling that today it was

[2] Founder of Filigranes Editions.

somewhat frowned upon to evoke notions like sensation, mystery, wonder. As if these words were today dusty or dated. However, in our respective photographic experiments, this research was always very strong. So we decided to put together our images – to not create new ones for the occasion but to produce unpublished sequences and mix them without saying who did what. As though the images replaced their authors to live a new life. And I was telling you that I like the idea that a photograph may have many lives. Taking an image from a previous book and associating it with others to create something different was a very interesting experience. Two writers, Hélène Giannecchini and Yannick Haenel, were also asked to write a text during a residency at the Maison Julien Gracq. It was not a critical text, but a literary narrative. They played exactly the same game as us. They co-signed their texts and you don't know who wrote what. The experience was really necessary to take the pictures out of their context and of their authors' lives. As if one were accessing a kind of fantasy world of the autonomous image.

RC: A few months ago, you took the plunge and published your first narrative: Histoire souterraine. *First, would you say it's a novel?*

AdC: No, it's not a novel, because everything is true. The purpose of this book was to tell something that I did not immediately acknowledge. This book is about a young man who is crushed to death by the subway on line 6. This young man was 24 years old. I read this news in *Le Parisien*. I started narrating that story, digging into it. I began to write about that, to search about this young man dragged to death along two metro stations. And then, little by little, I wrote by analogy, as I also sometimes do with photography. I mean, putting two images, or two sequences of different nature, in front of each other. At the same time, I began writing about a love story falling apart. I realized that through these tragedies, I was questioning disappearance. Something that has always interested me in photography as well: an act that reveals something that escapes you at the same time. I continued to write the story, and realized that this 24-year-old, this stranger from the metro, was the same age as my brother when he committed suicide in Singapore, and whose body I never saw again. I didn't have any pictures of him either. It was a dreadful tragedy to start mourning deprived of images and body. This story, through detours and fragments, sets images where I had not been able to see anything. The image of the fall, for example. Because my brother Charles jumped off the top of a building in Singapore. I'm convinced that images have a curative power even if they sometimes are only small plasters put on gaping wounds. As I lacked images for the book, I resorted to fiction, including citing films where bodies fall, as in *Vertigo*, or tales that resonate, such as *L'Inconnue de la Seine* [The unknown woman of the Seine], the death mask of a woman found around 1900 in the river Seine. The employee of the morgue had found her beautiful and had taken a cast of her face.

> *RC: In* Histoire souterraine *you only deal with things that aren't very funny. I'm not a literary critic, but your writing reminds me of Jean Echenoz. You can tell horrid stories but there is always, at some point, a little twist, a little irony, a form of nonchalance towards the subject that defuses the drama.*

AdC: Absolutely. This is an interesting point. To return to Bergman, who is important in my relationship to images, he is a filmmaker who arouses literary emotions. Although he deals with tragic themes, I always left his films with a feeling of intense joy. While the images are grave, they are always saved by beauty, and the power of life. Whether they tend to gravity or grace, one can always retain a form of intensity. That's what interests me in the images I take. Photography has the capacity to awaken wonder from something apparently dark.

> *RC: So, you apply the same principle to the text?*

AdC: To return to the text, yes. It's more difficult to be humorous in photography, even if I can find some photographers hilarious. In a very different category, Elliott Erwitt has always made me laugh a lot. Perhaps because he pays so much attention to what is ridiculous. I think our lives are full of ridicule that can overwhelm us or help us take some perhaps humorous distance from them.

RC: Parallel to Histoire souterraine, *you published* HS *with Filigranes. What is the link between the two books?*
AdC: I wrote this book and then I felt I had to find a photographic appendix. I originally thought of reusing footage from Hitchcock movies, to work with pictures that were not mine. Discussing this with a photographer named Pierre Liebaert, I was reminded that I had probably shot pictures at every moment of the story in Singapore, after the death of my brother when I went there, or during my love affair in Sicily. This was the case. I started collecting all these photographs and I came up with the idea of making a newspaper of sorts. The newspaper is the object of my daily work. It was a way to subvert the medium of my work and to produce my own little newspaper. The layout was designed by Pierre, who did a great job. We entrust our images as we entrust our children to someone we trust. The purpose of this newspaper with my images was to have the feelings of the book and the portraits of those whom we meet. No photography is captioned. Next to the text, which is extremely literal, these images may have softened it, questioned it, bringing a new fictional plot. The woman we see on page 4, is she really the lover from Sicily? Does the beautiful portrait of this young man represent my brother? In its dialogue with the text, the photograph remains ambiguous and incomplete. These images represent something or someone, but never care to identify them.

RC: Finally, your titles are always seemingly simple but really polysemic. Histoire souterraine *can be understood as a simple description of the fact that you talk about the metro, but also, when you've read the book, as a story that runs underground…*

AdC: It actually often happens underground, but also in the bizarre depths of memory. The challenge of *Histoire souterraine*, as one would say, was to bring the depth to the surface.

RC: At the same time, Après tout *can be understood at first glance as that frozen expression that basically means "it doesn't matter" but also as "at the end of everything".*

AdC: Or something that follows a serious event.

RC: Is it important to have this polysemy?
AdC: Yes, the titles I like are like multiple plugs, like images, trying to use words that don't lock the meaning in a frozen path. *Incidences*, for example, conjured up both the inconsequential and the so-called incidental light, which reflects. The consequence, the light. And yes, I like to find these titles that work like multi-layered images.

RC: Is it also related to your taste for Lacanian puns? The other day on Facebook, you spelled my name "Quoi Nier" *(what to deny). [Laughs]*

AdC: About *Fond de l'œil*, a journalist from a Swiss radio station, in perfect Lacanian style, heard "*font deuil*" (are grieving). Today, we didn't talk about the unconscious; I don't feel that it has good press these days. But in writing as in photography, it can have its little moments of brilliance. I think it was William Klein [see p. 178] who said that at 500th of a second, the unconscious is having a blast. You don't write the book you thought you were doing, like you never photograph what you planned to see.

26 May 2017

Since our conversation, Amaury da Cunha has published two new books:
Basse lumière, story, Éditions Filigranes, September 2018
Demeure, texts by Sylvie Gracia, Éditions h'Artpon, May 2018.

MISHKA HENNER

Mishka Henner was born in 1976 in Brussels. He lives and works in Manchester, Great Britain. He received an ICP Infinity Award in the Art category in 2013. He has been nominated for the Deutsche Börse Prize and the Pictet Prize. His work was exhibited at the Rencontres d'Arles in the exhibition "From Here On" in 2011, and at the Pompidou-Metz Centre for the exhibition "Views from Above" in 2013. His work is present in many collections, including the Pompidou Centre in Paris, the V&A in London and the New York Public Library. He is a member of the ABC Artists' Books Cooperative. He is the author of 15 books.

Mishka Henner turned to photography at the age of 27, after experimenting with various artistic mediums. The combination of a background in sociology and the shock of a major exhibition "Cruel and Tender" led him to take hold of a camera and practise something little known, a form of documentary photography. After a few years of doubts about the validity of his approach, random internet searches led him to turn to what he is now recognized for: appropriation supported by the practice of on-demand publishing. While it sometimes involves the use of "traditional" tools such as Photoshop, which allowed him to realize his iconoclastic *Less Américains,* Mishka Henner's work could never have emerged without the internet and specifically the emergence of the Google search engine and its variants – Street View and Earth. Humour is not absent from his work, though it is no more than an adjuvant to a reflection on what technology and networks allow, on how algorithms flatten the results of a research according to a mysterious alchemy of popularity and commercial interest. Pushing further, he lifts a corner of the veil on the uses offered by these tools, be they positive or questionable. In the end, Mishka Henner develops a powerful reflection on what photography is in the digital and network age. This conversation was held in public at the Henri Cartier-Bresson Foundation.

Rémi Coignet: *If you don't mind, can we consider your work in chronological order since 2010, in order to understand how you came to tackle Robert Frank's* The Americans. *You first studied sociology. How did you come to take an interest in photography, practise it and then decide to massacre it?*

Mishka Henner: Well, thank you for the invitation. I'm really happy to be here tonight. French is my mother tongue but I have lived in England for 32 years so my French is somewhat rusty. I apologize in advance.

RC: You're a very good speaker ...

MH: Actually, I was passionate about sociology. My grandparents were Communist activists in the 1930s, 1940s and 1950s and my mother was in Paris in 1968. She participated in all the events. That's why sociology was, for me, something really alive. It wasn't just an abstract theory; it was part of my family's memory. I was very good at it, but at the age of 21 or 22 I wanted to do something else in life than just study and do research. So I gave up sociology to start an artistic career. I tried theatre, I even moved to Paris to write a novel. But I was really bad, actually! [Audience laughs] I had all these pretty romantic ideas about what it's like to be an artist, that sort of thing. In fact, I spent much of my 20 years discovering what I wasn't. I tried a lot of different things – I tried my hand at painting, writing a novel, theatre ... but I never really found my place. And then one day, I went to see an exhibition at the Tate called "Cruel and Tender"[1], a huge exhibition on the history of documentary photography in the 20th century. I was extremely impressed for several reasons. To start with, I didn't know anything about photography, but the works that really impressed me were those of the New Topographics and the School of Dusseldorf, rather cold works. That is an almost anti-expressionist art form. Before I saw this exhibition, I thought that art should be expressionist, which means that, as an artist, you have to express what is inside yourself

[1] *The exhibition "Cruel and Tender" was held at Tate Modern in 2003. It questioned the place of documentary photography in 20th-century art. Curators: Emma Dexter and Thomas Weski.*

on the canvas in front of you. And what really impressed me was that photography, especially documentary, was a way to do the opposite. It was a way to discover things about oneself, about one's culture, just by holding out a mirror. It's a bit of a cliché, but the pictures of the New Topographics or the Dusseldorf School are so anti-expressionist that for me, in a sense, they tell a lot about culture, and I was really impressed. That's when I decided I wanted to become a photographer. Well, I had already decided several times that I was going to become a writer, a painter, etc. It was nonsense, but this time I really thought, wow! I found a language that I immediately understood. I didn't have to study it, I didn't have to read the texts on the wall. I saw these images, for example those of Robert Adams, and they touched me enormously because I saw a work made by someone who spent his time observing culture, that's it. I didn't know there was a role in art for that. That's how I discovered documentary photography and its history. In fact, that's what it is: people travel around the world, be it at the next street corner or in the antipodes, and they reflect on the culture that is before them.

RC: So you spent a few years – six years, it seems – working with, discovering and learning documentary photography. And after a few years you got tired of it. You chose to leave that photographic approach behind and work on images by appropriating existing photographs. Why?

MH: Because I started to lose confidence in some of the foundations of documentary photography – that is, in the man who handles the camera. I really started to doubt. I worked with a lot of people, I photographed them and knew them better and better over time ... but yes, I started to lose confidence in the camera, when I was handling it. I no longer had faith in that process. I began to think that the device, in a sense, was interrupting the relationship you could have with someone. What interested me most in these projects was the relationship I had with people. So, when I perceived that this interaction was based on the fact that I entered with my camera and that I alone made a profit from this exchange, that I alone had control ... I felt it wasn't a very healthy situation.

And on the other hand, like everyone else, I read a lot of newspapers, I watched the news, I was interested in the world, in geopolitical affairs. I didn't have much money, and I found it very frustrating not to be able to work in the field of geopolitics because of lack of funds, and not be able to travel around the world to carry out a project on American military bases, for example. This was happening just when internet really started to be a part of our lives. And of course, thanks to the internet and screenshots, you can travel around the world without needing a lot of money. All of a sudden, you can discover things you can't see if you're on Earth. Meaning that with the perspective of satellites and different data, we have access to things that are otherwise inaccessible ...

RC: How do internet and satellite views provide a vision that we didn't have until now?

MH: Well, it's a bit of a complicated question. I think the vision of documentary artists or photographers is just as relevant today as it was 50 years ago. I guess the world was different, of course, compared to today's networks, infrastructures, the links between things ... The world is undoubtedly much more global than it was 50 years ago. I also think that internet is a revolution because it brings us, the citizens, research tools that were for years and years limited to those who were working at huge international agencies, or perhaps the secret services, etc. Now, thanks to a simple search engine, we can find information that, as a citizen, is terribly important, crucial ... and even sometimes dangerous.

RC: We'll come back to it, but to proceed in a chronological order, in your first self-published book, Winning Mentality, *you Photoshopped your face on photos of winners of various and varied contests*[2]*. I see it as a denunciation of widespread competition. Is your work political, and what can art do in the face of power?*

[2] *For example, Green energy entrepreneur of the year, Miss Texas, the winner of the most beautiful begonia contest, or of the best rabbit breeder contest, etc.*

MH: Well, first of all, it started out as a joke. No doubt, those who are not very convinced by my work probably think that it's a big joke. But really, *Winning Mentality* started as a joke on Facebook. It was the beginning of it, and I noticed that the pictures that people put of themselves were aimed at trying to impress others. That is, they were trying to look really good… in English it's called "the pout" … You know, Victoria Beckham, for example? She's constantly pouting. [Audience laughs] So when Facebook was born, everyone was looking sulky, right? Everyone was really aware of the way they presented themselves, and so I, as a joke, started putting my passport photo. In Britain, you don't have the right to show any expression, you have to be completely neutral on your official pictures …

RC: Yes, in France as well.

MH: OK, so already, I was interested because … what is a neutral face? [Laughs] Where do we find it? On a passport, and as I was quite good at Photoshop, I was able to easily place my passport photo on the winners' images. What shocked me on the internet is that there are billions of winners. I found 6 million winners, and so you have to wonder where the losers are, as there are so many winners! [Audience laughs] It's absurd… and so I started posting these photos on Facebook, and the reactions… You have to understand that I had been working in the field of honest documentary photography for six years. How do you say "honest"?

RC: Sincere, honest.

MH: Sincere, yes. I wanted the work to be really honest, but it was always a battle to get the public to see it. [Laughs] I don't know, it sounds weird… Yet everything was sincere.

RC: You were trying to show a reality…

MH: Yeah. So I posted these pictures on the internet, and I never had reactions comparable to those that people posted with regard to these images. I didn't even think that we could make anything out of it ... How can I say? Not really in a political way, no, but to lead to some cultural reflection that would be also funny. In fact, comedians do that all the time, but I've never really seen that in documentary photography. And all of a sudden, I found it fascinating that ...

Agnès Sire[3]: Martin Parr ? [see Conversations 2, p. 148]

MH: Yes ...

AS: With his own head ...

MH: Yes, yes. But it's Martin Parr, so ... [Audience laughs]. So the reactions to this project gave me so much joy that I decided to make a book out of it. I made a selection of about 50 of these photos to make the book *Winning Mentality*, under the pen name Victor Starr, and I went to an art book fair with a single copy of the book. Indeed, print-on-demand allows for this. I brought the only existing copy of the book to this fair, and the head of the Tate's artist's books collection enters the room. She sees my book and she buys it immediately for their collection. It was my first step into this world. I didn't even think of this book as an art object. I saw it, as I told you, as a joke. But all of a sudden, it's as if the doors of the art world had opened up to me and I was told: "There is a place for you here. There's a place for this way of thinking." I did it seriously, but it was a joke ...

RC: Interesting!

MH: A serious joke.

RC: It all happened pretty quickly. We were talking about 2010. It's now 2017, and you've entered the art world very quickly, rather than documentary photography. It was quite fast.

[3] Agnès Sire was then the director of the Henri Cartier-Bresson Foundation. She is now the artistic director.

MH: Yes, but I think it's also documentary. It's funny because for me, art is a form of documentation, a documentary. I don't see a big division between the two. But when that door suddenly opened, I was also part of a cooperative of artists and ...

RC: Yes. ABC ...

MH: *ABC*. And for the first time in my life, I was surrounded by artists who worked in the same field. I was like a little boy in a candy store, I don't know how they say it in French. So, anything was possible. I began to get to know artists who had been active for a very long time, who had a great influence, but whom I discovered at the age of 35, like Ed Ruscha ...

RC: We're going to talk about it ...

MH: Or who else? Chris Burden, for example, or Cindy Sherman. Artists who really made me feel like I was having fun. You know, I think ...

RC: Isn't this the definition of the artist, to have fun?

MH: Yes, I think so. Yes, yes, but we forget it too often.

RC: And so, like many contemporary artists, you made a book after Ed Ruscha, Fifty-One US Military Outposts. *Why do you think Ruscha's books attract contemporary artists so much?*

MH: Because I think that often, it's the simplest gestures that have the most influence. Someone like Ruscha opened a door. And he knows that too, I think ... Well, I don't know him, I never told him about this, but it feels to me that in his earliest books, *Twentysix Gasoline Stations*, *Thirtyfour Parking Lots*, etc., we see someone who was reacting to what were the dominant ideas in photography at the time.

RC: Indeed ...

MH: Designing a book like *Twentysix Gasoline Stations* is a deliberate act. There is no wilful beauty in there, there is no perfection of the prints. The books themselves weren't really carefully designed, he had them pulled in a printing press specializing in restaurant menus, catalogues, stuff like that. And it's an integral part of his choices.

RC : All right.

MH : I think his books were a great source of inspiration to artists – my colleagues or myself, for example – because he has a rather rebellious side, and also a precise thought, a focus so well defined that in fact, he creates his own world ... Each of his books has its own world. It's a work in itself, even if the subject is terribly banal. For someone like me, it's a strong inspiration.

RC: We were talking about the "Cruel and Tender" exhibition earlier, so we could also talk about Lewis Baltz. *[see* Conversations, *p. 30]* *With Ed Ruscha or Lewis Baltz, there's a desire for neutrality in the image. But to move forward in the discussion, and to come to your appropriation of Frank's* The Americans *and also to evoke Henri Cartier-Bresson, do you see a difference between an approach in which the author affirms a vision of the world, and another in which they display an attempt at neutrality?*

MH: I don't think we can be neutral. It's impossible. And yet, this is what makes appropriation so interesting: the choice I myself make is not at all the one you would make. It's impossible to be neutral in that sense ...

RC: But that's what the Bechers or Ruscha tried, for example. They tried to assert neutrality.

MH: Yes, maybe, but I don't know. Have they tried to assert neutrality? Is that true?

RC: That's my feeling.

MH: That would be a surprise ...

RC: Well, it seems to me that in Henri Cartier-Bresson or Robert Frank, there's an affirmation from a point of view, a subjectivity, while ...

MH: Yes, but it's so obvious ... When we see a picture of the Bechers, we know immediately and exactly what they did.

AS: It's the question of style.

MH: Their style is terribly well defined.

AS: It's not quite the same thing.

MH: How? Isn't that the same thing?

AS: The style, yes, it's not ...

MH: No, but neutrality ... I don't quite understand the question.

RC: I meant we're in a lineage. There may be a desire with the Bechers to assert neutrality, even if one of their images is immediately identifiable. Whereas in Robert Frank, there's obviously going to be a subjectivity, immediately noticeable ...

MH: Ah, OK. Yes. OK, I get it ...

RC: And I think the same is true of Henri Cartier-Bresson.

MH: Yes. But I would say it differently ... Rather, it is the choice of a fairly rigid structure, much like with Sol LeWitt. That is, the structure and rules determined by the artist condition the aesthetics.

RC: Right.

MH: With the Bechers, you can see that they had a very rigid structure. They established rules that they chose to follow. And you can see them in their pictures. We can deconstruct them, understand them. With Frank and Cartier-Bresson,

I think it's entirely different, much more impulsive. But I'm not so interested. [Laughs] I started the discussion by saying that I had discovered for the first time in the exhibition "Cruel and Tender" that an anti-expressive art was possible. Well, it's a contradiction, because it's impossible not to be ... everything is expressive. And yet, I still think it's a possible choice for an artist. Do we want our works to be the expression of our personal sensation? How important is this question? I guess what I'm trying to say is that self-expression, the expression of our own feelings, also is a stylistic choice.

AS: The substance and the form?

MH: How?

AS: This is the famous question of substance and form.

MH: Oh yes? [Laughs] If you choose to express your being, you should know that there will certainly be a static stylistic aspect ... in which, in fact, I don't really believe anymore. Thus I was attracted to the works in which the artist seemed to erase their ...

RC: Their personality?

MH: Yes, or ...

AS: Their vision?

MH: As a gesture, even, the notion of erasing one's personality from the work is impossible. But I don't know ... Excuse me. It's difficult for me to explain myself in French and much easier in English. But what I would like to say is that when you work on appropriation, in fact, you're working with cultural styles that already exist. This means that it's not me who imposes a style on the subject. It already has its own style in itself, and, as an artist, it's fascinating because the creative process is much richer. Indeed, for each project, I discover a new aesthetic. I think it's a problem for many documentary photographers:

no matter what subject they're working on, they impose a style that eventually defines them. For many artists, this is very important. I don't care, I'm not interested.

RC: OK, but maybe it's also a question of the times. I think Robert Frank in his day was totally contemporary. He used 35mm, a Leica, like Henri Cartier-Bresson. They didn't use wet-collodion, they were modern. And so, is it not important, as an artist, as an author, to be contemporary with one's time?

MH: Well, yes. But I would also say that when I was working with a camera, I was a bit of a prisoner of the style of other photographers that I admired so at one point, I ...
Well, I'll be honest now because ...

RC: Yes, for once. [Audience laughs]

AS: It's about time! [Audience laughs]

MH: I had a certain crisis with photography. At one point, I was actually repeating other people's style. But I felt that it was, how to say, restrictive; it was a limit.

RC: Right.

MH: There's something else, to be honest. It seems to me that documentary photography, at that point in my life, was a way of seeking a certain authenticity in the world. That is, the device encourages you to open up to the world and meet people. It's a cliché you hear all the time, but it's true. I knew many photographers. All my friends were photographers. And I could see that, in fact, even those who according to me had the most authentic lives ... war photographers, for example: what could be more authentic than witnessing the most extreme part of man? But I realized that they spent most of their time on their screen. Because in war, not much happens. Most of the time, you're waiting for an event. And while they were waiting, they were on the internet. They would send emails, or they would look for press publishers to submit their photos to, or they would edit their images, they would add information to the metadata.

I realized that they, like everyone else, spent their lives on their screens.
So, all of a sudden, I thought of the screen as an interface with the world. In fact, it's like an elephant in a room. If now our relationship to the world is happening through the screen, how can I, as an artist, ignore this fact? So let's forget this completely ridiculous idea according to which photography, the camera, encourages an authentic relationship with the world. On the contrary, today our authentic relationship to the world is established through the screen, isn't it? You go shopping, you write your love letters, you build relationships through it. People have sex through the screen. So many elements of our lives go through the screen. And so, I thought, "Wow, if I want to use, handle a contemporary tool, it will be the screen."

RC: Yes, the reality is now the screen.

MH: Yes. After reading for much of my youth French theorists like Jean Baudrillard, Paul Virilio, etc., this notion made a lot of sense, you see?

RC: Yes. And I was wondering something as I was looking at your images in Dutch Landscapes. *In most countries on Google Earth, sensitive areas, military zones, etc. are just pixelated, but in the Netherlands, they chose to apply colour polygons of sorts. I was wondering if you thought, like Broomberg and Chanarin [see* Conversations, *p. 52 and* Conversations 2, *p. 40] that there are aesthetic strategies of power?*

MH: Well, again, what shocked me with *Dutch Landscapes* is that I asked myself: "What's going on here?" I had done the series "Fifty-One US Military Outposts", which showed 51 American bases in 50 countries around the world.

RC: So, as many as they are US states.

MH: No, there are 50 states. [Laughs]

RC: Oh yes, of course, sorry! [Laughs]

MH: But Britain is the 51st state, of course! What struck me when I worked on this project was the incredible visibility of the world. I then set out to search for the censored places. And I discovered that there are a lot of them in most countries. But of all the countries in the world, the Dutch are the only ones who have chosen a rather ridiculous style [Audience laughs] that I otherwise find very pretty. But I don't know if, when they designed this censorship, they thought the public was illiterate about satellite images.
In other words, is the public so stupid [Audience chuckles] or is it so unable to read satellite images that it will not perceive this pixelization? Or, this is also a possibility: it was the first Friday of the month, the day they invite children to the parents' office and they let the kids carry out the censorship ... In short, whatever ... I found this pattern really super-interesting because it represented a collision between the digital and the analogue as an aesthetic style. This reality fascinated me.

RC: And this relates to my next question. Are we merely uneducated in the face of satellite or automatically produced images, and should we learn a new way to read images?

MH: I don't think it's a question of "will". We're constantly learning. If you have children, you see the relationship they have to images, it's completely different from the one we had, which I had. And yet, I grew up in a house where there was always a computer ...

RC: You're young ...

MH: But our children now, even in school, are taught how to handle images. My daughter is five years old. They already use a screen on which they manipulate the images with their fingers. It's a completely different relationship. The image has now become a dynamic object: we can tear it, we can add a hat on a head, all this stuff ... [Laughs]

RC: Yes.

MH: Do you know Snapchat?

RC: Snapchat? Yes, of course.

MH: I never understood anything about Snapchat. [Laughs]

RC: Neither did I, but my 12-year-old daughter uses it.

MH: I don't understand it at all. It's a different world. The idea that the image only exists for three seconds. That's it, it's over: someone sees her and she disappears. Yes, we're going through a radical change right now.

RC: I'd like to talk for a moment about your film Photographers. *This is a compilation or montage of films in which photography and the photographic act are important; so there are excerpts from* Blow Up, Window on Court, *etc.*
What was the meaning of this piece?

MH: I made it with a friend photographer[4], and every time we met we told each other stories that we had lived while working. Gradually, the character of the photographer began to really interest us. Who's the photographer? What character is he or she? We began to study the topic. This character is full of clichés and stereotypes. And the best place to find these stereotypes and clichés is cinema. So, we watched a hundred movies in which a photographer appears. It was wonderfully funny because out of a hundred films, a third were devoted to the war photographer. That's a cliché. The war photographer. He's always a guy, always ...

RC: Yes, and about a third of your 10-minute film is devoted to the war photographer.

MH: Yes, the film is divided into three parts. The war photographer, the fashion photographer and then the photographer as a voyeur. You can practically categorize all films that have a photographer character. We made

[4] *David Oates.*

this observation and we kept only the scenes where the camera stared only at the photographer, where we see him or her only as a character. Then we tried to find a link to make it interesting to watch. And, yes ... that's all.

RC: OK. So we'll soon come to Less Américains, *but I'd like us to go first to* No Man's Land, *a book I discovered at Offprint at the Beaux-Arts in Paris in 2012. The book is made up of pictures of prostitutes in southern Italy that you found on Google Street View ...*

MH: We don't know if they're prostitutes. It cannot be said.

RC: Yes, it's true.

MH: It's still important to say!

RC: All right. So, women ...

MH: Because I'm not saying they're prostitutes.

RC: No, I know. You're right to correct me. So, we see scantily clad women on the side of a road in southern Italy or Spain. [Audience laughs] Maybe we can put it that way?
So I discovered your book at the fair, and a few minutes later I saw Txema Salvans's book, The Waiting Game, *which deals with exactly the same subject: lightly dressed ladies on the side of a road in Spain. But he used a view camera, I believe ... Very composed images. I saw these two works and I thought, "Does it still make sense to make these images today when we can just retrieve them from the internet, on Google?"*
And I know that Cartier-Bresson photographed prostitutes in Spain or Mexico. But maybe today, there is no longer any need to stroll the streets, or to go to the side of the road, to spend money to make these kinds of images. What do you think?

MH: No, I think there's room for everything, don't you think?

RC: Yes, of course. Everyone does what they want.

MH: Yes. I think there are several layers in this work. I can start by saying that Google Street View, when you think about it, is a really amazing project. When you think of Atget's influence, a guy who took to the streets of Paris a hundred years ago. Think of the importance of these images today when right now, there are a hundred cars travelling the world with 15 cameras on their rooftops documenting our world – the world that exists along the streets, it must be noted. It's not a full documentation, but it's still an extraordinary fact that could only develop at the time of the internet. At a time when we know how to manage a gigantic number of images. It's really extraordinary already as a documentation project. Secondly, my wife continued traditional photography ... We worked together for six years, and she went on. She worked with prostitutes in Manchester for a year ...

RC: We need to explain that No Man's Land *comes from there. Because you were working with your wife on prostitutes in Manchester.*

MH: That's it, I came up with this project because of that. We got to know the prostitutes quite well and there was a huge problem: how to photograph them? When you know them, when you know the experiences they have. When you know how they manage to survive, finding life strategies, what can a picture of these lives represent? In my opinion, a photo, a portrait, does not represent anything like such a situation. But my wife really had a big problem: she couldn't find a way to represent everything we had learned from their lives. All their conflicts, all their dilemmas, all their strategies, all that. And after a year and a half, I suggested to my wife that, perhaps, the solution was to do a job on the places where these women worked. And so, somewhat by chance, I went to Google Street View and looked at the places where we knew they were working, the streets behind Manchester's main train station. And there I see, before my eyes, one of the women we knew captured by the Street View camera ...

RC: Unbelievable ...

MH: So the car was passing behind the station and, interesting fact, Street View uses a wide-angle lens. So the human shape is always small in the shot. In addition, the cameras are high because they're placed on the roof of the car. This gives a very interesting perspective. In fact, we see more of the landscape that surrounds the human shape than humans themselves. Because of legal problems in Germany, Google had to invent an algorithm that blurs any face. So the face of any character that appears on Street View is erased. And frankly, I saw the picture and I thought, "Wow! This is the solution to your problem, to this problem." In fact, when the female shape is so isolated in the landscape, so vulnerable, so alienated… You say alienated?

RC: Yes.

MH: … It's deeply moving. Not only about prostitution, the life of the prostitute, but also regarding the lives of all of us in this hyper-technological world where we are constantly monitored since devices constantly observe us. I found it fascinating. A door was open. And at that point, I started doing more research. I discovered networks, forums on the internet where men shared information about where and how to find prostitutes, all over the world. But that's not all: they also used Street View often.

RC: And from there, you yourself were able to look for images in relation to these networks of guys looking for information …

MH: Yes, there were so many elements. It was so dark. I was so much, it was, it was…

RC: Disgusting?

MH: And at that time, I loved Michel Houellebecq. I was reading *Atomised*… What is the French title, *Les Particules Elémentaires*? *Elementary Particles*, right?

RC: Yes, that's right.

MH: I was reading this book and it really was a shock. I thought, "Wow, this project is so immoral that it has to be realized, because, especially in the world of documentary photography, there are all these ethical rules." It's so ridiculous.

RC: And actually, you've had a lot of criticism, I think, with this project.

MH: Oh yes, we can say that!

RC: How did you react to the classic photographers who found your way of doing things immoral?

MH: There was a Pulitzer-nominated photographer who said I was a conceptual skiver. [Audience laughs]

RC: That's not wrong, is it? [Audience laughs]

MH: Really? [Chuckles] I don't know...

RC: Ah, I'm joking!

MH: But I really liked it, actually. I thought I might put it on my business card. [Audience laughs]

RC: Conceptual skiver?

MH: Yes.

RC: You'd be pretty proud of that, then.

MH: Yes, because the guy didn't get it!

RC: Well, that's what I was telling you earlier. When I saw your book and then Txema Salvans's book, I found his work useless. There's no point in spending six years with a view camera by the road side.

MH: I don't know ... His pictures are better. [Laughs]

RC: Yes, they are better than Google's.

MH: His photos are more beautiful than mine.

RC: Sure.

MH: But I didn't make *No Man's Land* to make beautiful pictures. That's also true.

RC: And then you did No Man's Land 2.

MH: Yes. To tell you the truth, almost all my projects are published on demand. And I can tell you, there was no real demand there. [Audience laughs]

RC: That's the problem with the distribution of this type of book.

MH: So, with *No Man's Land,* I spend months on the internet looking for pictures, imagine that. I wasn't very proud of it. But my wife is of unwavering support. And she thought it was an incredible project. So, I made a book... a copy cost me about 30 to 40 euros. I put it on my website and went on to my next project. Immediately, however, a woman who ran an erotic blog in the US, in Los Angeles – I don't know how she came across my book [Audience laughs], but she wrote a pretty nice review. And suddenly, it blew up. There were feminists ... feminist sex workers, that's how they call themselves ...

RC: So, feminist sex workers.

MH: Yes, who launched a campaign to have the book banned. There was only one copy of this book [Audience laughs] that no one had bought. No one cared. Look, my experience is that people had nothing to do with my work. [Audience laughs] And all of a sudden, I started selling a lot of books. [Chuckles] Well, a lot... let's say 50. And then lawyers write to me saying, "Look, we've been contacted by this group of feminist sex workers, they say what you're doing is illegal. What's your reply?" I sent them links to the websites of artists who have been working with appropriated images since the early 20th century. [Chuckles] Furthermore, they claimed I had stolen the title of the book, *No Man's Land*, from a book of memoirs written by a prostitute. Well, I wasn't aware of it, but they told me that the title was protected by copyright. So I did a search on Amazon to find all the books titled *No Man's Land*. [Audience laughs]. There were 800 of them! [Audience laughs] And between 5 to 10 per cent written by prostitutes. I told them, "Look, if I stole this title, well, you'll need to write to all these people as well!" [Laughs]

RC: Well, that's a lot of people.

MH: Yes, it would give them a lot of work. [Audience laughs]. Then, after a while, critics began to take the book seriously. It was nominated for the Deutsche Börse, one of Europe's most important photography awards, and that's when book sales stopped. The more critics talked about the book, the less I sold. [Audience laughs] It was really weird, and I never understood why. During the Deutsche Börse exhibition at the Photographer's Gallery in London, the bookstore asked me to send in 60 books, and in the end, they gave me 54 books back. [Audience laughs] After three months of exhibition! I don't understand, but I'm happy to tell you because the general perception is that I've made a lot of money with this project, when on the contrary, I made none at all.

RC: Yes, if you could make money making books, you'd know, right? So, all this leads us to Less Américains. *We've seen the process that led you from documentary photography to appropriation. How did you ever decide to make your own version of – or to put it another way, and wickedly, to trash – Robert Frank's* The Americans?

MH: As you can see, I think a lot about photography, about what it is today. What does it mean? What is it in the digital age? What is memory these days? And at the time ...

RC: Three years ago, right?

MH: No. Five years now. So, I'm pretty clumsy and I broke a lot of hard drives. [Audience chuckles] It's true. And of course, when you break a hard drive, it's screwed up. You lose everything on it ...

RC: You lose your memory.

MH: Yes, you've lost your memory, exactly that! [Audience laughs] And I found it quite interesting already as a metaphor. We can philosophize about that, can't we? Why do you care so much about these memories? Anyway, it was 2012, and if I remember correctly, it was in 2009 that the important exhibition of *The Americans* crossed the United States. It was associated with a very large book, *Looking In*[5], which was an analysis of this project ...

RC: Which I love.

MH: It was like the Talmud! [Chuckles] You know? That's how I saw it. It was like creating a religion around *The Americans*. So, as someone who thinks about photography today, trying to find an urgent and vital language, I was somewhat frustrated that so much attention was being paid to this book. I thought that would spark nostalgia in a photography community that is quite sensitive to that feeling. [Chuckles] In fact, on one hand it really surprised me that no one had erased the book. [Laughs] Of course, Rauschenberg had done it with de Kooning, and I found the gesture really interesting. I must say that at the time, I read a lot of John Cage's writings. I was fascinated by his ideas and, of course, John Cage and Rauschenberg are part of the same family in a sense. I thought, wow! Photography never had its "Erased de Kooning" moment. At the time, I was teaching photography at a university in England near where I lived. I don't know the situation in France, but in England, students are not so interested. [Laughs] I mean, I was giving them practical work to do but they didn't come to my classes and so I had plenty of free time. I was waiting for them so I could

[5] Looking In: Robert Frank's The Americans, *Steidl, 2009, 528 pages. Edited by Sarah Greenough.*

give them a critique of their work. But since they weren't coming, I went to the college library. I took a copy of Frank's book, scanned it and started to immerse myself in it. I started with a photo, and as a gesture, it was already really super-interesting. The scanners that the college had were really good, so you could get a super-high-resolution image ...

RC: I find that when you look at the image that's right behind us on the screen, you see details that you wouldn't notice if you looked at the full image.

MH: Yes, but now, for me, in hindsight, what interests me in this project is the notion that each of us would erase different elements. This means only one thing: everyone looks differently. Moreover, it's impossible today to look at an image, or even the world, in the same way as in the past. From a scientific point of view, the way the vision works is really interesting. The eye is a muscle that keeps moving. And so, what interested me in this work was that by erasing, I chose certain elements. Your choice would certainly be different from mine.

RC: I was talking earlier about Broomberg and Chanarin. They told me, about Holy Bible[6]*, that it was their interpretation of the Bible and that anyone else could provide a different version of it.*

MH: Yes.

RC: So perhaps any other artist could have a different interpretation of The Americans ...

MH: But it's not just about the artist, it's also about the reader. Each reader has his or her own interpretation. That's what's beautiful about art. I think art is one of the few spaces now where you are not told how to think, or how to interpret things. [Sighs] How can I say that? It seems to me that this is one of our great strengths in culture today, but it's still ambiguous. I don't know what to add to that.

[6] *Adam Broomberg & Olivier Chanarin,* Holy Bible, *Mack, 722 pages, 2013.*

RC: Well, look, we're going to have to finish soon. Unfortunately, we didn't have time to talk about Photography Is[7]*, which is one of your favourite works. It repertories the first 3,000 results when typing "photography is" in Google. The result is hilarious, because it shows that everyone has a different definition of photography and that Google doesn't know how to define it other than by algorithms and page views.*
But since we don't have time to talk about Photography Is, *I'd like to quickly touch on* _IMG01, *a book you made after* Less Américains *in which you used a photo of the First World War. It shows Australian soldiers, five of them if I remember correctly, in the middle of a half-destroyed forest near Ypres in Belgium. The book contains a print of the image. First, why did you specifically choose this photo?*

MH: I stumbled upon this image by chance and it struck me. I thought the ruins of the landscape were a metaphor for the ruins of the analogue, in a sense. It's not very deep, I grant you that. [Chuckles] But to be clear, I opened this image in Notepad. You know, what is it? It's a software designed to write computer codes. And in fact, now all digital images are text code. There's no direct link to light, right? They're only computer codes. So, I had the ambition to make the most contemporary photography book there is. [Audience laughs]

RC: With no images?

MH: Well yes, it's an image, but an image you can't read because you don't have the means to do so. Today, the images are made to be read by the machines. Right?

RC: Broomberg and Chanarin, again, say the same thing.

MH: Yes. But I cheated a little, because when you open this image in Word, it's 250,000 pages long! [Chuckles]

[7] *Photography Is*, 2010, was presented at the exhibition "What's photography?" held at the photography gallery of the Centre Georges Pompidou in 2015. Curated by Clément Chéroux and Karolina Ziebinska Lewandowska.

RC: You made it into a book of "only" 740 ...

MH: Yes, because that's the maximum allowed with the print-on-demand that I use. I wasn't going to make a book of 250,000 pages.

RC: No, that would have been a shame. It would have been a waste of paper. [Laughs]

MH: Yes. There would be no more trees. In fact, it might be interesting, because there are no trees in the photo: they were all felled. [Audience laughs] Anyways. A writer, a young English artist, really super-intelligent and brilliant, Lewis Bush, was fascinated by my choice of image. I had no idea, but he taught me that the photographer who made this image during the Second World War was Frank Hurley. He followed Australian soldiers on behalf of the government. But he was fired because he was manipulating the photos in post-production. [Chuckles] The images weren't dramatic enough for him, so he would alter them a little after the shooting.

RC: There are people who have had problems with that at the World Press Photo ...

MH: Yes, indeed. So, Lewis Bush found it super-interesting that I had chosen this particular image, the photographer having been fired because of it. But frankly, I didn't know at first. [Chuckles]

RC: So what you've transcribed is the content of the image. Are we again ignorant, again uneducated? Because most of us are unable to read the images in text form.

MH: Yes, that's what I'm wondering. I've never tried it myself, but, who knows, maybe in 50 years, our children will be able to read it. [Laughs] Probably not, but ... I don't know. [Laughs]

RC: Thank you, Mishka. If you have any questions ...

Young girl in the audience: You use new technologies as a medium, and in doing so you make us think not only about the subject but also about how they transform our daily lives. Are you going to turn to other technologies? For example, are you trying to analyse the technology of smartphones, Google Map and of all the images they produce? Are you trying to introduce them into your artistic practice?

MH: No, not really. I guess the question is: what influences do new technologies have on my practice as an artist? I would say that at that time, because we're talking about works that I did five or seven years ago, I was deeply interested in the consequences of new technologies on documentary photography ... And the result of these new technologies on aesthetics also attracted me a lot. But it's been a long time since I've worked on a project that uses satellite images or Street View. I'm now interested in other things. In fact, a few years ago I started working on how we look, vision, how the eye works. I bought an eye tracking machine that follows and observes precisely where your eye looks, how it travels an image, and I started a work on that. I find it truly fascinating. The aesthetic is different, it's true, yes. Technology, in that sense, has an influence on aesthetics, but I do other things as well. I also work differently. I use my hands as well, I paint. I'm not a painter, but I use painting for another project ... [Laughs]

R.C: Maybe we don't have enough time to talk about that, but it seems to me that one of the questions your work asks is "What is being contemporary?" And thus, assess that you can't photograph today like Robert Frank and that perhaps it's Google Street View or satellite views that are the way to express yourself today.`

MH : Listen, frankly, when I started working with satellite images in 2010, I thought that within five years everyone would be working with that ...

A.S.: That would be a shame! [Laughs]

MH: The internet is so rich. There are billions and billions of satellite images. I honestly thought it would be much more widespread as a strategy… but actually, no, not at all…

RC: Oh, a fair number of you have appropriated this material. This reminds me of Jorge Luis Borgès, the Argentinian writer who imagined in one of his short stories[8] a country in which one lays a map on a scale that covers the whole country, resulting in the reality of the country no longer corresponding to what is shown on the map. Is that what you're talking about?

MH: Yes, it was through Baudrillard that I discovered this short story. It's a beautiful idea. It's quite dark and dystopian. I find it very interesting, of course, because there's so much information today that anyone can say anything and it becomes a reality. It's unbelievable.

Woman in the audience: Good evening and congratulations for your work. I've seen astronomy photos in your work; do you want to tell us a little bit about it?

RC: This is your Astronomical *project. These are images that represent space from the Sun to Pluto and each page represents I don't know how many kilometres.*

MH: One billion kilometres.

RC: Yes, 1 billion kilometres, and there are 12 volumes, if I remember correctly…

MH: Twelve volumes, yes.

RC: In total, there are 6,000 pages, something like that, and most of the pages are black, so it's just the void between

[8] *Jorge Luis Borges: "De la rigueur de la science" [On rigor in science], in* L'Auteur et autres textes *[The author and other texts], Paris, Gallimard, Collection l'Imaginaire, 1982.*

the Sun and the planets. The question I would like to ask you about it is: is it to show that we are nothing, microbes? [Laughs]

MH: That's the pessimistic interpretation! [Laughs] I believe that one of documentary photography's biggest problems is the issue of scale. So, as someone from the field of sociology, I find it fascinating that there are now ways to show the macro of society. Not the micro, the macro. I've used these tools to explore that notion. Can we talk about society from the point of view of volume, the very large, rather than individual moments or individuals? I've been exploring this issue for a long time, maybe four or five years. *Astronomical* was part of that reflection.
And I also worked on the artist's book as a field of expression. I was fascinated by it. The book is a wonderful vehicle for ideas, isn't it? In the history of art, there's a rich history of the artist's book. And the print-on-demand technology allowed me to create a model on the scale of the solar system, so I used print-on-demand. If you're a writer, but you're not particularly good [Chuckles] or you're having trouble finding a publishing house, you can self-publish. It's not at all expensive. A book of 500 pages costs 6 euros, and I would fill a book of 500 pages with black ink. It cost me 6 euros, but it cost 50 euros for the printing, so after three years, they told me: "What exactly are you doing, sir? For every book we print for you, we're losing 40 euros!" [Laughs] They print so many books, it's like a farm! There are so many authors who want to print their own books that they print thousands and thousands of them every month, so mine went under the radar for a long time. [Audience laughs] *Astronomical* was part of this notion of exploring the book as a form, to express ideas visually, but it also had to do with the scale of things. How to use this format to talk about something huge rather than small. Of course, I know that the tiny is part of the big and the big, part of the tiny. [Laughs] But in the history of documentary photography, there aren't so many works that speak of the immensity.

RC: There was another question, I think, madam?

Woman in the audience: Yes. I wondered whether, after all these years, you were attracted to a particular field.

MH: That's an interesting question, because right now, I'm wondering about many things. What am I supposed to do? What is the role of the artist? What's the point? In fact, I think that the artist is someone who manages to find their place in art because it's the place where he or she finds a way to, how to say ...

Woman in the audience: To express yourself?

MH: It's not just about expression. Something doesn't feel quite right. I wouldn't feel very comfortable in other fields. But I think it's because I'm really very critical of myself, the world, or the culture. I'm an immigrant, so I have this perception that the world before me does not belong to me. I don't have a sense of belonging, which creates a gap. And I feel there's a certain element of criticism in that. That's what I continue to explore. I'm really sorry, but it's hard to explain myself in French.

Woman in the audience: Artists are always so demanding of themselves. [Chuckles]

RC: Finally, to explain what you said about your immigrant situation, you were telling me this afternoon that your family is partly from Poland, you were born in Brussels, you have French nationality, and you live in England. So there is movement there, not perpetual motion, but certainly determinant ...

MH: My mother was a Polish political refugee in France in the 1960s, so I'm the child of a refugee. If I compare myself to the friends I grew up with in Manchester, I have a slightly different, open way of looking at things.

RC: Certainly. It's added richness.

9 February 2017

WILLIAM KLEIN

William Klein was born in 1928 in New York. After studying sociology at the New York City College, he served in the military from 1946 to 1948, first in Germany and then in France. In 1948, he moved to Paris where he has lived and worked ever since. After enrolling at the Sorbonne, he studied for some time in Fernand Léger's studio. At the beginning of the 1950s, he became interested in kinetic art and experimented with abstract photography – a dozen of these photographs made the cover of the Italian magazine Domus. *In 1954, he returned to New York and in 1956 released the founding publication,* Life Is Good and Good For You in New York: Trance, Witness, Revels. *An extended title often summed up to* New York. *The book won the Nadar Prize in 1957. Klein has subsequently released three more books on cities:* Rome *(1959),* Moscow *(1964) and* Tokyo *(1964).*

In the 1960s, he moved away from photography and turned to cinema. He is the author of some twenty documentary and fiction films, including Who Are You, Polly Maggoo? *(1966), recipient of the Jean-Vigo Award, and* Muhammad Ali, the Greatest, *shot in two steps in 1964-65 and 1974. In the mid-1980s he initiated the documentary series* Contacts *in which famous photographers decipher their contact sheets, generally a hidden aspect of the photographic practice. He only returned to the photobook in 1989 with* Close up.

William Klein is the author of some fifteen books, including the reeditions of his cities classics. This figure does not consider his many exhibition catalogues and monographs.

It might definitely be a truism, but let's risk it: with his *New York*, William Klein revolutionised the history of photography in 1956. He sent Ansel Adams and his *Zone System* overboard. Even Walker Evans took a blow. Everything that made the conditions of a good photo: precise framing, concern for the most careful print with a range of greys are rejected in favour of the "affirmation of the artist's absolute subjectivity and freedom to use his tool without any rules other than the ones he assigned for himself." Joined two years later in 1958 by Robert Frank and his *The Americans*, he paved the way for a photographic genre that I call, for lack of a better word, "first-person photography", and that could be opposed

to the so-called neutrality of the School of Dusseldorf, for example. What Klein has invented runs through the second half of the 20th century to the present day. Many tried with relative success, but very few artists have found their own way of expressing their subjectivity to produce masterpieces.
On a pleasant sunny January afternoon, a wonderful conversation with a Master of Masters in his apartment near the Luxembourg garden of Paris, with Pierre-Louis Denis, artistic director and Tiffanie Pascal, in charge of communications and production at William Klein's studio.

> Rémi Coignet: *The first time I saw one of your pieces,* The French, *must have been in 1982, in the auditorium of the National School of Photography in Arles. I was thirteen. Someone told me that there was a film about Roland-Garros by a great photographer, William Klein. And I said, "Cool, let's go."*

William Klein: You were thirteen?

> *RC: Yes. So, I was very young and ignorant. I played a little tennis and watched the Roland Garros games on TV. I saw* The French *and understood that you could represent the world differently than the media conventions. I've never forgotten the movie. It's always been on my mind.*

WK: You grew up in Arles? It's a beautiful city.

> *RC: Yes. And when I saw the film again a few weeks ago to prepare for our meeting, I felt that* The French *is a theatre...*

WK: A theatre?

> *RC: Yes, it's an enclosure, a closed place, a theatre.*

WK: I'd have to see this movie again. I don't know what I think about it anymore. That was a long time ago, in 1981.

RC: And I thought that almost all your works, be it your books, New York, Moscow, Tokyo, *but your films as well, were conceived as theatres in which you either record or make your characters act. What's your feeling about this?*

WK: Sure, I would agree.
I was offered *The French* and I accepted it without really knowing what I was going to find. I was a tennis fan.
I loved tennis, contrary to what he says. [William Klein Giggles]
I love tennis, but it's not all I hate![1] [Laughs] I would have liked to be friends with these great players I admired, but that wasn't the case, except perhaps with Yannick Noah, a bit.So, the first work of mine you knew is *The French*.
Not bad.

Pierre-Louis Denis: *It's also the first film of William's I saw, because I play tennis.*

RC: If you will, let's go back a little bit. We were talking about how I discovered your work. I'm not going to go over your biography. You know it better than I do.

WK: Yes.

RC: But in the late 1940s, you studied for a while with Fernand Léger. What did you learn from him?

WK: From Léger? First, that it was possible to talk about art "normally." He saw our paintings once a week and gave advice. He said, "That's good, it's strong, it's tough." Things like that. Before I met him, if I was talking about art, I would say the same thing you said at thirteen. I was amazed that such a great painter could speak of art as he did. Have you seen any pictures of Léger?

RC: Yes, he was tall, very big.

[1] *William Klein refers to the book* I love fashion and it's all I hate *by Loïc Prigent (Grasset, 2016) that I brought to him.*

WK: He was tough and he would say, "That's good, that's good." So, I was surprised he could talk so naturally about art.
When I was a kid, I used to go to the Guggenheim in New York and I didn't like the way they spoke about art.
And finally, Léger spoke about it how I wanted to. Above all, Léger brought us back to the quattrocento. The students talked about the avant-garde. But he took us back to Piero della Francesca, to Cimabue, to all these painters we didn't know, or knew unevenly. I also discovered Masaccio and it was a revelation. We were all obsessed with Paul Klee, Picasso, etc. And the funny thing is, when Léger was telling us about the quattrocento, we'd go to bookstores to steal rare books that taught us about Masaccio and the others.
When I returned to New York in 1947…

RC: You went back in 1947 at the end of your military service?

WK: Yes, I was a soldier and there was a very well organized government program for American servicemen known as the G.I. bill of rights. The government considered young soldiers who had spent two years in the army eligible to resume their studies or their job, which was financed by the State for two years. So once I was demobilized, thanks to this G.I bill of rights, I could choose a place to study painting. And what was in Paris? The Beaux Arts, the Grande Chaumière [William Klein giggles], the studios of André Lhote and Fernand Léger. So for me, as they say, the choice was obvious. I first decided to go to André Lhote's, whose discourse on art impressed me, though not as much as discussing painting and art with Léger. André Lhote was an art critic, he told us about painting. We worked in his studio and we kind of followed his analysis, but I thought it was pretty dry and I wasn't getting a kick out it. Whereas with Léger, yes.

RC: And what did Léger bring you that has nurtured your work? Did he teach you freedom or whatever?

WK: I knew who Léger was, which wasn't the case for most people. [Giggles] Léger wasn't appreciated; he didn't have many followers, at least not among the young students in painting, who liked Picasso and Paul Klee, period. Léger wasn't on their agenda. He was a surprise.After demobilization, I was in the South at some point and got lucky. I rented a house where I had an atelier in Golfe-Juan on the coast. And every morning, Picasso was there, at the café, smoking a cigarette and drinking a coffee. One day, I went to see him with my paintings. Obviously, it was tempting to meet Picasso and show him what I was doing. How old was I? 22 or 23, something like that.

RC: And what did he tell you?

WK: I could see him smoking at the café by the water. I had a large suitcase, so I put some paintings in it, went downstairs and said, "Look, excuse me for bothering you, I hope I'm not bothering you too much. I'd like to show you what I do. Would you be nice enough to give me your opinion? Do you think I can have a career as a painter?" He had seen me come in with my large suitcase and replied, "Hoho, I thought you were a salesman trying to sell me something! [Laughs] Then he said, "Sure, let's put the canvases on the chairs." And that's what we did: we took over the café, setting the paintings out left and right. He looked and then said, "What do you want me to say? You're a painter, so paint." And I asked him, "But do you think I really am a painter?" And he replied, "Yes, I don't talk nonsense!" And I said, "I was afraid you'd said that to be nice." And he said, "That's not my style!" [Giggles] and he advised me again, "Paint, go ahead, that's all." Then he added: "Are you free this afternoon? We're hanging an exhibition at the Picasso Museum in Antibes." I said, "Of course!" So, I went there. And at one point, he asked, "What do you think of the hanging?" What did you want me to say to him besides that it was beautiful? Still, I did say something because I saw that there were some large paintings of fishermen on their boats. And I told him that I thought it was a pity that he wasn't producing more large format canvases like "Guernica". To which he replied, "But that's quite a job!" In fact, he was painting women on a chair or an armchair by the dozens. And he made tons of them. But he didn't make many large canvases with many characters and scenes. And I knew *Guernica* by heart because the painting was exhibited for years at the Museum of Modern Art in New York [MoMA].

RC: Yes.

WK: *Guernica* finally returned to Spain. But *Guernica,* which was displayed at the entrance of the second or third floor at MoMA was the only major composition of its kind. For me, it was really the masterpiece of masterpieces.

RC: Let's move forward a little bit. In the beginning of the 1950s, you were interested in kinetic art and experimented with abstract photography; some of these made the cover of Domus *magazine...*

WK: Two books came out at the time. One was the Gyorgy Kepes[2] and the other by László Moholy-Nagy[3], and for me, they were truly a revelation.The works of these two, their talk, were truly exciting. It was the first time I was seriously looking at what could be done with photography.

RC: So, you started doing these photographic experiments influenced by Moholy-Nagy and, I believe it was in 1954, Alexander Liberman offers you a contract with Vogue.

WK. I was part of an exhibition at the Salon des réalités nouvelles. He saw the show and he wanted to meet me. So, I went to *Vogue.*

RC: Here or in New York?

WK: Here in Paris. And he said to me, "Do you want to work for *Vogue*?" So, I said, "Doing what?" He told me, "We'll see, you can become assistant art director, work with me, or do something else." We met again and he said, "I think the best you could do for *Vogue* is photography. Do you have a project?"

[2] *Gyorgy Kepes,* Language of Vision, *Paul Theobald, Chicago, 1944.*

[3] *László Moholy-Nagy,* Vision in Motion, *Paul Theobald, Chicago, 1947.*

And I said yes! I was pretty pretentious. I was around 25 years old and I thought that the pictures I made and the books I loved and that inspired me could be applied to New York. Because my view of the city was different from when I lived there. Living in Paris for two years proved to me that a city could be different from New York. And I thought I could make a book out of the pictures I was taking and that I was fiddling with, laying them out on pages. It was very pretentious. I thought I'd be able to make a book, when I'd never done one before. I had already made some layouts and I told myself that I'd be able to make a book about New York. I told Liberman who replied, "You think you can do a book about New York?"
And I said yes! [William Klein giggles]. To my surprise, he said, "We can fund this book. We'll give you a line of credit in a photo store; you can take papers, chemicals, an enlarger, whatever you need. You make the pictures first in New York and then you can work here in Paris."
And I said, "Right, I'm going to do that." I would spend all my time taking pictures in New York and show them to Liberman every week. He was enthusiastic. But after a while, he explained, "These pictures you make of New York for the book you're projecting are all fine, but you know, we're a fashion magazine. So, you also should try to make fashion shots!"
I didn't have much insight into how to deal with fashion. Through Liberman, I looked at what was being done and I noticed two great photographers: Irving Penn and Richard Avedon. Penn worked for *Vogue* and they regularly published his portfolios like the small trades, for example. Et voila, I did fashion photos.
I met people in New York I showed my pictures of the city to. I was in contact with one or two publishers who were puzzled. They didn't see a book in them. They felt that the high contrasts and my style at the time weren't suitable for a book.
I returned to Paris where I got married to a young woman. The second thing that the American army offered, if you got married abroad, was to pay for a trip from Paris to New York. So I went back, and discovered the city differently.

RC: Yes, you hadn't been back to New York since 1947. You go back and you start taking these pictures. You had stayed in Paris and in Italy, worked with Léger and in photographic abstraction, and you truly invented a form of photography that did not exist before. Zone System, *Ansel Adams, even Walker Evans, you threw them all overboard. Is this a form of invention of the photographer's absolute subjectivity about their subject?*

WK: I was doing photography without any photographic training. So, I was dealing with the negatives I had and thought there was something to do with them, like how I was looking at the city. All the prints I made and showed to the New York publishers weren't successful. They would tell me, "You can't make a book with these pictures, it's not possible." And when I came back to Paris, I thought that perhaps, there might be an opportunity here to find a publisher, someone who would appreciate this way of photographing. I looked at what was coming out and there was the collection, "Petite Planète" ...

RC: Chris Marker...

WK: It was published by Editions du Seuil. So I got on the phone and found out that the guy who was behind these little books was Chris Marker. I told him, "I have these pictures of New York and I'm thinking of making a book out of that."

RC: I just wanted to ask you this: everyone knows about Chris Marker's artistic work, but what kind of an editor was he? He's edited dozens of books.

WK: Chris Marker conceived the collection "Petite Planète." They were paperbacks and his idea was to show cities from this or that country in different ways. So, he'd come up with a book about Athens, or Istanbul, for example. It was intended for students. They were tips on how to get by living cheaply in these cities. And it was a perfect fit to meet a guy doing that.
He looked at my work, and it was the opposite of the New York publishers. He said to me, "We're making a book with these pictures, and if Le Seuil doesn't take it, I'll give them my resignation!" This guy resigned every month. He was

their pocket genius, and at Le Seuil, they were smart enough to go along with what he proposed.

You're asking me what kind of an editor he was? Well, he was the kind of artist who made movies, books and wrote.

He published a novel[4] by the way. So he said, "Let's go." I started working from the pictures I had. And speaking of the practical stuff, *Vogue* was great to have, because I had no technical knowledge but I had noticed a small room where they had a copy machine, which was high-quality for the time; and I was able to make layouts as I wanted. The book was made possible thanks to the *Vogue* copy machine! [Laughs]

What's funny about Vogue and Liberman is that he was just a guy who came from Russia. He was no revolutionary, he even fled Moscow to Western Europe. He worked for a trendy magazine in the 1930s and 1940s. He did reports on the Spanish Civil War and stuff like that. Liberman, a Moscow-born man, like Brodovitch at *Harper's Bazaar*, was the artistic director of a fashion magazine. He thought my pictures were good, interesting. And he encouraged my work.

RC: From this first book, typography plays an essential role, and it will be the case in all your books, as in your film credits. What role does it play for you?

WK: At the time, painting was entering the Pop age and typography was key. I even deliberately conceived some of my photographs like that. For a day, I would cover the city's typography all over the place. There's even a picture I really like, where is it in the book? [Tiffanie and Pierre-Louis flip through the 1956 edition of the *New York* book]

Tiffanie Pascal: *We're going to find it.*

PLD: Oh yes, here it is.

WK: There, it was typography day.

Happy Days Bar, New York 1954. This photo is a bit due to chance. I was there, focusing and framing, preparing

[4] *Chris Marker,* Le Cœur net, *Le Seuil, Paris, 1949.*

the picture, when this guy came from the rear of the café and got into the frame. I couldn't see the guy, I was focused on the window. It's a happy coincidence.

RC: Is it a bit like the "Cadillac" image?

WK: Yes and no. No, because for the "Cadillac," I saw people in the window while he happened to be behind the letters. But typography, letters, for me was indispensable.

RC: I understand that they are all over your images, perhaps like in Gun, Gun, Gun *as well. But even on the covers of your books, typography is very important, isn't it?*

WK: Yes. One thing I was told when I paid attention to the publishing process is that Robert Delpire, who was one of the most important figures in photo publishing, selected the photos based on the contact sheets of Henri Cartier-Bresson and even later of Sebastião Salgado. He made one of Salgado's very first books and he made a very, very contrasting book, with a lot of black.
Cartier-Bresson was perfect for Delpire. But he still did Robert Frank's *Les Américains*, which was very far from Cartier-Bresson. With Delpire, we never designed books directly together. We did co-editions. I did *Contacts* with an Italian publisher[5] and Delpire made a French version. He took on books originally conceived with other publishers. Like *Tokyo*, which was done by a Japanese publisher, etc.
I couldn't stand the idea of someone like Delpire, who was the best, looking at my contacts. I wanted to choose myself.

RC: I will try to move on, I have so many questions for you. When you release New York *again in 1995, it has nothing to do with the first edition.*

WK: Sure it does, a little! [Giggles]

[5] *William Klein,* Contacts, *Contrasto, Rome, 2008.*

RC: Yes, but it's not a facsimile. You made a completely different book, you deleted a lot of images, you added a few, and most importantly, they are printed full bleed. The design and layout are very different. Why this choice for a radically new version?

WK: The first one was a very graphically accentuated book, rather than a photographic one. And the second is more a photographic book. For the first, I was in fact influenced by Moholy-Nagy and Kepes. David Campany said the other day that Moholy-Nagy and Kepes's revolutionary work on photography was probably due to the fact that the Hungarian language has nothing to do with any of the other European languages. So, to express themselves, these people turned to abstraction rather than follow the "normal" method to design layouts. It's Campany's theory, I don't know if it's true.

PLD: It's a theory, an idea.

WK: I have another idea, and you can take it any way you want. There are two kinds of photography: there is Jewish photography and goy photography. [Giggles] And in America, the ultimate goy is Ansel Adams. As for the Jewish photographers, you know them, they include none others than Robert Frank and Diane Arbus.

PLD: I'm also thinking of Leon Levinstein who is a little less well-known.

WK: Jewish photographers are the street, the urban life, and goy photography is the landscape. Ansel Adams is the typical goy photographer. A Jew can't take pictures like that.

RC: It's an extremely interesting theory. But, one thing that strikes me is that you stayed in Paris and in Italy, working with abstraction, influenced by Moholy-Nagy as you said. And then you go back to New York and you're actually inventing something that no one's ever done before: no more framing, no more focus, no more rules.

PLD: Rémi asks if you were aware that you were inventing something new?

RC: It's a revolution.

WK: I thought, because, as I said, I was influenced by Moholy-Nagy and Kepes, that something else could be done with photographs and with books.

PLD: Had you ever seen pictures of Ansel Adams or of other photographers before you did your book?

WK: Oh yes, of course! I've often said that the MoMA in New York was my second home. And there, you could really see a panorama of all forms of arts, photography[6], design, or South American painting, which was then much appreciated.
But at the time it wasn't like today. We went to the MoMA with Pierre-Louis not so long ago, and there was a line. I was also at the MoMA for the "Picasso Matisse" exhibition and there was an unbelievable crowd. The line outside was going around the block! It was never like that before! The MoMA, if I remember correctly, was empty. I'd go there after school with some friends to see films in the basement and we were open to everything that was presented, in cinema, in painting.
Don't forget that MoMA was an extraordinary place. There was *Guernica*, we already talked about it, there was Le Douanier Rousseau, and paintings you didn't see in Paris. Now, in Paris, you see Jeff Koons at the Louvre. Besides, he took one of my pictures to make a sculpture. We're attacking him for plagiarism.

RC: Yes, I understand that he is very good at using the works of others. But how was the New York *book received? It wasn't published in the United States but in France, and I believe there were also an Italian and an English edition.*

WK: There were three editions. There was Chris Marker and Le Seuil in Paris; in England, there was a somewhat avant-garde

[6] *Which was avant-garde for the time. From 1940, the MoMA established a specific photography department, founded by Beaumont Newhall.*

photographic journal that published the book in English; and in Italy, a friend of mine, publisher Giangiacomo Feltrinelli. Do you know him?

RC: Yes of course, with his translation of Boris Pasternak's Doctor Zhivago *and his tragic end...*

WK: He was not a publisher when I met him. He later became one because he had money.

RC: And at the time, it was in 1956, how was the book received? How did you interpret its reception?

WK: *New York* had quite an impact in Paris. I was saying the other day that *Le Monde* published a rectangle on the front page at the bottom. They wrote about *New York*[7]. It was extraordinary.

RC: Let's move on to Rome, *if you will. As you tell it in the preface, in 1957-1958, you dared to get in touch with Federico Fellini who was passing through Paris.*

WK: When *New York* came out, I was a Fellini fan and I wanted to meet him and possibly work with him. So, I called his hotel and I met him. It was easy in those days, it's not like today where you have to go through...

RC: Yes, agents, publicists. But it seems that he told you, "Come with me to Rome, you will be my assistant on my next film." And you replied that you did not know anything about the job of assistant."

WK: Yes, but you know, even Fellini who was an international star was having a hard time making movies. Because his movies didn't work that well. And cinema is different from what you think. So, he had plans to make *The Nights of Cabiria*, but the film was delayed because they had problems with the producers and money. I accompanied Fellini when I was

[7] *« Férocité et Banalité », in* Le Monde, *1 December 1956, article written by Robert Coiplet.*

in Rome, two or three times. Once for a casting of hookers and... what do you call it? Pimps. Things like that, but I never worked on a movie with Fellini.

RC: You haven't worked on The Nights of Cabiria?

WK: No.

RC: I was wondering if Fellini had been your master in cinema, because your first personal film, Broadway by Light, *came out about the same time as your work on Rome. I was wondering if it came from watching Fellini work...*

WK: I've never seen Fellini at work. He said to me, "Come to Rome, you will be my assistant." But he was just a guy who told jokes. He made this proposition to me when he already had five or six assistants, so it never happened.

RC: In the book Rome, *as in the other books on cities, there are chapters. One of them is called "Eternal City," "Città Eterna" in Italian, and you have slipped a picture of the EUR district, built by Mussolini.*

WK: Yes, it's Mussolini's Coliseum.

RC: Is it just irony, or is it acknowledging that it is now part of the Eternal City?

WK: I don't know what's accepted or not.

RC: No, but I mean accepted by you.

TP: Did you do it out of irony?

WK: Of course! Mussolini's Coliseum is a joke.

RC: Another question about Rome. *I just reviewed the image there, flipping through the original edition, but in the edition you made with Contrasto, the opening page, precisely of the chapter on the Eternal City, shows this photo of an advertisement for Coca-Cola. In the re-edition, it is even more obvious because it opens the chapter. Is this a form of denunciation, or a mise en abime of the merchants of the temple?*

WK: This wall is a kind of compilation of all the inscriptions that can be found in Italy.

PLD: There is "totocalcio," and old inscriptions...

WK: There's something in Hebrew too.

RC: When you reissued New York, *you made a totally different object, and for the reissue of Rome, you made some changes in the images, for example the great series of people on Vespas is presented differently. But in a separate booklet, you have kept not only your captions, but also the original texts. Why?*

PLD: Not only: for New York, *you also rewrote the captions.*

TP: For Rome, *you used exactly the same captions and texts.*

WK: My wife selected all the texts about the city at Rome's municipal library.

PLD: Oh really?

RC: And you gathered them in a small booklet.

WK: I don't know. I think it was the publisher who had the thought of making this booklet.

RC: Then, in 1964, you published Moscow. *For me, it's the most mysterious of your books...*

WK: What's mysterious? [William Klein giggles]

RC: We're in the middle of the Cold War, you're American. What drives you to the USSR? Did you have a press or editorial commission?

WK: No. I simply made books about cities, but every time it's been, what do you call it? A portrait of sorts, a description of how we live. So, Rome, Moscow or Tokyo, these are very different cultures illustrated in a book about each of these cities.

RC: What surprises me about Moscow *is that at the time, we were in the middle of the Cold War, and there were Western intellectuals who were invited by the Communist Party...*

WK: Me?

RC: No, I don't know about you. But French intellectuals, Jean-Paul Sartre or whoever, would go to Moscow and come back and say, "It's magnificent, communism is great." And I feel that among your books on cities, this one is in a way the most neutral.

WK: Yes, it doesn't have New York's excitement. I represent people's lives quietly. I see *Moscow* as a very quiet book, made in a place few people could travel to at the time, and in the context of a highly polarised situation. The book seems to me neither for nor against the communist regime. You see people in parks, playing chess, you see, it seems to me, life as it goes, without judgment. Did you want me to take a stand for or against communism?

RC: Not at all, I don't want anything. But I have the impression that, in a time of frontal opposition, you have been very neutral.

WK: I have to say that what I knew about cultures outside of America was Paris. Rome, Moscow, Tokyo, all these cities were for me portraits of the way people lived in these places. And for *Moscow*, don't forget that I grew up with Russian novels. It was a culture I knew quite well from literature. I was obsessed with Russian novels. I read everything I could. So, covering Moscow was marvellous for me.

PLD: And you were free enough to take all the pictures you wanted?

RC: Or was there some kind of "guide" to tell you, "No, no! Not this!"?

WK: No, I was surprised. I never had a problem while working on *Moscow*. [William Klein flips through the book] I'm looking for a picture of some street with small, old houses. So, there, I photographed this street and people would say to me, "Why are you photographing this street, they're just old houses. Go to the centre, go here or there." Photographing an ordinary street? Passers-by thought it wasn't great enough. They'd say, "Go to the centre, go to the Red Square." Stuff like that. That's an example. [William Klein continues to flip through the book] Here's another one: the girl in the bikini. It struck me. It's on the edge of the Moskva River. It's the beach...

RC: Yes, there is a sense of freedom.

WK: I didn't think I could photograph a girl in a bikini in Moscow, but I was quite surprised. It's a portrait of a young girl, her father and her grandmother. And I was stunned that no one said no to me.

RC: I have a side question: out of the four books on cities, Moscow *is the only one not to have been reissued.*

WK: That's the way it is!

RC: Would you like to?

WK: I couldn't care less! [General laughter]

RC: In Moscow, *you keep the principle of chapters, but it is the first of your books with almost all full-bleed images.*

WK: So?

RC: Does it coincide with an aesthetic move in the construction of your books?

WK: I have to say that *Moscow* is a gentle book. I loved the Russians very much, I loved Russia very much, and there is no charge, no mockery in this book.

RC: From an aesthetic perspective related to the layout, is this change an evolution?

PLD: There are also many in Tokyo.

RC: Tokyo came out shortly after. Is it a new aesthetic choice? The format is a little bigger too.

WK: It's the only one that's been released in large format.

RC: Are you thinking differently in terms of design? Do you think it's more interesting to display the photos full bleed?

WK: For *Moscow,* I'm not proving anything. I don't want to prove anything, I show Moscow...

RC: If I'm stressing the point, it's because afterwards, whether it is in Close up, *which is the first with all full-bleed images , or in the reedition of* New York, *or again in* Paris+Klein, *this type of layout becomes a kind of "trademark": the image covers the entire page.*

WK: I don't know. I didn't want to prove anything by doing *Moscow*. I was showing...

TP: What Rémi is saying is that you'll keep this way of expressing yourself in the following books.

PLD: You preserved this book format. You did Close up, *the reedition of* New York, Paris, *the retrospective, and so, does it become a means to find the perfect balance to show your pictures?*

WK: I don't have a theory about it.

RC: Okay, but it's a change. So, just after Moscow *you published* Tokyo. *First, why did you go to Tokyo?*

WK: I was invited to Tokyo by a publisher. My books were well received there. There were many young photographers in Tokyo who were influenced by my work. This was not the case in Rome or elsewhere. No, the Japanese had a rather quiet photographic style at the time. It changed after, because people like Daido Moriyama [see *Conversations 1*, p. 200] were very influenced by my photos.

RC: If my information is correct, when you were in Tokyo, you were using the darkroom of the group Vivo (Eikoh Hosoe, Kikuji Kawada and Shomei Tomatsu, notably) to process your films.

WK: Yes, yes. They pissed me off because I didn't want people to see my contacts before I did.

RC: I'm not going to bother you too long. You said you didn't want people to see your contacts before you did. Is this when the Japanese discovered your work on New York or Rome?

WK: [William Klein giggles] No, they knew it well.

RC: And very soon after arriving in Tokyo, even though you wrote that you wanted to be there like a Barbarian who doesn't understand anything[8], very quickly you found yourself in contact with the local avant-garde, Butô dancers notably, Tatsumi Hijikata or Kazuo Ohno.

PLD: Did this happen through Hosoe?

WK: No, no. The Japanese have eyes everywhere and these dancers saw what I was doing in photography.

[8] *"In Tokyo, I thought: everything to see, nothing to interpret, I'll be the Barbarian in Tokyo. Convinced already that I wouldn't understand, glad not to have to try, I certainly didn't want to judge.", in the preface of the French edition of* Tokyo, *published by Delpire in 1964.*

TP: Did they actually know about you? They asked you to come and see them?

WK: Yes.

RC: And when you perform with them and Yoshito Ohno in the city's traffic, in the middle of cars, the image that opens the book...

WK: I made these images on the last day of my stay in Tokyo. I did this photo shoot with the Butô dancers. They thought I was going to photograph them in their studio. To which I replied, "No, we're going to go out on the street and we'll improvise."

RC: Okay. This partly answers my question: Did you follow them or did you tell them, 'let's do this performance together?' Because even though you're behind the camera, you participate in the performance by dancing at their pace.

WK: It was a happening, yes.

RC: Do you have any idea why your work so strongly influenced the next Japanese generation, Moriyama, Takuma Nakahira and others? Do you know why?

WK: Why not? [Laughs]

TP: It's true that the Provoke *generation claims to have been influenced by your photos*[9]*. Do you have any idea why it clicked in the spot for them?*

WK: The Japanese are always looking left and right for what can be of interest to them. But I had seen Japanese magazines at the time. And I had noticed that the last four or five pages of the magazines were reproductions of international publications that they found of interest. They went to great

[10] *See the 1967 article by Takuma Nakahira about William Klein, reproduced in English in the book,* Provoke, *published by Steidl in 2016 to coincide with the exhibition "Provoke: Between Protest Performance" at Le Bal, Paris.*

lengths to be aware of everything that could be published anywhere in the world.

RC: So, you're saying that they were isolated on their islands and at the same time, looking at what was happening elsewhere.

WK: Yes.

RC: One last thing about the cities. Akio Nagasawa [see Conversations *2, p. 124] republished* Tokyo *and it is the only one that is a facsimile of the original. Why is that?*

WK: Well, yes. For *Tokyo*, the difference is Akio's quality. He did a splendid job. Do you know him?

RC: Yes, I know him quite well, I would say he's a friend.

WK: He is a fine one.

RC: He's doing a wonderful job. Then after Tokyo, *for almost twenty-five years, you did not publish any books (except exhibition catalogues or monographs). Why is that? You didn't want to? No more time for that?*

WK: I did a few books but not about cities. I did something in Turin.

RC: But that's a lot later. It's after Close up. *The next book after* Tokyo *is* Close up *in 1989*

TP: Perhaps, you were devoting yourself to film during that time.

RC: We were about to talk about your movies.

WK: We just found out there's a movie theatre in New York that wants to show twelve films.

RC: Twelve is nearly all your films.

WK: Some of them, very little known.

RC: So, I'd like to ask you a couple of questions about your films. Since we have this long period of cinema. Since the mid-1950s, you had a contract with Vogue, *you were working with Liberman, and in 1966, you made* Who are you Polly Maggoo?, *a satire of the fashion world.*

WK: Not really, not only.

RC: No, it's also, among other things, a critique of the stupidity of French television at the time, for example. I saw it again recently. The film is even visionary about the contemporary top model system. And it opens with a fashion show taking place in one of André Bloc's habitable sculptures in Meudon, near Paris. The women editors are settling in and everyone is waiting for the arrival of some high-profile personality, whom we guess is the editor-in-chief of a major magazine. It's a caricature of Diana Vreeland, isn't it?

WK: Well, yes, clearly! Diana Vreeland. Who was the editor before her?

TP: Jessica Daves was the editor before Diana Vreeland.

WK: Jessica Daves wasn't chic, she didn't look good and she didn't have any theories. Diana Vreeland was a go-getter who thought she would make a change in the way we consider fashion.
Diana Vreeland has a daughter, or a daughter-in-law, I don't remember, who made a movie about her[10] and they used images from *Polly Maggoo*. So it's impossible to make a caricature of fashion, because it is itselft a caricature.

RC: Yes, I think you'll also see that in the little book I brought you, fashion is cartoonish. But how did Diana Vreeland react

[10] Diana Vreeland: The Eye has to travel, *2011, a documentary by Lisa Immordino Vreeland and Bent-Jorgen Perimutt.*

to this "tribute"? And more broadly, how was the film received in the fashion world?

WK: They always take advantage of everything, so they took advantage of the film too! [Giggles]

RC: Much later, in 1994, you published the book In and Out of Fashion.

WK: Yes.

RC: I wonder if deep down, you're not an anarchist who uses any available opportunities to do things your very own way?

WK: I couldn't say.

RC: Because from Polly Maggoo, *you are "In and out of Fashion." You work for* Vogue *and you make this movie. Let's move on. Perhaps I'm wrong, I see your work as not overtly political. You worked for fashion, and then you made fun of it. And, from* New York *to* Mister Freedom *and the documentaries you did for the ORTF*[11]*, there seems to be an underlying rejection of consumerism.*

WK: *Mister Freedom*, it's Trump!

RC: And de Gaulle coming out of the ceiling, it's fantastic!

TP: Rémi thinks there is an underlying rejection of consumerism in your work.

WK: Oh yes, I agree.

RC: And you made two very political films, Muhammad Ali The Greatest *and you were part of* Far from Vietnam *with Chris Marker, Jean-Luc Godard, Agnès Varda and Alain Resnais, among others.*[12] *Why, as for Richard Avedon,*

[11] *Office de Radiodiffusion Télévision Française, the former national broadcasting network in France, now called France Télévision.*

was it important to offer your reputation and artistic know-how to serve the fight for civil rights and against the Vietnam War?

WK: Why? Why not?

TP: There is a political side to your work.

WK: But of course.

RC: Can you explain why at that point it was important to be involved in this film?

WK: Because first of all, the Vietnam War was a horror. And I wanted to denounce it, of course. And if I'm making films, I need to be able to deal with topics that concern me. And again, Chris Marker had something to do with it.

RC: Yes.

WK: Chris Marker is behind *Far from Vietnam.*

RC: Yes, it's a collective film where each one shot their own sequence. There is one question to which I couldn't find an answer to. Was the final editing done by Chris Marker or was it also a collective effort?

WK: Chris Marker was contacted by students who organized political meetings. They were showing movies that were very bad. Then they asked Marker to make a film and his reply was, "No, I don't want to, but I'm going to ask my friends." And he asked six or seven directors to each shoot a sequence. I did the shooting that you saw in New York.

TP: But did Chris Marker do the final editing?

WK: Yes. everyone made their fifteen-, twenty- or thirty-minute film and he edited it all together. But at some point, it was

[12] Far from Vietnam, *1967. Film by Chris Marker, Joris Ivens, Claude Lelouch, Alain Resnais, Agnès Varda, Jean-Luc Godard and William Klein.*

too much. He had problems. He didn't want to go on. He asked me if I wouldn't finish the editing, and I said, "No, it's up to you!" [William Klein laughs] So yes, he did the final editing.

RC: To say a couple of words about Mister Freedom, *which I find hilarious, when, for example, Mister Freedom enters the American embassy in Paris, which is in fact a vast supermarket presented by the ambassador as the cultural department. But apart from that, I was wondering whether, for you, American comics, super-hero movies are (or were) propaganda, just like* The Little Red Book *or the* Manifesto of the Communist Party*?*

WK: You know, for that movie, *Mister Freedom*, unlike all the super-hero movies, I did say that the adventure was financed by a fascist movement... Because Superman, Batman, Spiderman, all that, you never know who, what power supports them financially. Whereas in the film, the financier of *Mister Freedom* is a fascist, Doctor Freedom, it's obvious.

RC: I'd like to talk about the "Contacts" film series that you started in the mid-1980s, in which famous photographers, starting with you, show their contact sheets and explain their selection. Why was it important at the time to show the backstage? When photographers, first of all yourself, and as you have already said, were reluctant to show their contacts?

WK: Why was it important? Well, it seems obvious. I thought that even though I didn't like to show my contacts, it was an important way to approach photography.

RC: Yes of course. I was an intern at Magnum Photos...

WK: You were an intern at Magnum?

RC: Yes, when I was very young, about 20 years old. And I spent hours watching Josef Koudelka's contacts because it was exciting. And shortly after launching the series "Contacts," you started to paint enlarged contacts with acrylic.

WK: Yes.

RC: And obviously there is plastic beauty in these pieces. But I wonder If it's not a way to link your work on film, be it photographic or cinematographic, with your beginnings as a painter, or even if it's not a way to reject the somewhat stupid debate of the time that basically claimed, "The painter does something with his hand whereas the photographer just presses a button."

WK: Yes, you can say that.

RC: And to say one is no better than the other...

WK: I don't know. I say nothing. I think it's beautiful.

RC: It's certainly beautiful and at the same time, it seems that in the painted contacts we see the end of the previous image and the beginning of the next one. It's also a relationship to cinematographic film.

WK: Listen, we're going to stop.

TP: William is tired.

WK: We've been a long way since *The French*!

RC: Yes, you're right. But if you're not too tired, I'd like to ask you two more questions.

WK: OK, go ahead.

RC: In 1989, you republished another book, Close up, *twenty-five years after* Tokyo. *The book's title is perfectly appropriate. Where did you get the idea to fit as many people as possible into the frame?*

WK: I've always done that.

RC: Yes, and already, in the New York *notes, you say that you're buying your first wide-angle. And if we take* Paris+Klein, *there are all these photos of various events. What do you like about this whole concept of having a lot of people in the picture?*

WK: It's because when you go out on the street to take pictures, you don't have the opportunity to bring everything you see and everything you feel into the picture. So, I'm getting as close as I can to this set of sensations and signs. Since the beginning, it's a way for me to work. I started with one Rolleiflex. And when I got a 35mm camera, I could change lenses. I often said that when I started working on the book about New York, I went to a photo shop and told them, "I can't put enough stuff in the picture." They said to me, "Well, try this one," and they lent me a 28 mm lens. I went out on the street and I was knocked out. I could in fact put a lot more stuff in the photo. All this thanks to a salesman in a photo shop who dropped a wide-angle lens in my hand!

RC: Great! My very last question. We said two words about Muhammad Ali. His mantra was "Float like a butterfly, sting like a bee." You could say that of your work as well, right?

WK: [William Klein giggles] Listen, I don't mind being compared to Muhammad Ali but it's not the case. He was world heavyweight champion, I wasn't.

RC: You may be world heavyweight champion in the photography category.

WK: Muhammad Ali was such an image man.

RC: Oh yes, he had an incredible sense of communication.

WK: Great, even!

RC: Couldn't your tactic be broadly summed as follows: you walk the streets, and all of a sudden, you start clicking. Would you agree?

WK: Yes, yes, yes. It suits me very well.

RC: Thank you very much. Thank you so much.

19 January 2018

SUSAN MEISELAS

Susan Meiselas was born in 1948 in Baltimore, USA. She lives in New York. After graduating in Visual Studies from Harvard University, she joined Magnum in 1976. Her work is now part of most major public collections in the United States as well as internationally. She is the recipient of multiple awards, including the Robert Capa Gold Medal in 1978, the Leica Medal of Excellence in 1982, the Hasselblad Award in 1994 and a Guggenheim Fellowship in 2015. She has authored or edited dozens of books.

Susan Meiselas's practice is altogether extremely generous, unique, pioneering and modest. Generous in the sense that she has tried, sometimes over decades, to return what she "took" from her subjects. Unique because she means to contextualize her practice "in history", reaching beyond the front-page headlines, shedding some light on the whys and wherefores of events. Pioneering because, while in the last few years there have been increasing numbers of books compiling authored photographs, documents and found photographs, they often deliver charming fictions, individual micro-stories or lazy attempts at revisiting history. Nonetheless, that inclination towards exhaustiveness dear to Susan Meiselas is sensed in the output of various authors. Consider, among others, Carlos Spottorno [see p. 304], Mathieu Asselin, Henk Wildschut, Laia Abril or even the entire body of Edmund Clark's work [see p. 62]. And finally, modest because Susan Meiselas willingly grants greater space to documentation than to her own images, as in the case of her work in Kurdistan, retracing a century of the history of the Kurdish people.

I met her for the first time at the end of January 2018, at the Kurdish Institute of Paris, where she was running a two-day workshop. Approximately 10 "students" were in the room. Some were working on their computers on layout, others were selecting images and documents to describe their personal stories within the larger history of the Kurds. Susan wandered from one to the next, giving advice on layout here, suggesting a selection there. Each participant would produce a small book that would be included in her exhibition premiering in the following few days at Jeu de Paume. She took part in these participative workshops in every city with a Kurd diaspora she had the opportunity to visit in Europe and in the Middle East. Two days later, I had a conversation with this great lady in her hotel lobby, close to Place de la Madeleine. She would spend the following week hanging her show.

Rémi Coignet: *At the moment, I am very interested in the relationship between photography and power. Be it the use of photography by powers, the strategies used by photographers to counter this use, or the power of the photographer over his or her subject.*

Susan Meiselas: Yes, that is very complex.

RC: Yes, very much so. It is a vast subject and I think that you took part in it from your first book, Carnival Strippers, *in which you refuse to use this power of the photographer: the words of the girls, of the clients and of the bosses are as important as your own images. What do you think?*

SM: Yes, I think you're exactly right. I wasn't trying to find an equivalence. Words and pictures are different. But I felt that their words could complement the photographs to contextualize them.

RC: Another aspect of your work is to always try to give back something to your subjects. I read somewhere that you showed your contact sheets to the carnival strippers so they could choose the prints they wanted.

SM: Yes.

RC: And later, you used other exchange strategies, in Nicaragua or in Kurdistan. How is that notion of exchange important for you and why?

SM: Yes, exchange or dialogue. I think my instinct very early on was to share what I was seeing. Sometimes you can do that quite easily with Polaroid film. When there was no Polaroid film and only digital cameras, the idea of physical exchange, whether of a contact sheet or a print, was the one thing I could offer. The process of sharing a contact sheet can sometimes be difficult, because people don't understand the photographer's selection process; so, inviting them to point, literally by placing their initials on the pictures that they liked, was a signal. Giving a photograph in the case of the strippers was more about allowing them to see their working lives in my photographs. Most often, they would give it to the men who shared their life. So that is where choosing a portrait, bringing and giving the print for them to give it away to another person, were particularly nice moments.

But, from the very earliest project I did at 44 Irving Street in the boarding house where I lived, I wanted to know what people saw in my seeing of them. And how they saw themselves differently than or much like I did. Did I capture something in them that they could recognize? The exchange was very early on part of my practice; but not always, of course, because I can't always do that. Technology changed all that. You have more capacity in some ways, but it is quite different to see an image on a digital screen, upload an image for someone else to print it, than to physically give them something. Particularly when it was a Polaroid, because you have to remember a Polaroid is a daguerreotype; it is a "one and only". And when you're giving it, you're giving something away forever. In fact, when I did a project in Cova da Moura, a neighbourhood outside Lisbon in Portugal, I went back to some of the people I had given the photographs to, asking if I could reproduce the photographs I had given them so I could make some murals for the streets. That was a whole new process for me, to return to the photograph and the person, and involving them in the public representation of the work.

RC: This also relates to what you did in Nicaragua, returning 10 or 15 years later and ...

SM: Yes, with the murals, though in that case, I didn't actually ask the people who were in the photographs about hanging the murals. I was thinking about history, and whether or not a particular image captured a moment in history, and whether others might remember the larger history from which those images came. So, it was a somewhat different process, similar in one sense, but they were placed back in the landscape [in Nicaragua] where I had actually made the photographs. In Cova da Moura, I may have made the picture anywhere in the community, but the important thing was giving the person their photograph and then inviting them to share the enlarged photograph publicly. Very often, they would place them in front of their homes, so it was both public and very intimate.

> *RC:* Nicaragua June 1978 – July 1979 *has a very different structure than* Carnival Strippers. *It opens with your 70 photographs, very strong, without any captions. The second section is mostly textual, with captions – a chronology of a country's history starting with the arrival of the Spanish in 1524 and ending with the victory of the Sandinistas in 1979 – along with a series of historical texts, including 20th-century diplomatic messages. Why this structural choice? Was the point to strike the readers with the images first, and then give them keys to understanding the context?*

SM: That's a nice term, "keys". Keys to unlock the mystery behind or around the photographs. In some ways, that was a much different process for me than *Carnival Strippers*, which took me three summers to complete. I was speaking the same immersive language, but there, time was moving very fast in a process no one had any idea where it would lead to. So, stitching together the photographs when I came home a year or so later, they were like fragments of a process. Part of me wanted to recreate that feeling of flow from which the photographs came, of time moving very fast, very cinematically. I wanted the reader to just experience that sense of emergency, but at the same time there were limits. The technology to print in colour was quite expensive and certainly not as good as the one we have today. In those days, if you wanted to do

a colour book, and *Nicaragua* was published in French, Spanish and English, you had to separate the text or publish each book independently, as you would now for a co-publication in French and English, unless you do a bilingual edition. There was no capacity to integrate the text without it being very expensive. So, for me, it was a choice that was both economic and aesthetic.
When faced with the economic decision, I thought about how I could create another form with similar results.
If you really look carefully at *Nicaragua*, there are blank pages, and I just reconstituted those blanks in the second part with the black-and-white thumbnails, so you know where you stand in the flow of time. And those texts are also very different than in *Carnival Strippers* because in that one, it was mostly exchanges between the women, the women and their managers and the women with the clients.
The textual elements in *Nicaragua* were much more diverse, broader historically, including not just the protagonists. They also included statistics, poems, unpublished letters, all kinds of diverse materials, which is very much in line with what I did in Kurdistan much later. It was my first experience of an experimental process.

RC: Obviously, it is the matrix of your subsequent work.

SM: Well, yes. I discovered a way of working with much richer primary materials than just voice recordings. The voices in *Strippers* were woven into a collage, but they were recordings that had been transcribed to become text. The sound is very rich because you hear the interplay between various perspectives. *Nicaragua* was really another kind of experiment, and graphically important, because you could juxtapose a poem, statistic or oral story. It's a different approach to mixing languages.

RC: I also think that in the title of the book, the dates "June 1978 – July 1979" are as important as "Nicaragua", because they frame a given period of time that you situate in a much larger history with the texts.

SM: Yes, this is true. But when we reprinted the book in 2008 (it had been out of print for a fair amount of time), we were able to put a CD-ROM of the film *Pictures from a Revolution* that I did 10 years after, when I returned to find the people I had originally shot in the photographs. It was quite interesting to stretch the book in time, though we didn't change the chronology that related to the photographs. Then, in the third edition, which just came out last autumn, I customized an app called "Look and Listen" and cut up our film into 20 or so sequences. In the book, you see a little eye icon under some of the photographs, which indicates that the photograph can trigger a clip from the film, to see the person in the photograph become alive, speaking, engaging ...

RC: This is a form of augmented reality.

SM: Exactly. It was quite fun to use augmented reality, to watch as people look at the photographs and suddenly decide to interrupt turning the pages of the book to look into a new flow of images, to watch a film clip that brings them closer to what I was thinking about when I made the pictures, or to hear the person in the picture. It is a way to invite the reader to engage more. At least, I hope so.

RC: Yes, and as I was saying, I see this book, Nicaragua, *as the matrix of what would be your practice over the years: producing objects that relate to social and human sciences or history. Though I have the feeling that photography is always first for you. Does photographing an event then lead you to explore all the facts that may have led to that event, using documents, archives, etc.? Is it the way you work?*

SM: I think the photograph is always at the centre and the connecting point. Not always, but in the best cases, it leads me somewhere else, beyond the image itself or the series of images. If I dwell with it within me to find what more I can do with it. It's interesting how these things relate. You know, there are connections between the thinking behind *Nicaragua* and *Kurdistan*. *Nicaragua*, however, was done during a specific period, and *Kurdistan* portrays 100 years of history.

It is not a time that I have lived through, which is very different from reporting on a time I have personally recorded. *Encounters with the Dani* is a similar approach from what I have learned from working in Kurdistan. Though the history is a very different one, there are similarities, points of connections. I'm migrating forms which are interrelated. I don't know if the work will be felt in the same way at Jeu de Paume.

RC: I saw the exhibition views from Barcelona.

SM: Oh, you did?

RC: Yes. The images from Barcelona, which I received from Jeu de Paume, give me a hint of what the exhibition will be. As I remember, you wrote in Prince Street Girls *that you were very busy in Latin America from the mid-1970s to the mid-1980s. Besides* Nicaragua June 1978 – July 1979, *you edited two books on the matter:* El Salvador: Work of Thirty Photographers *and* Chile from Within. *Was your motivation mainly to describe the struggles of the people fighting against dictatorships, or to denounce the US imperialism on the subcontinent as well?*

SM: Well, I think it is a mix of both. I wouldn't say that I authored books, I co-curated them. I collaborated with small groups to make them. They were a representation of the work by many photographers, 30 from El Salvador, 15 from Chile. A smaller group was involved in the actual editing, sequencing and thinking about the books. But it was quite intentional on my part not to be the author, the curator or the editor of these books. For me, it was comfortable to be the author of *Nicaragua* but it was not appropriate for *El Salvador* and *Chile*.

But yes, there was a dynamic that has to do with US imperialism and the power of the people to counter it. It's about power and the counter-desire to transform things. Not just to rebel against but to transform, or even to be part of the creation of a new society. It was very moving in that period, to believe that it was possible.

RC: I have the feeling that you don't have a huge ego. Whether in these books you co-curated about Latin America, or in Encounters with Dani, *the main part is not your photographs. Is the message more important than the messenger?*

SM: It is not just the message. It is more about a meaningful relationship through collaborations of which, again, I'm only one element out of many in these situations. You can be very singular and sometimes very solo, but this was history in the making by many, many people, and everyone was contributing, so that seemed like the right expression.

RC: Do you consider your work to be political?

SM: It depends on what you mean by political. Yes, to reveal what is hidden, to portray those who are forgotten, in some ways, that is very political. But if you mean "ideological" by "political", then no. I don't go places to prove something. I hope I'm always discovering something from being somewhere, and then I try to find a way to bring people closer to the complexity of a situation. What do you think you mean when you ask about "political"?

RC: Maybe this brings us to the next question. I don't mean to debate over the notion of the so-called concerned photographer, but for example, with Kurdistan, it is the century-old history of a people that have no land or nation. If you are not concerned with a cause, you are perhaps committed to helping them? That is what I mean here by political.

SM: Well, so there are two different words, "committed" and "help". And "help" is a strange word. Of course, it has been deeply meaningful to dig into history and learn how consistently, for over a century, the Kurdish people have desired and fought to have their own homeland. They sustain an identification as a community despite the context of living as minorities within multinational states.
It is deeply moving to me that they self-identify and have fought for so long, essentially for so little. And so, it seemed valuable

to make that history more visible to those who came from different parts of Kurdistan, who often didn't even know each other's stories, and of course to Western, European or American nations and peoples who had very little opportunity to know about them. The first edition of the book came out in 1997, following the Gulf War of 1991; Kurdistan had slipped back away into the shadows. Of course, the Kurdish question became a focus again after 2003, when the Americans, the British and others fought Saddam and the war in Iraq was unleashed. Reflecting now on the title, it should have been "Kurdistan: In the Shadow of Histories", because it's not just a single history, it is multiple, compressed histories. I was trying to bring something to surface to be seen, to be felt. It's not a direct line like «What do you do?», which would be more of an advocacy position. Now, what do I feel today with the bombing of Afrin[1]? It's horrific. Do I identify with the people who were in the streets protesting yesterday? Of course! I think they have to do something, be present ... what else can they do? What does a human do to protest against a specific power, or a complex set of powers at work? What can we do if we become only spectators? That doesn't mean you always know the answer to what to do. It goes back to the famous question: "What can be done?"

RC: But you always try to do something.

SM: I try to do something if I feel like I can be engaged in a meaningful way and participate and contribute in some small way.

RC: I was talking a few weeks ago with Dayanita Singh, [see p. 280] *and I was asking her (this was, for me, a very innocent question) if it had been difficult for her to be a woman photographer in India when she started in the 1980s. She immediately replied: "I do not define myself as a 'woman photographer'. If I am brave, if I go to war, it has to do with my personality, not my gender." You went to war, you also have*

[1] *Turkish military intervention in early 2018 in the north-west of Syria in a Kurdish enclave, then held by the Kurdish forces of the YPG.*

a body of work called "Archives of Abuse", and one of your last books released in the autumn is also about violence suffered by women. I'm not asking you to comment on her point of view, but would you define yourself as a "woman photographer"?

SM: I understand Dayanita's response and it is one that many women give. They hope that the work they do is of value independently of the fact that it might be a woman's view. That doesn't mean that my choices of what I commit to or portray are not impacted by being a woman or that my desire to support other women, which I do consistently, isn't because I'm a woman. But when you're a "woman at war", which of course, for a period of my life, I was seen as, you get defined either as the "woman photographer" or the "war photographer". Neither is my choice. I just want to be encountering and engaging expressively in such a way that people can find that what I am offering back is something that can be meaningful to them.
It's like a seesaw, you know, back and forth. There is no question that the first work I did, *Carnival Strippers*, was impacted by the conversations from that period of early feminism. I was shocked in some ways by how the women I would never have known otherwise responded. It was important to me that there was a difference between the feminists speaking on behalf of these women, and that the working women had their own strong voices to share.

RC: In the texts included in Carnival Strippers, *you can often tell that they feel in a position of power when they're on stage.*

SM: Yes, so I don't want to just flatten something into rhetoric. I really wanted to make a discovery. I had no idea what they thought until we really spent time together. So, right now, there are lots of conversations back and forth, in favour or against #MeToo, which clearly represents an important moment for women. Maybe globally, some women can speak louder and others less so in other kinds of environments.
You know, to find the way to portray, depict or replace a moment in time in greater perspective, you are best off being invisible to do the work. It may be more effective for what

it is that you are trying to do. And sometimes, you have to speak loudly.

RC: I have a somewhat provocative question: is a museum of art, or a museum of photography, the venue to exhibit a body of work that is partly historical or ethnological? Or should we be satisfied that these venues not only show black-and-white photographs in black wooden frames, two horizontal, one vertical, etc., but also allow the public to try and understand the complexity of the world instead of just admiring the beauty of horror and the virtuosity of the photographer depicting that horror?

SM: Well, this is the choice of those museums, not those of us who are making the work. So it is a question for the Jeu de Paume to decide that this is the time to give me the opportunity to have a show. And I think that how the audience responds will tell us a lot. Maybe it will draw a different kind of audience. I have certainly had experiences in museums that become very important forums for the people who see themselves portrayed on their walls. If you think of a museum as a place that you can be a part of, versus a space that is not inclusive of who you are, it's a fundamentally different context. There was a young man yesterday who was participating in the Kurdish workshop; he had taken the initiative of volunteering to bring new migrants to France into museums, which is not the most obvious place they would go. He arranged for special tours and opportunities to go to the great Parisian museums. Now, those museums may not be useful to them in the same way that finding a shelter or possibly finding a job would be, but he feels that it is one of the most important aspects of French culture to share.
It is an experiment and a mystery what will happen and what it may mean to them.

RC: Would you happen to know French photographer Matthew Pernot? [see Conversations*, p. 206].*

SM: Yes, a little bit of his work.

RC: He was exhibited at the Jeu de Paume three or four years ago. He worked for maybe two decades on a gypsy family from Arles, and for the opening he had invited the entire family to come to the Jeu de Paume see their portraits on the museum walls. It was their first time in the subway, or on Place de la Concorde… They were so happy to see how the trust they had put in him over the years was rendered, given back.

SM: Six months ago, I showed the *Prince Street Girls* work for the first time in a very small gallery in New York. The girls were all there and they celebrated seeing themselves on the walls. But I had no idea how they would feel until they were in the room. And you know, they ended up photographing themselves in front of the photographs of themselves. They are now 50 and they were 10 years old at that time. So, you never know what people will feel!
The Kurdish workshop was an invitation to contribute stories that will be on the wall in one week's time. These are small windows of possibilities, to break down what can sometimes feel like walls that exclude people.

RC: You always try to reach to audiences that would not naturally meet: wealthy Westerners who can buy a photobook or easily visit a museum, and at the same time the people whose story you told. Hence, with this last workshop, the participants will enter the museum.

SM: Yes, the Kurds who participated will be there. They are not artists. The 10 stories they contribute come from different Kurdish communities, from Syria, Iran, Iraq and Turkey. They have different professions. One is a doctor; another is a parliamentarian. They tell the stories of how they encountered France, how they left their country, what they left behind, the difficult transition, etc. One of these stories is something as simple as a young man from Iraq saying that he couldn't adjust to French food – something the French cannot even imagine! It is very difficult for him, so he describes his search to find something he can make Kurdish food with, just for himself at home. He could not find the proper rice! This is a small story within history at large.

Another project in the workshop is about a young woman who is now quite well known as a human rights lawyer, talking about how when she was young in Syria, her father forbade her to study beyond high school. Finally, it was her uncle, who is part of the Muslim brotherhood and living in Saudi Arabia in exile from Syria, who challenged her father and said he never had read in the Koran that women could not be educated. So, her uncle convinced the father to let her go on and study at university, where she passed the exams. Then, her father challenged her again and said, "But I want you to be a schoolteacher." She said, "No, I want to be a lawyer." The wonderful lines in her book is when she saw Mahatma Gandhi at the United Nations and said to herself, "Why not me representing Kurdistan some day in the future?" She was only 16 years old! It is an incredible story and she is now a human rights lawyer speaking on French television. Wild! So, you know, this was one of the great surprises of the workshop. Friday morning, at the beginning of the workshop (and we had only two days), I had no idea who would come in the door, who would be willing to spend the time and try to find some photographs and tell some part of their life. The range was completely wild. That is the discovery part; it is very rich, very special.

RC: As we already said, documented testimonies are very important in your practice and in your books. We were talking earlier about the use of photography by the powers in place. Is the use of these documents, these old photographs, a way to fight the use of photography by these powers?

SM: I'm not quite sure how to answer that ... I'm not sure if I fully understand what you mean. "Use" is a funny word, what does it mean? I feel that this is where it is really still a mystery. First, there is this show comprising 40 years of my working life, very disparate material. It's not like I'm a colour photographer and you always know I'm going to work with a certain kind of camera format or whatever.
There is a thread in my own search, trying to make sense of where I am and what I can do with whatever I have experienced in the past. The question is: "What can I do with the work?"

But there will be different approaches. There will be on one hand the classic, black-and-white photographs in black frames with *Carnival Strippers*, and sound, which is in English, to allow the audience to hear their voices. And in another context, I display the photographs from Nicaragua and deconstruct the process of how they were selected and published in the media, because I want people to think about what they see or do not see in the media.

RC: That was one of my next questions. Whether it is in books like In History, *or in exhibitions, you display magazine covers or report spreads. I'm sure this is not about vanity. But are these documents considered in the same way as any other document, or are they also a way to show how the subjects you dealt with, the images you made, were used at the time? Or is it even a criticism of the press, which is a power as well?*

SM: Yes, the press is a power, but it also, at one time, portrayed the protagonists countering the power. So they played a dual role. It is the power to portray absence. Because the protagonists are not always in control of their representation. Likewise, photographers may make photographs for which they can never find a place to show them. Whether it is a magazine or a museum, it is a complex network in which the right timing needs to be found to make their representation possible. So of course, when the Sandinistas triumphed over Somoza, more people were interested in Nicaragua, and the book was possible because of their triumph, not because of mine as a photographer. This is very clear.

RC: One question about Encounters with the Dani, *a fascinating book to me. These people were discovered in 1938 in New Guinea, living like in the Stone Age. The discovery would attract explorers, ethnologists, government attention and later, tourists, hence destroying in 70 years a society that had survived thousands of years. And changing their way of life, instilling a desire for money and consumption in them, transforming their rituals into tourist attractions. As a human being, do you look at this coldly or do you feel that it is quite sad that a culture that has lived for thousands and thousands of years can disappear so quickly, and that now these people have to earn money for a living. What's your personal feeling about this?*

SM: It is complex because there was a moment when I faced a very simple question – which was, having spent some time in the Baliem Valley, would I leave my flashlight (which I needed) for them? Did they need it? Was that an appropriate gift? In Latin America, I would always travel with pencils to give away, for example. I'm saying this that way because of course, it felt tragic to see people performing for tourists rituals that they no longer value or do for themselves and that their children didn't know about, except through those performances for tourists.
But you can't roll the world backwards. Is there more gain for us now that we are all endlessly connected and obsessed with our iPhones and digital connectivity? Are we better humans because of this? I mean, everything is faster, more fluid... something can go viral before people can even think twice. We used to say that: think twice before doing anything. I don't know if this is a better world. Of course, the impact of the missionaries was devastating. It was a slow process initially, but now it has speeded up. Perhaps this was inevitable?

RC: I was also wondering whether Encounters with the Dani *might be a metaphor for what we, Europeans, inflicted in so many places throughout the world, in Africa, in America, in the course of the last five or six centuries...*

SM: Sure, of course. But it's not merely a metaphor, it's not just symbolic. It's only that the Baliem Valley in West Papua was so small that you could visualize those changes. We can search into archives, as if we needed to look for proof. But we know that there's plenty of evidence of what has been done upon peoples around the world. So, what do we do now? The migrations into Europe, first from North Africa, obviously more recently from Syria, this massive migration north is connected to the devastation from the colonial period and the lack of investment since then. We are living in a world which is in total turmoil. We can talk about globalization, the impact on the working class; we can talk about colonialism and the impact on migration patterns now. I think that the world is in crisis, destabilized and distrustful. When I look back on the period of the 1970s, we were very optimistic about the possibility of the world transforming and rebalancing, putting an end to the Cold War.

RC: From your first book to the last, we have been talking about this for a while now – documentation is increasingly taking up more space. Do you think that photography alone is unable to attest objectively, or say, conceptually, to reality?

SM: I think photographs are windows, and you probably need houses to shelter them, though not necessarily mansions. But you definitely need to build around them. I'm not only thinking of them; they need to be placed well. Many times, I've said that you can't just take a photograph, you have to place the photograph. You must make the space for a photograph. The space can be physical – we talked about magazines, museums or streets... public life cannot just be left to advertising, but to other kinds of opportunities to engage as well. How do we disrupt and break through our little glass houses? It's funny, I wanted to say "caves", but caves are usually dark. I feel there is often darkness in the bubbles that we live in.

RC: About the issue of text, again. You produced two books, In History *and* On the Front Line, *in which your work is largely explained. Are you worried that it could be misunderstood?*

SM: Yes. *In History* was really the first time people wrote about my work. *On the Frontline* is slightly different because it comes from a conversation, much like the one we're having now. The only difference is that on the floor, there were long visual sequences of photographs and Mark Holborn was interviewing me. Without seeing or reading his questions, you read my responses, which were edited by him. Your own readers are going to read this without seeing the images, which is also interesting. One never knows how well that works, but you always want the work to speak. Whether it's a single photograph

that can function as such, or a sequence, or contextualization with sound – each of these forms is a response to my feeling that something needs more if it does, but it doesn't always. I don't know, maybe I over-contextualize, maybe the work speaks with the photographs alone.
Right now, I'm producing a very small little book that will be released right at the time of the Jeu de Paume. It's about one photograph, from *A Room of Their Own*, which we are calling *A View of a Room*, because when we put that photograph on view at the Photographer's Gallery in London, we asked people to write a comment about it. Hundreds of responses were made to that one photograph. I love people writing by hand all the things they imagined and saw in that one photograph. It's a very simple idea, but it shows you the richness of the dialogue: they spent the time, they "listened" to the photograph, it spoke to them in some way and they respond in whatever way they do. That's the mystery of photography really. That is the true power of a photograph, that it does or can speak to us.

RC: This is such a nice project.

SM: Yes, I find interesting this idea of speaking without a message but letting a photograph be a trigger for our memory, shaping our thinking in some way. It's much more mysterious than didactically purposeful.

RC: I realize I forgot to type a couple of questions I wanted to ask you about Pandora's Box. *So I will improvise. This one is for me the most aesthetic of your books, with its full bleed images, fake leather and latex pages, very little text compared with* Carnival Strippers. *What is the status of this particular piece in you work?*

SM: The status? I think it relates deeply with the rest. It is the connective tissue to two different projects. On one hand, it is about looking 20 years later at the sex industry in America, which was a surprise for me to discover. On the other, it deeply connects me back to some of what I experienced in Latin America – those terrible stories of people interrogated and tortured, images that I hadn't made. Images I never even saw until we all saw the pictures from Abu Ghraib. The work in *Pandora's Box* was done almost a decade before then, but it speaks to the terror of torture. It is particularly complicated, because in this case, human beings are acting by choice. I don't know how people will make that connection. Will they be disturbed by it? Many people whom I worked with in Latin America, knowing that I had documented mass graves and massacres, even in Anfal in Kurdistan[2] where important human rights abuses occurred, found it quite difficult to make the transition to seeing the S&M work from *Pandora's Box*. And yet, I think there is something deeply connected to my own desire to observe. Whether or not it sufficiently makes sense for anyone else, it was important work for me to allow myself to go closer, to face something that is really still deeply difficult to understand.

> *RC: And yet, each time someone looks at a situation, they change it ...*

SM: Yes, to some degree.

> *RC: In* Pandora's Box, *the mistress and the client usually play together. And by your very presence, you are changing their games, right?*

SM: That's a good question. They would say, as would I, that they are unquestionably performing for each other. I didn't feel that they were performing for me. It's strange how you can tell very quickly when people perform for you. Some people like to provoke interaction, others don't. I suppose I'm disinclined to ever ask someone to come and perform again if I've missed something. For example, already in *Carnival Strippers*, obviously there are certain habitual movements that you can anticipate, like someone moving to the door to tease the audience. You know that's what they might do, but I would never ask somebody, "I missed it, could you just do that again?"

[2] *Kurd genocide perpetrated in 1988 by Saddam Hussein's regime, causing over 100 ,000 civilian casualties.*

That may be the way films are made. I guess I'm not really a portraitist, which involves a different kind of directing. What I'm saying is that I have a sixth sense when someone is giving you a look that they think you want to see. And if I'm patient enough, I wait until they forget a little bit the reason for me to be there. This is very subtle. Sometimes you capture "it", sometimes you don't. But if you wait, there comes a moment of revelation that feels true to what you think you're seeing. Maybe it's a truer moment when they perform. I remember photographing Civil War re-enactments, which is not a part of this show at all ... But I found them really perplexing. People were probably re-enacting what they had seen in photographs or in films, not necessarily their lived experience. That is a wild construct.

RC: To finish on a somewhat lighter note, we talked about Prince Street Girls *and the exhibitions you recently had. The images are from the mid-1970s and you just published the work in a very nice small book. Is there a form of nostalgia for these bygone days, maybe days of innocence?*

SM: I'm not sure what you mean. What is the innocence?

RC: I mean before going to the war, before discovering all the horror in the world.

SM: A room of Their Own *is about horrors that you're not seeing, but the response, which is the retreat from the horrors, the recovery or the attempt to recover, I don't know if this is "innocence". For me, coming back to the encounter through photography, again, is the key work of being present in a place, trying to find an entry point that feels appropriate. A place that can be accounted for, because there is so much pain! It's not possible, however, to open the "Pandora's box"[3] within each of these life stories. You need to try to find a way to represent that place so that other people can imagine the importance, the deep value of that place. And in a way, it circles back to the time of my first photography*

[3] *Susan Meiselas's book* Pandora's Box *is named after the S&M club that she photographed.*

course, because my first work is "44 Irving Street", which is where I retreated to find a place then: a room in a boarding house, but with neighbours I didn't know. In some strange ways, it is very similar to A Room of Their Own. *The refuge is not a place where they know anyone. They live in their own room, rooms that are relatively bare. And yet, I am struck by the portrait of the rooms as a kind of expression of their capacity to recover and to hopefully move on.*

RC: A Room of Their Own *is also a collaborative work, because you have ...*

SM: Not in the same way as in "44 Irving Street", where I asked each person to respond to the image that I had made of them. In this case, it was much more to respond to the notion of refuge. I gave them a photograph of their room not knowing whether it was something they would want to keep as a memory. Would they want to remember that specific period of their life? Moving often, with nothing but themselves, and with the hope of being able to move on? It's interesting how the photograph is again a trigger. Or perhaps it's something to forget.

RC: I guess this is a good conclusion.

SM: Yes . Is it something to be remembered, or is it something to be forgotten?

28 January 2018

PINO MUSI

Self-taught photographer Pino Musi was born in Salerno in 1958 and now lives in Paris. His work is present in many public and private collections, including the Rolla Foundation, the Sandretto Re Rebaudengo Foundation and the Fotografia di Modena Foundation. In 2012 his series "Facecity" was exhibited at the Venice Architecture Biennale. He is the recipient of multiple awards. In 1997 the book Mario Botta seen by Pino Musi, *conceived with graphic designer Werner Jeker, received an award at the Frankfurt Book Fair; in 2003* Libro *received the Oscar Goldoni Prize for the best photography book published in Italy. Since 2011, he has taught at the Fotografia di Modena Foundation as part of the Master of Higher Education in Contemporary Image. Pino Musi is the author of 21 books to date.*

There's no need to hide it: Pino Musi is one of my closest friends. An excellent reason, it seems, to take this opportunity to understand the strength and coherence of his work. His practice astonishingly mixes a coldness inspired by Swiss graphic design and German photography with a very Mediterranean sensual theatricality. While you can't change your nature, you do shape your personality. Whether he photographs architecture, operating rooms or the landscape in Brittany, the two dimensions are inseparable. Even more interesting is the fact that his subject, far from ever being a pretext, serves as a means to reflect on representation and space. The notion of theatre is always a basis for his work. Conversation in my library on occasion of the release of his latest book, *Acre*, published by GwinZegal.

> Rémi Coignet: *You're from Salerno near Naples. It seems that the art scene, especially in theatre, was central in your training. What was going on in Naples and Salerno in the late 1970s and 1980s?*

Pino Musi: It was extraordinarily effervescent. The university was amazing. One of the most important Italian art critics, Filiberto Menna, from Salerno, taught there. He was truly one of the most important figures in art criticism in Italy. Around him, a series of people shared his analytical vision of art, such as Angelo Trimarco and Achille Bonito Oliva. They evolved in and according to the cultural atmosphere of that period. In addition, we had in Naples one of the most important galleries in the world, Lucio Amelio's Modern Art Agency. He was the first, perhaps in Europe, but certainly in Italy, to show Joseph Beuys or Andy Warhol. Talented young people flocked around this gallery. Mario Martone was doing amazing performances. He later became a major stage and film director in Italy. I participated with him in a theatre biennale in Venice in 1982. He was performing with actors at the Scuola Grande di San Giovanni Evangelista and I had my first exhibition called "Maschere e Persone" [Masks and people], a series on popular religious and pagan rituals in southern Italy.

RC: And you made a book with it, published by the Venice Biennale.

PM: Yes. So, there was this effervescence, and moreover, Salerno, thanks to the university and Filiberto Menna, had a festival of experimental theatre, one of the most – if not the most – important festivals in Italy called Rassegna Nuove Tendenze. They hired Giuseppe Bartolucci, a great expert in avant-garde theatre who lived in Rome, and he hosted the festival for two weeks every summer. We could see the best international troupes, the Living Theatre, Peter Brook, Bob Wilson, Jérôme Savary, Tadeusz Kantor, Richard Foreman, Il Carrozzone from Florence, Eugenio Barba's Odin Teatret, the first Roberto Benigni, etc. And I was doing theatre pictures at that time. On the other hand, I was the mascot of sorts of a theatre company called TeatroGruppo, interested in both theatrical experimentation and the discovery of popular traditions. We had a spot, an underground where we met almost every weekend until 4 or 5 in the morning. There were intellectually vibrant people there. So I was really used to talking to them, exchanging together in a group. There really was a cultural ferment that has now become very rare, but which has been instrumental in my training.

RC: How did you come to photography?

PM: I started at 14, following a series of very dramatic family problems. And I found in photography an activity that taught me a lot, in which everything appeared in the dark, like in the theatre. All my ghosts were with me in these two passions. At that time, my great passion was the darkroom; I'd spend hours in there. I had a little enlarger at my mother's and I was experimenting with chemistry and all that stuff. All these ghosts kept me company in this very dramatic moment in my family life.

RC: Is photography a theatre?

PM: Maybe ... it seems to me that it is. I think there are similar conditions at work in photography and in the theatre. The scenario is important. Though the actors as much as the photographer must take some distance from it. There is light and shadow. There are always apparitions. And you have to build with all these elements. You also stage and perform in photography. For me, photography must always be inspired by the methods of other art forms, and other visual disciplines in particular, to better articulate its language. I also had a great love for cinema, Bergman in particular. Later, my relationship to light, to space, to time, changed.

RC: I would like to go back to your first book, Strani Tipi, *published in 1980. You were 22, which at the time was a very young age to publish. It comprises close-ups of shop window mannequins. What is your subject for this book? And what is the meaning of the little plastic figurine that pierces the pages?*

PM: I already knew, without any clear awareness, that the book was not a place that could host an already structured work, simply slipping photos in, but somewhere for invention and creation. Actually, I saw the book as a theatre stage, the crucible for a composition. I fell in love with this novel by Blaise Cendrars, *Rhapsodies gitanes*, in which, very close to the conclusion, precisely in the chapter entitled "L'enfer" [Hell], he invites "all desperate lovers" to contemplate, in the casting room at Chez Jean, the "infinitely tragic, buffoonish and comforting" spectacle of the liquefaction of the wax heads of female mannequins. So, what I tried to do with this small work in the form of a book was to stage, to articulate a photographic work as if it were a small theatrical play. And I chose to make these portraits of mannequins that would be like a zombie population in the city. And in the end, I decided to use these little masks. I cut off part of the pages and integrated them into the body of the book. There were 150 copies. There was a printer close to my building. I found a very nice Italian translation of Cendrars's book, which this printer had typeset. I went all over the supermarkets to buy these figurines and I created this population, somewhat parallel to the human being. Nothing new, but for me, the interesting thing was not the photos themselves, but the proposal I was making with the book. And that stuck with me. The photograph is very important, but just as important as the non-directive relationship between the pages of text and the images. A whole little architecture to invent.

RC: I was going to ask you later, but if photography is a theatre, is the book an architecture?

PM: Yes, of course. I've always thought so. I started collecting photobooks around the age of 23 or 24. In Milan there was a bookstore that I loved very much, Milano Libri, and I spent my time there, selecting books. But I didn't like catalogues so much. It's weird that I've always loved books with an interesting construction. I started collecting on the basis of a whole series of ideas I had about the book: it must be a place of confrontation between different languages, but above all it must have interesting mechanics, an intuitive layout and a printing quality that values the photographic work. Finally, the content, its most important part, must work well with these various elements. So, I started collecting books that fit these criteria. Later, I would buy books in the United States, at Moe's in Berkeley, California. They sold very good books, like Avedon's *Observations* or *Nothing Personal*. They were a bit damaged and I could have them at relatively low prices. I knew a bookbinder in Como who would fix them for me for cheap. I always thought the book was the place to be for my work.

RC: Since we're talking about this, who are the photographers who have influenced you?

PM: I was rather influenced by the cinema; I mentioned Bergman. I spent time studying the light of different directors of photography, such as Sven Nykvist, Vilmos Zsigmond, Gordon Willis, Néstor Almendros. My influences also come from theatre, with directors like Jerzy Grotowski, whose statement on the body is present in nearly all of my work – even if the human being is almost never present. But the body is always there. If you look at my architecture photos, the volumes are bodies. And even when the body is absent, there's always something of a ghostly presence. So, it's always there.
I had a few, not very frequent but very dense, discussions with Grotowski about this. As far as photography is concerned, I like Avedon very much. When I started making carbon prints, I had just seen an exhibition, "In the American West", with these beautiful prints that moved me. Several authors have influenced me along the way: of course, Walker Evans, Karl Hugo Schmölz, Lewis Baltz, Lynne Cohen, artists like Ellsworth Kelly, Carl Andre … but I've always tried to find my own way. I've mixed all these moods in the way I photograph, moods that have mingled in me through my formative years and which very gently infused in my head until culminating in a whole series of encounters – with architecture, for example – and in defining a method.

RC: Does this intellectual weaving serve to articulate the relationship between the coldness and the expressiveness of your images?

PM: Yes. This is fundamental, because coldness is really a tension of the gaze and a method that I use in my work. It allows me to be very focused on what I want and what I don't want. I'm used to a selection mental exercise that turns into a practical exercise through the camera. This came in my first years of practice. Before photographing architecture,

I already had that structure, the habit of combining the method of intellectual reflection with the practical method. I have never considered one over the other. I've always made them travel together. And all the practical experiments I conducted were always parallel to my intellectual reflection.

RC: After Maschere e Persone, *we must wait 12 years for your next book,* Mario Botta Seen by Pino Musi. *How did you come to architectural photography?*

PM: I came to it completely by chance. I was always open to other languages, and architecture was one of them, but I wasn't paying any specific attention to it. I'm not trained as an architect, but I had a strong interest in space and its translation into photographic images. Space is central to all my work. By chance, I met Mario Botta in Salerno at a conference and I did his portrait with a seat called "Seconda". However, I changed the scale of the chair by placing him in the back, against a white background, and the seat seemed like a house. Instead of being a mere utilitarian object, by changing the scale, Botta seemed to fit into this structure that looked like a house. It was nothing special, but he appreciated this intuition of the change of scale. And we started talking and, somewhat as a challenge, he said to me: "Would you be interested in photographing one of my architectures?" I said, "But I don't know anything about architecture!" He then offered to take me to Chambéry, where he had conceived a theatre. It was 1985, and I started taking these photographs of architecture but without any awareness, instinctively. I saved 10 pictures at most out of the thousand I took! But we continued to exchange with Mario...

RC: Were you already using a view camera?

PM: No, I was working with a whole series of different formats. Later, I started to like the view camera and have used it for years now, because it gives a very reflexive slowness to my work. I must take my time and I like that very much. But originally, I would work equally with various devices. And very gently, we reached an almost fraternal relationship with Botta.

He appreciated my Mediterranean light on his very structured architecture, and he loved the fact that I used natural light, a very raw light that I would put into dialogue with the shade. I never liked sharp contrasts. Even with a strong light contrast, I have always sought to smooth out the transition between light and shadow. And he really liked that idea. After many years, we had our differences and I decided to move on. I didn't want to be someone's photographer. I truly collaborated a lot with him on very important projects, very important exhibitions. We made books together; I made him some wonderful prints. I contributed to his success. And he's been instrumental in making me grow. I owe him my understanding of architecture, and so many of the encounters I made: Jean Petit, Pontus Hultén, Werner Oechslin and all the others.

> *RC: Jean Petit published* Ronchamp Le Corbusier *with your photographs. And while he's a reference for those of us who are interested in Le Corbusier, he's not necessarily very well known in the world of photography. Could you tell us more about him?*

PM: Jean was really part of Corbu's circle. He knew everyone, Xenakis, everyone who revolved around this great architect. Imagine, his house near Geneva was a temple. There were many prototypes of Charlotte Perriand and Jean Prouvé, and magnificent carpets by Corbu. He had incredible correspondences with all these people. Above all, he was an amazing graphic designer and a true scenographer of that world. At some point, he was the artistic director of Adriano Olivetti's Edizioni Comunittà. Can you imagine? Olivetti was one of the best Italian patrons of culture, an industrialist with extraordinary qualities. Thanks to Jean Petit, I began to love Paris. He was born in Paris, in La Villette, and later moved to Switzerland. He was a dear friend of Robert Doisneau. Once, the three of us took a tour together of all the bistros where Doisneau had shot his images. Jean was like a father to me. We'd meet up and he'd say, "Pino, you shouldn't become too German!" [Laughs] It was a time when I started to appreciate the culture of the German photographers who had worked on industrial heritage and architecture, like Werner Mantz, etc. I made extraordinary discoveries thanks to him. He took me to Lombard-Fuertes, which was a beautiful silkscreen workshop. You know, Corbu had those colours he loved, purple, red… And that workshop had some sort of patent to use them. Jean also made book-objects with the new realists, César, Arman. He would make sculptures out of the pages. I've always had a passion for book making. I've always wanted to understand how toys are dismantled. I would always read who was the printer, who was the graphic designer in the colophons, and I always wanted to understand why these people were important. Thanks to Jean, this passion became even stronger, because he knew perfectly all about the different types of printing techniques, graphic design, etc. It was about the time when I met Werner Jeker and started to work with him, and also with Bruno Monguzzi, etc. I've worked with many very good graphic designers in Europe. And it further increased my love for the book.

RC: In 1998 you published Oxymoron, *a book about the industrial world. It is printed in tritone, a black-and-white reproduction technique that would hence become the trademark of your book making. What are the specificities of this printing technique?*

PM: I discovered tritone when it first appeared. Before, the technique was duotone, and many printers still use it. Tritone is somewhat more complex. We're talking about black-and-white photography. When composing a range of grey in three tones, you usually have black, a more or less dark grey and a very light grey. Black is the skeleton. It's the sketch of the image. The second tone will provide the skin of the image and the third tone, the highest, will soften the light tones. The fine balancing of these three tones delivers the best solution to print a black-and-white photo. It opens huge possibilities to work on the intermediate tones: you can push the different forces during printing and find the right mix of the three. It was as interesting to me as when I would dismantle toys when I was 14. What's the point of this technique? What does it mean? There was a very important printer of Italian origin who lived in Switzerland, Roberto Forlano. He was in Ticino. He was really a great master of tritone, but also of printing supervision.

He taught me how to do it. And then, little by little, I improved the method. From *Oxymoron*, I started to think about it and decided to make the tritone separation for *Attraverso* myself. And my best books, the most recent ones, are those with my own tritone separations.

RC: And that relates to the notion of passage that you support between the blacks, the greys and the whites…

PM: Yes, because it really allows me to respect the original. I can't stand the idea that the book is just a document from the original photo. For me, the book has an autonomous identity and therefore it must have nuances, something that expresses that identity. Printing in a way that reflects this identity is very important. That's why with tritone, I have initiated a new relationship with the content of the book, adopting various tritone balances. For example, as you have noticed, the latest book is colder than previous ones, because you have to respect the climate of each book. This allows another way for the author to work on the book. I find it very interesting. It's important to know all these elements in order to exchange conclusively with the other people involved in the making of the book, the graphic designer, or the printer.

RC: In 2002 you published a book about Giuseppe Terragni[1], one of the architects of Fascism. What drew you to the subject?

PM: It's one of the most interesting jobs I've done on architecture, along with *Facecity*. In fact, it's about meta-photography: this is when I started to think about the use of digital. The images are totally fake, like in *Facecity*. Since it had come to be, I felt that the digital should not be a mere commodity replacing the analogue. It needed to have its own identity. And for me, its identity is to connect very strongly with the essence of the project. So, I selected projects the meaning of which could be played with the digital.
For the work on Terragni, which is called "ipotesi (su Terragni)"[2],

[1] *Giuseppe Terragni (1904-1943) was an Italian modernist architect.*

[2] *Assumptions (about Terragni).*

what did I do? I looked at all the original drawings of his various buildings and then idealized his architecture. I went to photograph the facades of his projects in mid-August, when the streets are empty and the buildings closed, because I wanted to convey the climate of absence, of temporal suspension of this rationalist architecture. The shooting, the perspectives, are modified according to his drawings. For example, the facade of the Sant'Elia asylum is quite long, but it's at the corner of two streets. It's impossible to look at it frontally as I had perceived it in the drawings. So, I made a whole series of changes. I took pictures and unified them to show the frontality, because the perspective only allowed to look at it sideways. I made a whole series of moves in order to make the photographic perspective believable. I then digitally processed them with subtle changes in relation to the drawings. I made my own projection of it. I idealized the architecture of Terragni. It's an assumption, what this architecture could be. These photos are more related to the drawings than to the actual documentation of the architecture. That's why I'm calling it meta-photography. It "seems" to be photography, but it's not. It's a complete mental construction, with slight changes compared with the reality in order to be able to visualize it. But if you look at it, it looks like a photograph. The same goes for the following project, *Facecity*.

RC: Yes, I see Facecity *as a fiction because what we see is not reality. You once explained to me that you had removed a tree in Photoshop, for example. So, the digital allows for this fiction, and what does fiction allow in photography?*

PM: The essence of the project, the strength of the project, if the project requires it! Fiction is not gratuitous, it's not Photoshop retouching. For example, with Terragni, my idea was to link in a very strong way a form of hyper-reality to the original drawing. *Facecity* follows a similar idea. This book was born out of a proposition from David Chipperfield and Fulvio Irace for the Venice Biennale to work on the notion of cooperation between all the architects of the so-called "typographical architecture" in Milan in the 1950s. There were almost 20 of them and they worked on the notion of the facade as a typographical grid. Each one de-structured it according to their fancy. Other Italian photographers, and Gabriele Basilico is an important example, have worked on the document. I didn't want to go into that direction; I wanted to work on meaning. So, with a friend who writes electronic music scores, we selected facades, over 20 of them, only facades conceived according to that grid. But it was almost impossible to photograph them all frontally. I made some spotting photos, then he built the sequence with all the encounters of the different facades.

RC: The book is here. [Pino takes Facecity *and unfolds the leporello]*

PM: Each encounter is perfectly projected in this score and you can play it because it's musical writing. It's like a roll where all the drawings contribute to write the score. I re-photographed the original facades with a view camera, then proceeded to deform them subtly to get the frontality and deleted all the elements that generated visual confusion in order to keep the rhythm going. And when you look at the roll of *Facecity*[3], the encounter of the different photos of facades creates other facades. So, everything is wrong but true at the same time! It's like the rhetoric about Terragni. It starts from a substance, a very strong meaning. It allows us to feel the essence of the work better than with documentary photos. It's not exactly a document, it doesn't exist. *Facecity* took me months of work with a collaborator. Almost no one understood it, but it was a huge process. Initially, the roll was 1 metre high by 15 metres long, and the book is a leporello, which perfectly respects the concept of the roll that was exhibited at the biennale.

RC: You were talking about frontality, and in 2003 you published Metonimie *with small agricultural constructions in the Naples countryside. My feeling is that from there, your photography becomes more frontal. What would you say?*

PM: I came to frontality when I was working with Botta. But Mario was obsessed with symmetry and I didn't like.

[3] *As an exhibition,* Facecity *was presented as a roll of 1x15m long.*

I'm interested in frontality, not in symmetry. For me, frontality is a vis-à-vis: looking at architecture in the eye, and it is a very subtle exercise because frontality is not elementary. There are subtle distances through which frontality will express very precise movements of planes. In the case of *Metonimie*, I wanted the frontality of this cube-like construction to be like an arrow that would clearly show the surrounding landscape. The building is a signal, but it also invites the viewer to look at what surrounds it. The cube is fixed, the rest moves...

RC: They are small farming buildings.

PM: Yes, made by peasants with the lava stone from Vesuvius at the beginning of the 20th century. These are very minimalist cubes of astonishing force. But they're located in places that are very difficult to reach. The distance from the background was very important to me. I didn't want to be too close to the buildings and turn them into sculptures, as in the Bechers' photographs. For me, they had to be a trajectory allowing us to see the surrounding landscape. So, I chose to stand not too close to them so that the facades could guide you into the landscape.

RC: In 2005 you published La Fotografia ri-gardea la Scuola, *a truly experimental book.*

PM: Yes, it is, a book made, ideally, with young students. An association of Neapolitan artists, Aporema per l'Arte, is involved in artistic workshops in very risky high schools in the suburbs of Naples, we're talking about Scampia, Pianura... There, the schools are attended, among others, by the sons of the *camorristi*[4]. These are true war zones. So, imagine these artists who are committed to doing workshops there... I had the idea to go to the school at a very specific time of the day (a method also used for *Attraverso*), in the laps of time between the end of school life and the absence of any activity, and take pictures of the place just before or just after the boys invaded

[4] *Members of the Camorra, the Neapolitan mafia.*

the school. And you see weird stuff, you can't tell whether it's a prison, or a place like that. Then, I decided to make an open book that all the boys could write or draw on...

RC: Does this explain the blank pages that you can't even open and the images in folds?

PM: There is one photo that describes the climate of this work. A boy got up one morning, the son of a *camorrista*, and nearly painted the entire school with gouache! It's altogether an expression of freedom and an amazing sign of violence. [Pino looks for the page] It is a gesture that aims at demonstrating a form of power, at frightening the others... The origin of this project was to give the boys a medium to help them think about the space of the school where they spend a large part of their day, and, at the same time, to suggest that they should not be drawing on the school walls but rather on the book.

RC: But why do you have these folded pages that don't open?

PM: With the team at Aporema, we decided that the book should be hidden in parts, in the same way that the boys hide themselves behind a series of behaviours. Leave parts that are not declared, not open. Then the boys could draw on the book, or "spy" on it and imagine something. A book is a place you need to discover.

RC: In 2008 you made Steel City ILVA, *your only colour book. What's your relationship with colour?*

PM: I don't particularly like using colour. I love some of the photographers who use colour, Eggleston, for example, but I don't have a great attraction to colour. *Steel City* is an actual commission, which is different from *Oxymoron*. Then, I was working for the ILVA steel mills, one of the largest in Europe at the time, and photographed the entire steel cycle for years. I had become an expert on the subject. While I was producing this corporate photobook about ILVA, I was designing *Oxymoron*. Both are photographed only in the light of fire. Steel mills are generally represented as archaeology, somewhat removed from production. The production is dangerous, but I took the risk of getting involved. And while I was doing the documentation for ILVA, I was making *Oxymoron* with the same ideology, but not as a commission. Which means that in this black-and-white book, I photographed the slightly dusty dimension of hell, the *fucina di Efesto*[5]. In *Oxymoron*, there is a beautiful text by Werner Oechslin, who taught at Zurich Polytechnic and is one of the greatest experts in Baroque.

RC: In 2011 you published two really large books with FMR: Italia Bellezza Eterna, *on archaeology, and* Italia Bellezza e Fede, *on religious architecture. How important is classical culture to a photographer?*

PM: It's huge. I think that in Italy, instead of drawing their inspiration from other cultural emergencies from abroad, the new American landscape, for example, photographers should work on their own cultural history. We have a stunning history of art and I think it's wonderful to reflect on it.
And if photographers would commit to rereading our great history of art, that would be wonderful for us. I found immense stimulation in looking into these topics. It's wonderful to read the Colosseum anew and to exit fully from the stereotypes of the tourist image. For me, it was a very interesting challenge. It's stimulating to re-read our history, our classical culture.
I did it in churches too. You know, in all the churches, the light is ruined because they've added artificial lighting everywhere. This is horrible! So I had all the lamps turned off, only the natural light remained. It was the cancellation of a redundant abomination due to a total lack of culture.
Similarly, I've developed assumptions for the reading of Pompeii. Pompeii is generally read through the statues, the monuments. I've done a lot of work on Pompeii's domestic and urban spaces. It's not true that you can no longer read a place because everything has collapsed. No, there is still a sketch of the space that you can understand and read anew, and I did it in Pompeii in articulation with the domestic space. I removed the colours to restore the strength of the space. I took away the decoration.

[5] *The forge of Hephaistos.*

It may seem heretical to take pictures of Pompeii without delivering the Pompeian red. But for me, it's good: removing the decor makes it possible to understand the space. And it's a way of thinking about our culture. So instead of taking pictures in the manner of Stephen Shore, we could try to read anew, with intellectual autonomy, our culture that comes from there, and not from modernism. You see, I don't think there is, in Italian photography, the same sense of urgency that can be found in German or American photography. I find that it would be a good idea if we returned to our culture instead of producing simulacra.

RC: You told me the other day that from then on, you reached the age of maturity in your books. How so?

PM: By practising an exercise that is, as we said earlier, at the same time intellectual and practical, you will define where you are in the scenario. And maturity, for me, is a very clear definition of the place that must be mine in this scenario. Where the photographer should stand. From then on, I'm very focused, I easily find the perfect spot to respect the project as I have defined it. Maturity for me is to no longer be making placement mistakes. For each project, I know where I need to be and what is my function within the space of the project.

RC: In 2012 comes Attraverso – Through, *with buildings commissioned by the town of Salerno to star architects such as Zaha Hadid, and that were never completed because of political incompetence. What did you want to express with that book?*

PM: There is the city, and there are these new architectures that are juvenile bodies within that city. What do photographers normally do? They take these young bodies and place them in the centre to celebrate the city's new beacons. But these bodies are only healthy if they have a skin, if they are completed. If they remain construction sites, they will age and quickly die. A skeleton cannot survive. But while the city is ugly, it is alive. *Attraverso* reverses perspectives. Instead of looking at the bodies supposed to become beacons for the city, I went into aged bodies, even though they were designed by David Chipperfield or Zaha Hadid. And I looked at the city *atttraverso*, through the construction sites. I knew I had to look for openings, scores inside these bodies. And I found a score of filled and blank spaces, the "screens" that act as hyphens between the images. I thus focused on the city, which, even though it is ugly, is more lively, more exhilarating than the bodies that were meant to renovate the vision of it, and make no sense because of their unfinished condition. If you watch closely, some of the images inside the Chipperfield building seem to have been taken in a cemetery. And that screen is also theatre. The frontality of the theatre is there. *Attraverso* is not an open gaze at a subject, but through an object, which changes the perception of these various bodies.

> *RC: Like in* La Fotografia ri-guarda la Scuola*, where the pictures are on folds; and a bit like in* Operating Theatre*, where if you just flip through the book, you don't see much. Is it important to show and to hide?*

PM: Yes. I think that books are unfinished objects. *Operating Theatre* does not judge; it initiates a debate, but it is never a book that forces you to start and to finish. I can't stand books that want to be finished, that contain a vast number of photos that tell you the same thing a thousand times! I feel that we need to send a message, and people take what they want from it. *Operating Theatre* offers room for reflection, like the book about the school, which is an open space letting children in. Similarly, *Attraverso* remains open: in the end, we don't know whether this architecture will be completed. It's a suggestion. And there are pages in each of them that hide something: they are in limbo. I always have this notion of limbo. An apparent void hides something articulate.

> *RC: You talked about books with a lot of images. The radicality of* Operating Theatre *is that there are only eight photographs in the book.*

PM: Designing *Operating Theatre* took time because the work was originally conceived to be exhibited. It was acquired

by very important foundations and the images are very large, 1.5 metres by 2. It therefore takes a large space to exhibit the eight images. The content is so rich that you can't place them very close to each other. It's necessary to have a physical space that really allows you to enter the images and create relationships. Each photo explodes on itself. It breaks down into several images. You have several elements to relate and you can disassemble each part of the image. In the perspective of the book, I spoke with Antonello Scotti, one of my dearest friends, an artist who is also a poet. And we were thinking about the mechanics of the book. We found possible connections, the 4 millimetres of the spine with the 4 millimetres of the plate, the cover sheet that isn't really a cover sheet but becomes a rigid structure that maintains the book... and the seam is made with suture thread. The idea is that each page is a separate plate. We wanted it to be difficult to read! It was meant to be an inconvenient object. We thought about it very calmly, we took a long time to do it. We chose texts by Antonin Artaud from Gallimard's Quarto [collection] because in my culture, Artaud is truly fundamental. Moreover, he's very close to all the issues at stake in this book: the history of electroshocks, flogging and the resurrection of the body. Which is why Artaud is in a dialogue with other texts in the book, both scientific and philosophical.
The texts don't accompany the images. There is no grid and it's not about graphic design. It's like "*poesia visive*"[6]. There's a composition of words and you must find the relationship between them. Antonello designed it more as an open textual relationship than merely a text that would accompany the images. This book deals with a complex set of notions.

RC: What was of interest to you in the operating room?

PM: Again, in the rhetoric on maturity, there are several elements. First, I wanted to know if I was able to find the right distance within five minutes and understand what I wanted. So, I decided to wait, to think about it so as to enter the operating room with a very specific notion of the space. Very quickly,

[6] *Visual poetry.*

I realized that I should not have a static perspective but change position with each new intervention, with each change of the scenario, because it was indeed a theatre. It's the same room I've photographed every time, but it changes according to the elements of the medical scenography. Each intervention requires a complete change of medical equipment: if it's an operation on a joint, for example, a specific machine is brought in. The elements of the set design were constantly changing, so I couldn't stay static. I had to rotate at the same time as the elements. It was very interesting, with the protocol that I had determined, which was to take only one photo for each type of intervention. It was a very quick exercise. I would enter the room and I had to immediately understand the relationship between the different volumes. Architecture, again!
And I had to create a very specific relationship with the notion of the melee, which has taken place but is over when I am present. All that was left were traces. And these traces had to be very clear. Clarity is very important for me, it's one of the essential elements in my photography. Everything must be clear, recognizable. Similarly, the composition must ask questions without providing answers. However, the elements must be clear and sharp. The gloves, the light, the blood, the name of the Zeiss machine, nothing should be nebulous, so that the reader can relate everything together. It was necessary to represent and stage the notion of the hope of saving oneself that's part of human weakness, but where, in the end, when nothing else seems possible, you will wait for a miracle staring at the portrait of Padre Pio rather than at that of the Madonna.
You remember that weird episode with Lesley A. Martin [Creative director at Aperture, see *Conversations*, p. 192] in Arles, who said, "No, no, no, I don't want to see that!" when we showed her the book? What's scary is to touch upon the fact that you could find yourself in that situation. Because this is not Doctors Without Borders or first responders in war zones. That, you can accept, because it's far from you. There, no, and it's much more frightening than the unknown. For me, it was an interesting reaction. We see war images all the time and we tolerate them, but we don't accept what is an integral part of our life. These are a series of very interesting questions.

RC: In 2014 we did Three Days in Tharoul *together. Well, I didn't do much except pick you as a guest photographer and lend a hand in the kitchen. The project, initiated by Fabrice Wagner*[7] *and carried out with the complicity of Philippe Malcorps, Hanane Housni and Pierre Liebaert, was a form of performance, producing a single-copy book in three days, including shooting, layout, printing and binding. How did you approach the project?*

PM: It was an extraordinary happening.

RC: Yes, a performance.

PM: Yes. It was about putting us to the test. But the cool atmosphere, and especially this friendly relationship between all of us, allowed us to play with the idea of a book. I find that amazing. Apart from the subject, which was secondary, not very important, it was the performance that was interesting. This community idea of producing together, experimenting, dialoguing, of being part of a community reflecting on a project. It brought me back to the days of theatre when I would stay up until 4 in the morning talking to these people older than me. I sometimes say that I don't give a damn about the image of the lone photographer. I don't care, it distresses me. I like working in a group, I like when you move something together and you achieve a result. That's what's beautiful.
The idea of the "book on demand" is also stimulating because I think it can be an interesting activity: creating groups that organize themselves to produce artists' books for collectors. For example, there would be three or four of us and you would ask us to make a book for you. You'd choose your subject, your wife or your house, and we'd make you an amazing book. And most of all, you'd pay us! Not a bad idea! [Laughs]

RC: RVB Books made a book with a Dutch photographer who goes to people's homes and makes them private books.

[7] Fabrice Wagner was then the publisher of Le Caillou Bleu.

PM: In Rome in the 1500s, there was a publisher who made books "on demand" with the *incisione* technique[8]. You wanted a book about the Colosseum, he made you a copy and got paid a lot of money for it. In an abstract way, this could be an interesting operating process.
However, the strongest aspect of our book, the truly great side of it, was that it was not a book "on demand" but the community idea of being there, in Tharoul, working, eating, making music together. And the challenge was a success probably because the climate, the atmosphere, was right. That's what makes you think. If it hadn't been for Pierre making us laugh or Philippe who selected beers and wines, maybe we wouldn't have been so relaxed. We could have made several mistakes and not got the book done by the Monday. Those who came to Tharoul after us have also succeeded in carrying out their projects. This means that this community experience is feasible and allows you to work better on projects when concentration is not oppressive. It relates to the ideal of the Bauhaus, where they played, created and danced together. They weren't working in fearful rigidity. If you work with fear, you only come up with bullshit. If you're relaxed, maybe you're getting better results.

RC: Finally, you've just - and maybe this is another community relationship, with Jérôme Sother in this case - published Acre, *with GwinZegal, the fruit of a residency at this art centre in Brittany. First, what do you mean by that title?*

PM: The title comes first and foremost from the unit of surface measurement. In addition, the four letters lend themselves to be mounted on the cover, like planimetry. With the graphic designer, Claire Schvartz, we thought that the cover could become like the planimetry of the agricultural field, with different farming buildings. You can read "acre", you can read "crea", you can read "reca". You can give different meanings to these letters. So, *Acre* is the unit of measurement of agricultural land, but it is also the word for acrid, pollution, in French. All these elements filter through the images without being directly represented. Consider that Brittany has rather serious

[8] *Engraving.*

pollution problems due to pesticides and livestock farming. It was Jérôme who had the intuition about the title, I immediately liked it very much! And it was perfect to introduce the organizational structure of the book. From this title, we selected the colour of the cover. We wanted the slightly acidic green, and the acidic yellow of the typography as well. Inside, we wanted these hallucinated blank spaces, without a grid. Somewhat like a hallucinating and grotesque journey, never seeing anyone, encountering such bizarre and surreal situations. This is a very difficult territory to define.

RC: In the very careful editing of the book, we first see farms that have barely changed in the last 50 or 100 years, then the agri-food industry, and finally, suburban areas that imitate the architectural style of old farms. As I was telling you the other day, I see a "Pasolinian" aspect in this book, with a dying traditional culture and the consumer society that replaces it. What would you say?

PM: You can read it that way even if it isn't what I am claiming. This is perhaps somewhat of a strong interpretation of the work. Yesterday, I was again reading Pasolini's texts and he said, among other things, that the different cultures (peasant, proletarian, labour) continued to conform to their own ancient models: repression was meant to obtain their verbal agreement from the peasants, the proletarians or the labourers. Today, on the other hand, compliance to the models imposed by the centre is total and unconditional. Real cultural models are denied. The abjuration is accomplished. It can therefore be said that the "tolerance" of the hedonistic ideology defended by the new power is the most terrible repression in human history.
It's as if you were in these hypnotic cycles that put you to sleep. Pasolini was in fact completely on the opposite end of what Marx claimed, who thought that peasant culture didn't allow for the evolution of history. Pasolini was against that idea. Such permanence was for him the strength of peasant culture. So that's your interpretation – it can be found in the work, but it's not my assumption.

RC: Pasolini's contradiction is that he was both a Marxist and missed traditional life. I see no regrets in your work, but an observation.

PM: Yes. I guess you do find in this work the slow cycles, moments suspended in time where nothing develops. It's terrifying, but at the same time this suspension allows that culture to live on its own. Even if now, there is the oppression of the agri-food factory. The other day in Saint-Brieuc, there were two debates that interested me a lot. One was with Rural Studio architects, an American and an Italian who work in Alabama with students from the local university. They build houses from recovered materials with and for the most underprivileged in the poorest parts of the state. And they create gardens to feed them. They do moving things. Then, there was a meeting with the Janin brothers. They're located near Lyon. They're peasants but also architects who reflect upon and completely rethink the farm as a living place. They do "land art". Twice a year, they hold huge parties. They have created a whole debate around the issue of the regeneration of agricultural culture as a place to gather. For me, it's a wonderful opportunity to make the issue central again. And that could save us from the oppression of the agri-food industry.

21 March 2017

Since the conversation, Pino Musi has published four new books: *Border Soundscapes*, text by Marie Rebecchi, Artphilein, 2019; *Grecia Antica*, text by Flaminio Gualdoni, FMR, 2019; *Sottotraccia*, texts by Giovanni Columbu, Marco Delogu and Valerio Magrelli, Fondazione de Sardegna and Punctum Press, 2019; and *Carlo Mollino: Architect and Storyteller* (collective), photographs, drawings, plans and documents by Carlo Mollino, texts by Napoleone Ferrari and Michelangelo Sabatino, contemporary photographs by Pino Musi, Park Books, 2020.

SOPHIE RISTELHUEBER

Sophie Ristelhueber was born in 1949 in Paris, where she lives and works. After studying at the Sorbonne and working in the press and in publishing, she turned to photography and film, co-publishing Intérieurs *with François Hers in 1981, and co-directing* San Clemente *with Raymond Depardon in 1982. She published her first individual book,* Beyrouth, photographies, *with Éditions Hazan in 1984. During the second half of the 1980s, she was part of the DATAR photographic commission. Her work is notably present in prestigious public collections such as the Centre Pompidou or the Maison Européenne de la Photographie in Paris, the Museum of Fine Arts in Boston and the Victoria and Albert Museum in London. In 2010 she was the recipient of the prestigious Deutsche Börse Photography Foundation Prize for her exhibition "Opérations" at the Jeu de Paume. To this day, excluding catalogues and co-editions, she is the author of 13 artist's books, including the mythical* Fait.

The work of Sophie Ristelhueber is now widely recognized for what it deeply stands for: the work of an artist inspired by the real, who develops her own themes and questioning – the eternal cycle, the wound and its suture, the trace. While never explicit, a strong political commitment also underpins the oeuvre. Nevertheless, her work has been the subject of often contradictory misunderstandings and criticisms. She has been somewhat derogatorily labelled as a reporter while also being accused of aestheticizing the violence of the world, when she conceptually embraces much wider fields. To these, she has often replied in the press and in two major books, *Opérations* [1] and *Sophie Ristelhueber: La guerre intérieure* [the internal war][2]. When we first talked on the telephone, she told me that she would gladly meet me, but had no desire to give the same responses to questions she has been asked a thousand times already. In short, she challenged me to approach her work from an original perspective. Then, she uttered the following sentence,

[1] *Sophie Ristelhueber,* Opérations, *Thames and Hudson, 2009.*

[2] *Catherine Grenier,* Sophie Ristelhueber – La guerre intérieure, *revised edition, Les Presses du Réel & JRP Ringier, 2019.*

left unresolved: "To think that I am a literary mind, or at least I was ..." And I thought that her relationship to words, to text and literature, could be a fertile approach to her practice, an aspect that, to my knowledge, has been little touched on. Conversation on a spring morning in her vast studio in the 9th arrondissement of Paris.

Rémi Coignet: *You have studied modern literature, followed the seminars of Roland Barthes and Gérard Genette and, as you have said on several occasions, devoted a memoir to Alain Robbe-Grillet and his novel* Jealousy[3].

Sophie Ristelhueber: That's correct.

RC: What interested you at the age of 22 or 23 in his writing?

SR: Let's say 20, 21 years old. It's hard for me to remember why I made that choice. Especially since the *nouveau roman* was no longer fashionable at the time. It picked up again afterwards, but in the 1970s ... In my literary studies, Robbe-Grillet was never discussed. I think it was rather the whole literary movement that interested me. And when I think back to this choice of the *nouveau roman* through *Jealousy*, I can only have an amused smile at the ambiguity of the term jealousy.

RC: Certainly!

SR: Because it's both a feeling and a Venetian blind that allows you to see without being seen. So, there could already be issues of light, photography and framing. Which I didn't realize when I chose it. It's an enigma for me, in 2019, to issue any comment on that. Frankly, I could find the name of the professor with whom I defended this essay, but...

RC: I'll tell you about Robbe-Grillet later. I too studied literature and quickly re-immersed myself in his work and thinking

[3] *Alain Robbe-Grillet,* Jealousy, *Grove Press, 1959.*

for this conversation. It's amusing that the first of his books that I drew from my library was The Voyeur. *A term you reject for yourself. And then I took* Jealousy. *And in both books, there is a geometric, cold description of the frame that in some way can be found in your work…*

SR: Yes! Of course. We can in fact connect what I've become today by finding it logical to have started with Robbe-Grillet. Both by the profusion of details, but also, by what I think is very important and driving in my work: the ambivalence of things. When Robbe-Grillet describes a scene in a way that is meant to be exhaustive, in the next chapter there is a slight detail that will change the whole thing.

RC: Absolutely.

SR: And in my work as an artist – which I prefer to the word "photographer", which always bothers me – I believe that everything was already in place from the beginning.

RC: Without trying to piece together your biography, which has already been done elsewhere, I would still like, if only to enlighten the readers, to return to your first book, Intérieurs…

SR: Oh yes, I forgot to put it on the pile! Do you know it?

RC: Sure. You made it in 1981 together with François Hers.

SR: Yes.

RC: About this project on social housing in Belgium, he had you in mind to write a text.

SR: Yes, and it's worth noting because my move to the image dates from *Intérieurs*.

RC: To do this work, I think you lived a few weeks with a family, and you met many others. Why did you give up writing to take hold of a camera?

SR: It was the involvement, almost even physical, the immersion in a family that I did not know, that led me to make this choice. The family lived in social housing that was not in the suburbs but in the heart of Brussels, next to the Court House.

RC: That architectural monster in the heart of Brussels… [Sophie Ristelhueber laughs]

SR: I was literally absorbed by this family, which, like any family, had problems and conflicts. And I found myself, at barely 30 years old, becoming the confidante, the witness, the attentive ear for every member of the family. The children were teenagers, the mother was older than me and the father was gone. I thought, "I will never have the necessary literary mastery to transcribe all this." Also considering that it was not in the nature of the project to be a sociological study.
This stay with them deeply disturbed me. I had made small sketches of the different parts of the apartment and I had taken a camera with me to ask them to use it and capture their favourite corners of the house, because I myself didn't photograph. Which they never did. And then I found myself in a nightclub with the eldest son… And then I thought of one of my reference books, which is *Let Us Now Praise Famous Men* by James Agee and Walker Evans[4]. And I told myself that I would never have the genius of Agee, with whom the description of a closet becomes a poem… I continued to make visits, on my own or with François Hers, who photographed the rooms emptied of all their inhabitants. And as I continued to talk with them, I was struck by the way they stood in the space of their homes. Very neat but highly decorated interiors. As if their dwellers were going to be swallowed by their wallpapers and then, with a 35mm camera, I started to take pictures of them. And I went on!
I think I did an honest and honourable job. But what was truly new was what François Hers did, who photographed the interiors in colour like crime scenes, with escapes to the outdoor

[4] *James Agee, Walker Evans,* Let Us Now Praise Famous Men, *first American edition, Houghton Mifflin Harcourt, 1941.*

landscape. The exhibition at the Centre Pompidou[5] had great success. It happened by chance for me, but for him it was well deserved. Suddenly, I realized that successful work could end up in a museum, and that made me want to continue. But to finance my photography work, I lived by other means – other jobs, sometimes related to literature, for over 10 years.

RC: Indeed, you've worked a lot in publishing…

SR: Yes, rewriting, iconography and everything else you do in publishing. I also performed less glorious tasks, such as repainting apartments, an activity I ended up excelling at! I say this to reassure the younger generations of artists…

RC: Your following book, Beirut, *published in 1984, heralds the originality of your approach and raises several issues that will permeate through the course of your practice. First, you place as incipit an excerpt from Lucretius'* De Rerum Natura, *which may deal with destruction in the beginning but ends for me on a rather optimistic note[6]. Later, you used excerpts from Thucydides'* The Ecclesiastes *and* The History of the Peloponnesian War. *Why such interest in Ancient Greek literature?*

SR: *Beirut* was the first time I was using a text from Ancient Greece, after a long process to understand what it was that I wanted to express. And decide whether I wanted to put words in it, and if so, how to place them. At first, Éric Hazan[7] put me in touch with Jean-Christophe Bailly, the significance of whose work we now understand. This guy is great. He wrote for me a text about the notion of the ruin, which I must have somewhere in one of my famous white boxes, but which I didn't use because I didn't want a comment on the ruin. In Beirut,

[5] *"Intérieurs": Exhibition at the CCI/Centre Georges Pompidou, 1981. And a book published by Editions des Archives d'Architecture Moderne, Brussels, 1981.*

[6] *"After nearly falling, it [the Earth] regains its balance and its habitual place."*

[7] *The French publisher of* Beyrouth, Photographies *and* Fait. *Published in the same year, their English versions,* Beirut *and* Aftermath, *were published with Thames & Hudson.*

I had taken "topographical" notes on the locations I was working on at the end of 1982. The civil war was far from over. There was the famous demarcation line, the green line that had to be crossed to get to the city centre still largely mined. For example, at the museum checkpoint, an emblematic position along the demarcation line, I had listed the various belligerents. The situation kept changing, and when I returned to Paris my "captions" were already obsolete. The Palestinians had left, but it was still a back-and-forth of all the parties involved. At that time, I had not yet forgotten the Sorbonne and my literary studies from which, probably, came the interest in ancient texts. Like *Ecclesiastes* that I used in *Mémoires du Lot* to remind us that everything is an eternal restart. Which wasn't meant in a pessimistic tone.

RC: What about The History of the Peloponnesian War*?*

SR: For this destruction to take place, man had to build. We've added a few layers since the Peloponnesian War, we've destroyed others, yet we keep going and we start over. The choice of Lucretius for *Beirut* allowed me to place myself in a much broader spectrum of human history than that of this civil war that had become emblematic. Even today, for people born in the 21st century, the name Beirut is still associated with destruction, urban catastrophe...

RC: Yes, you can walk into a teenager's room and say, "It's like Beirut in here..."

SR: Yes, they'll understand!

RC: Beirut *opens with a half-destroyed building that reads "Jupiter".*

SR: It was a commercial for a beer, I think, but I'm not sure exactly.

RC: And it ends with a view of the ruins of Jupiter's temple in Baalbek...

SR: Which is the only image in the book to have been made outside Beirut.

> *RC: Is this assumed editorial choice a sign of the repetition of infinite cycles or a touch of black humour? I wondered ...*

SR: Considering how I was at the time, I don't see myself using black humour. I think I'm more serious than that.

> *RC: Going back to Jupiter – and Jupiter is lightning – who is present at the beginning and at the end of your book, as a back-and-forth between modern and ancient ruins that would be spotted again in "Dead Set" [2001] for example, how was this received?*

SR: *Beirut* raised much debate, as did *Intérieurs*, but it shocked people and was even violently criticized, with comments such as: "How can you afford to make aesthetic photos, to make art in times of war? How can you erase people?"
I never wanted to reply to this kind of criticism, nor justify my aesthetic choices.
There are, moreover, very beautiful images that I didn't select at the time because they couldn't find their place then.
In 2016 I pulled out some of them for an exhibition[8] because they could evoke Aleppo, Syria, which was then in turmoil.
I didn't exactly "pull them out", because in fact they had never lived before.

> *RC:* Beirut *thus inaugurates a series of misunderstandings about your work. Generalities or approximations were brought forward. You've been called a reporter, you've been accused of aestheticizing ruins, long before the upsurge of the poetry of ruin and the so-called "aftermath photography" of the 2000s. It took a while for critics to admit that your work is part of the field of art, which is for me obvious.*

SR: Yes, we can say that I've inaugurated a new genre in photography.

[8] *At the Jérôme Poggi Gallery, Paris, who represents Sophie Ristelhueber in France.*

RC: About Aftermath, *a reporter wrote: "It contains no words, no captions." This is inaccurate, to say the least, since the book opens and closes with two carefully laid out double-pages extracted from General Clausewitz's military strategy treatise*[9].

SR: Specifically, Clausewitz's words about war, taken from the middle of sentences and which I use as a kind of "wrapping paper" for my book and the images, which are not images of war but traces of war. It's complicated.
When I left Paris I knew what I wanted to do with this war ... without knowing, on the other hand, what I was going to find there to feed my intuition. While the term "obsession" is overused, that's what it was all about. It's something I *had* to do.

RC: That's one aspect of your approach that intrigues me. For some projects, when you leave Paris you know exactly what you are looking for – this is the case for Aftermath. *But in other cases, such as* Irak, *you told Catherine Grenier that you had exhausted your driver roaming across the country in search of what you call a "Ristelhueber". I wonder, what's the difference between leaving knowing what you're looking for, and having to find it once you've arrived?*

SR: It depends. In the summer of 1982 I had no television, and the desire to go there was born from one or two press images that had struck me. They represented all the tragedies of Beirut, the crying women, the dead and, in the background, the crumbling architecture. This is the setting I embraced, because I thought that treating it without any human presence paradoxically allowed stronger evocation. In the picture you're showing me, if we consider this little figure there, lost in a corner of the image, you'll wonder who he is: a soldier? A militiaman? A Christian? A Palestinian? etc. But looking at the naked architecture so tremendously marked by man that I showed, I don't think it can be said that it is bare of human presence. That's impossible!

[9] *Carl von Clausewitz,* On War, *1832.*

Of course, I must adapt my approach. For example, for *Aftermath* I thought I would only do aerial views. But when I got there I quickly realized that it was just as interesting to find traces on the ground from the top of my 1.75 metres, and that the work should be the combination of the two.

RC: By considering humans through their absence, your plastic approach could compare to a metonymy... And it seems that Robbe-Grillet can contribute to an understanding of your approach. While doing some research, I came across an archive from INA [National Audiovisual Institute][10] where, about his cine-novels, he was saying: "It is not a question of refusing all anecdotes but to refuse the anecdotal code in power, meaning this organization which is called realism and which is only a code, because it changes according to the eras and genres." So, should we replace "anecdotal code" with, say, "photojournalism"? Would you say that to hold onto the rhetoric that is yours, you're putting yourself outside of the code of realism?

SR: The statement can be made, but I won't claim it as a standard. I do what I need to do because I feel that it is right and that I *must* do it. But then, everyone is free to interpret my work and put it in a box.

RC: On the contrary, I'm not trying to put you in a box. You've had enough of it..

SR: Oh yes! But at the same time, I guess I'm unclassifiable. [Smiles]

RC: I believe so. But I'm trying to understand or express the difference between a codified, stereotyped representation and an artistic representation of the real – with quotation marks wherever it might be needed.

SR: In Kuwait, during my walks, I happened to encounter corpses that were nothing but bones: given the 50° local temperature,

[10] *"Alain Robbe-Grillet et le ciné-roman," in the television programme* Italiques, *8 February 1974 (www.ina.fr/video/I00013333).*

the uniform remained as new but there was nothing left of the person. I didn't take any pictures. Not that I was indifferent to the sight of these deceased, but it didn't fit into my work. On the other hand, when I saw the little Scottish blanket thrown nonchalantly on a trench, I did photograph that to evoke this soldier.

RC: As in Beirut, with this half-ripped apartment where you can see the wallpaper on the wall and a carpet hanging in mid-air…

SR: Yes, we imagine the family.

RC: If you don't mind, let's look at the formal aspects of your books. You designed the Beirut *dummy yourself, with the format…*

SR: From Gallimard's "White" collection. Let's move back to that time. I was in Beirut in November and December 1982, I designed the work in 1983, I showed the dummy to Éric Hazan and the book came out in early 1984, which is for me the date of the work. Indeed, for me, the date of a work always coincides with when it begins to live on a wall of a museum and in a book. But the formulation I used at the end of the book is totally clumsy: [She takes the book in hand] "Made in Beirut in December 1982." This suggests that the book was printed in Beirut. As if I were a printer!

RC: And I think that other than the cover…

SR: Yes, I went there with my dummy with the Gallimard cover titled "Beyrouth" and instead of "novel" it was written "photographs". Éric Hazan, who didn't know me at all, said, "Sophie, I take everything but the cover." Graphic designer Dominique Carré[11], who was working for Hazan at the time, invented this montage on tracing paper with one of my images. Well, 10 years later, Éric Hazan will take my cover as I had designed it originally for *Aftermath.*

[11] *He founded Éditions Dominique Carré in 1989.*

RC: Do you always design your book dummies?

SR: Yes. Except for *La Liste*, for which I worked with a graphic designer, Jean-Marc Ballée, whom I had asked to channel the spirit of "La Campagne" [1997]. Meaning, like a stack of images, regardless of the value of one relative to another. And he had the genius to figure out how to do it, and to find the printer who agreed to bind all these sheets, none of which were the same size.

RC: Playing with different paper sizes inside the book was very fashionable in the late 2000s and early 2010s. But to my knowledge, La Liste[12] *is one of the very first books to toy with the technique. I imagine this is no coincidence since, as you've just said, it is inspired by the notion of stacking in "La Campagne", where you had not hung but…*

SR: Yes, set on the floor, leaning against the wall, overlapping images printed in large format and pasted to soft cardboard. With each book project, I determine a format, often quite small. *Beirut* took from that of Gallimard's White collection, which today no longer seems that small. But this was a novelty, because the books published in photography at the time were usually in large formats. Then, there was *Aftermath* and *WB*, which came more than a decade later. These two books have an identical dummy; I designed them as brothers because they both deal with the earth in the generic sense of the term.

RC: And back to that stunning dummy of Aftermath*?*

SR: I've said everything about this book… but I can tell you an anecdote.
For the printing of the book, I went one first time to the printing press in northern Italy near Padua. I arrive, and they had started to print tests on a catastrophic glossy paper… I had the press stopped, thinking I was really daring, but the printer just asked me what was wrong. I said, "Nothing feels the way my dummy with photocopy paper does." So he went to get two sheets

[12] *Sophie Ristelhueber,* La Liste, *Éditions de L'Hôtel des Arts, Toulon, 2000.*

and said, "I think I have what you need." We did some successful tests and he added, "The problem is I don't have the paper in stock, so you'll have to come back in three weeks." Éric Hazan was obviously not happy because it was, for him, an additional cost, but when I came back with the book finally printed, he took me in his arms and said, "You were right!"

RC: It's a nice reward for being stubborn, isn't it?

SR: Yes, the relationships between the different stakeholders involved in the making of a book are always a bit complicated. And I regret that there was a misunderstanding about the graphic conception of *Aftermath*. It was mine and not, as indicated in the colophon, that of Atalante, the company newly founded by Xavier Barral, to whom Éric Hazan had asked to help me load my book on the computer because I didn't know how to use computers then. On the other hand, it was Xavier who gave me the beautiful idea to tinge the edges of the book in black.

RC: Most of your books are small or even tiny, while your prints or wall installations are often quite large. Perhaps the most striking contrast is Every One[13]*: the book is 14 centimetres high and the prints nearly 3 metres. Why this choice?*

SR: Probably because of my closeness to books, which are, in my mind, objects that you take with you, that you put in your pocket. For *Every One*, the images on the walls had to be extremely large in order to remove the human scale and avoid identifying with the bodies and faces depicted. I have only half-succeeded because, when I observe public reaction to these tableaux in museums, I can see that everyone is stepping back.

RC: Me first.

[13] *Sophie Ristelhueber,* Every One, *1994. The piece produced in Parisian hospitals represents details of sutured bodies as metaphor for the conflicts of the time. The 14 unique photographs were exhibited in various museums, including the Centraal Museum in Utrecht and the Museum of Fine Arts in Boston, and collected in a very small book published in approximately 500 copies in French and the same number in English.*

SR: Even before the *Every One* image at the Pompidou Centre, which represents a scar on a man's head magnified 10 times, everyone got tense. I had probably anticipated this reaction by making this little book printed on Bible paper, soft and silky. You could walk out of the exhibition with a more intimate object in your pocket, sold for a few francs at the museum.

RC: Does this establish different relationships to the work?

SR: Yes, but these two forms complement each other. They are not in opposition. For example, for the show "Mémoires du Lot", which I conceived with Gloria Friedmann, we exhibited in Les Arques in a small, still active church. While my large prints were hanging on the side walls, my little book was offered in piles at the entrance to the church, to be taken as a prayer or song book that could be kept. This is probably the smallest book I've ever done[14].

RC: Simple curiosity: two books that are for me, to borrow your expression, true "Ristelhuebers", do not appear in your bibliographies: La Route de la betterave *[1992] and* Pilat *[1994]. Why?*

SR: I should probably integrate them. These are commission jobs, for which I had constraints that I needed to take into account, contrary to my personal commissions. While I designed the book *Pilat itinéraires* myself, *La Route de la betterave* was laid out by Philippe Bissière. To consider the horizon line in the successive landscapes, as I had asked him to, he suggested a small accordion book.

RC: It's a leporello…

SR: Yes. Back to the *Pilat* commission, the work, consisting of selecting 40 points of view on the territory of the Natural Park, was very important in my fantasy life. Indeed, there was a disturbing similarity between these landscapes and those I had seen the previous year in Yugoslavia at the beginning

[14] *Sophie Ristelhueber,* Mémoires du Lot, *1990, 24 pages, edition of 350 numbered copies.*

of the civil war. I then decided to return to Yugoslavia, and more specifically to Bosnia-Herzegovina, to photograph these landscapes which, beyond their bucolic dimension, had now become mass graves. This work became "La Campagne". A piece that was based on this ambivalence.

RC: In contrast to these commissions, a few of your important pieces, such as "Vulaines" [1989], "La Campagne" [1997] that we have just discussed or "Dead Set" [2001], did not become books. Why? Since Operations *in 2007, your last artist's book [not to be confused with the monograph from the Jeu de Paume, which is also called* Operations[15]*], you have made films, sound pieces and other photographs... None of these pieces were suitable as books?*

SR: No, I didn't feel it was necessary. That said, half of "Vulaines" is in the book *Les Barricades mystérieuses*[16]. It wasn't at the time necessary with the "Vulaines" series, with which I inaugurated the large formats. A choice that came from the photograph of a red children's bed that I blew up to a 1:1 scale to make the viewer want to lie down.
As for "Sunset Years"[17], the 20 large format prints on the wall were enough. I don't always feel the need to give two lives to a work, that of the book and that of the installation.

RC: Going back to your beginnings, after Beirut *you were involved in the DATAR photographic mission for which you conducted two shooting campaigns. One was on mid-mountain landscapes seen from the railway tracks, appearing in the two books published by the mission*[18]*, with completely different editorial choices. For example,*

[15] *Sophie Ristelhueber,* Operations, *Éditions Le Quartier, 2009, edition of 450 numbered copies.*

[16] *« Sophie Ristelhueber, Les Barricades mystérieuses, Cabinet des Estampes, Musée d'Art et d'Histoire, Geneva, 1995.*

[17] *"Sunset Years," exhibition at the Jérôme Poggi Gallery, Paris, 23 March to 3 May 2019.*

[18] Paysages, Photographies/La Mission photographique de la Datar, travaux en cours, *Éditions Hazan, Paris, 1985;* Paysages, Photographies en France, les années quatre-vingt, *Editions Hazan, Paris, 1989.*

it doesn't include the colour series that you shot on the Côte d'Azur during the second campaign. Why?

SR: I don't have an answer for that, but it was in fact my decision, since it was the photographers themselves who had to decide what images could be published or exhibited.
The DATAR mission was the only opportunity I had to work within a group. I was able to forge or deepen many friendships[19]. It was warm, and needed, because these long and lonely "campaigns" were tough.

RC: As for your second campaign, made in colour on the Côte d'Azur, it was never published?

SR: Nowhere. I then went from medium format to the 4x5 view camera. I don't know why I haven't done anything with it until today, but one could see it as the draft of what would later be *La Liste*.

RC: Actually, it reminds me of Mémoires du Lot, *for which you proceeded from the workshop, without going out on field.*

SR: I did go out on the field, I went scouting. I didn't take pictures, but I had the hotel rooms, the rain, and the eternal question: "What am I doing here?" While doing research at the Cahors Municipal Library about the area, in particular about the prehistoric caves, I found inspiration and wrote these few lines that start the artist's book: "I met the rhinoceros, the mammoth and the Homo sapiens on the banks of the Lot. The world was not a landscape."
With these words, I illustrated my point by bringing together images I had made previously that apparently had nothing to do with each other: the Duomo in Milan, a rhinoceros from the Jardin des Plantes in Paris, Masada above the Dead Sea, etc.

RC: Mémoires du Lot *is an almost metaphysical memory! This work therefore comes after "Vulaines" and just before*

[19] *The group included Lewis Baltz, Robert Doisneau, Gabriele Basilico, Christian Milovanoff, Raymond Depardon, Dominique Auerbach, Holger Trülzsch.*

Aftermath. *And while much was said about the importance of the suture in your work, less has been noted about that of memory. "Vulaines" dealt with family memory even if anyone can project what they want...*

SR: Yes, this family home that hasn't changed for more than a century was probably the original matrix... It was open from spring to autumn and I used to go there often.

RC: Considering these three series together – "Vulaines", "Mémoires du Lot" and "Aftermath", in which you show the traces before they fade into the desert winds – I wonder whether there wouldn't be for you in art a Promethean desire to preserve memory?

SR: No, I don't believe so. Today I tell myself that all this work and my tiny contribution to the development of shapes will also go to dust. I'll be curious to know what will be left of it in a hundred years.

RC: You have often explained that Aftermath, *like other pieces, was born from a photo seen in the press. Here, an image from the first Gulf War seen in* Time Magazine *if I remember correctly, which, before convincing you to go and see for yourself, triggered a phenomenon of reminiscence, reminding you of* Dust Breeding *by Marcel Duchamp and Man Ray.*

SR: I can't even talk about *Dust Breeding* anymore; it's been so much talked about. But indeed, the image inhabited me.

RC: Are history, memory or literature the necessary conditions for the implementation of your work?

SR: Perhaps. But the implementation is first and foremost a way for me to avoid exploding, through a controlled shaping of my emotions. For example, in the 1990s, my most militant years, the Balkan conflict overlapped with Rwanda's, with civil wars in the most atrocious sense of the term. There is an interview with Michel Guerrin in *Le Monde des débats* where I said: "How to create, explore social facts, preserve the anger that is in me without falling into militancy? How can we pay tribute while creating? Tell of a suffering that will exist forever? That's how I envision creation connected to the existing world."[20]

RC: My question was about the notion of deflection As Bruno Latour writes very well in the fictitious dialogue at the beginning of Operations*: "It is not committed art, but at the same time, your Sophie is not disengaged either." [Sophie Ristelhueber smiles]*

SR: Ah, I forgot that passage!

RC: That sentence struck me. Your work is often part of a political context. You just said that during the 1990s, you were particularly committed. And we were many to be shocked and outraged by the wars in Rwanda and Bosnia, without really knowing what to do. Going back to Every One*, this work is a metaphor. So, does the need for the detour, through the literary form of the metaphor or through a pre-existing artistic form, allow you to approach reality while avoiding "the anecdotal code"?*

SR: Yes, I hope so. *Every One* is really emblematic of the way I transpose a reality. With this work, I was in hospitals in Paris and not in the field. The people depicted didn't necessarily suffer war trauma, and I used a text by Thucydides about the Peloponnesian War. Frankly, we're a long way from Sarajevo. And you know what? The first articles and accounts about the work claimed: "Sophie Ristelhueber went to photograph in Sarajevo." At first, it put me off and I thought, "But I don't give them any leads, nothing is said." And later, I thought, "Girl, you get exactly what you wanted, because that's what you're talking about." The journalists dropped Thucydides and went straight to the point. But in fact, as nothing spoke directly of Sarajevo and the Balkans, it was very good that they referred to that on their own. Conclusion: mission accomplished!

[20] Le Monde des débats, *"Les 30/40 ans, une génération culturelle", p. 6-7, June 1993.*

RC: Like your image A cause de l'élevage de poussière, *which raises the question of scale, which is also present in* Aftermath…

SR: Unlike Man Ray who mentioned it, mine is a true aerial view made by myself, though I didn't use it in the book or the wall installation for *Aftermath*.

RC: Yes, you only disclosed it much later, in 2007. But your version is like a matrix, right? And especially for me, it raises the notion of scale that permeates Aftermath *with alternating aerial views..*

SR: … And ground views, so sometimes you don't know where you are.
But it can be in my own images that I find inspiration to deal with other situations. Thus, when I photographed from the plane the traces of scars on the ground created by the trenches in the desert, I understood how I was going to deal with the civil war in the Balkans, where I had been three months before and where I will return.

RC: I have one last quite trivial question regarding Aftermath. *The book, on the second-hand market, costs a small fortune.*

SR: Used to – because now I think it's gone down. It's interesting to see, because at a given time it was worth several thousand euros, though it had been printed in several thousand copies. I like this paradox of making artist's books with large traditional publishing houses, which allows us to emerge from confidentiality.

RC: And the English title…

SR: The English title *Aftermath* was imposed on me by the English publisher Thames & Hudson.

RC: Whereas the French title, Fait *[Done] is totally polysemic.*

SR: This is all the more curious, because the English use the word "fait", for example in the expression kept in French "*fait accompli.*" That said, this *Aftermath* title has become a genre in which new generations rushed into.

RC: Yes, you have "done"...

SR: I made. [Smiles]

RC: Returning to the relationship between literature and your plastic work, and, in particular, to the book Les Barricades mystérieuses, *I'd like to talk about the text by Laurence Sterne*[21]*, reproduced in screen print on the cover. I read: "To know the character of a man, it would suffice to take a chair and go quietly to sit in front of him as one would before a glassed beehive, in order to contemplate his naked soul." And, at the end of the excerpt: "It would suffice to take one's pen and ink and put on paper strictly what one would have seen, under oath."*
In this text, the verb in the conditional tense: "it would suffice", to be found in the first and last sentences of the excerpt, particularly interests me. Doesn't this conditionality say that any attempt to exhaust the meaning of things is impossible?

SR: That's exactly what it is. I treated "Vulaines" as a self-portrait. I then looked at this genre in literature. *Tristram Shandy* in the 18th century was one of the very first books in which an author, Laurence Sterne in this case, spoke of himself with irony and distance. I found myself in there. And indeed, the conditional attests to this impossible mission.

RC: I purposely used the phrase "any attempt at exhaustion is impossible" because it obviously relates to Georges Perec. To my knowledge, you have never referred to his work...

SR: No, but I read it. And if it has any form of influence on me, it would be in an underlying way.

RC: I came to think about Perec when I saw your work, not because of the lists, but because of the geographical

[21] *Laurence Sterne,* The Life and Opinions of Tristram Shandy, *1759.*

proximity between your Luxembourg garden and his Place Saint-Sulpice. In Penser/Classer, *[Think/classify] he writes these lines that I find interesting: "There are things that are different and yet a bit the same; they can be assembled in series within which they can be distinguished." You've often referred to your "obsessions". Does organizing them in series allow you to make them identifiable to the public?*

SR: It is common in photography to proceed in series. For me, these series can offer very different forms and content.
For example, the exhibition "La Liste" in Toulon, which, in addition to images made in the Var region that were directly pasted to the walls like posters, also presented soundtracks. The sound could be heard inside as well as outside the art centre on the boulevard, releasing the voice of Michel Piccoli reciting a thousand names of places located in the Var. The list had no apparent logic, it was not alphabetical, it named small rivers, mountains, big cities, villages, localities, etc.
The choice was not neutral: it was the recognizable voice of a well-known actor who interpreted this litany. I wanted to see if words could exhaust a place or an action. And the answer is obviously no! This project also has a political dimension. Toulon at the time was a Front National constituency; the atmosphere in town was anything but friendly. The recording lasted over an hour and the entire exhibition could be visited before the list of names was finished.

RC: Is that a form of arbitrariness?

SR: No doubt. It was a commission from the Toulon art centre, I could do what I wanted, but I had to stick geographically to the Var department. One morning, in my hotel, I woke up, I grabbed the damn map of the department, and thought, "What is the Var?" And I started reading out loud the words that were before my eyes. I then realized that the list would be part of the piece: naming without ever exhausting anything.

RC: It does look like The List *is one of your more political works, even if it isn't obvious at first sight. As you said, it was a far-right town, but your commission came from the department, ran by the moderate right. Could it also deal with something of an electoral list?*

SR: Well, on the day of the exhibition opening, officials did ask me: "Why did you call it *The List*?" And I replied, "Well, what's happening here a few months from now?"[22]

RC: In the exhibition, there is also a triptych of blue, white and red photographs. And the invitation card to the opening was a backlit road view with palm trees…

SR: Yes, when I made that photo that was used for the invitation card, I thought that the murder of MP Yann Piat must have been committed on a similar kind of road…[23]
I worked a lot for this exhibition/installation and the book, but it was a flop: no one from the art world came, precisely because it was Toulon.

RC: You pay close attention to your hangings. In Toulon, you played with the mouldings, the fireplaces and the door frames to paste your photographs. You did the same in Arles a few years later, with "Eleven Blowups" in the former official apartment of the governor of the Bank of France…

SR: For the exhibition in Arles[24], I was searching for a lived-in, bourgeois apartment.
I had refused the proposal from the Rencontres to exhibit in the Ateliers SNCF, already in ruins, and told them that there was no sense to add ruin to ruin. I was lucky enough to meet the mayor, who told me that the building of the Bank of France was available.
For this installation, the shutters were drawn as they do in the South, and it took a little time to adapt to see that the pieces were coming out from the wallpapers. I have always paid

[22] *Municipal elections were to be held.*

[23] *Yann Piat was a French politician. Initially a member of the far-right National Front party, she quit to join UDF (Union for French Democracy). She was murdered in 1994 in Hyères.*

[24] *Rencontres d'Arles, 2006.*

great attention to the modes of presentation of my work. The scenography of the exhibition is part of the piece.

RC: When I saw the exhibition, I thought of Martha Rosler's "Bringing the War Home"...

SR: That's true, even though it's very different. We both play on ambiguity. She, within the very image, and I, between the image and the setting.

RC: Speaking of this relationship between artists, the flop of The List *reminded me of Lewis Baltz,* [see Conversations p. 30] *with whom you were friends at the time of the DATAR mission, and who told me that no one had seen the exhibition "New Topographics" because it was held in Rochester, a city where no one ever went. And he added that he couldn't believe his ears when, 10 years later, people started telling him that it was the most important exhibition of his life.*

SR: Ah, Lewis! He was a part of the DATAR missionaries, I loved him very much. Later, when I did *Fait*, he had this nice expression in English: "But Sophie, what is left to do?"

RC: For me, beyond the bond between two individuals, there is also a strong closeness between your respective works.

SR: I agree.

RC: If you are fine with it, we can talk about Le Luxembourg, *an invitation to exhibit from Noëlle Chabert, curator at the Zadkine Museum, close to the Luxembourg Gardens. Again, perhaps subliminally, it is an autobiographical piece...*

SR: Yes.

RC: To open the book that accompanies this exhibition[25]*, you have placed a portrait of you at the age of 10, with the École des Mines in the background.*

SR: Only attentive people can make the connection. I always have difficulty accepting an invitation to exhibit, especially when it requires me to design new work. I'm often on the defensive, because I want everything to be fair! I'm not interested in exhibiting for the sake of exhibiting. When I arrived in this overloaded museum and in her office that was the size of this table, I didn't know what proposal to make to Noëlle Chabert. It took me a while to realize that the museum, like the apartment of my childhood, was located on the edge of the Luxembourg Gardens. And I remembered my father, who on the rare occasions he looked after us on Sundays would say, "So girls, what are we going to do?" And he would add, "Why don't we pay a visit to our dear old Luxembourg?" Suddenly, I understood how this territory of my childhood connected me with Zadkine and his studio house. That's how the project was born.

RC: The autobiographic dimension appears only allusively, except through the portrait in the book.

SR: I wondered how I was going to approach this garden that I knew by heart since I had been visiting it in my childhood, and as an adult I walk through it whenever I can. I looked for ways to look at it differently, knowing that the first time I would go back there with this exhibition project in mind, everything would fall into place.

RC: It seems to me that with this work, you are saying, you are demonstrating (I don't know which is the right verb to use) that you can represent in a comparable way Kuwait, Iraq or the Luxembourg Gardens – in other words, a place you don't know or a place familiar to you with the same point of view. Eschewing the picturesque. You don't show, for example, the small boats on the pond. All we see is bitumen cutting off the sandy path. Is it an affirmation that the power of the gaze, of the artistic approach, outweighs the anecdote?

SR: I don't see it as a statement, a claim that would be established from the start and then implemented. But there is obviously a similar logic in my approach. In *Le Luxembourg*, there are

[25] Le Luxembourg, *Musée Zadkine, Paris-Musées, 2002.*

large scars, large deserted patches, and a loss of scale as well. So, I do see the Sophie who was in Iraq shortly before.

RC: For this book, you asked Jean Echenoz for a text.

SR: Yes, by a complicated path. Since I felt like I was talking about myself, I gathered some documents about my parents, about myself as a child, and I had given them to Emmanuel Carrère whom I knew a little, asking him if it would amuse him to write a fictional text about this child from the Luxembourg Gardens who later made pieces such as *Aftermath* and *Irak*. And I added, "What happened to her? I leave it to your imagination because I have no idea." Emmanuel told me he was going to think about it, but nothing came of it. I can't remember how I connected with Jean Echenoz. His reply was: "Listen, the little girl means nothing to me, but as a provincial arriving in Paris, the Luxembourg was my park and I always wanted to do something about the statues of the queens around the large pond." So, he wrote that text.

RC: I really like the books of Jean Echenoz. In this text, he describes in an objective, almost detective way the statues of the 20 queens. But this desire for "clinical" objectivity – when talking about your work, words are "loaded," if I may say – [Sophie Ristelhueber smiles] is deliberately shattered against descriptions titled as "expression". So, it reads, for example, "Expression: Unkind" or "Expression: Doubtful". This is bending towards interpretation, subjectivity, right? There is a drop of tongue-in-cheek humour, quite characteristic of his writing, in this text, which defuses his subject matter. And in these portraits of queens, this is manifested in three or four instances by the mention: "Presence of big breasts".

SR: The words by Jean Echenoz were printed on small frames that I had placed in the museum gardens. An academic, Christine Jérusalem, has devoted a whole book to Jean Echenoz[26], including a chapter about *Le Luxembourg*. Her text on Echenoz's writing is quite interesting.

RC: And yourself, while your work may seem cold and neutral, you offer ambivalent and offbeat interpretations.

SR: That's right. The Iraqi triptych dated 2001 has long coexisted in one of my white boxes with a text by Tolstoy, which I ended up using years later in my video *Le Chardon* [The thistle][27] shot in Vercors, an important region of the Resistance. Eventually *Irak* went out alone, and that was fine.
Texts are always important to me and I have been collecting them for a long time. For *Le Luxembourg*, the text about space [reproduced on the cover] from a book by Meša Selimović[28], an author from the Balkans, literally haunted me: "Space takes us over. We possess of it what the eye can browse. But it exhausts us, frightens us, calls us, chases us."
Not only did I use a very small extract for *Le Luxembourg*, but just after the exhibition, I was invited to Japan to participate in the Echigo-Tsumari Triennial. This same text, in a longer version, was translated into Japanese so that the dwellers of the village in which I had chosen to perform could read it. It was called "The Tunnel". The text was half a sheet in its Japanese version and I still managed to get it read by some locals: there was me, the French, the Balkanite through his original text from the 1960s, and the Japanese who grew rice. We were all gathered around this story about space, enriched by their comments and their reading of it. I don't speak a word of Japanese, but I've been told that depending on whether you're a woman or a man, you don't use exactly the same words. Each had therefore slightly adapted the text. In addition, there is a more sophisticated, noble Japanese language, and an everyday Japanese. I've never been able to appreciate the subtleties brought forward by the 14 people who read this text and who appropriated it. Their voices could be heard

[26] *Christine Jérusalem and Jean-Bernard Vray,* Jean Echenoz: "Une tentative modeste de décrire le monde", *Presses Universitaires de Saint-Étienne, 2006.*

[27] *Preface to Tolstoy's last novel,* Hadji Murat, *1904. The triptych was entitled by Sophie Ristelhueber* Le Chardon, *which would also become the title to the video shot in the Vercors region in 2007.*

[28] *Meša Selimović,* Death and the Dervish, *Northwestern University Press, 1996, for the American edition. First published in 1966.*

from the exit of a disused tunnel at the exit of the village. This shows, since we are talking about words and books, how my Selimović lived and circulated.

RC: And with the sound piece The Tunnel, *I believe you have also designed a very small book, with very few copies.*

SR: Yes, I did it for the participants and offered them their copy. It was indeed a very limited edition.

RC: After Japan, you designed WB *from a photo seen in the press, as you did for* Aftermath.

SR: Yes, it was again from one of the images I keep in my white boxes. That one represented a settlement on the West Bank with completely symmetrical and repetitive buildings that don't lend themselves to daydreaming. Looking at it, it became clear to me that I had to talk about separation, in a reality all the more painful because it is located in the Holy Land, a place where the three monotheistic religions meet. When I got there in 2003, I didn't know how I was going to give shape to this notion of separation. And the wall that was beginning to be built was formally too obvious, even caricatural, for me to want to use it.

RC: Even before the trenches or the barricades, what caught my attention in the book WB *is the fact that the images are studded with conventional signs, such as yellow stripes at the side of the roads or road signs that have lost their meaning. Beyond the context of the Israeli-Palestinian conflict, isn't the subject matter of this book the loss of meaning?*

SR: Yes. However, I would say more about the diversion of meaning than its loss. All these obstacles that had been put in place to prevent the use of roads and paths – rocks, mounds of earth, trenches, etc. – were incredibly violent actions to signify a desire for separation. Even more so since all this was set in a rather idyllic, bucolic landscape. This is what I called the reversal of the landscape against itself.

RC: And you used a map…

SR: Yes, it was a road map where I would note the locations where I had travelled and the obstacles I had encountered. I later discovered that the United Nations had drawn up an official map of these blockades, which I found even more shocking because all these devices were known and precisely spotted.

RC: On the cover of the book WB, *you are seen prostrate on the platform of the car from which you shot your images. Is this to counter the cliché image of you as a bushwhacker in your fatigues, always ready to jump on a plane to "cover" a conflict [Sophie Ristelhueber smiles]. It seems that many artists suffer from being assigned to a position. Sophie Calle* [see p. 48]*was telling me that people, still today, are asking her: "So, do you follow people in the street?", though it has been 30 or 40 years since she followed anyone. How then, did you get around?*

SR: I worked with a "fixer", Rachel Leah Jones, a great American-Israeli woman who spoke Arabic. All those kilometres and back-and-forth on the platform I had installed on the roof of the SUV, it was tiring. But what really depleted us was the absurdity of the situation, of what we saw. It was really depressing. Even more so for Rachel, who lived in Tel Aviv, so close. As for me, in this photograph used for the cover of the book, I was like a patty asking myself, "What am I doing here, devastated, on the roof of this car? Am I thinking that it's nice 'to stand safe and sound on the shore, watching others struggle amid wild currents and furious winds?'... "[29]

RC: It reminds me of the cover of Details of the World[30], *about which it was said that the little wild boar running away...*

SR: That it was me, yes.

RC: Since the two books are of the same format, I wondered if there was not a self-portrait in diptych...

[29] WB, *Thames & Hudson, Paris and London, 2005.*

[30] English edition: *Details of the World*, Museum of Fine Arts, Boston (USA), 2001.

SR: Yes, the baby boar is really a self-portrait because it didn't know where it was going, but it was going there! Only an artist, not a graphic designer, can make this kind of very personal choice. I made it run across the cover with its snout stumbling on the book title and its tail slipped between my name and the title on the back cover.

RC: On the back cover of WB, *you complete your purpose by quoting a famous phrase from Lucretius… What is striking is to leave Beirut and to arrive on the West Bank to find Lucretius again*[31]. *In the first mention in* Beirut, *Lucretius' text ends on an optimistic note, the possibility of rebirth; whereas in* WB, *there is the feeling that there's no more hope…*

SR: Some, still… because if I write that I'm at war, it means that some action is possible. But it's true that this text is less optimistic, and with the sentence about the shore, I question myself, by saying, "But in the name of what have I mounted this platform, have I recorded these cuts, these modes of separation and all this misfortune that is not directly relevant to me?"

RC: What differentiates your commitment according to the situations you are dealing with?

SR: The situations themselves. What concerned me in the Balkans was that it was happening in the heart of Europe, with our first cousins killing each other. And what were we doing? Or what weren't we doing? I participated in protests in Paris where there were 40 of us, small groups.
As for the Israeli–Palestinian conflict, it is exactly my age. It is so deeply entrenched in the international landscape that it is difficult to see what its resolution might be. This question inspired me the project for another piece with the UN resolutions about Palestine. It may be noted that the last resolution

[31] The full text composed by Sophie Ristelhueber is: "What am I doing here, devastated, on the roof of that car? Am I thinking that 'it's nice to stand safe and sound on the shore watching others struggle amid the wild currents and furious winds?' Not that there is any pleasure to be drawn from someone else's misfortune. But it is pleasant to be preserved from such despair'? No doubt, as an artist, I too am at war."

that explicitly names it dates back to the 1970s. Afterwards, it is only about the Middle East; the word "Palestine" is no longer stated in the title of the resolutions. Words are important.

RC: One year after WB, *you published* Eleven Blowups. *Should this title be considered a reference to Ed Ruscha?*

SR: No ... while I'm a fan of Ruscha, I didn't make the connection. One might also think that it was related to the film *Blow-Up* by Michelangelo Antonioni. But no, for me, it was eleven explosions.

RC: As is often the case, one image was the trigger for this work: that of the crater of the explosion that caused the death of Lebanese Prime Minister Rafic Hariri in Beirut.

SR: An image seen on TV. I wasn't expecting it. I had just hung "WB" at MAMCO in Geneva. I was still in that story, a little down. And there comes the image of this crater that forces its way in; meanwhile in Iraq, there were daily bombings that were terribly deadly. But what could be done? Return to Iraq? The information I could gather indicated that I was going to find myself stuck in the green zone because the rest of the country had become too dangerous for Westerners. Then, I turned to Reuters, and they tell me that they have repatriated to London all their images (photos and videos) made during the bombings of the last three years. So, I went to London to watch the full rushes from 2003 to 2006 on the topic. Nothing was usable as it was, but they were my inspiration to create new images made of material taken from my own photos from Iraq or elsewhere.

RC: So, can we say that you're making a detour through fiction?

SR: Yes. In this work, everything is true, and everything is false. It's not difficult to see that it's totally theatrical. It's easy to see in an image that the sunlight, for example, comes from both the left and the right.

RC: As often, you slipped an excerpt from an ancient text into the artist's book you made. Here, you're quoting the Marshal of Saxony[32]*: "War is a science covered with darkness in the obscurity of which one does not walk in confidence.. [...] All sciences have principles and rules, war has none." If I indulge in a quick textual analysis, it can be understood that if war has no rules, neither does the contemporary artist, apart from those they set for themselves. And if we use the word "science" in its classical 18th-century meaning, it refers to a technique or a craft. In your case, could we then refer to "the science of the artist" to describe your practice from the beginning? Knowing you and your concern to be fair, I can't imagine you searching on the internet for an incidental, convenient quote...*

SR: No, of course. I read the original edition of the Marshal of Saxony's book at the Sainte-Geneviève Library in Paris. I asked for it; the book came, beautiful. I love all these experiences. Whether it is putting both feet on the ground, going to the library or facing for hours and days in the basement of Reuters images of horror. But I manage to get through all this – like when I did *Every One*, and attended surgical procedures in operating rooms – I could handle it because I knew what I was looking for.
At the moment, I'm not tempted by other experiences, or to react to the immediate news; I'm focusing on the UN resolutions, which should take the form of a book, which I would like to be like a huge brick, an object that will question: "What have we done with all this?"

RC: And these resolutions bring us back to the refugee tents set up in 1995 in front of the European headquarters of the United Nations in Geneva, and on which you had screen-printed excerpts from resolutions. In view of the installation, the institution was confronted with its own impotence[33].

[32] *The Marshal of Saxony was a soldier who served under Louis XV. The text selected by Sophie Ristelhueber is an excerpt from* My Daydreams, *The Hague, 1756.*

[33] *The installation "Résolutions" by Sophie Ristelhueber was part of the exhibition "Peace Dialogues" curated by Adelina von Fürstenberg, Geneva, 1995.*

In the same register, the relationship of words to the real, we can mention your artist's book, Operations[34]. *It comprises a list of names of military operations conducted around the world, mostly between the 1980s and 2007, although the oldest dates from 1946. And you have laid out this list of names in an original typographical composition.*

SR: In parallel to the book, there is a video installation showing the words according to the same broken-down layout as in the book, and a soundtrack broadcasting Jean-Claude Risset's[35] ascending chromatic range. It is a sound that never stops, evolving in a kind of endless repetition. The music sounds like the noise of a drone, and it can actually drive you crazy.

RC: I would like to note the first and last names of the operations that you mention: "Days of Penitence" and "Urgent Fury". Does this choice, necessarily meaningful – like Jupiter at the beginning and the end of Beirut *– reflect your state of mind, at some point, in the face of the disconnection of language with reality, of violence…*

SR: I wouldn't say disconnected from reality, but able to conceal it, yes! The use of a text can be genius when it comes from Selimović: it makes us move forward. But it may as well, as with the UN resolutions, allow a community to hide itself behind the words.

RC: While preparing our interview, I saw an exhibition about Allan Sekula: "Photography, A Wonderfully Inadequate Medium"[36]. Would you take that assertion for your own?

[34] *Sophie Ristelhueber,* Opérations, *Le Quartier, Centre d'art de Quimper, limited edition of 450 copies, 2007.*

[35] *Jean-Claude Risset (1938-2016), French composer and a pioneer in computer sound, which he notably introduced at IRCAM (Institute for Research and Coordination in Acoustics/Music).*

[36] *Exhibition conceived by Marie Muracciole at the Marian Goodman Gallery, London, May 2019.*

SR: Yes, it suits me because I have an extremely ambiguous relationship with photography myself. And it bothers me to be defined as a photographer. Why? I don't know. It's stupid. But I don't want to be framed. I made videos, sound pieces…

RC: Videos, sound pieces and… cross-stitching, even?

SR: Cross-stitching, indeed. I used the technique for two pieces; one, "Stitches", about portmanteau words that evoke war, and a series entitled "Untitled", for which I embroidered words or sentences through which I bring forth some of the complex realities of the contemporary world: "Palestinians remain sceptical", "The Turkish issue", "Warm and heavy weather"… I've used a lot of different techniques, but at the same time, even if I've said many times – including to myself – that I was finished with photography, I still came back to it, even quite recently with my "Sunset Years", thinking to myself: "What a wonderful way to express yourself."

10 June 2019

DAYANITA SINGH

Born in 1961 in India, Dayanita Singh lives and works in Delhi. She studied visual communication at the National Institute of Design in Ahmedabad and documentary photography at the ICP (International Center of Photography) in New York City. Her work is included in multiple prestigious public and private collections, including MoMA in New York, the Art Institute of Chicago, the Centre Pompidou in Paris and the National Gallery of Modern Art in New Delhi. She is notably the recipient of the Prince Claus Award and the Robert Gardner Fellowship, and in November 2017, her book Museum Bhavan *won the Paris Photo–Aperture Foundation Photobook of the Year Award. To date, she has authored a dozen books.*

Dayanita Singh explores multiple themes: friendship, long-term work commitment, the necessity to draw life lessons from our encounters, a taste for the archives and memory, and above all, a consuming passion for the book. With all that, she constructs her oeuvre like a living museum. Add to that convictions and unwavering determination, and you get a stunningly delicate body of work. On the day following her conference held at Le Bal, on a pleasant yet already fresh late September morning, we met for tea in the garden of the well-named Eldorado Hotel. Two months later, *Bhavan Museum*, her latest released book, won the prestigious Paris Photo–Aperture Foundation book Award.

Rémi Coignet: *In 1986 you published your first book,* Zakir Hussain, *about the famous musician. I have to say it is the only book of yours I could not consult. You followed Zakir Hussain for three years, if I'm right.*

Dayanita Singh: No, six. Six winters.

RC: What did you learn from him?

DS: I think I learned life lessons from him that I still follow. I really learned focus from him. To just focus on what you're doing. You know, when I met him, I wanted to practise photography, and also calligraphy, and learn how to play the flute, and be a type designer. But watching him so closely, which was a huge privilege, really made me understand the importance of focus and rigour. It doesn't matter how talented you are. The rigour is really important. And Zakir is a genius. He didn't practise every day. He would be with his tabla somewhere, and in the middle of a conversation, he would start calculating his beats. He is one with what he does. Everything else is secondary. So, I think that at the age of 18, to have that kind of mentoring is invaluable.

RC: Was it before or after that book that you met Mary Ellen Mark? How important was it for you to meet her?

DS: Again, it was very important to have met Mary Ellen Mark, because she really advised me to go to New York to the ICP and spoke to my mother – because you know, money was a problem – on the importance of leaving India. And she said: "I know all the men in your profession, they'll never let you be a photographer, so you must get out."

RC: Photographers in India?

DS: Yes. At that time, all the photographers I knew were only men. And I think from her too, I learned tenacity. If you really want something, you can make it happen. There's nothing casual. So that was also very important learning.

RC: You were just speaking about this: what does it mean being a woman photographer in India? Then, or even today?

DS: I don't define myself as a woman photographer.

RC: OK.

DS: I do not participate in any exhibitions or books, as much as I can help it, about women photographers. But in those days, I used to feel bad, because, you know, I wasn't taken seriously.

And now I say thank God they didn't take me seriously, because I could really do my own thing, I played my own part.
There was no problem, we were all great friends. I think it still might be like that. I don't know. I mean, I don't care. But it was good that I didn't become part of the boys' club. I wanted to, of course, very badly, I wanted to go out drinking with them and dress like them. But I was able to do my own thing.
So, it was very good for me, it was very lucky that I didn't get accepted by them.

RC: And why do you not want to be part of women photographers' books or shows?

DS: I don't think the gender is really relevant to how one photographs. Not at all. If it's about bravery or going to a war, that has to do with my personality. That has nothing to do with my gender. If it's about photographing at night, that also has to do with the kind of person you are. I'm so annoyed with the issue of women's photography and women photographers, that I have made the Anna Atkins Award for the best Indian male photographer[1]. [Laughs] It's 50,000 rupees [around 650 euros], and that's no small amount of money. Just for the men to think a little about what does it mean to call someone a "woman photographer". I know that practise has entirely to do with your personality. And then, why the women photographers? Why not the third sex? Why could we not have a category for the queer photographers? Right? Why do we have to make these categories in the first place?

RC: Your second book, Myself Mona Ahmed, *since we are on the gender issue, was released only in 2001, published by Scalo. I have to say that when I read the book, I was amazed to discover that there are still 1 million eunuchs in India. This book is a story of friendship between you and him – or her…*

DS: Her.

[1] *Anna Atkins published the very first photography book in history,* Photographs of British Algae, *in 1843.*

RC: And you spent 13 years on it. My question is, but you already partially answered, is the gender question important for you?

DS: No. In fact, I know that book is a very important book, but I see it as a complete failure because at the end of it, people only know Mona as the eunuch. They don't know her as the very unique person she was. She was exceptional. I don't know how. It's not that she was highly educated, but it's really from Mona that I learned how to live your life on your own terms. How you can live outside the box. She chose to live in a graveyard. She wanted to live in an open space. She didn't like to be in an enclosed space. She was a misfit in any society, not just the eunuch society. She passed away two weeks ago.

RC: Oh, I'm sorry about that.

DS: Yes. It was awful. I was on video call with her when she passed away. Even if it was great that they wrote about her in the newspapers in India, it made me cringe, however, when they wrote "the famous, iconic *hijra*" – which is the word used for people who are neither man nor woman. To some, I was able to say: "Could you change the word to 'eunuch'?" Because her gender was not everything. I think the book was really a failure because in the end, you still think of her as a eunuch and not as this exceptional spirit who had the courage that maybe hundreds of men and women would not have.

RC: But I'm not sure it's a failure, because the reader also discovers the amazing story of her daughter. And one thing that strikes me in the book is the emails she sent to Walter Keller [Publisher of Scalo]. So, you have this, let's say, very traditional caste of eunuchs, and at the same time, she was using the internet. Could it be seen as a mirror of today's India?

DS: I don't know, but that was Mona. Mona was a lot of different people. There were many different sides to her. Even today I was telling a writer that he could write at least four different books about Mona. Because she had so many facets to her personality and she was very interested in technology. In those days, you had to connect to the internet through the telephone and there was a sound when the connection happened. You remember that?

RC: Yes, yes. [Both mimicking the sound of a 56K modem and laughing]

DS: And she loved that. And what she liked about the internet was that I was not correcting what she was saying. You know, because then, I would have become an editor. I was just her transcriber. And I think this is the strength of the book. It is her story told the way she wanted ...

RC: And she always started her messages with: "Dear Mr Walter..."

DS: Yes, and she would end with "Blessings". She always said, "This is not my true story, I would make another book." She could constantly reinvent herself. I could have made 10 books on her.

RC: Your following book, Privacy, *the first published with Steidl, pictures high-society families in India. You had been working during the previous 10 years as a photojournalist...*

DS: Not 10, three years.

RC: OK. Is this book a will to escape the stereotypical depiction of India? I mean, crowded trains, Varanasi, poverty...

DS: Yes, absolutely. I was a photojournalist for two or three years from 1989 to about 1991–92, because I thought it was the only way to be a photographer. You didn't think of exhibitions or anything else, really. Either you were a fashion photographer, or you were a photojournalist; so, I think I reached a point where, with photojournalism, I realized that either I had to become an activist, like when I was working with the children or the prostitutes; or otherwise, I would be just another pimp.

And I couldn't bare that. I think there is something very sick here. Nothing changed for the girls that I was photographing. And nothing changed for the issue either. I was just becoming more and more well known, and every foreign photographer who came to India would be calling me, asking, “Could you arrange a meeting with the little child prostitutes?”

And I thought this was disgusting. Then I wondered, what am I going do? What am I going to photograph?

I thought that if I could photograph all my friends and their friends and give them prints, then those prints would hang in their homes, and if at the end of my life, 300 such homes had my portraits, that's it. I would be very happy. It's better than any exhibition in any museum, no? Because you live in people's family archives. So, that's what I started. I started photographing families in 1992, very slowly because film was expensive. With one roll I might shoot three or four families. I'd go to Calcutta, stay with friends for three weeks or a month. So, really living off my friends, sleeping on sofas or wherever I could, and making these portraits. And then the problem was to make the prints, because we used to buy 100-foot rolls of film and cut them up. So I was doing that. It was big enough to make a contact sheet. But to make prints was very expensive. Through Walter Keller, Robert Frank heard about this project of mine. And in 1997 I got a grant of 10,000 dollars from him. Today, if you give me 100 million, 10 times 100 million, nothing can be as important as those 10,000 dollars. So, from 1997 to 2001, I stretched that 10,000 dollars and was able to give people prints.

Most of the *Privacy* book actually comes from this money. Robert Frank didn't want anything; he didn't want any credit. I was so surprised! In the beginning, I told his lawyers, “Why is he doing that? What does he want from me? These are family portraits, I can't give them to him.” And they said that Robert said, “If you don't want them, you can throw them in the sea; it's for you to do what you want.” And I thought that is a great lesson in giving. You give, and the person does what they want, buy a car or an apartment. if someday I'm able to make a grant, I think it would be something in Mona's name.

RC: That's a beautiful story!

DS: But all because Robert Frank showed me that generosity. And you just pass it on, no?

RC: I have the feeling that the pictures on the walls, animals from Africa, Christ, Pandit Nehru ... are one important element in this book. What do they mean?

DS: It's very interesting that you ask about that, because in *Museum Bhavan,* I made a museum of photography; and again, like there is the notion of gender, there comes also the notion of nationality, of "Indian photography" – I can't stand it! We don't talk like this in the Western part of the world. But when it comes to my part of the world, then you see a Bangladeshi photography, etc. But why? If photography is this universal language, then why do you want to put categories? Anyway. I forgot what was the question ...

RC: The importance of all these images on the walls.

DS: Yes, then we started to have Indian photography shows, and I thought this is really bullshit because, consider Japanese photography, you can understand why you have a show of Japanese photography, because very important photography movements started there that influenced photographers all around the world, even today. So yes. But, nothing so radical happened with Indian photography; yes, there were a lot of photographers in India, so what? And then I thought that we do have a special connection to photography. And that's when I made this photo museum, the first book for it, because of how we live with images. A museum that can be visited privately. Because it's in *Privacy* that I started to notice the way people live with their imagery, and in *Privacy,* I started to photograph just the imagery, without the people. I didn't even completely register it at that time. It's only when this Indian photography bubble started about 2006 or 2007 that I went back to all that work to make a little booklet to show to curators; to show that if you really want to do something about photography from India, do your research and do something on our relationship with the images. It is a fantastic PhD study to be done. It would be a fantastic exhibition. But it requires a lot of research and it hasn't happened. So I did my own photography museum. And yes, the seed for the photography museum which is *Museum Bhavan* now was actually in *Privacy*. I am amazed you picked up on that.

RC: This is striking to me. What's the meaning of the following book you published, Chairs, *in which, as suggested in the tittle, one can only see chairs?*

DS: That's not only chairs. They are portraits, they have nationalities, they have genders. There's a ballerina chair, there's a grandfather chair. So there, I'm all for gender, nationalities and geography. But the interesting thing with the *Chairs* book was really the dissemination of it. And to me, that is the most significant aspect of photography. I was talking about it last night as well at Le Bal. Because photography is my medium, my raw material, the dissemination of the work becomes really important. If I were a sculptor or a painter, I don't think I would have been so focused on dissemination. And the *Chairs* book to me was a great example of how one could take dissemination away from the distributor. It is an artist's book that I wanted to distribute myself. And this is what I was told: "Oh! Come on, Dayanita, how are you going to distribute a thousand copies?" So, I told them to keep 500 for their trustees and people they had to send it out to, but none of these were to be sold. And they had to pay for the other 500 copies that I sent to 50 "distributors" around the world: so, for example, in Zurich, Urs Stahel got 10; Christoph Schifferli got 10; Jonathan Watkins in Birmingham got 10. And Jonathan said: "This is too elitist, I'm going to give the 10 books to the 10 first persons I meet today" – the bus conductor, the cleaner at his museum, the bookshop seller, the waiter at the café… Some people kept it in their drawers and only gave them away to people who were really interested.
And then I had the great honour of meeting Sol LeWitt in Connecticut. And I thought, what does one bring to a genius like Sol LeWitt? You can't just take flowers, somehow that's not enough. I knew he loved books and was a great master and supporter of the book. So, I took one of my 10 copies of *Chairs*. And he laughed and he gave it back to me and said

that I had to keep it, he had three already. [Laughs] All this because three of my distributors had thought they must give one to Sol LeWitt. So that *Chairs* book was very liberating for me to understand that there are other ways of dissemination. And this is something that only photography – maybe there are others also – but photography is made for. And I also learned that from my few years in photojournalism. And while years later, by the time of the *Chairs* book, I was very much part of the art world, it was not enough for me, because at the heart of my work is the book. To me, the exhibition was the catalogue of the images in the book, as if the book had been taken apart and put on the wall, which always made me feel a little uncomfortable. And I always wanted to insert my books into the frame. So that was the great thing with the *Chairs* book for me. Other than the format and the fact that it took 40 minutes to print at Steidl's. It was probably his fastest printed book. But beautifully printed. It was about dissemination and it was about friendship. And I still don't know where those books have gone; it could be that someone reviewed one and I don't know.

RC: There's a copy at the Maison Européenne de la Photographie's library here in Paris. [Chuckles] In 2007 you published Go Away Closer, *and I have the feeling this book was a turning point ...*

DS: Yes.

RC: And it heralded Sent a Letter.

DS: Yes.

RC: I mean that maybe you distanced yourself from a documentary style to move to something more "poetic", even if I don't like that word. What do you think?

DS: You're absolutely right. I think photographing empty spaces for *Privacy* was one big turning point in 2000, and then making *Go Away Closer* was a huge shift for me, and for that, I must say, I have to credit Urs Stahel. He had come to India and looked at a lot of my work. It was always in these separate sections, you

know, the family portraits, the chairs, etc. And he said, "You have to mix it up." And I said, "No, no, no, you can't have the pictures of prostitutes in the middle of the families. It's not right. How can we do that?" And he showed me a book that he had edited for Anders Petersen [see *Conversations*, p. 218] for Winterthur[2]. A beautiful book. It's a novel, really. You can feel the editing but you can't describe it. Not that the Swiss style is my cup of tea, it's something else. It's as though it was edited with an emotion. And then, at that same time, I was in Kolkata and I photographed the girl on the bed – you know, my friend's daughter, whom I'd been photographing since 1992. She was just running away and then laid down on the bed and I took the picture. And at that moment when I took the picture, the words "go away closer" came to me. I knew that I had photographed with that emotion before. But I hadn't done anything with those pictures because they were sidies – you know, pictures you take on the side. So I went back to Delhi and I took out all those photos, the sidies. And then I made prints and I went to my house in Goa where I have a lot of long tables, and I put Mahler's first symphony, second movement on repeat for a week, or two weeks I think, but 24 hours a day, even when I was sleeping. [Chuckles] And I think the key to editing is really the music you're listening to, or the silence. The sound has to be a very conscious choice, and that really affects the editing. Now, I can't even aspire to be Mahler's toenail. But if you set yourself up for that, that symphony, just that movement has all the human emotions in it. It's incredible, the gravitas, the humour ... You think of so many different emotions in that one piece ... And I wondered: can I do that in a book? And of course you can't do that in a book, and of course you can't do it in photography. But what is the harm in trying? And that's what *Go Away Closer* was: an attempt to see if one can just really edit with the emotion. I could even go so far as to say "edit by listening to the photographs". And not visually. So that was a big, big turning point for me, and again I'm amazed that you picked up on that.
And parallel to that, I had been making these books for friends

[2] *Anders Petersen,* Ich Dich lieben, du mich auch, *Fotomuseum Winterthur & Schaden, 2002.*

which formed *Sent a Letter*. Travelling with them and making two copies, one for my friends and the other for myself. That allowed me to mix up all these images. If I was making one for you, there would be a picture of the cross out there, the tea pot here. It's not like there would be a picture of you, but of your scarf on the chair, something like that. So, *Go Away Closer* really freed me; it allowed for *Sent a Letter* to take shape. I had been making those books since 2002. So, it was there already, this mixing, but I would never have imagined putting it out.

RC: You mean publishing them?

DS: Yes. It was just for me and one friend, whoever it was made for. It wasn't made to be shown. So when I made one for Gerhard Steidl [see *Conversations 2*, p. 210] from the Kolkata trip, he was so happy because he was really fed up with all the big books he was making, and he said: "We have to print it, I want to print all of them!" There were 32 books and I couldn't afford to make prints for 32 books! I said that I couldn't do that, and his reply was: "OK, so then we do seven." And that's how *Sent a Letter* was made. That's probably the answer to your next question.

RC: Yes. [Laughs] That's nice to hear you talk about music and editing. You'll see that in my book, it's a question I often ask photographers, whether editing is something that can compare to musical composition.

DS: Really?

RC: I was wondering whether your fascination with museums came from Sent a Letter.

DS: No, I've been fascinated with museums since the 1990s. It was really my way of accessing a place. So if I came to Paris, I would try to research and find out which were the house-museums here. I was fascinated by the house-museums of writers, musicians, composers. I went to Budapest to the Liszt museum, the Bartok museum, to photograph their houses, but also the view, and that was fantastic. I think museums are also part of me because in those days, not anymore, but then, middle-class homes had these sorts of wonder cabinets in the houses, a niche built in the wall with glass in front, usually sliding doors, and you would keep adding your souvenirs. So there would be an Eiffel Tower, a Japanese doll, an Air India maharaja figurine, little whisky bottles ... Because in those days travelling was such a big deal, you would make these little museums in your own house. I don't know, I just grew up in a house where, for example, all the keys of the house were in a glass case with labels, because my parents were like that, labelling things, organizing them. So I think the museum actually didn't come from just going to the museums, but probably from that cabinet in my house, which we were not allowed to touch.

> *RC: Coming back for a second to* Sent a Letter, *one volume is about a trip with Gerhard Steidl, for example. And he once said about you that you were "a genius of book making". What would you say about him?*

DS: I think he is the genius of printing and the idea of the book. Consider what he does for the great, the master photographers like Lewis Baltz [see *Conversations*, p. 30]. Now he isn't there anymore. A whole generation wouldn't really be able to access him, or only through a book here or there, perhaps. But he made that wonderful set with Baltz. And he made two sets like that for Eggleston, for Bruce Davidson, all the Robert Frank books. Can you think of any publisher in the world that has that kind of commitment to their authors? He was just in Kobe in Japan for an exhibition for Robert Frank. He goes himself with this roll under his arm and pastes it on the wall, and then it has to be destroyed because he doesn't want it to have value. So, he is also an exceptional mind. And he loves challenges. I think that's why we get along so well, because I'm always pushing things a little bit. He gets really annoyed with me, but then he's also very happy with what we do in the end. So, I'm very lucky, very, very lucky to have him as a publisher and to have Frith Street as a gallery, because neither one pushes me to do anything. You know how it is in the art world now, all these art fairs, how you can't say no to that exhibition. Nothing – I have no pressure. I feel really blessed to have Steidl on one hand and Jane Hamlyn on the other. I mean, what more could an artist, or a book artist, ask for? And even if the book and the gallery are two different worlds, Jane completely understands that the book has to be there. You cannot take the book away from me. You can take the gallery away from me, the museum away from me, but you cannot take the book away from me.

RC: The last volume in Sent a Letter *is called "Nona Singh" and is made up of pictures taken by your mother. I wonder how for you, public and private memory combine?*

DS: I'm sorry, I'm going to ask you to repeat that question because it's my mother's birthday today, and she'll be delighted that somebody sitting in Paris is asking. [Takes out her phone to record the repeated question.]
Oh, totally, because my mother was an obsessive photographer. I was her favourite subject since I was the first born.
So, photography was also something that annoyed me as a child, and possibly the last thing I wanted to do was to become a photographer. Because every departure was delayed by her picture making and I was a way for her to validate her experience as well as make beautiful images. But I think even my empty spaces are tributes to images I saw her make.
But your question was about public and private memory: totally; I'm unable to separate the two, and I suppose you could even think of it as a criticism of my work, that I can never be objective. If you say to me, "Dayanita, I have a project for us to do: a book on such and such, or on this museum" – if I don't have a connection to it, I really can't do it, and you can see it in the images that would come out of it. So, my commissioned work, the little that there is, is terrible, because there, I don't take risks, or at least I couldn't take risks. So, they are OK pictures but there is nothing more to them.

RC: They have no soul?

DS: Yes. And where does that soul come from? Where does that something else come from? I think that really comes from what you bring to it. And what you bring to it is not just your personal memory; it is also the books you read, and the music you listened to, and the architecture you have experienced. Earlier I talked a lot about music and literature, but I would like to add architecture to that. When you experience Geoffrey Bawa's Kandalama hotel, it's something that is bound to change the way you think of the book, the way you think of photographing. When you see [Kenzō] Tange's work in Japan, or the Kanazawa art museum, you go into these incredible architectural spaces. It does something inside. And then you'll bring all of that to your work, if you can. But I'm sure it'll come. So when younger people want to come and study with me (which I don't do because somehow I don't), I often give them *Austerlitz* to read ...

RC: Austerlitz *by W. G. Sebald?*

DS: Yes, that's my favourite photography book. If they don't get it, then we're not meant to be. And nobody comes back. Because for them, it's a writer's book. And I think it's a photobook. If I have to put on a table five books that have shaped how I think about photography, that would be the first one.

*RC: I had talks with Daniel Blaufuks, [**see* Conversations, *p. 42 and* Conversations 2, *p. 22**]. He's a Portuguese photographer who's really committed to Sebald and* Austerlitz.

DS: Really? There's a fantastic book, *Photography after Sebald*[3], please try to look at it.

RC: Can you explain the idea behind Museum of Chance *and* Museum Bhavan *in exhibition form? I have the feeling that the concept is difficult to understand for someone like me who could not experiment with it.*

DS: I know. So, *Museum of Chance* was the main museum, and I asked Gerhard Steidl if we could make a book for it. And he said yes. And then I worked with Walter Keller on the editing. Walter has always been a very important person in my life. And when we made the book ... there are 88 images

[3] Searching for Sebald: Photography after Sebald, *Institute of Cultural Inquiry, 2007*

in the book, and I asked Gerhard if we could have 88 different covers. And he said that I was completely crazy. And I said, "Gerhard, I want to make exhibitions where shipping and insurance isn't a big issue." And you know that if you want to have an exhibition in that hotel, you have to send prints over, you have to think about security, about insurance, about shipping, all kinds of things like loan agreements. But with *Museum of Chance*, you could walk into a bookshop and find maybe 5, 10 or 30 different covers and the bookseller could put up an exhibition with them. Someone in New York did that. Whereas when you order it on Amazon, you only know what you get when you get it.
But the idea was really to take the people away from online and to make them go to the bookshop. Because if you like the image of the man with the keys on the cover, you can't order that online. You need to go to the bookshop and look for it, and maybe you'll see another cover. So, the exhibitions happened by putting 88 books – 44 fronts, 44 backs – on the wall[4]. Initially with clips, and after that I developed this structure that is a very ...

RC: A wooden structure.

DS: Yes. Like a frame that you slip the book into and put on the wall. And then I built a suitcase that can contain 44 books. And you can put them on the wall, and you can keep changing the front and the back of the books displayed continuously. That became another kind of exhibition making. And I was very happy last year at the MMK [Museum of Modern Art] in Frankfurt. They had the *Museum of Chance* books on one wall, *Sent a Letter* on another wall and *File Room* on a third one. So the *Museum of Chance* book really convinced me that it was possible to make an exhibition with the book. An exhibition as glorious as an exhibition with silver prints. And so when I have exhibitions of the books in Bombay, in different places, I want them exactly like I used to have the exhibitions of my gelatin

[4] *Apparently, the deal made between Dayanita Singh and Steidl was not to do 88 covers, but 44, each with the same image embossed on the fronts, and a random choice of images for the backs.*

silver prints. I want to take away that distinction that's in people's mind about the print and the book. And I can do that because I work with Steidl. Because he can give me the quality that sometimes is even better than the print's.
And now that I make digital prints, there's no doubt in my mind: my heart is with the offset print, not with the digital print. When I made silver prints, yes, I loved that paper. But it's different with the digital print. I actually prefer offset, so now I call myself an offset artist. [Chuckles] So, *Museum of Chance* gave me the opportunity to have a proper exhibition, and then *Museum Bhavan* ...

RC: The idea is the same, no?

DS: No, it's different. Have you seen *Museum Bhavan*?

RC: Yes, of course.

DS: It's a leporello.

RC: Yes, in exhibition form.

DS: Yes, but with *Museum Bhavan,* I was able to make each box unique. You see, the problem with the book is that it's always so mass produced. If you don't get it here, you can get it somewhere else or you can order it online. And I thought, what is it that is stopping the book from having value? I think the book is the most undervalued thing. And in my dream world, I would have a very, very special book, and then there would be an e-version of the book, or a small paperback version. So, I really want to stretch the gap between hardback and paperback. I want the hardback to be as valuable as my prints. Someday ... There is no harm in dreaming. So, how do I make this book into such an object of desire? With *Museum of Chance*, there were 88 covers – you can make a calculation of how many covers exist of that in the end; they also had different cloths covering them. So, it's possible that there were unique ones, but maybe not. But with the *Museum Bhavan* book, I was able to make these boxes in India where each one is unique. So, you're forced to come to one of my events, or to go to a bookshop, to select your own box. And once you've started choosing your box, I've hooked you into my process, and it's really an invitation for you to be the curator of my work, for you to have an opening of my work. You could decide this Saturday to have a Dayanita Singh opening on your terrace if it's a lovely day. You do what you like with it. It's your book. You have an opening for it and you pack it away. This *Museum Bhavan* pocket museum idea really came because the larger museums that I'd been doing – which were almost like *Sent a Letter* on steroids, except that you could change the images on them all the time – were in fact meant to be for my house. I was going to live with all these museums. My house was going to be the Museum Bhavan. And gradually, the museums started to get acquired by other museums, which is something I hadn't anticipated. Then, when *Museum of Chance* was acquired by MoMA, I thought that on one hand it was great, it was fantastic, of course; but on the other hand, I felt: "But what do I have?" Again, the conversation with Gerhard: could we make a mini *Museum Bhavan*? And then came the idea of the boxes. He thought these boxes could be made in India, like for *Sent a Letter*. And I said, "No, Gerhard, this time I want 3,000 different boxes." And he said: "This is bullshit, this is just too much." And I know that the secret is to tell him all these things at night, so he can sleep over it. And in the morning, he came and said OK. I went back to India, spoke to my friend who did accordion books, and told her I wanted to make boxes and I wanted each one to be different. She then showed me this fabric that we had worked with before, which is the under-cloth of block printing. So, if this is the table, you put a sheet on it and then over it, you put the fabric to be printed. So each box is made from the fabric below, which is the accumulation of ...

RC: Ink.

DS: Yes, ink. And so that's why I don't know what colour your box is. But the ones that are black, it's because hundreds and hundreds of metres of material have been printed on them. So, it's not uniform anywhere. And no two boxes are the same! So now what you call my *Museum Bhavan,* is it unique? Is it mass produced? It's both. Is it a work of art? Is it a book?

RC: That's fantastic!

DS: Yes. That's why I'm doing this tour[5] and why I'm so excited by it. I don't even think everybody gets all the aspects of it. But I thought that if I'm so clear about this, it's really part of my work to move around, to talk about it.

RC: Talking about the work is still working.

DS: Yes. And in talking about the work, the suitcases came, which I will show tomorrow at the Tate; and the jacket came, which I wore last night with the nine pockets. And I don't know what else will come. It was wonderful in Zurich the other day, people were arguing with each other about the boxes, saying: "I saw this one first, I should have that." And I actually took a box from somebody else, because I saw a box that I loved and I had not seen before, it had a big red dot on it. So, I said: "Excuse me, but this one is for me." And the person, he was the Steidl representative, was really annoyed, saying: "You can't do that." And I said, "No, no, no, it's my book, I can do that." And I took it from him. [Chuckles]
It was really important for me that people chose their box. I believe that in that choice, I hook you in the process of my work; but also, you own it differently. It's like if you mail-ordered that scarf, for example, it's fine. But if you got that scarf when you went to Vietnam, it's then loaded with meaning, no?

RC: Certainly.

DS: It's the same for the people who bought the boxes yesterday. And the other aspect about the 10 to 20 people who may have bought the box last night is, can you imagine what a privilege

[5] *When I met Dayanita Singh in September 2017 in Paris, she had arrived from Milan, where she had presented her project at the MiCamera bookstore and gallery. She had given a conference the night before at Le Bal in Paris and was flying off to London and the Tate after our conversation, and probably to more European cities afterwards.*

it is for me as an artist to think that my box is now possibly curated in 10 or 20 homes? And if not today, maybe in a year, or maybe in 10 years. And then, if you have *Sent a Letter* as well ... Do you?

RC: Yes.

DS: Great, so now you have 16 exhibitions of my work – 15 of mine and 1 of my mother's. So, you could do a museum show of mine without asking me. Without paying any shipping or insurance, which are becoming really big issues with museum exhibitions. We have to think of other formats for the book. Because this *Bhavan Museum* experience, the box, the smell of the box, the opening of the box, that is not an online experience.

RC: True.

DS: You know, I could see that *Privacy* could be an online book, possibly. I would hate it, but it could be. But *Museum Bhavan* can't be ... it's a physical, tactile object that you have to hold in your hands and close to you if you want to see it; you can't just come to an exhibition and look like that. You have to come close to it or you get nothing. So, the scale of it is really important to me.

RC: I would like to come back to Dream Villa. *It is one of your only colour books ...*

DS: With *Blue Book.*

RC: True. All pictures are taken at night. I have to confess I never really understood the meaning of this book...

DS: *Dream Villa* is for me like a hallucinogenic experience of the night, because the night makes everything look so different. So it's all about where the light falls, and what the light does to the darkness. It was a kind of fictional idea, coming more from cinema really than from photography. So, the tittle *Dream Villa,* is it a dream? Is it a nightmare?

Am I hallucinating? Is it like some drug experience? Or is it like the horror that you get before or after an epileptic attack?
All those things were in my head and I was making those images to see what happens to colour in that darkness. *Blue Book* was made by accident, because I didn't know that I should be using tungsten films after daylight and so everything came out blue. And that's when I thought, maybe I can work in colour, because maybe I've found a way of my own with colour. But in *Dream Villa,* I went further into the night because in India, that light quality only lasts for 15 minutes – 15 minutes after sunset and before it becomes dark. I don't know if it would be the same in the light here, but in India it was very short, and this took me to *Dream Villa,* and then it became about the night and what happens at night to the scenes you know so well in the day. Binding and fabrication was another process. Because the printing was delicious, seductive, we made this book in which the gutter goes through the images, to irritate people.

RC: And the paper is very glossy.

DS: Yes, so you see the reflection on each side. And the binding is so tight you can't even open it flat. It's not really a functional book. In a way, someone could say that it's a book object: there are no page numbers, it doesn't lie flat, you can't see the full images, it's always reflecting the other side. And *Blue Book,* which would have made a beautiful large book, we made it as a book of postcards.

RC: In 2013 you published File Room. *Are archives museums?*

DS: Yes, archives are part of museums and I would love if archives became museums, but to be a museum I think a part of the collection has to be open to the public. And that doesn't happen with archives. But I'm trying with an archive in India to turn it into a museum, and it would be so easy to do it. It just means putting glass walls so that people can't access every part of the archive, but they could certainly walk through it, and that's an amazing experience. I worked in Venice with the state archive, and just the privilege of walking through 600 years, 700 years of records is immeasurable.

RC: I feel that File Room *is very polysemous. We can see it as a critic of bureaucracy, or instead as a celebration of the largest democracy on earth, or yet again as work inspired by Joseph Beuys, for example. What is your feeling?*

DS: There is an Indian musician, TM Krishna, whose music and voice I love. I asked him to launch the *File Room* for me and he said something amazing at the opening. He said: "Firstly, I don't know why we call Dayanita a black-and-white photographer because her photographs are everything but black and white. They exist in the grey area only." That was his reading. *File Room* is not a book about paper, it's a book about how our mind works and how we record all these stories in our mind. I thought it was incredible and I was very happy with that, making a book that anyone could make their completely own version of it. *File Room* is all those things you said, and more. To me a successful book is one in which people can really bring their story to it. And with the archives, I really have "archive fever". I cannot stop photographing archives; I made a book, exhibitions, screenings. I don't think anyone wants to see my archives anymore, but I can't stop photographing just because nobody is interested. I still photograph archives and I will make another book with archives, you can be sure. Maybe nobody got it, but last night I was also talking about embracing failure. Failure is such a capitalistic word. When we made *Museum Bhavan*, we had no idea if people would want this object. I'm sure Steidl has put a lot of money into it and I'm not sure he will recover it all. We don't know how much of it he will sell. But you still do it. And I guess that's the strength that comes from being an artist. After many, many years, I feel I have to do this, and maybe nobody is interested, but I can't help it. I can't help doing archives.

RC: For me, you're actually defining what it is to be an artist.

DS: Yes. You can't be doing your work thinking about whether people will want it or not.

RC: About Museum Bhavan *again, there are nine volumes ... [Dayanita Singh looks at her watch as she has a plane to catch at Roissy Airport] ... We will end soon. Each volume being the museum of something, the "Little Ladies Museum", the "Printing Press Museum", etc. Are you now trying to create typologies?*

DS: You know, when I started to make the "museums", I wanted to have the typologies of museums: museum of photography, museum of furniture ... because those could be existing museums. But by the time I came to *Museum of Chance*, I started to feel that I didn't have to do what museums do. I must free myself from all those typologies. And so I made *Museum of Chance*, which is really based on images that happened by chance and came together by chance. So I made the typologies at the start and then let them go.

RC: So that's why, for example, in the "Printing Press Museum", there's a portrait of Gerhard Steidl in the middle ... [Laughs]

DS: It's so important to dislocate the reader. People see a printing press, and another printing press, and suddenly ... I don't make the distinction; it's all meant to be together. But I can see that for the reader, it would suddenly startle them. Another example: the blank page, which as you know is important in a photobook. People would say, "Oh, ma'am, you left out one page, there's no image there." So yes, you must give yourself the freedom to play with your work, not take it so seriously all the time. And you know, if I feel like putting a bed in the middle of the "Printing Press Museum", I could do that too, because maybe I think a bed must be there for the printer. I don't have to justify it as long it feels right in the editing.

RC: This is my last question. Is the other defining notion of being an artist to be playful, to like to tease?

DS: But of course! Life would be so boring otherwise. And what would be the point? Because you must tease, provoke, challenge yourself, but also the viewer. Like *Dream Villa* – that clearly has provoked a lot of people who would ask, “Why did you do this to these images?” I think it’s fantastic. I like to pull the rug from under people’s feet all the time, and say, “OK, now what’s going to happen?” And then, something else happens. Because I’m always open to possibilities. I don’t say, “Well, let’s do the *Museum Bhavan* book and boxes, and then it’s over.” Not at all. A suitcase got made, the dress was made, and I don’t know what will happen by the time Sunday comes ...

29 September 2017

CARLOS SPOTTORNO

Carlos Spottorno was born in Budapest in 1971. He lives and works in Madrid, Spain. He is two-time winner of the World Press Photo, in 2003 and 2015. He also won the Kassel Photobook Award in 2013 for The Pigs*, received a Special Mention from the Paris Photo-Aperture Foundation PhotoBook Award for* La Grieta *in 2017, and was nominated for many other awards. He is the author of six books.*

Far from the image of the adventurer out in the field, Carlos Spottorno has the slightly old-fashioned elegance of a polyglot globetrotter, at ease in an upscale ski resort in the Swiss Alps as much as he is with migrants. It is no insult to him to say that his first books went somewhat unnoticed despite their quality. Perhaps the explanation lies in their classical form. While he is the most pleasant man there is, Carlos Spottorno is not without ambition when it comes to his practice. So, he decided to respond. When *The Pigs* was released in 2013, the small world of the photography book got passionate about this jubilant work: we had never seen such a taste for paradox blended with self-deprecation. To strike a chord, Spottorno applied the know-how acquired during his career in advertising to serve his personal work. In 2015, *Wealth Management*, a counterpart to the former, was just as well received.

In 2016, eager to reach out to an audience beyond the small, traditional photobook community, the ingenious Spaniard released *La Grieta* with journalist Guillermo Abril, the result of their joint reports at the borders of the European Union in the form of a graphic novel with specialist publisher Astiberri. The first print run of 3,000 copies sold out fast and soon had to be extended. The book, whose texts are crucial, has been translated into French, German, Italian and Japanese. Surprisingly, no British publisher has, it seems, expressed interest so far ... All these versions reach a print run probably unheard of for a photographer who is little known to the general public. This public conversation with Carlos Spottorno about his work and the theme "transgressing the forms of the photobook" took place at the Henri Cartier-Bresson Foundation.

Rémi Coignet: Carlos, even if I don't believe that, in photography as in literature, biography can explain the work, can you tell us what your life was like before becoming a photographer?

Carlos Spottorno: Good evening. Two minutes to thank you for coming here tonight. You're not at Photo London or at the Prix Niépce[1], so it's great to have you here. Thank you to the Foundation for inviting me. I am very happy; and besides, Paris is an important city for me. I lived here for two years as a teenager, a stay that left a lasting and deep mark on me. I agree with the question of the relationship of the biographical with the work. You told me about this before this conversation, and I understand why you are asking me. Two or three facts probably might be of interest to understand my relationship with the book. First, my parents – nothing very original. Parents do have a certain influence ... My father was a diplomat, which is why I was born in Budapest. We were thus living in Hungary at the time. My mother is a visual artist; she is not famous, but I was marked by her artistic sensibility. That's how I got interested in international affairs and politics from a very young age. As a teenager, I read the newspapers, I tried to understand, because my father pushed me there. When I was 14 years old, we would read the papers together during meals and we talked: "See what happened in China? ... You will see in a week, something else will happen in Russia." I've had this kind of thinking process since I was very, very young. And on the other hand, my mother's artistic bend led me to study fine arts, painting in particular ...

RC: You studied in Rome.

CS: I studied in Rome, that's right. I've lived there over several periods of time, nine years in all. So, yes, I feel a little bit Italian as well. Those two aspects are important to me. I studied painting, and obviously, I didn't become a painter. When I was old enough to work, I just think I realized that being alone

[1] *Both events were held on the same day as this conversation.*

in a workshop, without ever meeting anyone, was somewhat painful for me. And I looked for another way. I wanted to work, I wanted to earn money, like any other young person, I guess. I started working in advertising and for six years I was artistic director in a major advertising firm, creating adverts for TV or for magazines, with photography, design ... What's going on?

RC: It's raining.[2]

CS: I did this job for quite a while, and after a few years, I got bored too. I wanted to make a living from photography. Part of my job was to collaborate with photographers. I saw what they were doing, I liked it, and I wanted to do the same. For a few years, I did advertising photography, but the truth is that from the beginning, my goal was to practise documentary photography: to see the world, to know it, to understand it. I was talking about my father earlier, and I was interested in international relations, the relations between global powers. I want to understand macro-politics, macro-history. That's how I started to be able to create my own stories through photography.

RC: Before I get to our main topic, I would like to quickly mention your first books. What do they have in common?

CS: Which first ones are you talking about? There's *The Pigs* and *Wealth Management.*

RC: No, before that, China Western *and* History Seekers.

CS: One thing in common? With *History Seekers,* I don't know. Is there one thing in common, I'm not sure ...

RC: It's a form of typology.

[2] *In 2017 the Henri Cartier-Bresson Foundation was still housed in the artist's workshop, Impasse Lebouis in Montparnasse, and the conversation was held on the top floor, under a glass rooftop. The Foundation has since moved to a new home, 79 Rue des Archives in Le Marais.*

CS: Yes. They're portraits. I went to Egypt, thanks to a commission from the Spanish *National Geographic* to cover a story about Spanish archaeologists. I spent a month or so with them.
After doing the work that was expected of me, one day I thought: I will make a portrait of the Egyptian workers who are not archaeologists but who, in reality, are the ones who, with their own bare hands, discover these objects dating back 3,000 or 4,000 years. I then thought about making a book about these guys with turbans that find the objects that can then be seen in the Louvre.
After that, I wanted to make a very exotic story, on a topic I didn't know, something new. I searched like crazy for a story that had not yet been dealt with. And I felt like I found it in 2006, when I discovered that there was a region in China called Xinjiang[3]. It's a huge province, two or three times the size of France, populated by only 20 million people. In terms of China, it's obviously very, very little. This place is empty, mostly deserts and mountains. And the population is Muslim.
I did some further research, I looked – it was then a very little-known place. I looked for any books on the matter and couldn't find any. Some photographers had travelled there but there were no books. Which is a miracle in itself!
Any photographer, any writer, any bookmaker knows that all topics have already been dealt with. So, when you find one ...
Well, at least, I was not able to find anything about it.
It encouraged me to go and see. I made a book out of it that I still love today. I think it's very well done, it's a good book, but very classic.

RC: I'd like to say a word about the title of the book. I feel that in China Western, *there is already a characteristic feature of your approach that will be amplified in your following books: the play on paradox. Indeed, when we talk about westerns in the West, we think of the United States, cowboy movies, not of China. It seems to me that this taste for the combination of opposites is totally characteristic of your work. How do you feel about this?*

[3] *As we know, Xinjiang Province has since made the headlines.*

CS: I guess you're right, because when I search for the titles of my books, I think about it a lot. I work with the same method I used in advertising. When I searched for a title for *China Western*, I wanted one that could be understood by anyone. Quite naturally, English words, but that everyone can know. That is to say, China is understandable in almost any language, at least Western languages. And "western" is a geographical definition. Literally, the title indicates that it's about western China, but at the same time, it refers to western films, pioneer stories, cowboys, gold seekers, the Frontier, and confronting the "native Americans". And I found some connections with what may have happened in Xinjiang, where Muslim Uighurs are the local population; suddenly, the Chinese Hans burst in, searching for natural resources, and sometimes found themselves in conflict with the locals.

RC: OK. Let's get to The Pigs[4]*, published in 2013, which for me marks the turning point of subversion in your work. Again, your taste for the paradox right from the cover, with this "pig" title, and the photo of a romantic, colonial couple of tourists in front of a temple in Agrigento, Sicily.*

CS: That's right. This is a process inherited from the world of advertising that works. There are two or three things that work every time in advertising: humour, sex and paradox. And sometimes, we mix two: humour and paradox, for example. To get to the facts, when the financial crisis broke in Europe in 2007–8, it was particularly harsh in southern Europe. It was really hell in Spain in 2008–12. In 2012 I took all my money out of the bank and converted it into dollars because there was a real fear that Europe would disappear. In Spain at least, we all had that possibility in mind. And yes, I'd been reading *The Economist* for years, and I was thinking about these guys who every seven or eight weeks were doing a cover saying that the euro was going to collapse very, very soon.

[4] *The PIGS: derogatory acronym coined by Anglo-Saxon financiers and journalists of the magazine* The Economist *to qualify countries of Southern Europe (Portugal, Italy, Greece, Spain), among the most vulnerable during the sovereign debt crisis of the late 2000s.*

And at the same time, they were talking about southern European countries as PIGS. At first, I was a little offended. I didn't think it was very professional of them. I felt that *The Economist* was a serious newspaper that could be read in confidence and suddenly, they are using this vexing term, which I didn't like. My second thought was, "It's good, maybe they're right." After all, I too was very angry with what was happening at home. Of course, you're here tonight, you're thinking about your politicians, but if you saw ours, it's really hell. We certainly have a problem. All this triggered a reflection not only about Spain but about southern Europe as a whole. I wondered what these countries had in common, countries supposed to be the birthplace of the very idea of Europe and which today were called peripheral? I thought to myself: "Ah, there, Rome is the periphery of Europe, while Holland is the centre of it, they who were the barbarians 2,000 years ago!" But to be clear, I didn't want to be in a position of protest, like, "We're better." Not at all. On the contrary, I told myself that I was going to make a book in which I would show all these clichés, their banality depicted at leisure in the financial press. I was going to travel to these countries, I was going to photograph these clichés and I was going to see what would come out of them once collected. What will be our reaction? And now I remember very well a review you wrote when *The Pigs* was released.
Rémi wrote an article in which he said that I had used the technique of a judoka – that is, that I used the strength of the opponent to bring him down. And that's true. I think you summed up my point of view well. When you see this accumulation of clichés in the book, I guess in the end you think, "Well, maybe it's too much. They can't be as dirty as pigs: I went to Spain, it wasn't that bad, and I visited Venice, it wasn't that horrible. I was in Greece and it was still not bad." By accumulating, this is the reaction I hoped to produce, and I believe I have succeeded.

> *RC: And this cover [The book is circulating in the audience] with an elegant couple and a slanderous title, couldn't it suggest that it's the northern tourists who are the pigs?*

CS: I very meticulously avoided saying this, but of course, the cover image with these well-dressed tourists looking at a temple in Agrigento symbolizes, I believe, the relationship of northern Europe with southern Europe: a kind of fascination for a wonderful bygone world, and at the same time a fascination with what has been squandered. I think there's a love–hate relationship, no? We love it but we also say to ourselves: low and behold, we work so hard, and the southern countries are wasting our money. But in fact, this situation is very old. Already, Protestantism was born in reaction to the Catholic Church, which did the same: it took the money and then organized the Bacchanalia. [Laughs]

RC: Just out of curiosity, have you received criticism about The Pigs *from people who did not perceive the irony?*

CS: Well, I was very scared of that. I imagined that I would get a lot of criticism of the kind. None except for one. I remember a Greek woman who wrote, very angry, a comment under an article by Sean O'Hagan[5] of *The Guardian*. She basically said, "Ah, here's another photographer ready to insult his countrymen for fame and fortune." She clearly didn't understand.

RC: It seems that with The Pigs, *you accepted your advertising past and chose to use advertising strategies to present your work.*

CS: I think that's exactly what it is. It is true that often, when you work in advertising, you try to keep a low profile about it because it's a bit shameful. You see, advertising is very commercial; it has nothing to do with culture, with documentary or with books. For quite a while, I would say even about 10 years, I wouldn't hide it, because it's not easy to hide, but I wouldn't talk too much about it. And, besides, I kept doing advert pictures because I still had to pay the rent. And in fact, it was with *The Pigs* that, as you said, I accepted my advertising know-how and that things started to work much better for me. Instead of fighting my background, I began to understand

[5] *British journalist and photo critic.*

that this knowledge could work in my favour. And in the end, it worked – people understood and found the approach interesting. And as for me, I realized that I had found a way to express what I had in mind through a language that I understood and mastered. So why not? That's it: I came out of the advertising closet. [Laughs]

RC: To finish with The Pigs*: on the back cover, there's a fake ad for an imaginary bank, the WTF Bank. WTF is the acronym for "what the fuck", and* Wealth Management, *your following book, is supposed to be a commercial brochure for the WTF Bank. Was this book already in preparation when* The Pigs *came out?*

CS: No, not at all. The idea came to me later. I first designed *The Pigs* and had the idea to place this fake ad on the back cover. Then, quite simply, I got a commission from the magazine *El País Semanal*[6] to do a story about European tax havens. I was told, "Look, we have an article written by an economics expert, but we have no idea how to illustrate it. Can you think of a solution?" So I went to Switzerland and to Luxembourg. I had no idea, I didn't know what to do, but mentally, I started to see images with an atmosphere of dark thrillers, crime films … And started thinking about the story that way. I thought, "Here I am, I could photograph real scenes, but reminiscent of these films, and then I'll edit them as a fiction, though conceived with real documentary images." The concept is a bit twisted, but I think it worked well. It started with a successful commission. I had pictures that I liked very much, and I thought I'd make a book out of it. Maybe not a great book, not a very complex one, or too long, but I could work another year or two and make a little book that would be the flip side of *The Pigs*. So, while the lazy people were in *The Pigs*, napping for hours on end, in *Wealth Management* … Ah, I must explain that this is something I discovered in Luxembourg. I walked into a private bank pretending to be a potential customer. I was very well dressed in Burberry, a hat and all that, and I took a brochure. Private banks' brochures are luxury books, with a beautiful paper …

[6] *Weekly magazine of Spain's leading centre-left daily* El País.

RC: Excuse me, perhaps it should be said for people who have not seen it yet that Wealth Management *is in the form of a private banking commercial brochure.*

CS: That's it, with super-good quality paper. Often, instead of being cheap pictures from some photo bank, the illustrations are in black and white and authored by famous photographers. They never sign them, but you can find images for Swiss banks by Magnum photographers or maybe by some of you, if there are photographers here. You don't want credit for such images, but you accept the commission because they pay well. I thought that the format of brochures and the language of private banking were perfect mediums to explain that environment. I set out to spot their language on websites and in brochures. Their way of explaining: "Come to us, we will help you to not pay taxes. We're going to help you hide your money."

Taken out of context, some sentences are quite funny. I quote from memory, but phrases such as, "We will ask you questions that are not easy to answer." What does that mean? I went on reading and they basically explained, "When you have a lot of money, and reach a certain age, you have to think about your estate. Do you trust your wife, or do you not? And your children? Is one smarter than the others?" Yes, this is the kind of questions that private banks ask you. In other words, you need to prepare your estate, and then you have to think, "I have one child who's a jerk and the other who is super-intelligent. Everything will go to this one." This is the kind of rhetoric I discovered when I read these pamphlets. Again, ironically, I find them quite humorous.

RC: The book contains texts. For the most part, it is, as you said, pure corporate semantics from private banking, with the exception of the introductory text that you wrote, and which is very funny.

CS: Yes.

RC: It's a form of pastiche.

CS: Yes, I read their prose a lot and took it as a model to write the text …

RC: In a corporate language?

CS: In an advertising corporate language, which aims at reassuring the customer by saying, "Don't worry, we adapt to the circumstances, and even better, we can create the circumstances, we know how to do it."

RC: Why did you decide to pixelate the faces of the people who appear in your images?

CS: At first, I didn't intend to, but I have this friend, an English photographer, who has been working in Switzerland for years and who explained to me that he was … How do they say that …

RC: He was sued in court?

CS: Yes. Sued by lawyers, on several occasions. He had a lot of trouble, because he was photographing people in Switzerland and the Swiss are very belligerent, they have very good lawyers, a lot of money and time to waste to sue a simple photographer. I felt it would be really stupid to make a good book and then lose the house and have to tell my wife: "Yes, we don't have a house anymore, but I made a great book!" I figured it really wouldn't be a good idea. So I set out to hide the faces of the people photographed in order to protect myself. And I suddenly realized that the book was much more interesting that way. First of all, it protects me and it protects them. In fact, I don't know who they are. They look like gangsters, but I have no idea if that's the case or not. I also had to protect them from my insinuations. Then, what convinced me is that with this protocol, they really all seem guilty, because in the press usually only the culprits are pixelated. So in the book, as soon as you see them, they seem suspicious. In addition, hiding their identity works perfectly with the concept of hiding the money. Hiding from all is exactly what the very rich do.

RC: OK, there's the fact of protecting yourself and hiding. But I feel that in The Pigs *and* Wealth Management, *symbols matter more than the description of reality. Whether it's a Greek peasant sleeping under his olive tree or a woman in a mink coat in front of a Cartier boutique in Geneva, the symbol wins over the contingency of the real.*

CS: Yes, absolutely. These books don't deal with journalism. They are absolutely part of my interpretation. I'm interested in appearance, not in being. I don't even make the effort to know who they are, what they do. It's enough for me, in the specific case of these two books, to know what they look like, and whether they fit my story.

RC: A small question, by the way. Because I find that, somehow, The Pigs *and* Wealth Management *are a form of hoax ...*

CS: A form of what?

RC: A joke.

CS: Yes, a little.

RC: And therefore fabricated, right?

CS: Somewhat.

RC: Does that bring you closer to Joan Fontcuberta? *[see* Conversations 2, *p. 64]*

CS: Maybe ... I'm not an expert in Fontcuberta. I never studied with him. I've never been, say, in his circle of influence. But I imagine that his language, his way of understanding photography, has something to do with what I do. I know Fontcuberta worked in advertising, so there could be a connection there.

RC: Yes, indeed, he also started with advertising.

CS: Actually, I only met him recently. But I think yes, we have a similar understanding for some things.

RC: Let's move on to La Grieta *[The crack]. For this new book, you adopted the codes of the graphic novel. Why that?*

CS: Well, it's a long story. Where do I start?

RC: Wherever you want. [Laughs]

CS: OK. So, we must first explain that it started again with a commission from the magazine that regularly calls on me..

RC: El País Semanal.

CS: They asked Guillermo Abril (a journalist and co-author of the book) and myself to go and do a series of reports on the southern borders of Europe, because at that time, there were migrants jumping over the fences in Melilla in southern Spain, which you may not have heard of here, but in Spain, it was very important, of course.

RC: In Morocco, you mean? Melilla is not in southern Spain, but in Morocco.

CS: It's in Africa but not in Morocco, it's Spain! [Laughs] No, it's something to be said because in this case, is Gibraltar in Spain?

RC: Or England?

CS: In my opinion, it is in England. It is unfortunate, but that's the way it is. So yes, Melilla ... I was joking. This may be unfortunate for Moroccans but technically, the city is in Spain. It is not only Melilla but also Ceuta[7] in Morocco. Anyway, there were also rafts in the Mediterranean. It was 2013, a particularly deadly shipwreck had just occurred with almost

[7] Ceuta and Melilla are two Spanish enclaves along the Moroccan coast, just as Gibraltar is a British territory at the southern tip of Spain.

400 people drowned. These facts sparked the interest of the directors at *El País Semanal* to publish a story about the flow of migrants that was beginning to intensify at that time. Some images had not yet been seen. So, with Guillermo we covered that story. We went to Melilla, then travelled in the Mediterranean on an Italian ship and witnessed a rescue on board. We then went to the border between Greece, Bulgaria and Turkey, an important crossing place a few months prior, but nothing was happening there then, but we went there anyways. We didn't find much in Greece, however. Everything was forbidden, it was impossible to photograph. On the other hand, we had more success in Italy. The report was very well received. It made the headlines and about 20 pages. We also made a video that was very successful and for which we got a World Press Photo. This encouraged me to conceive a sequel, continuing to visit Europe's external borders to the east and north to investigate what was happening there. Were there any migrants in the Baltics too? What about Poland? What was the situation in Finland? A country with the longest external border in Europe with a single country: 1,300 kilometres of border with Russia. I prepared a file and got a grant from the BBVA Foundation, which allowed the project to continue with the support of *El País Semanal,* including the participation of Guillermo Abril, who is part of the editorial staff.
We continued the work but with the idea, in my mind, to make a book of it in the end. Let's just say I initiated the book project. Guillermo in that phase was not yet thinking about the book. He's a journalist who works for a magazine. He doesn't write for a daily newspaper and isn't a hot news specialist.
I was thinking of making a book of all these stories with all these images. In my mind, it was originally a traditional book, meaning choosing perhaps the 70 or 80 best images to be associated with a text by someone famous, possibly a politician, or a philosopher. In short, a truly traditional book. The truth is I was not then seriously thinking about the book format. And at one point, I thought that if I did a book like that, it would surely be good, well done and interesting, but what audience would it reach? Could it reach a significant number of readers? I came to this because I had the idea of conveying a specific message through a book that would be somewhat activist.

A book that would seek to explain the challenges facing the European Union and to convince – without verging into propaganda or the pamphlet – that the EU is not so bad, that it should not be lost. And that I, at least, didn't want to lose it. So, I wanted to get that message across and spread it massively. I was afraid I wouldn't go very far with a photography book. I already had some experience with photography books, and I knew how it went. *The Pigs*, which was very successful, sold 3,500 copies, which is quite a lot as such; but if you think in absolute terms, it's not really much.

RC: It's a lot for a photography book, but at the same time it's nothing.

CS: It's nothing, you're right. But I'm a comics and graphic novel reader. I'm no expert but I read the popular titles, the ones that many people know. It's a genre that I've always liked and I've always wanted to practise but I thought it was impossible; because when you try to make a graphic novel with photos, it immediately becomes a photonovel, and I absolutely wanted to avoid that, because I don't like it at all… If I see a book that looks like a photonovel, I immediately close it. And that's when I found a way to process the images of *La Grieta* …

RC: Yes, it's very interesting; can you tell us about the technique you used? How did you treat your photos for them to look almost like a drawing?

CS: I didn't want them to lose their photographic essence. At first, I tried to use software that creates pseudo-illustrations from the photos, but I didn't like the result, precisely because they looked fake. It was neither a drawing nor a photo. I didn't like it. I thought it had no character. So I looked for a way to process images that made them much flatter, with a combination of Lightroom and Photoshop. Photoshop especially. On the one hand, I strongly contrasted the white and black, and on the other, applied very little contrast to the colours. Then, I flattened the images, and you get that result. I still remember the day I found the solution. I then felt completely encouraged to undertake the book, because I had found a way of making it pleasant to the eye that I really liked and that I imagined could also please others as well, and that, furthermore, took me really very far from the photonovel.

RC: Can you tell us what is the crack that gives the book its title? And even when you read the book, you understand that there are several of them.

CS: Yes, in fact, I still wonder if "The crack" is the right title or if it shouldn't be "The cracks". Maybe there are, indeed, several of them. We have imagined the external border of the European Union as a crack that separates it from the rest of the world. And this crack widens, expands by the day. There is so much pressure that has had some consequences within the EU. The two most important pressure points are immigration and Russia, which are creating cracks within the European Union. I mean, countries react very differently. Not everyone agrees on how these issues should be dealt with. This is particularly clear with Hungary or Poland. And today, the most obvious crack is Brexit. So, it's clear that a whole series of small cracks are weakening the European wall. So much for the observation. I wondered if one day the whole European construction would be destroyed, if the whole structure was in danger of collapsing. The first crack is the outer border you never think about. Europe is thought of as a borderless space, when in fact, it has a huge border. Over 10,000 kilometres guarded by many soldiers and policemen ... and very heavily monitored.

RC: How many images are in the book?

CS: There are about 755.

RC: This is huge compared to the average in a photobook. Generally, a book has 40 or 60 images, 80 max.

CS: Yes, the way you choose photos, how you build the editing is completely different, although the basis, really, is the same as for any book. I mean that we look for the most powerful images, the strongest, the ones that tell the most, the most iconic in a way. But then, in this case, you need to sew them together to build various stories and finally connect all the stories. So, it's true, the editing work was very, very long, very complicated.

RC: Indeed – for a year, we didn't see you.

CS: That's right. The work was built on a skeleton of stories arranged according to the chronology of the events we experienced. I built the sequences and layout that are the basis for the storytelling. Then Guillermo wrote the texts. These are fundamental to stitching the chapters together and bringing the images to life. While in a comic book the script often precedes the drawing, here it is the images that translate our memory into narrative before the text comes to take its exact place.

RC: One thing I find remarkable about La Grieta *is that you don't hesitate to crop some of the images harshly, sometimes in squares, or in panoramic views, etc. Is the story more important than the author's vanity?*

CS: Yes and no. Because the author's vanity is so great that they want to make a book that everyone sees! [Laughs] But the vanity isn't based on the photo, it is based on something else. There's probably a little bit of vanity. But yes, we know that photographers generally don't like to see their images reframed, modified… But from the beginning, I thought we shouldn't think about what we're destroying, but what it is we're building. And it was so clear to me that I was doing something much more important than the images themselves, that I had no qualms about it. I made a choice very quickly and never regretted it.

RC: Do you consider The Pigs, Wealth Management *and* La Grieta *to be fictions based on reality?*

CS: *The Pigs* and *Wealth Management,* certainly. *La Grieta,* no. I don't think it's fiction, because we respected the laws of journalism – that is, the facts. For *Wealth Management,*

I made it clear that I don't know who the people represented are. Here, it's exactly the opposite. People are who they say they are, their names sometimes appear, and we've been very, very scrupulous in respecting the facts.

RC: You're saying that you've been very scrupulous, and that's the truth, but Guillermo Abril's text in the book is very different from the journalistic canon; it incorporates the form of "new journalism" heralded by Tom Wolfe. It describes what you see, which is journalistic, but also what you do, what you think. What is the purpose of this first-person account?

CS: Well ...

RC: I'm thinking, for example, about the moment when you join an Italian navy ship and Guillermo writes: "We try to get into the military helicopter nonchalantly, but our wheeled suitcases betray us: we are not war reporters."

CS: Yes, that's the point. For us, it has always been important to point out that we are ordinary people who find themselves in an exceptional situation. You see, we're not the mega-built-up, super-strong war reporters who have seen it all – that's not the case. But wait, what were you saying?

RC: The question was about first-person storytelling or deviating from the usual codes of journalism.

CS: On one hand, I would say that it's a journalistic code. Kapuściński[8] spent his entire career as a journalist writing in the first person in the form of a diary. It's one way of practising journalism that indeed includes interpretation. We are there in the narrative, the storytelling. We thought about it intensely. What are we going to do? Will it be a story or not? For a narrative to be easy to read, you must always be able to follow a character or event whose evolution you can perceive. And since our various characters are usually only visible on one page or so before they disappear, we needed to find

[8] *Ryszard Kapuściński (1932–2007) was a Polish writer and journalist.*

someone to follow. In this case, it is about us. We are the vehicle of the story. When a factual narrative comes kind of out of the blue, we are always there to re-establish the narrative pattern.

RC: So, to try to bring together the three books, The Pigs, Wealth Management *and* La Grieta, *what does applying existing forms foreign to the usual canon of the photobook allow you to do?*

CS: What does that allow me to do?

RC: Yes.

CS: First, it allows me to tell a very, very complex story with much more nuance and detail than in a traditional photography book with shorter text not directly related to the images. This makes you lose a lot of details. And here, my goal was to explain to the reader – I always had a young audience in mind ...

RC: Are you talking about La Grieta*?*

CS: Yes, I'm talking about *La Grieta*. I imagined a young reader, twenty or so. And I knew that if it did the job for a 20-year-old, it would just as well do so for someone in their forties or fifties. None of us have much time these days. We still read, of course, but some of the stories sometimes lend to a certain laziness. And I was actually trying to tell a lot of things within an hour and a half. This is what this form allows me to do: to deliver a panoramic picture of the current situation of the European Union in an hour and a half.

RC: OK, but if you like, my question was somewhat broader, because it also included The Pigs *and* Wealth Management. *So, using formats that are not traditionally those of the photobook, what else can it bring? When you take hold of a model other than, say, the blank page on the left, the photo on the right, the white margin, etc.*

CS: What can we do? We can do anything! That's exactly what it is. It's very personal, I think. I like to invent, and I'm not so keen on repeating patterns so much. I'm not saying that I'm systematically inventing something, that I'll always find new forms. No; but I do try to innovate every time because otherwise, I get bored. We'll see, but for now, I have the feeling that the relationship I established between the image and the text will leave a trace. I think that, one way or another, I will further my reflections on the matter. I'm not sure that I understand the question "What does it allow?" because it allows me to do anything and to explore ... It allows me to tell and create, it gives me strength, it encourages me to continue.

RC: I titled this conversation "Subverting Editorial Forms". We'll see – maybe the public will have their opinion. Perhaps my proposal is too strong, and we're almost at the end of this conversation, but do you see yourself as upsetting the rules with your books?

CS: Well, maybe I do, but I'm not doing it on purpose. That is, I'm not trying to provoke a revolution. I'm trying to find a solution to a problem, or to a subject that I'm looking at, for which I have to provide an answer. I'm quite capable of designing a traditional book from a selection of images, but I have one fear: that no one will read it. So, I'm trying to break that curse. And if this anxiety leads me to invent by upsetting the formats, well, so much the better! I'm quite happy about that. Because, in the end, you are the critics – you, the readers, have the last word. Did we invent something or did we not? It seems so to me, maybe. It wasn't the goal, but it was much welcomed. [Laughs]

RC: In Spain, La Grieta *was an instant success. Did you expect it?*

CS: I'd be lying if I told you I didn't. [Laughs] What if I said yes ...

RC: I should point out that the first print run in Spain was 3,000 and the success was skyrocketing.

CS: That's right. The book was immediately a great success. We reprinted less than a month after the release because the booksellers were reordering copies. The most interesting aspect is that it was mostly popular in the comics world. The buyers are mostly comic book readers. And it will probably be the same here ... we'll see, I don't know yet.

RC: We'll talk about it later ...

CS: We'll talk about it later, of course. But I have the feeling that comics readers and authors have enjoyed the project, perhaps because they don't see me as a real threat. [Laughs] I'm still a tourist in comics land, after all! [Laughs] We'll see if I'll continue in that vein. Maybe I can do it, I don't know. However, if we look at the causes for this success, I think they are primarily related to the subject, which is, I believe, interesting. It's a great story, very difficult to make. Going from Africa to the Arctic is still a great story conceived in "real" images. It's a mega-production and it is attractive because we're not so used to that anymore. This language was well received by the comics world in Spain; here, we will see. And then, there will be the reaction of the photography world. I'm quite curious about that. For starters, I'm here tonight, at the Henri Cartier-Bresson Foundation. Not bad! I mean, from this moment on, I want to consider the project as a success in the field of photography. [Laughs]

RC: You were already here in Paris last week to promote the book, and I have to say that this simple word, "promotion", is almost incongruous in the world of the photobook. Because promoting a photobook basically boils down to sending a copy to 10 journalists around the world and signing books at fairs and bookstores. And we're very happy if we have a buzz on the blogs. That's what promotion basically sums up to. You know the world of the photobook as well as I do. And when you told me the programme that Gallimard, your French publisher, had prepared for you, I was amazed. You've done several TV shows, including 28 Minutes *on ARTE, two radio shows on France Inter, an article in* Libération *... I don't know, you've had something like a dozen gigs in a couple of days. It's pretty amazing when you live* *in the small world of photography. What is it that's missing in the traditional photobook to attract mainstream media?*

CS: So here, we really are hitting the spot, that's the real topic of the conversation. What is really missing? Of course, I've wondered about that. I'll tell you an anecdote that really moved me. The magazine *El País Semanal* – everything always, always starts with *El País Semanal*, I don't know why. [Laughs]

RC: That's your life.

CS: Right, that's my life. So, they sent me out for the portrait of an author who writes bestsellers. An Englishman who lives in Mallorca in a great castle, an incredible property. My job was simply to make a portrait of a famous writer. The reporter was asking him questions, and for three hours I listened to him telling his story: the beginnings of his career, which today resulted in 270 million books sold. That's it: I spent three hours with someone who sold 270 million books! I came out of there thinking, "Something's wrong, it's not possible. I'm happy when I sell 3,000!' [Laughs] 'Something's not right." So, I started thinking about the bestseller phenomenon: what is a bestseller? Does it exist in the field of photography? I realized that there are bestsellers in any other artistic practice. In films, with bestsellers with dinosaurs, and also *Apocalypse Now*, which was both of high cultural quality and very popular. This implies that there is such a thing as quality bestsellers. Pink Floyd's records were bestsellers, but it was also quality music. Or The Doors, or even the Beatles. The same happens in painting, literature, music, and of course, in the world of comics as well. Just think of *Tintin*. I don't know how many millions *Tintin* books have been sold.

RC: Tens of millions of them probably.

CS: Tens of millions, maybe hundreds of millions over the years. But is there such a thing in the photo world? I was thinking about it a lot.

RC: There's Yann Arthus-Bertrand.

CS: Yann Arthus-Bertrand, that's it. The bestselling artist in the photo world is Yann Arthus-Bertrand. In the 1990s I think everyone had a book by Yann Arthus-Bertrand. I had one myself.

Someone in the audience: 2.5 million copies.

CS: Ah, 2.5 million. That's a bestseller. There is of course also Sebastian Salgado. Another bestselling artist, but not only with a single book – all his books are great successes. I don't have the figures for Salgado's sales. I have no idea.
Let me be clear, I wasn't looking for the recipe to make a bestseller. No, I was wondering about the commonalities between popular works that are also intellectually high-standing. From there, I thought that what was missing very often (I would say almost always) in the photobooks – including in Yann Arthus-Bertrand's – is a narrative, a story. That is, a traditionally conceived story that begins with "Once upon a time ..." Then, a conflict, and in the end, either everyone dies, or everyone is happy.
In short, storytelling. Surprising events, characters to follow ... Jeffrey Archer, the writer I mentioned, told us: "Look, 40 years ago I found a writing technique whereby, when you get to the bottom right of the page, it's impossible not to be compelled to continue to the top left of the following page. And for 40 years, I've been writing the same book, with different titles."
That's exactly what he said. [Laughs] Though it may not necessarily be the only way to do it. And then I thought: a narrative, that's what's really missing in photography in general and in my own books. There is never a story, a narrative.
When in fact, people like to read. Even those who never open a book in winter will read two or three 500-page bestsellers over the summer. They like to read when the story is easy to understand, when it's interesting, when they learn something. And I think people like to learn. I like it. There are graphic novels that I loved, like Guy Delisle's *Pyongyang*[9]. These are first-person stories that narrate the facts and have taught me things.
For example, I learned about Iran from reading *Persepolis*[10].
I have spent years reading about this country and never

[9] *Guy Delisle,* Pyongyang, *L'Association, 2003.*

[10] *Marjane Satrapi,* Persepolis, *Pantheon Books, 2003*

understood it. The day I read *Persepolis*, everything became clear. I understood the Iranian Revolution within a couple of hours. That's why there is a market and an appreciative audience. Because within two hours, it's possible to learn in an interesting manner, pleasant or unpleasant, but in any case accessible.

RC: So, you need to find a narrative? A form of storytelling?

CS: That's what it takes.

RC: This is one of the questions I'm passionate about right now in photography and in photobooks: how to tell a story with photography, even if it means mixing it with other elements – that is, not just the author's photo, but also found documents, archives… in short, elements that expand the narrative possibilities of photography alone. The new ways that authors are currently looking for to tell stories with photography.

CS: When I was working on *La Grieta*, I told very few people about it. Most of them were saying no, I was wrong, photography is not for storytelling. It's a different language. And I wondered why do we believe in this divine law that photography would not be fitted for storytelling? I find the mere notion of that thought to be limiting. It couldn't be. The truth is, there are storytelling photobooks these days, and we were both talking about them today. Their format is very different from mine, but look at *Ville de Calais*[11], a wonderful book that you showed me.

RC: The author is Henk Wildschut, a Dutch photographer. If you haven't seen it yet, I invite you to have a look at this book about the Calais "jungle".

CS: Formally, his book is more traditional. It combines photos and text. But the text is narrative, it is written in such a way that you want to go on to the next page.

[11] *Henk Wildschut,* Ville de Calais, *self-published for the English version, Gwinzegal for the French edition, 2017.*

RC: As you were saying about Marjane Satrapi's Persepolis, *I discovered things about Calais, of course ...*

CS: You didn't know anything?

RC: I didn't know anything about the reality of the camp. Like everyone else, I had seen reports on TV, read the newspapers, listened to the radio, heard about the so-called "jungle", etc. But this book reveals a real economy, real social relations with businesses being set up ...

CS: A real estate market ...

RC: It's crazy! A cigarette shop, restaurants, a hairdresser, etc. A real economy is taking place before our eyes, but I had never heard of it before Henk's book.

CS: That's it, exactly right. But this is truly a rarity in the world of the photobook. Often, we see books that are formally fine, the images are superb. But sometimes, ironically, if I can be a little mean, what we see is what I call the "Leroy Merlin book": various papers and elements, hard to open ... And the content £is often quite poor in terms of story. That raises suspicion, you see. How many are they that can hold comparison with *Ville de Calais*?
On the other hand, in the world of comics, I often find interesting books. But production is the most important. However, I want to make it clear that this language is not the only one that can be used. There are others, I'm sure of that.
I specifically mentioned *Ville de Calais* because it's an example of a book less extreme in graphic terms than *La Grieta*, but from a narrative standpoint, it's perfect. I love it, and I would like all the books to be of that quality.

RC: Two years ago, we were at the Kassel Photobook Festival. You were presenting Wealth Management *and Martin Parr [see* Conversations 2, *p. 148] challenged you by asking if there was a life after pastiche. Is* La Grieta *somehow a form of answer to that question?*

CS: Yes indeed, because I remember very well that he was the only one to raise his hand and he asked me this rather wicked question. We talked, he's super-friendly like that, but ... At the time, I replied, "Ah, wait and see, the next book won't be a pastiche." It wasn't possible in the end; I still committed a pastiche! It's not exactly one, but as I said, I'm once again using a language that isn't the usual language of traditional photography. So, in fact, probably for me, there is no life after the pastiche! [Laughs] I can't escape it.

RC: We could stop here. It would be a very good conclusion. One more thing, though: you've already explored the forms of the magazine, the commercial brochure, and the graphic novel. Do you already know what your next book will be like?

CS: No, I really have no idea.

18 May 2017

KATJA STUKE & OLIVER SIEBER

Artists, curators and teachers Katja Stuke, born in 1968, and Oliver Sieber, born in 1966, both live and work in Düsseldorf. They have been collaborating since 1999 while also developing individual projects. Their work is included in many public and private collections. In 2014 Oliver won the Paris Photo–Aperture PhotoBook of the Year Award for Imaginary Club *and in 2016, they jointly received the LUMA Dummy Book Award at Rencontres d'Arles. To date, they are the authors of 47 zines, an essential practice for them, and have published nearly 16 books jointly or separately.*

Katja Stuke and Oliver Sieber's practice is at once simple and complex. Simple, because their main subjects are contemporary culture understood in its broadest sense, from mass media to urban subcultures and economics, and an in-depth reflection about the photographic medium.
Complex, because while they alternatively work together or separately, their production can take on multiple incarnations: the same project can successively adopt the shape of a zine, a video, a blog, an exhibition, stickers on the walls of cities or a book released in 5 or 1,000 copies. Paper, however, remains central to their practice. After years of crossing paths with them and a few more exchanges at the Cité des Arts in Paris during their residency, I had a conversation with them in my library to try to tie everything together.

Rémi Coignet: *Preparing for a conversation is never easy. But I must admit that in your case, it's a whole new story considering how abundant and non-linear your practice is. I guess the easiest for me is to start talking about paper, a medium you use in multiple ways: zines, books and even stickers. How is this material so important in your work?*

Katja Stuke: I think paper is a crucial aspect in photography. When you produce something, you need to have some material, and what's photography's material? Paper, right?

Oliver Sieber: There is something funny about book lovers. Some people start by smelling the book, others don't. So sometimes, the first step to friendship can be with someone who smells books before they even read it. You say that we work in so many directions, but in fact, the book is most often our focus. Even if we also think in terms of video and works for the wall. Sometimes, the exhibition can be somewhat disappointing: you frame the image and it can no longer be touched, it is no longer reachable. I feel that touching the physical object is an important factor for me, and for you too, Katja.

KS: Yes, the book is much more real because we do these different scrapbooks and all various paper objects. For example, when we work with students, we always want them to print their images. It's not fun for me to look at a photo on an iPad, unless it's for a valid reason. You have to at least see it printed in order to work with it.

OS: The selection of paper is crucial. You articulate a specific purpose when you use newspaper stock, for example. You can establish contrasts between elements in a book by using various papers. I think it is one important reason to think about the use of different qualities of paper.

KS: It's not that we are not using computers and digital equipment. Actually, I was always a bit crappy at doing layouts, for example, but I'm super happy that computers can help me with them or prepare printing files. And yes, images need to be touched, you need to organize the pages on a table, to juxtapose and work with them, rather than in an abstract way on a computer screen.

RC: For you, what is important is to publish, it isn't the size of the print run. For example, there are only five copies of Japanese Lesson. *Why is the number of copies secondary? We know that many artists want their work to be widely seen and received by as many people as possible…*

KS: This is a discussion between us. I still believe that part of the work is making many copies. On the other hand, we wanted to finish *Japanese Lesson* without having to wait until we could produce a larger print run of it. It is 1,200 pages, and everybody knows how difficult it is to find funding for such projects. So, in a way, we understand this edition to be the work. And this may have given me a different understanding of what a book is.

OS: Sometimes, we agree to do very small editions that allow us to think better about the project, to bring it to look and feel like we want. With *You and Me*, we won the Arles LUMA Dummy Book Award, so it was easier to find a publisher and to print a larger edition. Also, about the book as a democratic thing, I'm not quite certain that it is truly democratic. Even when it is sold 50 euros for a print run of 500 copies. For many people, this would be expensive; you might print 1,500 copies to reduce printing costs, but then, this means that you have to find 1,500 people who will want to buy it ...

KS: This is not so important to me; I'm more interested in the notions of photography, the edition and the original. If you print an edition of five copies, it still has the feeling of being an original. But if you print 1,000, it's something different. For *Japanese Lesson*, we made dummies, and while we were working in Japan, we also produced zines that allowed us to get a sense of the editing and printing for the book. We have kept those, because they feel akin to an original piece. I think that's the difference between 10 or 10,000 copies. On one hand, the feel of the original, on the other, the copy of a copy.

RC: But wasn't photography conceived from its invention to be reproduced? And early in its history, to be so in books?

KS: Yes, that's right, and we do discuss this a lot when we do editions. It also has to do with the market, especially in Japan where they don't care about limited editions. And yet, it's also nice to own one single object that no one else has. If you want to produce a creative image, you frame it and hang it on the wall; then, it has a different audience and takes on a different meaning.

RC: You mentioned them already, so let's talk about the zines. There have been 46 of them so far since 1999, if I'm not mistaken and if you haven't produced a new one since we last met a few days ago at Cité des Arts [Laughs], the latest one being Moving with Books. *What is their function? Do they translate an urgency to publish, or to test an assumption?*

OS: In the beginning, it was a mix of various notions. One of them being to reach out to the audience. So, we would print our zines, only four pages, and we would go have a coffee and show it to people around in the café. The material which we used in the zines came from our archive.

RC: An archive you owned or of your own work?

OS: Of our own work. We were wondering what to do with this archive, how to organize it, or how to process the images. So, Katja and I delved into them and started thinking about how to connect our images with a title. And this reflection about our work led to the construction of new meaning. We would then discuss our work with people and sometimes they bought our production.

KS: It was also for us a way to structure our own thoughts; to start a conversation, and to compare or juxtapose what we were each working on. Through this, we figured out that we were both exploring similar topics. Over time, the idea of the zines changed. We created topics specifically for the zine, using it as a playground to toy with our ideas. For example, there was one zine we made when Polaroid declared bankruptcy; we bought an old passport photo camera and the last Polaroid films we could find. We organized a party, took some portraits and made a zine out of that material. It is a truly playful way to think about photography.

OS: By the way, we called it *Instant Böhm*. It was not all about photography, it was also about products that we offered during the party. When you think about instant products, they came in the 1950s and contributed to changes in society.

RC: Are the zines the starting point of your collaboration?

KS and OS: Yes.

OS: You are censoring me, Katja! [Laughs]

KS: No …

OS: She's always double-checking when I'm going too far with my explanations.

RC: Please go on, Oliver.

KS: It's fine, no problem. [Laughs]

OS: Of course not, she's my better half.

RC: The last zine to date is Moving with Books. *You have also designed a piece,* Fax from the Library, *which comes in various formats (video, installation, etc.) for which you selected an image from various books in your library and subsequently faxed them, right? Tell me if I'm wrong …*

KS: Yes, well, it's not exactly a proper fax. A fax is by definition the copy of a document sent somewhere through a telephone line. We slightly modified the function of the object.
What we did was to make a copy and send it through a telephone line to a blog we created on Tumblr.

RC: Watching the Fax from the Library *video, in any case, is quite frustrating for anyone who knows the history of photography, because the images are only on the screen for a split second: we start thinking "Yes, of course, I know that image," and by the time we acknowledge what we are looking at, it's already vanished, replaced by another. How important is it for you to rely on a visual library, digging into the immense body of more than 150 years of photography? [Laughs]*

KS: Well, we didn't one day decide that this or that was "important". It was a need from the beginning. Both of us bought books and magazines; we also went to the cinema or listened to the radio and to music. We love the diversity of this material and want to be surrounded with it, and in a way, it all shapes how we understand photography.

OS: I've already forgotten the question.

RC: How important is it for you to rely on a library and on 150 years of photography history?

OS: We are here sitting in your library for this conversation, and it's a perfect place. Actually, we have lots of books in common ...

RC: I saw that in Moving with Books ... *[Laughs]*

OS: So, it's quite nice to be here. I feel comfortable because there are so many friends and interesting photography books. It is important to have many books around. Not only the idea of the book, but the very object. Not its representation on the computer, but to feel the paper, the weight of the book.

RC: This reminds me of a personal anecdote. My daughter sometimes asks me why I have so many books that I don't look at. I tell her that they are tools; sometimes, I need to look at one image by Lewis Baltz [see Conversations, *p. 30], so I look for the Lewis Baltz book.*

KS: Yes. And to see that the three of us share many books in common means that we are talking the same language. We don't need to explain generalities. For example, if people don't have too many photobooks or books in general, or if they have a different visual education or background, then we need to prepare what we want to say and what we mean when we use a specific term or look at a specific image. That's an important difference.

RC: These two projects, "Fax from the Library" and "Moving with Books" inevitably evoke memory. What is your relationship with the notion of memory, which is obviously different from that of history? And I would like to add that the notion of memory is not explicit in your work, even if for me it runs through from the very beginning to the most recent projects.

KS: I don't believe it's anything conscious. I think it's something that we put together, as if we were concocting a soup with various selected ingredients, to put it very basically. These various memories, these bits and pieces of images, music, films, of what we've seen on the street or in adverts, we gather it all together into one big bundle of knowledge. So perhaps, it's not so much about memory as it is about a visual language.

OS: You mentioned *Fax from the Library* and *Moving with Books*. It's very interesting to be thinking about memory regarding these projects. Sometimes I don't need to look in the book because I know what's in there. If I see here Richard Avedon [points to the library], I know how the images will be inside, so I don't need to open it.
But with *Fax from the Library*, you open the book and you see images that maybe you have never seen or understood before. Which is why it's important to own the books and to revisit them again and again if you really mean to understand them and the images inside. This might be a strange approach to memory but *Fax from the Library* could be a good way to reach out to the books in the library and revisit them.

KS: About *Fax from the Library*: the idea of the black-and-white copy totally changes the images and makes them into new images. At times, there's just a little thing left from the original. It is perhaps the memory or the trace of the image. So I think that making a copy of something is an interesting thought. It's like reminiscing an idea or a memory in a new form.

OS: We are very lucky to have access to the memory of the times when the fax was invented. You could communicate with images, though the quality was so bad, you just got a glimpse of them and they needed to be talked about, explained ...

But that fuelled new ideas, a base for communication. And even if you could just imagine that there might be a little figure there, in the missing information, there was freedom to think about the image because it was not fixed. If you focus on the notion of image, it can be interesting to reduce the quality of your own work as much as possible to see how it transforms or if it isn't sometimes even better.

RC: The other day, you told me that someone said that the printing quality of Moving with Books *was fantastic…*

OS: Yes, but it is merely a Xerox on nice office paper. It was interesting to see some people who focused only on the black matte.

KS: Maybe it was the first time these people paid any attention to printing quality. I had the impression that some were impressed because they had never actually thought about it before.

RC: About what you were saying, it seems that an important aspect of your work is that printing quality is less important than the actual work. What would you say?

OS: Well, you can't really generalize. One and the other need to be somehow coherent in the end. It's also a combination. We were so happy when we started working with zines in 1999: for the first time, we could print double-sided in colour using the early inkjet printers. It was like going into the darkroom for the very first time and processing your first black-and-white image. It looked real, whatever that means. Today, it's not so interesting anymore because you can send your file anywhere. Printing technology is so advanced right now that it's only a half-surprise when the book is good. Now, it's a different matter when you return to the copy machine…

RC: You told me the other day that at some point, when you were making zines in colour, the technology got so good, you decided to return to black and white.

KS: I think that's still why we do the zines, because, as I said before, it's a playground to try out things. With books like *Japanese Lesson*, we discovered a different way to reproduce. The book has a very good digital quality. But with the zines, our approach is experimental; we can test new things; and yes, we are back to black-and-white Xerox now. I think that's important for us because in the studio, we both have many options, we can choose many different sizes and materials and we like to produce by ourselves. We don't want to give a file to a lab, go there to check the colours, and again to fetch the object. It's quite important for us to produce it ourselves and to work with the machines on our own. Now, we're into making photocopies; this could change in the next month. We'll see.

OS: I need to touch the editions that we conceive, the printing we do, which, by the way, involves lots of manual work. Sometimes, I order my book via "print-on-demand" online, I get it in a package, and it feels like it was someone else who did it.

KS: Once you printed your own book...

RC: Do you mean with Blurb?

OS: Or something like that... But I really like to going to the print shop and standing next to the machine, talking to the printer, getting a feeling of the whole thing. And going to the bookbinders to check on details and talk to them. They're often very interesting people, and then you see some new machine and you think "Oh, I want to do something with this machine, it could lead to interesting stuff." If you merely order it online and get your package back, you get a book done by someone else.

RC: I don't want to be too cliché, but aren't you "man machines", like Kraftwerk?

KS: Perhaps this is a Düsseldorf thing! [Laughs]

OS: Yes, Kraftwerk is always nearby, at every street corner.

KS: We don't complain.

OS: No, we don't.

RC: So this wasn't such a stupid idea after all... I was thinking these last few days, "No, no, you can't ask this stupid question," but your previous replies brought it back to mind.

OS: These stories of robots and man machines become somewhat more realistic and human when you live in Düsseldorf, go to cafes or go shopping, and Florian Schneider[1] is standing next to you in line. It puts things in perspective somehow. We probably see it a little bit differently than our Japanese friends who come to study music.

RC: We began talking about paper, but this is reductive because it seems to me that fundamentally, the notion that irrigates your work is that of the incarnation – the term can be considered in any of its meanings, including the divine – of the image: you take pictures and you print or express them in one way or another on stickers, zines, books, prints, photocopies, videos, etc. How do you feel about the notion of incarnation in your work?

KS: Well, I think that's both the good and bad part about photography. We often call it "the three different states", like in chemistry or physics. For example, steam, water and ice. There are different forms; you can produce and present photography in many different ways. This is great, as well as a challenge. You must think about taking the photograph, you must think about the appropriate way to show it, stickers for example. And sometimes, with time, it can change. For some of our pieces, we've found different ways: at the beginning, *Fax* was a Tumblr blog, then it was a movie. We feel that photography's great quality is to allow for multiple forms of production and presentation.

[1] One of the founders and main members of the band Kraftwerk, founded in Düsseldorf in 1970, a major influence in electronic music.

RC: This refers to Walter Benjamin and reproduction…

KS: Why not…

OS: Katja, you said why not…?

KS: But it wasn't a question.

RC: No, not really, just a remark in passing. So, Katja, you make videos and then you make books with them. And together with Oliver, you photograph and make videos that are mash-ups of Hollywood movies like O.I.F. *or of Japanese culture. What is your position regarding the status of the image today?*

KS: Perhaps I should start by explaining why I make these videos. One day, I was watching these gymnasts on television during the Olympic Games, and I was really surprised to see one-minute-long portrait sequences. Because usually, TV is always fast and moving. I started to take photos of these portraits, or rather, to transform these images into portraits, which they weren't meant to be. This came from when I was younger; I was impressed by Hitchcock because of his very structured storyboards. He had a very clear vision of the images needed for his films. So I would take screenshots of his movies from the TV. And since I don't need to rely on others' films to make images, I started to shoot my own movies. Film is maybe my way of looking at and perceiving what is happening on the street. Then, I determine specific frames and print photographs of them.
Film and the moving image are always influential in our creation of images and imagery of the present time. That's why there is this close relationship between film and photo for us.
And since you mentioned *O.I.F.*, it is the German acronym for "original in colour". It is a technical mention in newspapers that they need to specify when printing colour images in black and white. That's where the title of the zine came from.
At the time, colour photos of California and New York were reproduced similarly. We were trying to understand the American landscape, and what we knew about America. We had seen so many movies that we had a clear vision of how

California should look like. We went there to try to clarify that vision. Was it right or was reality different? And how was our idea of California shaped by the movies we'd seen?

RC: Which brings me to the following: today, we know the world through images. For instance, the other day, there was a yellow-jacket guy who said on TV that he had never come to Paris before, this was his first time. But we all know the Brooklyn Bridge and Hollywood without necessarily having been there.

KS: Yes, but we still need to understand what we're looking at. For instance, I now see on Instagram images of people from China or Japan, South America or Africa, and I have some idea of what life might be like there. Still, I need to understand that these are images made for a public audience and I must interpret them. For this, I need to have some knowledge in other fields, it's not so easy. But you can still communicate through images, since you can share a similar visual culture. For example, we all know the Eiffel Tower in Paris, but we don't necessarily know other smaller mysterious places, or we have no images of them. We don't see the full reality; it's important to be aware of the fact that it's one among several perspectives.

RC: Oliver, do you think that it's the role of the artist today to reach out behind the image?

OS: With *O.I.F.*, I think it's interesting to compare between having the book or not. If you look at *Once Upon a Time in America*, and you are so moved by the movie, you travel to Brooklyn or Queens and you find yourself kind of standing inside the movie. This isn't easy to describe, but it's important somehow, when you think of images, to realize that they are only representations; you can compare them with your experience of what you see and explore, and think about how they relate to your own life.

RC: I was just showing Katja this little book, Paris *by Hans-Peter Feldmann, whose work I really like, and we were talking about Paris and the suburbs the other day.*

It's a brilliant book, but what is Paris to him? Postcards of the Eiffel Tower. Maybe, at one point, it is one way to sum up Paris.

KS: Yes, but I think that was Feldman's point; it's quite good, and I imagine he was being mischievous about it.

RC: Of course.

OS: You know when you told me to cross the "border" to leave the centre of Paris, I felt a certain freedom going there; because inside Paris, I feel like I'm on holiday, relaxed. It was very good to see something different, alternative realities ...

RC: Sure, Paris is a beautiful city, but it seems difficult to make photos that wouldn't be cliché, right?

KS: I guess so. When you take a photo of Paris, the reference to the cliché is always there. Whether you reproduce it, or say "I don't want a cliché, it's not my purpose," it's always still somehow there when you take a photo of Paris. You must deal with the image people have in their heads of Paris. On the other hand, it's so easy to live in Paris and not see the Eiffel Tower at all, it's not so difficult ...

OS: I think people are always producing stereotypes of ideas. Even when you go to the Cité des 4000[2] in La Courneuve, you always have in mind images with a sheep in the front; some of them are so boring, others try to get closer, and thus deeper. I guess if you're thinking about producing something on Paris, it would have to be a form of commission. With someone asking you "What do you think about Paris?" or "Would you want to work on Paris?" You would really need to dig deep into your consciousness to really express what it is you want to express about Paris, or about any city. In the same way, when you are invited for an exhibition on specific topics, you really need to try to get rid of certain preconceived ideas.

[2] *A social housing estate in the suburbs of Paris.*

RC: I don't mean to say that it's not the same for you, Oliver, but Katja is really good at taking photos – even on the streets of Paris – of things seemingly with "no interest" and making them interesting, not through what they show but through the way you are looking at them.

KS: But that's mostly the fun stuff I do for Instagram. You haven't yet seen all the other photos we've made in Paris.

RC: I say Paris, but I could have said Tokyo. You are able to look at humble things and find interesting subjects there, on a street corner.

KS: Maybe that's because of what we talked about before: the memory of all the images we have in our brain. You learn by yourself to adopt a particular perspective or view. It's not as if I was looking for anything special. If you were standing with 9 other people at a street corner, you'd have 10 different perspectives and views of the same place.

RC: The other day, Katja, you showed me two of the sketchbooks you're constantly composing, one for You and Me *and the other about Japan. They are made up with cards, drawings, photos taken from books, images of pop culture, excerpts from encyclopaedia or Wikipedia – in short, various elements that are like a basis for reflection. Somehow, this relates to the notion of library, but in what way is it necessary to rely on knowledge, on intuitions before even starting to work?*

KS: Tough question. We've always made sketchbooks. When we went to New York the first time, or to Japan, I just wanted to keep all these memories, and it was something to collect all of them, and nice pictures. It's like going to the flea market to search for old postcards that become souvenirs of the places we visited. The sketchbooks became research tools. You can collect all these screenshots and do all these things on the computer, but then you can't talk about it, it remains in the computer. You need something like a sketchbook, a physical object to engage the conversation. I can show them to Oliver and we can discuss them. He can contribute new ideas and we include them. The scrapbook for *You and Me* was a tool to consider what to keep and what to remove in our photographic work. We were dealing with the Bosnian War, and we knew we didn't want it to be the main subject, but we needed information about it. We read books and did some research. The sketchbook was a container in which we poured all that information, and though it is part of the project, it's not all included in the final result.

> *RC: Maybe they should remain private, but they are beautiful and could be published as they are.*

KS: Some are private. For *You and Me*, I started to write my notes in English because I knew we were going to have an exhibition in Chicago. From the beginning, I thought it could be exhibited and the audience would have an opportunity to leaf through it. I felt from the beginning that it could be made public. In the end, we displayed some pages in the exhibition and on a screen so the audience could see it. When you exhibit published books, people can manipulate them; but this is a fragile object, which makes it more difficult to handle for obvious preservation reasons.

OS: What I like about these scrapbooks is that they contain many different elements that do not necessarily relate to each other, other than through the connections that we create. So I glue something here, and a new element comes up there, which contributes to developing new associations. This brings up a new idea that will lead to another, and again. And the object builds up nicely. Katja does most of it, I add some notes.

KS: Yes, we discuss topics and I start by inserting the elements chronologically. And as Oliver said, several unrelated topics can come together. This is how we work. We're not scientists or researchers. We're artists, we have the freedom to create associations and connections between things that you wouldn't usually think as connected. Especially in *You and Me*: the project came about through a private connection. We knew someone who had come from Bosnia to Germany and then went to America. I think the work is about finding connections between these three countries and also discovering other stories or finding other people who experienced similar stories but made different decisions.

RC: One of your references is The Mechanical Bride *by Marshall McLuhan [1951], where he takes as a starting point adverts or newspaper articles. One of the essay's main points is that it can be read in no particular order: like a proto-expression of the internet rhizome, the web. Is this notion that goes against the rational explanations that you appreciate so much (encyclopaedia, etc.), but also coincides with the multiple formats of your pieces (zines, Tumblr, video, mash-ups, cartography, etc.), stimulating for you?*

KS: I'm not an expert in philosophy nor in Marshall McLuhan's oeuvre, but as you said, we like to have an "umbrella theme" under which we collect several topics to fuel ideas.
We collect and gather all these impressions into a visual library. Some we have an emotional feeling for, others we know well, or yet others grabbed us from the moment we saw them. This is what is always influencing the work, even if it can make it sometimes difficult to find the final format.
Regarding *The Mechanical Bride*, there were the brides, and then I wasn't so interested in the different types of portraits of women in the ads. So I focused on these Japanese idol figures. I made stickers and photographed them wherever I had pasted them, also considering the reaction of passers-by.
The whole project comprises zines, wallpapers and videos. Different ways to articulate an idea and turning it into an artwork. That's the way I think, and that's the way the world functions today: you can take your ideas from various sources, from books, from the internet ... I don't know how I would work without the internet today. Searching for any piece of information would take hours, years even, going to the library and finding out it doesn't carry the one book you're looking for and then having to go to Paris or Japan to find it – when it's now so easy to pull all these strings together with the internet.
About *Encyclopaedia*[3], what we're talking about is another

[3] *Katja Stuke & Oliver Sieber,* Encyclopedia, *Böhm Kobayashi, 2010.*

properly emotional mash-up of different topics and ideas, of music and manga. And we put it in alphabetical order to give some sense of structure, but they are also just loose topics collected from the world we live in.

RC: "Mash-up" is a very important word, in both of your practices.

OS: I was just thinking of how I understand the word "rhizome". It's maybe that you can really get lost in this kind of mad world. I really like that sometimes. You start from point A, and you have no idea how you end up at point B. Then, you need to pull yourself together and think, because you can go crazy when you keep drifting away. I can get a little weak and soft and not know what to produce, but at some point I must decide ... I see some books here ... and maybe I don't concretely look into them, but the title *Concrete Octopus*[4] is an interesting metaphor: while the octopus is alive, it has a central point (the body) from which the tentacles extend. And I think the most important thing for me is to stay connected with my internal system. You can exchange with other systems, but if you want to create interesting work, it's important to have a centre. I feel it's important to explain our work to the audience because people don't necessarily see what is at the core of our respective practices.

RC: Well, I don't want to be obnoxious, but it maybe because of your rhizome-like practices that you're difficult artists. Your approach is non-linear. You don't only think in terms of books and exhibitions, but also in videos or Katja pastes stickers on the street ... Since the work can assume various formats, it may be difficult for some people to understand the purpose, but I find it really interesting. I was talking about the incarnation of the image earlier, and this is maybe what makes your work sometime difficult to grasp. It takes on many incarnations.

OS: What's the solution, then?

[4] *Osamu Kanemura,* Concrete Octopus, *Pierre von Kleist and Osiris, 2017.*

KS: I guess there's none. For example, conversations like this one or working on an exhibition place our practice into a structure that we can't, as artists, define, because of the way we work. We never say: "This is the idea!" And focus on that to reach the final result. Sometimes it's very different from the initial idea. For example, *Imaginary Club*: Oliver had started making portraits of people he thought were interesting, meanwhile also photographing the surrounding locations. He did this nearly everywhere we travelled – in Japan, Finland, America, Spain, China… In all kinds of places north of the equator, I would say. He gathered all this material together in a book, and that's the initial format of the project. While he was putting it together, we started talking about what it was about. Was it about subcultures? But then, they are all very different. Should he explain what punk is or where it comes from? So he started looking for all these links, videos, references to fashion, to cinema, etc. This makes it very clear: on one hand, you can understand it the way you want; but including this bundle of information brings another layer of reading to the book. In Japanese books, the artist usually writes a statement of 8 to 10 sentences. But in the case of Oliver, his statement for *Imaginary Club* was 12 pages of tweets and comments.

RC: Imaginary Club *brings us back to your first book, Oliver,* Deutsch/SkinsModsTeds/Übungsräume *(Rehearsal rooms). In 2002 you already were dealing with subcultures (skins, mods, etc.). What attracted you to them?*

OS: The starting point was a mixed tape from my childhood, because music is central to me. I was listening again to my old mixed tapes from the 1980s, I was quite attracted to the two-tone movement in England, and also to the rockabilly scene. That's what I grew up with, it shaped me. And punk also. Fifteen years later, I was amazed that there were still people like me following that music, and who expressed it visually through their style. So I would go to the concerts and watch the crowds, and then I started taking portraits. That's how it started.

RC: A topic you're still working on today, almost?

OS: Well, kind of ... [Laughs]

RC: Is there still something happening? Are new generations still attracted by these movements? Or are they the same people still listening to the same music and living according to the same style? As to your work, there were various incarnations: Imaginary Club 1 *and* Imaginary Club 2, *but also* J_Subs, *and then the very big* Imaginary Club *in 2013... Why such a long-term interest in the matter?*

OS: Well, I'm not really sure that I'm still working on it or whether it's reached its peak with *Imaginary Club*. This book is an extension of the former projects, because it doesn't only deal with the 1950s and 1960s; it also includes the 1980s with post-punk, gothic and the new wave ... It also came from an interest in Japanese youth culture, because they were really into 1970s glam rock, and I started to do some research into that influence. It led me to the new wave, post-punk, movements – which I didn't actually take part in when I was younger.

KS: For example, Oliver did these portraits in Germany, and he went on to do *J_Subs* with similar groups in Japan.

RC: But this was years later?

KS: Six years later. That was the second part of the work... They're both very close. When you go to Japan and you see that these subcultures are still alive – and I'm not talking about the people who dress like that as a fashion trend, but about those who live the subculture, with their shops, their record stores, their clubs, their hairdressers – I think that as an artist, you develop a different strategy in your work. Oliver invited people to the studio in Germany; in Japan, we'd go to the gigs and I was his assistant. And the work developed like this. There are still other subcultures in Japan. I think that's how you work as an artist: you develop a project, you make a book or an exhibition with it, and then you go on, but it's all connected in the end. So perhaps a project is something that can only be furthered, in a way.

OS: Yes, well, I'm considering changing path ...

KS: It's not a conscious decision. When we met anarchists in Japan, we didn't decide that we would now connect these works.

OS: I guess it's a process. We're getting older, but it's also a process in the artistic life. With *Imaginary Club*, we travelled a great deal and I didn't necessarily know where to start when we would stop somewhere. But there was always music and concerts, so everywhere we went, it felt comfortable, it's a good starting place for research. For me sometimes, the black-and-white images are more important than the portraits, but no one talks about them.

RC: I did ...[5] *[Laughs]*

OS: Going to these concerts today, I sometimes feel that I'm done with them. In Düsseldorf, when you go to punk concerts, people are at least 60 years old; they don't dance, so it's kind of boring. It was very good to experience concerts in California because you saw very young people dancing to the music. They really loved it and they saw something of their life within the music. Now I feel a little uncomfortable going to hip-hop concerts, where people are too young. I think I was the right age when I started doing this. I was connected to the people and the bands, some younger, others older. Now, we've reached this activist idea of considering what really matters.

RC: I'd like to go back a little. Just after your first book, you published Character Thieves, *in which you show your characters on the side of their living environment, as in the previous one, the one on rehearsal rooms. And in* Imaginary Club *as well. How important is it to put things in context?*

OS: In the first book, the rehearsal rooms were not those of the people I portrayed. It was the publisher's decision, who didn't want to put only portraits in the book. I think

[5] *Review of* Imaginary Club *published in* Polka Magazine, *No. 25, March-April 2014, p. 200.*

these rooms were very special rooms for each band. They were building their own little society in there. Like a darkroom. You go there with your friends, uncontrolled. It's a space of freedom. Which is why the rehearsal rooms fit perfectly with subcultures and counterculture movements. With *Character Thieves*, I was interested in the cosplay community and people who dress like they were in a film or a manga. They usually avoid showing where they live because their so-called "real life" happens on the internet, or with their friends in special places. They disconnect their everyday environment from their fantasy character.
I love the scene in the film *Men in Black* where Will Smith enters the kitchen and you see little aliens making tea. And it feels quite normal. If I went to your kitchen and there where little aliens making tea, I think I would think it's normal, and I might even say "Oh, please, could I also have a cup?" and then come back to the conversation. I sometimes imagine people running around in cosplay. A nice fantasy, and a normal thing for me. I like to be surrounded by different kinds of characters and people. I wanted to explore the contrast and articulation of people who live in their parents' living room while expressing their inner selves by acting different. I went to meet them and wanted to describe our encounter. I felt really close to their world, inside their homes, their shopping stores and their character. For me, it all seems very normal. It felt closer than the world I explored in *Imaginary Club*.

KS: But wasn't it also about identity? I remember you said that some people think they're hiding something because they're dressing up as fictional character. But I understand when you say that you see much clearer about a person's identity from the character they select. You learn so much more about the person than when you make a traditional portrait. Quite often, they select their character in terms of its identity.

OS: Yes, and gender issues come up when dealing with cartoons and manga as well. So, I felt that I could come closer to these people through the cosplay.

RC: Not talking only about Character Thieves, *but also about the* Imaginary Club *series, do you feel comfortable or accept an affiliation with the German tradition of typology?*

OS: I can say yes or no ... I never thought of building a typology. I may have, but it was never intentionally.

RC: So, Oliver has been working for years on subcultures, and you, Katja, you went the opposite way, taking an interest in men in suits, be it with Suits vs. Fact & Fiction *[2008] or* Eleven to Liverpool Street *[2011]. Is it the other side of the same coin? And why was it interesting to you?*

KS: Yes, I think *Men in Suits* is part of a bigger project, because in the beginning, I made videos on the streets wherever I went, and later I would select certain frames and put them together. The main idea was about surveillance and CCTV, and I made this one book about it, *Konnte Sein*. Later, I focused only on one place. I was in London in the financial district, and it was really a surprise to see only men in suits there. There were empty streets and men in suits. It was an interesting image. Perfect for photography. I started filming, I had two days and spent most of them in the City.
Oliver was working on *SkinsModsTeds*, and you know the mods have their own suit culture, like the Beatles and others.
So the suit is not a unique uniform. While I was filming, there was a scandal in Britain. The *Financial Times* did a cover about a Russian spy who lived in London, looked like Daniel Craig, James Bond, and wore these fancy suits. So I quickly made the decision to take as many portraits of men in suits as I could, and combine them with found material from various archives. It was the easiest project to come up with, find the combinations, do the layout, and even an exhibition in the end. So *Men in Suits* is part of this whole CCTV series.
We returned to London a few years later and went back to the same neighbourhood to see what was happening. It was at the time of the G20 summit and we happened to end up in a protest. I guess focusing on specific spaces or places shapes the way I work. For closer connection. But while it's easy to take these photographs and videos, making the subsequent

selection of frames and re-photographing them from the screen can often take up to a year to finish. Which means that the project is still in progress.

RC: That's an important question. You often work with video and make books out of them. Is this a way not to decide on the decisive moment, to postpone the moment of selection?

KS: It's one of the aspects. It's easy to work that way. I find this space or that person interesting, follow them for a while, and decide later. But it also has to do with the printing of the photographs, because the raster is an integral part of the project. I move the image. It's not just a photograph, it's a photograph of an image that was on a screen at some point, and that changes the viewer's perception[6]. They need to wonder where the image comes from. Some people think I use material from the news or surveillance imagery. What is important is what the photograph looks like, and not that I work on the street. I display them as tableaus or grids of 12 or 15 images to evoke a surveillance room.

RC: CCTV and video are at the core of your work since the beginning, so... we are no longer talking about photography but about images and what they do to our world, right?

KS: Yes, and how they are received, translated, understood and assessed.

OS: While there is nothing original in that, when you extract images from a video, you cannot trust the image that comes out, because you create arbitrary relationships between situations and people. You make people look like friends when they've never met and were only passing by.

KS: I could adapt my process, by making a snapshot on the street and carefully choosing the moment when I'm quite aware that I'm manipulating, bringing people into contact with each other who have no connection at all.

[6] *Katja Stuke's images are often rastered from the video transfer.*

RC: Let's consider Nationalfeiertag. *I believe this book is important because you mix a selection of video images with excerpts from newspapers published in Hong Kong.*

KS: I guess it has to do with memory because working in that space was my first idea when I was in Beijing. There are always these nice connections, even when we work separately. We went to Beijing because Oliver wanted to find some Chinese punks. We went to the clubs at night, and during the day, I would go to Tiananmen Square. I was wondering what people knew about what had happened there, since there is no mention of the events in Chinese schools and history books. That was my idea. But even if you look at a person attentively, you never know anything about what's in their mind. Then I decided to make 100 portraits and tried to figure out what they know or could remember. And we went to Hong Kong three or four years later, on the day of the anniversary of the massacre. The second part of the book focuses on young Hong Kong students who were demonstrating to keep the memory of the event alive.

RC: OK, let's change subject... I think your ego (or private life) almost never appears in your work. And yet, you published You and Me *in 2017. But this apparently autobiographical title is immediately counterbalanced with encounters, travels and questions. Is the You more important than the Me?*

OS: Aleksandar Hemon wrote that there's no Me without You.

KS: He's the author who wrote the text for the book, an American writer who came from Bosnia to the US in the 1990s.

OS: "There can never be Me without You." I really like the sentence that ends his text. You must always continue a dialogue and if you're lucky, you'll end up meeting your Me.

KS: *You and Me* is not about us. Various elements come together. It's about much more than our trip and the research we did. When we started working on the project, it was about the dialogue and connections between countries, and the music perhaps, and the past, and different stories. We were retracing the story of a refugee from the Bosnian War. What we hadn't planned is, while in the US, coming across historical facts and places related to the 1960s civil rights movement. The connection between these two historical events occurred while we were travelling. Again, our research is not historically scientific. We have a very personal connection with the people, memories and places. They are important.

OS: We are probably quite lucky to be able to do what we want. The example of hip-hop music and Public Enemy is rather evocative. While we were going to Memphis and Birmingham, I realized that Public Enemy connected with me to the story. I was listening to their music for 20 years, but I wasn't particularly thinking about segregation, the Black Panther and racism. And years later, we're travelling to these places, and it suddenly all comes together. It all made sense to me because I liked that music, and because I was there, in the middle of nowhere in America, in Birmingham that I had never heard about before. Suddenly there were people who had been on the side of Martin Luther King, and there I was standing in a place where history was made. That's a good reason to travel to photograph, to be artists in the world.

KS:And there is the weird connection between *You and Me* and *O.I.F.* On our first trip to America, we were focusing on movie locations. It's a nice, kind of romantic approach to the country. But on this other trip, the story we had in mind was quite different: the Bosnian War and how America was connected to it, the green cards, Bill Clinton and the politics of his time. And these facts are connected to Germany and the people who found shelter there before migrating to the US. So you see totally different realities depending on the subjects you have in mind. As we said before, if the three of us were standing at a street corner in Paris, we would each see different details. During this trip, we visited cities we had never been to. We had only determined the first stop, thinking that we would see what would happen next and how topics and people can be connected. And we found people in America that have strong connections to places and people in Bosnia. That was very important.

RC: But at the same time, you had carefully prepared your sketchbooks... [Laughs]

KS: Yes, but not everything is written! If you look at the sketchbooks, there are many topics that are not in the final work. It would have been too confusing.

RC: In 2013 you started the ANT!FOTO *project. It comes in various formats: exhibition book, zines, posters and a manifesto. What was the purpose of the project?*

KS: It was first an exhibition. The office of cultural affairs in Düsseldorf offered us a space and a small budget to curate a photography exhibition. We took the opportunity because we are always really interested in the works of other artists, we don't always focus on our own work. We are always curious of everything that happens in the photo world. We often talk together about the different approaches to photography and the various forms it takes, and we missed these debates in Düsseldorf. We wanted to bring together different practices and reflections about photography in that exhibition.

OS: We felt a form of frustration because every time you say you are from Düsseldorf, people's reaction usually is: "Oh, Düsseldorf is such an important city for photography!" And we wonder what they're talking about, because photography is not very present in the city. It is only the story of a few people, that's it. There was no collection until very recently. Well, now they bought the large Kicken Collection[7]. For the first time, we have a major collection in Düsseldorf. Before, there was no public policy for collecting and preserving photography. So, we couldn't really understand what people were talking about ...

[7] *Annette and Rudolf Kicken (1947-2014) are major German photography collectors and gallerists.*

KS: Oliver, that's not true! Because we knew, we just couldn't accept it ... If you talk about photography in Düsseldorf, you're only talking about the Bechers and the Becher school, a kind of monoculture. We know and appreciate the work of the Bechers but we weren't ready to accept that they would be the only perspective in photography in Düsseldorf.

OS: We talked with people from the city's cultural affairs and they asked us to deliver our vision of photography; they gave us a space where we could invite many people from different schools representing a diversity of reflections about photography. We did it from 2010 to 2013, and wrote the *ANT!FOTO* manifesto in 2013.

KS: Yes, at the end of it. We produced exhibitions and a magazine with interviews with the artists. And because of the title, some people told us that we should write a manifesto; we said no, explaining that we wouldn't, we had a vision but no manifesto as such. However, we found the idea pleasant, and we wrote one and sent it to many people, asking them to respond to it. It became the last magazine we did, with many reactions to our reflections and assumptions. It allowed for very interesting conversations with artists, authors and curators from all over Europe and America and a few from Japan.

RC: So the point wasn't to throw away photography?

OS: No, of course not! Because we deeply love photography. We wanted to show photography from different perspectives and various angles.

KS: Sometimes you need to have a provocative title. [Smiles] We never, however, thought of it as a provocation ...

RC: Now, Japan ... It's been one your focuses since 2005. What attracted you there?

KS: We first went there as tourists, and we were lucky to get a grant and stay there for three months the following year.

Basically, different things brought us there. For one, it was to have a different perspective on photography. And Japan is a really good place to think about photography: so many bookshops, not so many galleries and only a few museums. I believe their approach through bookmaking is very important. Then there were various topics: *J_Subs* and the *Character zines*; and we met so many nice, interesting people, some of whom became friends. Though we did not expect it in the beginning, we were able to establish a very personal, intimate perspective on Japanese issues.

OS: When you get a grant, you're just thrown into a place and you must deal with the situation. And then they tell you that you have eight weeks to come up with an exhibition, there is 1,500 square metres of space, please fill it. You're a bit shaken about it all ... But it was also very nice to see that there was a strong interest in music from some of the people we encountered. It made it easier to communicate. Some of them are very much interested in the Düsseldorf music scene ... It's something in common ... It felt like digging into an archive of subcultures that are somewhat forgotten about here. But in Japan, they preserve all kinds of music and fashion as well. You can get anything you like there. It was nice to discover again scenes and movements that are preserved there but not here. And I started to make some portraits and compare them to the work done eight years prior. It was a strange feeling.

KS: Well, when you talk about music and Düsseldorf, it might be interesting to add that we have quite an important Japanese community in Düsseldorf. It's not as if we had travelled to Japan and that was it. When we came back home, we could still experience it, in nice local restaurants, bookshops and convenience stores. There are a lot of Japanese people who come to study at the Düsseldorf music academy. So there are good exchanges between us and the Japanese, some of whom are now our friends. It is therefore not so strange for us to go to Japan again and again each year. We still bring back new material and images; we see new details and aspects. I believe this was a very positive influence for us.

RC: Let's go right to the point: was the relationship between Germany and Japan during the Second World War a topic of interest?

KS: In fact, no. You might think about it when you're in Japan, when you go to a bookstore or meet some people, and you wonder "Wow, what went on?" I think the Germans and the Japanese have very distinctive ways of dealing with history. Culturally, they have a totally different way of relating to their past. For us, however, it was never a topic we dealt with. Maybe people are now increasingly aware of the fact that we are working with activists, but it's never been a topic in our work.

RC: I didn't mean to be obnoxious with that question. Now, if we look at Japanese Lesson, *and if I got it right, could we say, in short, that you focused on segregation in Tokyo, and on neighbourhoods that a Western eye could consider as ghettos, where "second-class" citizens are confined.*[8]

KS: I would never call "second-class" citizens people living in discriminated and stigmatized neighbourhoods.

OS: I agree; we would never refer to people in those terms. But yes, there are strange words and ideas about certain populations in Japan.

KS: I think it's a bit like the caste system in India.

OS: Just one word, when we arrived in Japan in 2005 for the first time, we felt very comfortable being in a certain neighbourhood, although it was a very difficult one. We like to go back there, again and again, to do some research in these old areas. Somehow, we connect with lots of people there, it's just a nice community. We're into it.

[8] *Since medieval times, the Japanese term* buraku *refers to these deprived neighborhoods and* burkumin *to their discriminated dwellers, originally for complex issues relating to "impure" trades linked notably to death and blood. Today, their residents are still among the poorest.*

KS: I think this clarifies what we were talking about earlier. Our practice is very personal, but it's not about our personal life. We always build strong personal connections in these neighbourhoods, meeting and exchanging with the people who tell us about their lives. The initial approach is always very personal, not historical or analytical.

> *RC: To make it clear to the audience, for* Japanese Lesson, *you made maps of these neighbourhoods and walked along these limits looking both in the inside and the outside, noting the differences. In other words, you have conceived a kind of topographical approach. Why?*

OS: Well, for some reason, it's kind of logical and even easy, because these districts are historical remnants from the past and their "borders" are visible. Even Google Maps shows you exactly where they are. If you live inside these areas, you are more discriminated than if you live nearby, on the other side of the "border". So, to think of these tiny differences resulting from the fact of living 5 metres inside or outside was a trigger for us. Because this, in itself, determines whether or not you get a job. Likewise for your postal address, your father's profession, your name, surname… Everything is so fragile and you're being judged and supervised by some higher authority… You may have no idea that you're being categorized like this as a human being, stacked on a shelf. Our interest was really to think about these notions of inside and outside. Walking along these borders in these neighbourhoods allows for an understanding of how they shape your identity.

KS: At the time we discovered that system, it was already vanishing. In China, they have a social rating concept. They supervise everything, they check your social media, your WeChat.[9] If you cross the street at the green light, you get a better job or are allowed to travel … This represents the most perverted version of high-tech surveillance, and it's spreading everywhere in the world.

[9] *The Chinese equivalent to WhatsApp.*

Depending on where you live, your social origins, your fate will be different compared to a person living in the other side of the city. It's the same here and I guess it's the same all over the world. But it comes with a different face in different places. We are here in Paris at the moment, working on various projects, and this idea of finding connections, similarities, in different countries is very stimulating. But we don't want to teach anyone a lesson. However, for us, finding connections between Tokyo and Paris, or Japan, Asia and Europe, is interesting in our working process. For example, finding connections between activists … but I might be going too far …

RC: About the title Japanese Lesson, *what is the lesson?*

OS: We were asked that question last week in Hamburg where we opened the project exhibition.

KS: There is so much information … So, the one lesson could be about Japanese photography, because for so many years now, we have talked so much about photography, the different approaches, the image and memory … I think that's something that has shaped our perspective on photography, and learning about Japanese photography likewise shapes our perception of the medium.

OS: I think that when we tell our students about Japanese photography, we do this for one main reason: to trigger some fire in them, because you really feel it there, with all the books they make, how they take photographs, how they intensely think about photography and their practice. It's encouraging, and a fire always stems from a spark.

RC: Katja, could you tell us something about Cry Minami? *I won't go into details, but it's about a Japanese singer who one day decided to shave her hair, and in order not to lose her contract, had to show up on TV, in tears, to apologize for having destroyed her public image … Why did this inspire you?*

KS: It's again about imagery, what we see in the media and how the information gets to us. The first thing I thought about when

I saw this Japanese woman with her hair shaved, were the women in France and Holland after the Second World War whose heads were shaved because they had had some affair with German soldiers. My thought was that shaving a woman's hair is a strong symbol of punishment.

RC: But she did it voluntarily, right?

KS: It seems so, though it isn't clear. Did she really do it on her own? Or did the management decide this might be a clever marketing move? Obviously, shaving a woman's hair is always a form of punishment, and crying publicly on TV is not something you usually see on European TV. This was a strong image for me, so I started thinking about what I could make out of this new, strong image. I always liked this idea of images in the street, you know, stickers ... We gathered information about Hilario Gidez. He was a black man who was killed by the Nazis in the 1930s and I found out about him because someone did stickers about this story. Since then, I've been convinced of the power of stickers. There's so much information on the streets, on lamp poles or traffic lights! I like to use a photograph and move it to another environment. Then, you start thinking about other forms: should it be placed in a book, in an exhibition or in the street? That's just the creative process.

RC: So you created the stickers of Cry Minami *and you pasted them in Tokyo, and other cities in the world, including down the boulevard near my home. [Laughs] Were the reactions any different from one place to another in the world?*

KS: It's hard for me to tell because you don't always know if anyone saw it – whether in London, New York or elsewhere. But in the case of *Cry Minami*, I pasted the stickers on the streets of Paris. As you know, there are many Japanese who travel to Paris. So, a young Japanese woman took a photo of the sticker and posted it on Twitter, and some of our Japanese friends told us that the post had generated fascinating reactions: some of them were utterly racist, some were directly referring to the Second World War ... even provoking theories like

"It was placed next to a Japanese restaurant as a warning not to go there or your hair will be shaved"; others wondered why her. And that's just the issues I'm dealing with: how do people react and why?

RC: In 2018, Oliver, you made a Xerox called Looking at Imaginary Club. *Are you nostalgic?*

OS: I was a little bit disappointed because the book sold out immediately, and I didn't have the time to think about it or discuss it with people. No one wanted to write about it, and that was frustrating because it was constantly on my mind. I wanted to further reflect about the work and have these conversations. Even when it's not through your own words, it's useful to reflect on your practice. So I started a process over several days consisting of photographing myself while looking at my book again, and then producing a Xerox book of that experience. I'm constantly trying to raise debate about my work, notably because of censorship. Regarding China[10], it seems quite interesting to me to think about the original *Imaginary Club*, and the fact that the decision to close my exhibition forces me to take my practice further. It may not even be the refusal to exhibit my work that compels me to do so; it's interesting to think about censorship in general and the people who apply it, to send their ideology out into the world. But at some point, they need to be stopped. I don't know who can do that. I think I'm getting more and more ... not angry, but convinced of where my place is or will be with my form of activism in the world ... it's really important to me.

[10] *In December 2018, a few days before this conversation, the well-known Lianzhou Festival opened in China. A few hours before the opening, local censors came to various exhibition spaces to take down images that had previously been "authorized" by the central authorities. In Oliver Sieber's exhibition about subcultures, only six photographs were left hanging. The directors and curators, in agreement with the artist, then decided to cancel the exhibition that had been stripped of its meaning. The amusing, ludicrous and grotesque aspect of this censorship, relayed via social networks by the Western journalists present in China, was that posters announcing Oliver's exhibition were still displayed throughout the city even when the exhibition was made invisible. Thus, passers-by still had access to his work.*

And I don't really care so much about the fact that they didn't show my work. This generates a positive reaction to go further.

RC: But do you have any idea why the images of Imaginary Club *were censored? What could hurt them?*

OS: At some point I think it's arbitrary – anything could be the reason. It's just a matter of power, not about the images. This is about claiming: "I'm the boss here, and you do what I say." They probably didn't even research my images, perhaps only our biographies. I say "our", because we did an exhibition together in Japan that included Katja's series on Tiananmen … In the real world, no one cares about rockabilly hairdos and tattoos, so it can't be about that …

RC: And you even did photographs of young Chinese people with incredible looks at parties …

KS: Maybe that's not so dangerous. It's only fashion.

RC: Last year, in 2017, Oliver published For Sale, *with images of all the cameras you used over the years, mainly for* Imaginary Club *and its side projects. Are cameras useless today?*

OS: I like cameras … [Laughs] Unfortunately, it doesn't make any more sense to use all of them today. I have one I really like and I use it. But camera-less photography is also interesting.

KS: Well, but you must admit that you love cameras. When a new lens comes up, you start wondering what new idea of photography it will deliver for you. And then you'll say: "Now I need a new camera." It's a real, important issue for you. I believe you could never make a project with your smartphone.

OS: No, for me, when I wanted to make a certain portrait, I had to use a certain camera because they each have their specific features. Hence, for *SkinsModsTeds,* I used an 8x10 camera with Polaroid film, because this is what was appropriate for me at the time.

If you want to use the flash, all depends on the camera you use. I'm always looking for the right tool for the job. So, I did *For Sale* to see the connections between the photographs I took and the tools I used, and also the recordings I did. The sounds are so important, not because they're nice to listen to, but because they're quality checks somehow; if the sound is kind of bad, then the quality of the image may be so as well. So, the book deals with that matter as well.

RC: Right, the book comes with a CD of the recorded sounds of the shutter of each camera.

OS: Yes.

RC: The funny thing is that you used analogue cameras but the recording that you made of them is digital.

OS: We also recorded digital cameras.

RC: But the sound of digital cameras is fake, right?

OS: No, they also make noise, but it's not the shutter. It's the lens when it comes out. You can hear that.

RC: OK.

OS: They are still mechanical noises. Everything you hear is mechanical noise, and we decided to do this with a digital microphone because the other old, analogue systems are not good enough for this. If you have this small Ricoh camera that has a small, tiny click, it wouldn't work.[11]

RC: You needed to equalize.

OS: Yes, except that when you use an equalizer, you lose some of the details ...

KS: Yes, and you also "equalize" the needs ...

[11] *Oliver recorded these sounds with Axel Ganz, a musician from Düsseldorf.*

OS: Yes! We don't want that! In the same way we don't want to print our images all in the same format, in A4 for example. They would relate in a way that wouldn't work.

20 December 2018

PIERRE VON KLEIST
JOSÉ PEDRO CORTES & ANDRÉ PRINCIPE

The independent artist-run publishing house Pierre von Kleist, based in Lisbon, was founded in 2009 by Portuguese artists José Pedro Cortes and André Principe, both born in 1976 in Porto. They have published 35 books to date.

Pierre von Kleist rose to fame and was immediately established as a major actor on the international photobook scene with the publication of the facsimile of *Lisboa: cidade triste e alegre* by Victor Palla and Costa Martins: a masterpiece of Portuguese photography that could easily compare with William Klein's *New York* [see p. 178]. This journey into the past was but a small detour before pursuing publishing of contemporary photography – their own work and that of others close to them. Pierre von Kleist's editorial line could be defined as poetically committed in the contemporary world, or, as the two publishers would say, as "a dance between objectivity and subjectivity". Here, they revisit their editorial and personal journeys. They also tell of the necessity and of the difficulties of their double activity as artists and as publishers. This conversation was held in my library, on the day after Offprint Paris in 2018.

> Rémi Coignet: *The very first book released under the imprint Pierre von Kleist was Silence, by you, Zé Pedro*[1]*, in 2005 if I am not mistaken. That same year, André, you published your first book,* Tunnels, *with Booth-Clibborn. But I think it was in 2009 that Pierre von Kleist became…*

André Principe: Became an active cell, as they say in terrorism! But to talk about the beginning, the first time that the idea came up of creating a publishing house together, Zé and I, was when I was in the process of trying to find the publisher for my first book, *Tunnels*. We both lived in London in those days, and we were both very much into photobooks.

[1] *Zé Pedro, or Zé, is a diminutive for José Pedro.*

Let's go back a bit. We've known each other since we were three years old! We went to primary school together, to secondary school together and all that. And we shared an apartment in the 1980s and 1990s. We felt estranged from the world then, as there was no internet or good bookshops ... The only thing we could get our hands on were magazines and newspapers, like *Melody Maker*, *New Musical Express*, *i-D*, *Face* ... We were also into music, anything that we could get from abroad. This was like seeing what Kurt Cobain is wearing one week, but also being exposed to [Wolfgang] Tillmans and [Juergen] Teller without even knowing who they were. Every so often, we would find a book – let's say, *The Americans* by Robert Frank, something like that, and because we had so few books, we started to spend a lot of time with them. So, books have always been there.

Later, I went to film school and I felt frustrated with the process of making a film, the producers and everything. When I left film school, I decided that the photobook is a medium I wanted to always have in my life, to work with; I thought that it would be kind of like a film, but cheaper. In the years we both were living in London, I had an exhibition at the Centro Português de Fotografia, an important museum in Portugal at the time, curated by the great Tereza Siza. And there was going to be a book as well. I was the first one to have a show, so I was the first to go through the whole publishing process. I tried in London where I met Michael Mack [see *Conversations*, p. 180]. I just went there with my book ... this was in 2003 or 2004. Michael Mack said he would publish it, but only in two years. I was completely shocked, because as a young man, I could not wait two years!

I also went to Portugal to try to find a publishing house, though I had no idea how it worked there. It didn't take me long to find out that there was only one publishing house that released photobooks then, but I also found that they had no specific editorial line or any particular idea; the books that were published were the ones that came with money. I was a bit shocked by that.

RC: I think anyone would be shocked to discover the backstage of the publishing drama.

AP: So, with many difficulties, I finally managed to publish my book with Booth-Clibborn. It wasn't an easy process but I observed a lot and realized that in Portugal, there were not all the limitations I had to face with Booth-Clibborn, a subsidiary of Thames & Hudson. Soon after I finished making the book, I was going to have the show. Zé was already going through the whole process and was looking for a publisher. I told him about my experience and that we would always have this problem: we would always need to come up with the money, we would not have control over the design, the distribution would not be handled the way we wanted it to be; and in the end, they don't care because they have so many other things to deal with.
We started thinking that we would gain experience – this was not the only book we ever wanted to make, we were going to make a lot of books! And since we were always going to have this problem, why not do it ourselves?

José Pedro Cortes: There are also some parallel things; for one, we don't come from a specific art background.

RC: What did you study, Zé?

JPC: I first studied management...

RC: Which is a good thing if you want to manage a publishing company! [Laughs]

JPC: Yes! And then halfway through, I was also eventually drawn to do things with cinema and with photography. I started early with photography, but only received my master's later, at 27. Before that publishing house idea, when we were 19 or 21, we thought of creating a space like a gallery, to show our zines and bring other people in. And in a way, that idea turned into a publishing house. We knew for instance the books of Daniel Blaufuks. [see Conversations, p. 42 and Conversations 2, p. 22] There were a few people who were important to us in Portugal and Daniel was clearly one of them. André met him in film school. So, our aim was to create a structure, the idea being that there certainly was a small niche that we could fill.

So when we started to think about publishing books, and had the initial idea of creating a space, the point was to keep control over what we were doing, and since we didn't have the support of a school, or artists around us, it required some persistence.

AP: Actually, we were talking about this yesterday, we were talking about how, somehow, we swapped our initial idea. An important thing when we started, coming from the fast-publishing, magazine world, was to take photos and publish them immediately. When we were kids, the books would come out, and most of the time there was a large time lapse between the time the work was made and when it was finally published. For example, photos of Mexico taken in the 1970s would only be published in the 1990s. There was always this time gap. For us, young photographers who were not photographing when we were 10 years old, the notion of not being dependent on this or that publisher, to be able to do a body of work for 2 or 3 years and to publish it when it was completed, was very attractive. We wanted to photograph our times, and this was a very important reason why we wanted to have the publishing house. We didn't want the time of reflection, this passing time. This was very important in the beginning, as Zé was saying. However, I don't necessarily agree with him on this point. Visiting Offprint this year – and considering all that has happened in the self-publishing movement in the past 15 years, with the internet, social media etc. – it seems to me that the situation has reversed, meaning that images are not being published too fast: they are published immediately. You see kids in school making their fanzines, and upon graduation releasing their book; everything is published immediately as it is made, with no reflection. So, I may be overreacting, but as you know, it is a blow to the quality, to the seriousness of the work.

RC: Martin Parr [see Conversations 2, *p. 148] said the same thing a few years ago in Kassel*[2]*. We were having tea downstairs at the cafeteria, and he said: "Look upstairs [pointing to the fair], there are so many young people*

[2] The Kassel Fotobookfestival in Germany is the oldest festival exclusively concerned with photobooks. It celebrated its 10th anniversary in 2018.

trying to talk the lingua franca *of contemporary photography, but there are very few who are really interesting."*

AP: Right, and I was thinking about this: you take a photo and publish it immediately. But what happens when you work with analogue photography, which we still practice, between the shooting and the moment it is published? I am re-exploring all these mysterious processes. I was fighting that in the beginning, and now, I feel it's all going too fast. You know, the books that I'm excited about this year in Paris are Saul Leiter or Garry Winogrand. I like these. Looking back is also a reaction to what is happening. Books that took 20 years to do are again the sexier ones.

RC: Why did you choose the name Pierre von Kleist? I cannot remember precisely, and could not find it on your website, but you made up a biography, a man who was some kind of an adventurer…

JPC: A Second World War hero…

AP: And the world's most important photobook collector… His house got bombed during the war and that's how he lost his collection.

JPC: It's funny that, the other day, or maybe a year ago, we were looking into the emails we wrote when André was living in New York and I in Porto, in 2001. At the time, we were discussing opening the space and we were emailing suggestions of names for the venue. There were over 100 names, from the most bizarre to the most normal names for shopping centres in Portugal. Two names were very close to each other.

AP: Which ones?

JPC: John Fuller or Jack Bartok.

AP: We wanted a name that sounded great, really aristocratic in a way. Something that sounded so good that the guy must be doing great things. Obviously, it has to do with Heinrich von Kleist, whose work we've read, of course, but it's not a tribute to him. It's something more instinctive.

JPC: Here again, in a retrospective way, there was always a playful side to it. The point was neither to be serious, nor to be afraid of our endeavour. We needed to select a name and make up a biography, because in 2009, our project was still small. People didn't know we were behind it, even in Porto! It was not that we were afraid or that we wanted to keep it a secret. Still today, people are asking for Pierre at fairs. And we still receive emails now with "Dear Pierre ..." In 2009 we launched the website with the bio, and two or three days after, the first email we received was from a so-called Pierre von Kleist.

RC: Really?

AP: Really! He said his name was Pierre von Kleist, he lived in Uruguay and was on the internet with his kids looking for family history; he had googled his name and we had come up first. So, he was wondering if we were somehow connected [Laughs]. This would be a project for Daniel (Blaufuks), because the man was German and Jewish and emigrated to Uruguay. But let me say that the first sentence of the biography was: "Besides being a Second World War hero, PvK is the most important photobook collector of all times." It claimed that though he isn't famous, he has nevertheless written some of the most important texts ever written about photobooks. I even wrote a text, supposedly signed by Pierre, about a book that never existed and that would have been entitled "The 35 African Tribe Leaders". It was supposed to be one of those German ethnographic books from the 1920s or 1930s, but with a twist. In that text, I was implying that Ed Ruscha had borrowed his titles from there. I pretended that it was a mysterious book because it was called "The 35 African Tribe Leaders", but it comprised only 33 photographs of tribe leaders and three photos of swimming pools. This was a while ago, it was fun to make. Which is what matters, really.

RC: Yes of course, it's always important to have fun. In 2009 the name of Pierre von Kleist reached a broader audience.

That year you published three or four books, including the facsimile of Lisboa, cidade triste e alegre *by Victor Palla and Costa Martins. The book was originally published in 1959. It is a milestone in the Portuguese photobook history and came back to light thanks to Martin Parr and Gerry Badger*[3]*. What was your goal? To pay tribute to this remarkable volume? To make it available to an audience (including myself) who never saw the original?*

AP: It is a story more than it is an idea or an intention. With everything we do, there is a story, something happens. In 2005 we published Zé Pedro's first book. At the time, the idea of a publishing house was already there, but we weren't real active. Zé did his book by himself with some designers, and it was released under the Pierre von Kleist imprint: the idea and the logo were there, but the *modus operandi* was not established, nor was the distribution. Zé did it himself, the way I did with the Booth-Clibborn book. As you know, we were then living in different cities.

Then, in 2007/8, we moved to Lisbon in a house with some other people and the idea of launching the publishing house came back. But we needed money and projects. The Palla project (*Lisboa*) was not our idea initially. We had no experience with that kind of publication. It came about because I was making a documentary about Victor Palla[4]. I met him when he was alive. He asked me if I liked photography, and then he showed me the book *Lisboa*. I was blown away! I asked him if he had other material of that kind to show me, and where I could buy it. He told me that it was difficult to find. This is how the story started.

Palla then died. I kept in touch with his family and after that I contacted the Centro Português de Fotografia. The hype was coming up, and Zé and I were part of it…

In London we did the rounds of all the bookstores and all

[3] *Martin Parr and Gerry Badger,* The Photobook: A History, *Vol. 1, Phaidon Press, 2004.*

[4] *Victor Palla (1922–2006) is one of the most important Portuguese architects of his generation. His architectural oeuvre is in line with the International Style and modernism (e.g. Le Corbusier, Oscar Niemeyer). He was also a photographer, a painter, a graphic designer and a publisher.*

the galleries. There was Michael Mack, we knew about this. So, we put the family in touch with Steidl, or was it SteidlMack at the time? We were in the middle, sending messages back and forth to everyone. It seemed that they were going to publish *Lisboa* and we worked hard for that to happen. We were very happy because that was going to prove that Portuguese photobooks existed, that there was a history. Then, something went wrong. We met the family and asked when would the book be released, but we soon realized that it was never going to happen. Some were in favour, others were against. The book had been printed in photogravure, which could no longer be done. I remember Palla once telling me about people being too fetishist about it; he would have published it in Xerox copies if he could have...
So when that conversation came up, I told the family that their father and grandfather had once told me this, and it kind of put an end to the debate. It became clear that either we were going to do it, or it wouldn't happen. And I asked Zé whether we should consider doing it.

JPC: Again, there were these small events that happened one after the other and that led us to making the book, including meeting Gerry Badger. When we decided to make the book, at first we didn't even know how to reproduce it! When Victor Palla died, we went to his house with his daughter, and it was soon clear that there were no negatives. We decided to photograph the original book for the reprint. When we visited various printers in Portugal, they all said that it was impossible to make. And you know how important the binding is, especially for this book. We then asked one of the best printers, showing him the original book, telling him the same story. And he replied: "I know this book very well. As it happens, my wife is the daughter of a famous gallery owner who, in the 1980s, did a show with Victor Palla and published what some people consider the second edition of the book." In 1959 it was published in seven fascicles that people had to bind together themselves. And in 1982 he did a show called "Lisboa e Tejo e Tudo" [Lisbon and the Tagus and the Rest] at Galeria Ether. At the time, they had found 300 sets of the fascicles for which they conceived a new cover, with yellow letters, and thus revived the book.

They sold 300 copies internationally, which enabled the likes of Martin Parr and others to get a copy.

AP: His name was António Sena, by the way, and he is responsible for the recognition of the book in the 1980s. And by coincidence, the printer is married to his daughter and knew the whole story.

JPC: And he knows a lot; he helped us tremendously, trying out things with the ink and papers and all. About the same time, there was this Martin Parr and Gerry Badger book, and we wrote to Martin Parr. We told him about our plan with the book and asked whether he would want to write a text for it. It seemed important. He replied that he did not write the texts, Gerry did and does. We didn't know Gerry Badger, so we got in touch by email and he just said okay if we offered him the plane tickets to Lisbon. Gerry came to our flat that we were sharing with four other people and stayed with us. For three days we visited Victor Palla's archives, in his office; we showed Gerry some of the places seen by Palla. We worked a little bit, and we had lots of fun in Lisbon the three of us. That's how Gerry wrote this important text. He was very enthusiastic about the whole project.
Little by little, with support from the printer, Gerry contextualizing the work and a little bit of financial support that we managed to get to start, we launched the project. 2009 was the 50th anniversary of the first edition of the book, so we had this deadline to have the book ready by December, and not only December, a bit earlier for Paris Photo.
And we came with the zines ...

AP: ... and three copies of *Lisboa*.

> *RC: Yes, three copies only. I can remember when I saw the copies, I was waiting at Schaden's booth for the book to arrive. I was asking Markus who this Pierre von Kleist was, because the biography that you invented seemed a bit farfetched to me. And he told me they were young Portuguese artists.*

AP: Let me say one thing about the financial chaos it was to do this book. We were completely irresponsible and completely unaware of the mechanics of it. The book cost between 40,000 euros and 50,000 euros to make, with contracts for royalties etc. We had to raise that money and we knew nothing about that. We managed to organize presales to a bank for 500 copies, which raised more or less 25,000 euros, just half of the production costs. And as the deadline was approaching, the printer asked us to send him our VAT number and some money. Maybe he was wondering who these kids were and whether they actually had any money.

Peter von Kleist wasn't official, and we didn't know how to go about it. This guy perhaps freaked out at some point and said he wouldn't do one more thing before we set up a company. But he did help us through the process. And then he added that he would not give us the books unless we paid him first for the materials, and we were already late on that. And he also told us that the second payment was due 60 days after delivery of the book.

We didn't have that kind of money and had no clue what we were going to do. We went to banks to ask for loans, but they said no, even with our parents as guarantors. Nothing worked. So we convinced the guy to give us 100 copies before we gave him any money, just 100 copies for the book launch. And on that day, we sold 100 copies at 90 euros each, which meant we had 9,000 euros. The printer was a bit impressed; we went to Paris with only ... three copies. We didn't sell them, but showed them around, including to Jeffrey Ladd[5], whose blog at the time was quite important, and he selected it as his book of the year the following December ... Overnight, 100 to 200 people had bought their copy through our PayPal. I can still remember waking up one morning and checking our emails: there were 200 new emails, all new names ... I wondered what was happening! It was a different time then, a time when it was hard to find a resource online. And then I also saw that you had listed it

[5] *In 2007 Jeffrey Ladd created* 5B4, *the first critical blog to review photobooks. Jeffrey Ladd's book culture and the quality of his writing soon made* 5B4 *an international reference in the field. His work largely influenced my decision to launch* Des Livres et des photos *in 2008, hosted on* Le Monde*'s website. There was nothing of the kind in French back then, and I shared with him the idea of a journalistic approach to photobook reviews. While* 5B4 *is still online (http://5b4.blogspot.com), the blog was closed in 2013.*

on your blog for *Le Monde*. And suddenly, we felt this extreme explosion of sales.
I must add that Markus Schaden also helped us a lot. He was then the best bookseller, perhaps even of all time[6]. He bought many copies from us, helped us with the distribution and contributed to making our imprint known. This was actually the book that really made the international shift for us, also allowing us to meet many members of the photobook community. And it also allowed us to make new books. It took us one to two years to get to publish *Lisboa*, with very tough financial pressure as we just told you and also realising how ignorant we were. But through these lucky coincidences, the financial pressure was cleared out in one month. We paid our dues to the printer on time, a very happy ending. We had this hip book in our hands, we had our name around and we had this spare money to make other books ... and then came the post-Lisboa moment.

RC: Well, that was my next question: How do you find money for your new books? Do you wait for the previous ones to sell to have the money for the upcoming ones?

JPC: It depends, and it has shifted over the years. We've managed to create a system that lasts for two to three books, sometimes having to readjust along the process. Initially we started with small print runs and most of the books were financed by ourselves. Then we tried to recover our expenses through sales. Then we started with special editions. Right from the beginning, we were under pressure. We wanted each book to work, we felt responsible for the book to have a life, for the distribution to be good. We put care and effort into selling the special editions well. We're talking about a period where things were going well internationally for us, even though in the early 2010s there weren't that many book fairs like there are now.
In Portugal I started to give workshops with people who didn't even know *The Americans*! And now, they are book collectors.

[6] *He founded a brick-and-mortar bookstore in Cologne, Germany and was a pioneer of the online bookshop with schaden.com, active from 1998 to 2012. He played a fundamental role in the diffusion of high-end contemporary photobooks.*

There was an audience to build up and this was a full process: we had to be responsible for the money we were putting into it, and it was really important that each book release be made special. Suddenly finding ourselves at the helm of a company, and thus financially responsible for each title, forced us to be very practical and serious about it.
After two or three years, especially after the release of my second book, *Things Here and Things Still to Come*, and of *White Noise* by António Júlio Duarte, the amount of investment grew steadily, and it went well. We had to run after the horse a little faster, which gave us a bit of muscle ... And then again, after two or three years, we had to readjust to smaller print runs; sales were not doing too well. Not just for us, because there were more books available on the market.

RC: Yes, and there was the 2008/2009 economic crisis. Pierre von Kleist grew up with the crisis.

AP: After *Lisboa* we had some little money and we felt very responsible after what we'd been through. My book *Tunnels* was published with a print run of 3,000 copies, and whatever happened that I don't know about because Thames & Hudson's distribution is weird, 1,000 copies failed to be distributed back in 2005/2006. So we were aware of what happens to the books ...
After *Lisboa* we were very cautious about the print run of the books we published, mine or other authors'; they were small books and we did 300 copies, even if this meant that we wouldn't necessarily make our money back ...
We assumed the risk.
The 500 copies of *Lisboa* sold and we turned a profit.
This is what gave us the confidence to do larger hardcover books: we were then already aware of the financial montage needed, we knew how to handle projects, whether it was a print run of 500 or 1,000 copies. We were cautious, more experienced, even if sometimes we still made mistakes ... because you never know what will happen to a book.
JPC: Over a period of nine years, there are three types of books that we published: books for which we invest most of the money ourselves, which is over half of our catalogue; then, over a period of two years, we received a grant from the Portuguese

government that covered about 20 per cent of all the costs; and then, especially this year, there are publications conceived in collaboration with a museum or an institution, or co-published with a fellow publisher, for example the first book we did with Daniel Blaufuks, *Fábrica*. However, most of the process comes from our investment and the way we support the books. By the way, when we say investment, we're talking about the money for the books. If we were working for five months on a book thinking only about the money we would make, it would be a disaster. We're not talking about money that goes into our pockets. It goes directly into the making of the books.

AP: It's interesting, because out of need, out of financial circumstances, we both had to learn graphic design. Though we had a perfect understanding of bookmaking, we couldn't afford a graphic designer. So we learned to do everything ourselves, which is something I quite like.
I think it's part of our identity to be able to do everything by ourselves. We often compare ourselves to people of our generation like Mörel or RVB, but also to the older generation like Gösta Flemming at Journal Publishing, and van Zoetendaal. But you must keep in mind that we are artists: most of our time is spent taking photographs, doing shows or making films. Publishing is just another one of our activities! We have to manage all that ... For Pierre, we find the money, we do the editing and the design of the books, we distribute, we travel to fairs. So, this is one big thing we do among many other activities.

RC: Yes, and that's a real issue. Because regarding the financial aspect, we've been talking like businessmen, and thus about material matters: finding money, calculating the costs, going to the post office to send off the books ... Isn't this double activity boring, I mean as artists?

AP: It is, but you know, we are Portuguese artists! [Laughs] Pedro Costa is always talking about that. People are always telling him about creativity, and his response is: "Shit! What are you talking about? Sixty per cent of my time is spent paying my bills etc." Creativity is easy! But we don't have that privilege. The issue of costs is at the heart of our system. Of course, this is boring, but it is unimaginable for us to do it any differently. And in a way, there's a political aspect, and a form of responsibility, including financial, involved in bringing a creation into the public sphere, which I quite like.

JPC: Also, and this relates to what he was just saying: we see loads of examples in Portugal where tons of money are poured into books by institutions or more mainstream publishers, and that money goes straight down the drain, with no tangible result. So when you see an institution spending four times more money than we do to publish a book, pay for the graphic design and so many other things, and that in the end, half of the print run remains in the basement, then you understand the error. The problem is that the bigger financial means are delivered with total lack of thought about what to do with the book project. A fatal mix that destroys everything.

RC: I didn't want to go into this, but last time I was in Lisbon, I was amazed by the number of books published by the Gulbenkian Foundation.

AP: Well, let's talk about that! The same happens all over the place, but in Portugal most of the art books or artist monographs are published by and completely paid for by institutions. They are still very much working the old way, including producing bilingual editions. The artists are usually happy to have a book – it will often be their only book – so they want to do a kind of portfolio that will present their complete works. Which means assuming from the start that the book will not make money because this is not commercially feasible. Then, they give away this huge book, this portfolio, and it will not be considered an artwork as such.
We always compare books to children, and so we call these books abandoned children. We also say that this is not only about giving birth. It is about feeding and raising these children until they reach 18. They will then be able to lead their own life. This is what we try to do with our books: not just launch the book, have it in the shops, and "boom!", and then, at the end of the year, the leftover copies are remaindered. No way! They need to be taken care of. We see how much energy and

waste is happening in book production. So, for us, it is a political act to fight that, and thus to be rational about the amounts of books printed, deciding what to do with the books and how to fight for them.

JPC: People don't drive down to Portugal for the weekend like Germans can travel to Berlin. In the same way, you wouldn't hop on a train from Paris to Lisbon like you would to Brussels or London. No one does that. The biggest effort is not only in the book making. I personally think that there are many great things being done in Portugal in the arts. But while the books are good, the fact is that we are talking about something material. Yesterday, I was comparing it to film. Portugal has a great, internationally renowned cinema, because film has become immaterial: now, the process is digital. No need to carry your 35mm film rolls around to cinemas. They are in a file, with no geographical limitations. But with material objects, you must travel by plane with your load, show it around, talk about it, and this does require a real effort to be at the heart of a practice. Not just in Portugal, also internationally.

AP: Think about Portuguese photography. Paulo Nozolino, for example, was living in Paris. Each artist made it by themselves. Those are strong men who have strong work, but they were completely alone. There was no scene. So, what do we have today? You have Pierre von Kleist, which is us, plus André Cepeda, António Júlio Duarte, the authors we publish.
Pierre von Kleist is now the visible face, a very important face of Portuguese photography. But we're not even full-time publishers, we work with so little! Where are the strong Portuguese photography curators? Where are the businesses? Where are the Portuguese collectors? Where are the mainstream publishing houses? Where are the Taschens and Steidls? There's nothing. There's no scene. It's different elsewhere.
We still sell enough books. Here in Paris, we see the Dutch, they are there, we see 100 or 200 people from the Dutch scene; along with the Swedish, the Germans, the Swiss and so on.
But we don't have any of that in Portugal. It's just us. This means a lot less money available, with undeniable consequences on what we do and the way we do it.

RC: In some ways, your situation is comparable to that of our Spanish neighbours, with people at Blank Paper or NoPhoto/Phree having to do everything by themselves.

AP: Yes, I guess that would be the closest, though somewhat different. Spain is richer, bigger, and the country has achieved its regionalization. Which means that the regions enjoy substantial financial autonomy to support the arts and to have their own museums. The Spanish scene is much more diverse.

JPC: Yes, but I guess they have the same problems with printing, or money wasting. It happens everywhere.

RC: We've been talking quite a lot about money and the material issues. But what makes a good book project for Pierre von Kleist? I have the feeling that you would happily reject anything that looked like documentary style photography.

AP: I guess there is a Pierre von Kleist world, an idea of photography. First, I would like to say that we are an author's publishing house, along the line of *Cahiers du Cinéma* in the 1960s, and the politics of authors. This was always very important to us. We work with the authors and not on a project; we work on their vision of the world, book after book. Thus constituting a body of work rather than a large, sensational project. Then, about the work of the authors we work with, I guess you could say that it's always committed to the world we live in. It's not digital manipulation. It's always material extracted from the real world, specific places like Canada, Algeria ... We always want the authors to be dancing between the objective and the subjective. We don't believe in documents in the way that a passport is a document. We think the best documents are novels. What are the best documents about Russia in the 19th century? Tolstoy or Dostoevsky. And Bob Dylan or Leonard Cohen are the documentarists of the 1960s. Though it's not thought of as documents but as art, their work is in tune with the world we live in, and their commitment is poetically fair to this world.

RC: Other than yourselves, you mainly publish Portuguese photographers. Is this deliberate? I know that other nationalities are also present in your catalogue, but there is a small group around you with António Júlio Duarte, Daniel Blaufuks, André Cepeda ...

JPC: This was not our original idea. When we started, we knew some people we wanted to work with, and we were also talking to other people who are not Portuguese about making a book together. There are practical aspects in the way we run our projects: most of our editing process requires physical presence, time and discussions. And most of the people we publish become our friends. We were talking about money earlier. But when it comes to the books and their production, it becomes a lot more romantic, as André would say; with even sometimes that old-fashioned notion of bookmaking as a process of shared experiences between a group of individuals. And these experiences deliver a book. Therefore, we often work with Portuguese people. Also, we came to realize at a certain point that if these people hadn't come to us, they probably would never have had that book published, and they might have stopped everything.

AP: Yes, that's one of the reasons. And we also see authors and works in Portugal that we think are strong and need to be published. However, we know full well that if we don't take them on board, nobody will. We feel responsible for what is created back home. In the past, events may have happened that you don't know about, that nobody knows about, because they were lost in the periphery of the publishing process; so they don't really exist. The other aspect is indeed practical, but there are people from abroad, some of them you know, like Osamu Kanemura, Keiko Nomura and Nils Petter Löfstedt, with whom we are working.

RC: Well, let's talk about Japan. It is one of your major interests, both as authors and publishers. What attracts you to Japan and to Japanese photography?

JPC: I guess we both developed an interest in Japan before doing books. This came from various sources: cinema, poetry and photography. And through all that, Japan grew into

our lives. You know António Júlio Duarte's series, *Japan Drug*? He did it in 1997. We had no connection with him then. The fact that he was exploring Japan has nothing to do with why we chose to publish him. There was a previous version of that book and the edit was not very good. So when we saw the whole body of work, we knew we had to do another book. We told him: "Let's forget about those 27 pictures that you chose and let's do something bigger."
André started to travel to Japan in 2001 to make a documentary about Japanese photographers. I was invited in 2012 for the project "European Eyes on Japan". It happened gradually. We started to have Japanese distribution a few years ago and our books sell quite well. Our work is well considered in Japan, and we started to go there regularly, gradually building connections with more authors and publishers. In the end, there are a lot of ties that connect us, not only through our tastes, but also through what we have produced in the last nine years.

AP: I would like to say two things. One deals with Japanese photographers and their practice of photography, to which we feel close, like most of our authors do. Often their approach is – and I am going to use this completely overused word – diaristic, which no longer means anything anymore. Indeed, what does diaristic mean in Japan today? It means that they don't have a pre-set project; they practise daily, as they would a sport. That's what it means.

RC: That's what Daidō Moriyama always says *[see* Conversations, *p. 200].*

AP: It's not something like, "Dear diary, I fell in love…" or any secret intimacy. No, it's like sports. I come from sports, and physical activity was always more important to me than school: a discipline practised daily, like playing guitar or the piano every day. It's like thinking about photography as a martial art, approaching it as a physical activity. We've always behaved like that, with that spirit, and that's one thing we have in common with the Japanese. Secondly, for several economic reasons, gallery spaces are very small in Japan. And for all kinds of reasons, the photobook was traditionally the privileged, natural medium. Photographers understood from an early age that the book was essential. Which was also our case, as we already told you earlier. Growing up in Portugal, the photobook was always important because it wasn't easy to find. So, there are two strong connections: the nature of the photographer's practice, and the photobook as the ultimate medium. It all became clear to me in 2001. I was living in NYC and I went to see a show called "New York 71"; I didn't know who Daidō Moriyama was and the show was amazing. Additionally, public libraries work very well in New York, so I could borrow 10 or 20 books and keep them for a month. I could then leaf through all the Winogrands, the Friedlanders, etc.

RC: Yes, you told me when I visited your studio in Lisbon last spring.

AP: This really was how I learned, looking at books. Visiting the Daidō Moriyama show struck me deeply. And the books were exhibited there as well. Back home, I started to remember the photos I liked. I couldn't remember a single photo, just the feeling. This changed the way I looked at photography. The point is not to try to solve one single image equation, but to organize a set of elements to create this one body of work which is the book.

RC: Yes, and that's the interesting thing about books, we all agree on this: it's not about a single image but about editing and sequencing. I think that this relates to your conception: Lewis Baltz [see Conversations, *p. 30] was talking about "photography as this small and narrow space between literature and cinema".*

JPC: I agree, but I would say between poetry and cinema. Because if you think of literature, novels, there are structures, like in narratively structured films. You have a background that, in a sense, gives a better understanding, and this could compare with documentary, as André was saying, which is also my point of view.
The most criticized part of photography, and sometimes

its weakness, is non-narrative photography. A 2D representation where there is nothing to know. If you want to learn something, you must turn to photojournalism, or a photo novel, or whatever. I tend to play with an idea and build the book from that idea. We also work on the gaps between the images. It's important for us that the book be slightly ambiguous or carry a subjective view of reality; in the sense that we don't tell a story in a visible manner. We project an image, as with poetry. The image is a kind of fragmentation of reality. And then, by gathering them in blocks, they come together to constitute the book.

AP: We completely come from literature and books, as teenagers, and then as young adults, cinema was the thing. I studied cinema and psychology, but film was everything. We didn't come to photography through the fine arts but through literature and film. When we started editing books together, as I was just coming out of film school, my language was entirely filmic: I had studied editing and montage, so I would talk about *mise en scène* or dealing with what goes on off-screen. Wasn't it like that in the beginning, Zé? And we continue to practise that language. Should you be standing behind us while we're editing a book on the computer, you'd think that we're in a film editing process.

RC: It's interesting that in English, the term "editing" applies both to the selection of images for a book and of scenes for a film.

JPC: Indeed.

RC: When it comes to publishing one of your own books, for instance, how do you go about it? Do you, Zé Pedro, tell André: "I have this body of work that's ready now"?

AP: There's something to be said about this: it sucks to be your own publisher. Zé and I both suffer from this.

JPC: We've been friends for a long time. We knew each other as teenagers and shared similar interests. Then, in our thirties, we started to know each other as co-publishers, so that was another thing we had to discover. And now, André is my editor, my publisher and my friend. So, I think I went through phases, and in the beginning there was the excitement of making the book.

AP: To discover.

JPC: Yes, to discover the work. But at the start, you're sometimes afraid, nervous, defensive because of all the things we need to negotiate over time. You know, we worked on many books together over the years, and especially for the first books we would work very closely together. But as time went by, we started to work more individually. We've reached a point now where it's closer to the end of the process when we share and exchange on the editing, back and forth, again and again. And we do have strong opinions. So, we leave it to rest for a moment, allowing us time and distance, and then we go for it.

AP: We work differently with our own books than we do with other people's. With our authors, the process is much more collaborative. Zé and I exchange about it throughout. With our own books, each one of us will start to conceive a dummy; so, we're on our own for the earlier steps. Only after that do we show the project to the other, already in that form. With the other books, we create and work on that form together. And with some of the authors, we can even decide the body of work that we want to publish. Or decide whether to publish this Japanese series and not that American project, or both. So, regarding our own work, the first steps of the process are solitary, then we show it to the other, and then there's the time of the confrontation and exchange. And in the end, we meet on common ground.

> *RC: Perhaps because when you are dealing with your own book, it becomes much more emotional?*

AP: Yes, and we know that being able to turn to another person who does not have the same involvement in the work is a good thing, though you need to find the right timing for that. If Zé puts something together and shows me, I now know very quickly what he wants to do, and I can react to what is not working. I can see what he is trying to express, and I can think about what might be missing. Then we can work together. Again, it's difficult to publish your own book.

JPC: And even more of a stretch to sell it.

AP: I hope that, as a publisher, I can handle the whole thing: sell the book, defend the work. I can be warm and protect my author. I can even lie to them if sales are not too good. If they feel that the work is good, I can tell them that it isn't quite so. I can sense their needs and insecurities. I can protect them as a publisher, I can take the bullets for them and let them have the credit when reception is good. But when it's my own book, I take all the bullets, and no one is there to defend me. And as an author, when you finish your book, you just want to have a glass of wine. However, as a publisher, I still need to write the press release, photograph the book or go to the post office. You have no time to relax, take some distance, step back and enjoy it. No, you still need to take care of it.

JPC: It's basically as if we had created this island with its own working process, its own rules. We've talked many times about bringing our own book projects to other publishers. But we're now at a point where we feel like a deeply rooted tree. At some point, I was working on this book project, *Costa*, with another publisher, but it fell through because I suddenly realized how hard it was for me. I couldn't let go of the process, maybe disagree and in the end accept not really getting what I wanted. We did build this tree, and it is difficult to get it off the ground and go somewhere else. At some point we thought of hiring someone to handle our table in Paris. But we reached the conclusion that people buy our books because we are there, and they want to talk to us. Everything is connected in our practice, as artists, as publishers and as authors. Sometimes we sell our books because we ask people: "Would you want a signed copy? I'm the author." It's clearly a pleasure to be making a new book, to be in Paris, to show it, to go around looking at other people's books, to go to dinners and drink, fully knowing that the next day, you need to wake up early to be at our table. We live both worlds of the book.

AP: We see our authors when they come to Paris with a new book. They're so relaxed; they go see all the exhibitions. And I tell myself: "Oh man ... what the fuck!"
You know, we still think of 2009 as year 1, when we founded the company and released *Lisboa*. It will be 10 years next year. This is insane. It went so fast. On the plane on our way here, we were trying to tally it up. Daniel Blaufuks's new release, *1+1=1*, is our 30th book, or perhaps it's the 35th! I mean, how did we make it? You have to remember that we can't really do four or five books every year; we also make films, we photograph, we do shows. It's a lot.

RC: One technical question: do you work with a distributor?

AP: Right now, we have a distributor in Japan for 12 books, and one in the United Kingdom for 10 books. We cover distribution in Europe and in the United States directly to bookshops by ourselves. It has become a huge problem recently. In the last few days, we sold to two bookstores, one from Korea and one from China. There isn't one European bookstore that came up to us at Offprint and said they wanted our books. Some are gone, others are not asking for books; Kominek is among the very few. Which means that our books are nowhere. We don't know what to do about this. Maybe go back home and try to contact them. For some reason, distribution is suddenly again a big problem.

JPC: It's also a problem for small bookshops, and even for institutions like Le Bal. They're having problems, according to them.

RC: I was about to ask how many brick-and-mortar bookshops you work with ...

AP: We used to work with 20 to 30 bookshops. Nowadays less, but we're somewhat to blame. This year we each had two museum shows, so we were a little less active in the distribution than we usually are. And you need to be so active, you have to get them to reorder or it just fades away.

JPC: The books are in 20 shops?

AP: The new ones no, but in general yes.

JPC: We're talking about the new ones.

RC: Do you sell on Amazon?

AP: Not Amazon, nothing of that kind. They do book dumping, as you know, and we can't afford that. Our books are in small print runs and we can't sell them to shops at a fair price and have Amazon dump them. Their prices are not fair. Even for ourselves, and our online shop, which is growing quite well. If Amazon was there selling our books for less than us, that would fuck us up.

RC: Michael Mack told me the same thing.

AP: It makes sense.

JPC: We were talking with André about the beginnings of Offprint. We couldn't remember how many people were there; but I think only Mörel and us were there at the beginning. I'm not so sure if Kominek even existed. And Aron Mörel [see *Conversations 2*, p. 108] had perhaps only two books. Around 2003/2004, Yannick Bouillis[7] had the Shashin bookshop in Amsterdam and I contacted him when I published *Silence*. At the time, my girlfriend was Dutch. So I went to Amsterdam and gave him five copies; he paid for them and we stayed in touch. Then in 2009 we were still working on *Lisboa* and I was in Amsterdam – we had never met again since. I was walking in the streets and spotted a furniture shop. I ventured in, there was a corridor and at the end of it, I see JH Engström's *Haunts*, published with Steidl [see *Conversations*, p. 84 and 92].

[7] *Yannick Bouillis founded the Offprint photobook fair.*

I recognized the cover, so I walked in and there was Yannick. He tells me that the shop is not going well and that he's closing it. He tells me how difficult it is, etc. And then he tells me about this crazy idea he has: "We need to do something for all these people who publish books." I told him that he should drop me an email when he launched something. And later in 2009 I received this email from Yannick about this fair for small publishers. I thought that was the stupidest idea ever. He couldn't be serious ... Could we ever consider spending the money to go to Paris and make maybe 20 or 30 euros back? [Laughs] Who would buy our books? We said yes in the end. The process of *Lisboa* was going fast and we thought we could take it along. We were in Paris in 2010 for the first edition of Offprint. There were about 20 tables. Markus Schaden was there, as well as something like 15 publishers, and a few magazines.

RC: I remember well.

JPC: I was telling him the other day that on one hand, he could have written me an email anyway, and on the other, there are these small happy occurrences, like bumping into him on the street. And 10 years later, we're here at the École des Beaux Arts in Paris.

RC: I was amazed at the first Offprint. I knew Yannick by name because I bought a few books from him. I remember it was far from the city centre, near the Père Lachaise [cemetery]. They were so many young people around, many of them probably students, speaking Dutch, English, German ... I felt, right there and then, that something was changing for the photobook. So many interested young people. It was so crowded for the opening, with people pouring out on the street, and during the whole weekend. This was a turning point.

AP: Out of all the fairs we've been to, that one was where we made the most money ever. Something like 8,000 euros.

JPC: Yannick Bouillis and Markus Schaden were instrumental at the beginning of our story. During the first edition of Offprint,

I told Markus I had this dummy for my book about Israel, *Things Here and Things Still to Come*. We were selling a print for each pre-order and Markus saw it; in 5 to 10 minutes, he sent me 20 people, just like that… So many people. That's the Markus effect for you. But the days of the expert are over. The experts used to be Gerry Badger and Markus. Back then, to have your book on Markus's table was a very big thing. It was like being published. It was a form of validation, because people were going to pay attention to his selection. He cared for books. Things have changed. There are no more experts in that sense.

RC: Yes, the industry has grown democratic, in a way. Everyone thinks of themselves as expert or that they are able to select books. Anyone with an interest in books believes they know it all.

AP: It is also about the end of the underground. You would go to Markus's table then and wonder how on earth he could come up with this weird Bulgarian book… And another from Russia, and three from Japan. And they were all great. There was this notion that he was finding something for you, something you would never have found without Markus. But now, because of the internet, you just have windows to the world, one after the other. Nothing is hidden.

RC: A the same time, in the beginning I was hoping that the internet would be a great way to discover new unknown things from South America or Japan… It was the case for some time, but it no longer is, or rarely so. For me, at least. I feel we need to pay tribute to booksellers. No doubt Markus was a great one, but I still always discover books when I go to Yvon Lambert or to Le Bal.

AP: Yes, that's true, they are book curators.

Le 12 novembre 2018

DONOVAN WYLIE

Donovan Wylie was born in 1971 in Belfast, Northern Ireland, where he lives and works. He joined Magnum Photos in 1992. His work is present in the collections of the most prestigious museums of contemporary art, including the Metropolitan Museum of Art and the George Eastman Museum in New York; the National Gallery in Ontario; the Pompidou Centre in Paris; the Victoria and Albert Museum in London; and Pier 24 Photography in San Francisco, among others. In 2002 he received a BAFTA for his film, The Train, *and was nominated for the Deutsche Börse Photography Foundation Prize in 2010. To date, he is the author of 14 books.*

Donovan Wylie was a precocious photographer. He took his first pictures aged around 13 years old and published his first book, *32 Counties: Photographs of Ireland*, at 19 in 1989. Five more books were to follow, all in black and white, marked by both the British social documentary tradition and the influence of Walker Evans. Though quite interesting, this first part of his career is now overshadowed by his later works in colour, starting with *The Maze* (2004), which allowed him to develop the notion of "conflict architecture" associated with a strict photographic strategy. He focused on that theme for nearly a decade. One of the strengths of Donovan Wylie's work, besides his rigour, is that, from his own, local experience of the Northern Irish conflict, he is able to stretch his gaze out to distant events. More recently, he has been considering civilian issues in which violence, urban or topographical, is pregnant. Skype conversation between Paris and Göttingen.

Rémi Coignet: *So, you are at Steidl's in Göttingen, printing a new book.*

Donovan Wylie: Yes, printing the book and preparing an exhibition. It's the first time that I've conceive an exhibition here at Steidl's.

RC: What will the book and the exhibition be about?

DW: The book is a project I'd been talking about with Gerhard Steidl [see *Conversations 2*, p. 210] for a long time. It's about social housing defence structures[1]. The exhibition comes from a project I made in the US over the past two years.

RC: Is this the project in New Haven, parallel to Jim Goldberg's?[2]

DW: Yes, exactly. We're printing some of that work for a big show at Pier 24 in California.

RC: You were born in 1971 in Belfast in a country at war. Which was unique in the European Community and later in the European Union: both Ireland and Great Britain became members in 1973 and the war in Northern Ireland ended at the end of the 1990s. I don't like to relate artists' personal stories to their art, but have these facts influenced your approach to photography?

DW: My mother was very Catholic, and my father was Protestant ...

RC: And that's very special?

DW: Yes. Completely. At the time when I grew up, there were few from different backgrounds to get married. I think we all felt a little bit on the outside. We felt we didn't belong to one side or the other. My mother was an art teacher, my father was a painter. They met in art college. My dad became a filmmaker. Art was always in our life.
I discovered photography when I was really young, like 12, 13. One day, I went into my parent's bedroom, I can't remember why exactly, but I was looking for something, and I saw a camera lying on the bed. It looked beautiful. I picked it up and took it to my bedroom. I took it completely apart and I couldn't put it back together. I was worried my father would be upset but he wasn't, and that's when I sold my bicycle

[1] *The book* Housing Plans for the Future *released by Steidl in July 2018.*

[2] The book *A Good and Spacious Land* released by Yale University Press in 2017.

and bought a camera. I felt free. I felt that nobody could see what I was thinking, nobody could hear what I was saying. I felt I had total freedom. During the conflict, I felt people were being forced by different sides to have polarizing positions, and with the camera, you really felt you could be autonomous. I remember taking photographs for two years with no film in the camera. I only started putting film into it when people said, "Can we see your pictures?" Suddenly, I had to try to make a picture.

Before, it was instinct, I felt what I saw and the world we were in. It was the conflict that actually brought me to photography because it enabled me to be myself and not compromise my own feelings, my own sense of identity. It enabled me to be young and free, to feel things honestly and naturally, without stereotype or pressure. That's how I came to photography.

RC: I won't ask you if your work is political, as that seems obvious… but how do you see your work in a political frame?

DW: It's a good question, because I don't actively see it as political. I'm not an activist, but I work in the context of history. I'm a photographer in Northern Ireland. History made me become a photographer, which clearly implies that you're going to deal with real life, and real life is political. The hardest thing for me in photography has been to transcend the political. For example, *The Maze* is about a historical place, and a very political one.[3] But I couldn't represent it in that light because I didn't experience it. What I did learn, though, was that the architecture of it was very mechanical. I also learned something else: human architectural repetition can be a form of control. And that transcends politics. It brings into question the way in which human beings operate as a species. That interested me because it made me feel human and helped me to understand what it was to be human.

[3] *The Maze was a prison near Belfast that served as detention centre during the conflict for a few Loyalists and mostly Nationalists. It is regrettably known for the hunger strike initiated by IRA prisoners. Faced with Margaret Thatcher's inflexibility, the action led to the death of Bobby Sand. Built in 1971, the Maze was closed in 2000 before it was razed to the ground.*

I work in a political context but I'm not a political photographer; I'd say I'm probably more of a historical one.

> *RC: Your first book was called* 32 Counties: Photographs of Ireland, *thus including the 6 counties in Northern Ireland and the 26 counties in the Republic of Ireland. Was it a manifesto?*

DW: Not at all. No. I think everybody in Ireland, no matter what your political persuasion is, understands and welcomes the idea of being Irish. No, that book was about being 17 years old and travelling the island of Ireland and discovering it as a very young person. The last thing it had was a political angle.

> *RC: You published in 1989, at merely 18 years old ... This is quite young to publish ...*

DW: It was published in 1989 but I did it in late '87/88. Don't forget, coming from my background, coming from a mixed marriage, the conflict came from the outside of ourselves. I was living in a bubble. My parents created a world where art was my life, not politics. It was innocent. I had a strong ego. I wanted to make a book. I wanted to try to understand my identity. I wanted to take pictures like Walker Evans. That was my agenda.

> *RC: So you published a book very early on; how important is the book form in the presentation of your work?*

DW: I love the book. I love the photobook as much as the novel. The photobook is where I started, actually - where I discovered photography. It's probably my singular place of expression. I love the photobook because it connects with literature, with albums, with the notion of the storyteller. It's an intimate experience, you and the book. *The Maze*, as you know, was really designed and conceived as a book. It has been exhibited many times, and that was always a struggle because it wasn't made to be an exhibition. The whole point of the book was to be entrapped in a page, to be locked into a page, without knowing what's coming next. But with the gallery, you can see it all at once. So, the experience of the book, through a book, is important. The book is my essential vehicle of communication as an artist.

As we said earlier, I'm now printing for a show, working on similar pictures, but it's interesting that some of them are very large. It's very different from the book and at the same time very similar. The book and the wall have always been friends of mine, they're connected. In fact, I teach students to try to identify where they best feel themselves: the book or the wall? Because I feel that they are elements of identity for yourself as an artist. I believe they can both coexist. But I have a deep love for the photobook as a means of communication. Primarily its intimacy, linked with literature; and the tactility of it, the paper, the printing, all the various aspects of its conception. The book is permanent. One problem I have with exhibitions is that for every new show you have to create a new experience, which I find difficult. Whereas with the book, it's there… it's the closest thing I know to making a recorded album, a studio album. You know I'm here at Steidl's, and when I come here, I always feel like we're in a recording studio. Yesterday morning at 7 a.m. I was asleep… the phone rang and it was Gerhard. He said, "Come to the press." And you know it's a truly historical moment: you get up, you get dressed, you walk out of your room, and you enter the production area, the press. It is like walking into a studio to record your album. I always found it amazing when musical artists talk about making their 14th studio album. It compares with when you make a book, especially here, at Steidl's. You have that studio feeling because there are other artists coming in. There is this feeling that we're going to put something down, it's going to live. That's a special feeling tied to the photobook.

RC: Very interesting. And after 32 Counties, *in 1992 together with writer Robert McLiam Wilson, you published* The Dispossessed. *Not going as far as saying that it is a protest of the Thatcher era, can we say that you were "angry young men"*[4]*?*

[4] *Name given to a group of British writers in the 1950s who rejected the traditional elitist system. Their main characters, often underprivileged, fought against society and the Establishment.*

DW: Robert was, more than me. I was angry to make work. He was angry politically. But we were both pretty young, you know. I haven't seen him in a while, but back then, he was a genius writer. You need to understand that all my first publishers were literary publishers, they weren't art or photo publishers. So my world was that of writers, not photographers. I was studying photography, but my community was that of writers, and Robert was part of it. He was a very successful young novelist. As far as I was concerned, I wanted to make a project about feeling alone, and the book is based on George Orwell. Robert really wanted to write something equivalent to George Orwell's *Down and Out in Paris and London* ... I was just angry to be making pictures about being young, angry and feeling lonely ... not knowing how I was going to go about it, and at the same time trying to find a photographic voice. I was super, super young in my photographic life. If you look at some of the pictures in that book, you'll see that I was literally obsessed with Walker Evans. *Labour Anonymous* by Walker Evans: I was trying to get that same raw feeling that he so brilliantly succeeded in capturing. I really wanted to publish, but it was a tough one to make. Robert was slow. We helped each other a lot. We pushed each other a lot. We disagreed a lot. That book is a book about friendship more than anything.

RC: I don't want to spend too long on your books from the 1990s, but in 1994 you published Notes from Moscow *and in 1998 the book on New Age travellers,* Losing Ground. *What led you to these subjects?*

DW: I went to Russia because Robert said I should go. I had just joined Magnum Photos, I was 20 years old, and very young. And you know what? Going to Moscow at 20 was unbelievable for me. It was in 1991, Communism had collapsed. It was an extraordinary time. But I wasn't a photojournalist, I had never conceived a photographic story in my life. I didn't speak Russian; it was very difficult for me. I photographed Moscow like Walker Evans would have. I was walking around taking pictures of streets, of buildings, working in medium format, and Magnum was expecting stories. I simply didn't understand what they meant by "story". I'm not being critical about it;

I just didn't get it. They were good times. And how I found myself in Moscow was very funny: I had found a place to stay via an ad in the paper. I stayed with this woman and her family in the outskirts of Moscow, and it was just insane. Then, I met a friend called Igor ... he was a student. We became friends. I moved into his flat and we lived together for several years. We're still friends. One day, one evening, the news was on, the tanks were blasting parliament in Moscow[5], Yeltsin was in power, and at the same time Igor was telling me that Moscow was having its first reggae concert that same night. I had to go to the reggae concert – I was young, you know... Moscow was one of my universities. I was a very bad photojournalist. I didn't follow the news, but I lived the experience of being young in Moscow. Perhaps *Notes from Moscow* is not a good book because it was published by a literary publisher, Picador. Anyway, that's how I ended up in Moscow.
The travellers project, which was really important to me, was a true experience. I met these young people of my generation; and I was with Magnum, trying to photograph like an old Magnum photographer. I had dropped my Walker Evans and my medium format. I was shooting with 35mm. The experience and the work were really good. But to be honest with you, this was in the 1990s and I think I knew how to take a good picture, which isn't hard. I knew my voice and myself, and I knew what it was to be an outsider. I identified with that position and I photographed that. But I never had any education in critiquing and I was quite behind in that. So the 1990s was a period of big crisis for me... in fact, I gave up photography – I gave up the one thing that saved my life.

RC: These books made in the 1990s are in black and white and are produced in the British social documentary tradition. I was wondering if back then Chris Killip was a big influence for you.

DW: Chris Killip was and still is a big influence. If you look at those early books, you'll see huge copycat pictures

[5] *On 4 October 1993, during a political crisis opposing President Yeltsin and Parliament, the army surrounded the building before using force.*

of Chris Killip or Walker Evans. But when I joined Magnum, my picture style changed. I went into reportage and I loved it. But it was also problematic, because there was a new wave coming up in photography that I was not aware of, and I had to study it. After *Losing Ground*, I felt I needed to study photography. There was too much happening within the photo world, so many questions about the medium that you just couldn't ignore it. I realized I was behind and had to study. So what I did was I went to Martin Parr's house [see *Conversations 2*, p. 148], something like every two weeks or every month. And for two years, I basically studied every single book on his shelves. That's how *The Maze* was born, and that was a game changer for me.

RC: For your generation, it's odd not to have gone to photography school ...

DW: Well, there was no or very little education in photography when I was young. In the United Kingdom there was Newport, which Paul Seawright was running; you had the great English team with Martin [Parr], Paul Graham [see *Conversations*, p. 116] and Chris Killip, who went to teach at Harvard. But yes, education was very minimal ... It's different now. But it's absolutely essential if you want to be a contemporary photographer, and it's also related to the market ... Since the 1970s, photography was in a new development stage, in which I was finding a new platform and a new voice in a young medium. I would actually argue that Walker Evans influenced that; he influenced Ed Ruscha, not many people know that. And of course, Walker Evans discovered [Eugène] Atget, because he went to a lecture by James Joyce in Paris. So the whole literary connection was already there. Look at what Evans contributed. It led on to Robert Frank, his diaristic narrative, the perception of time, of light ... The main point was, however, that the medium had evolved in a way that I totally didn't understand. Rémi, to be honest with you, given my context, I thought it was impossible for me to go on with photography. So I thought, "Fuck photography! I can't do it!" I went on and made movies and did really well at it. I won awards.

But my heart was in photography. I knew I needed a subject I had a connection with, that I could represent clearly, and that was metaphorical as well. But I had no fucking clue what that was. At that time, remember, everybody was shooting their family or their feet. I really believed photography was over for me.

And then, completely out of the blue, this great woman, Louise Purbrick, asked me to photograph the Maze prison. This was just after the peace protests, the first ceasefire, the first released prisoners from the Maze...

> *RC: That was my next question: you were shooting in black and white, then you published* The Maze *and your style changed radically.*

DW: Yes, looking back, the first book was published in 1989 and the next one in 2004. Fifteen years. Fifteen years of wilderness. And when Louise invited me, I said no. I told her I couldn't go there. It represented so many things ... You know my parents came from different backgrounds and they found a way to be together. The conflict ruined many people's lives; even if you weren't directly concerned by it, you couldn't not be affected by it. So I didn't want to go there. She asked again. It was in partnership with a museum.

Then I went to Martin Parr's house for Christmas; we were talking... I told him I'd been offered this and he insisted: "You have to go and look at it!" and I did. From the moment I walked in, I felt I had to work there. But I didn't know how to photograph it. And *The Maze* began.

> *RC: And you radically changed your style: you used a large format camera and colour film ...*

DW: Two or three things. I didn't radically change, but I didn't know what to do. One of the first things I did was to buy a 4x5 view camera. I bought it in a bomb-damaged shop, so I got it cheap because it was bomb-damaged. You know, Rémi, I nearly never use the 35mm. My first camera was a Praktica. I got rid of it in a week and went straight on to the Yashica-Mat – loved it, stayed with it, moved on to a Mamiya 645 and then to the 4x5.

Then I went backwards by taking up photography and joined Magnum again.
I needed security, I wanted security. I went for a Leica, an interesting camera, and went to the Maze, except that I had no idea how to shoot it. I was obsessed with how to represent a place. I had a connection with that one because I was from Northern Ireland, but how to do it? I looked at Stephen Shore's *American Surfaces*.
There was a prison guard with me while I toured the prison and photographed surfaces in the hope that that they might reveal something deeper. It was an embarrassing disaster. Then I figured that I needed a view camera to take architectural images. I thought I could do it in a week. I went back to London, sent the films to the lab, the lab processed and scanned the films, and sent them back with a CD. For the first time, I was looking at my images on the computer. It was a form of digital photography that wasn't digital photography. I looked at the work and thought it was brilliant. Then I looked at it again; on Tuesday ... yes, it's good; on Wednesday ... it's not so bad; on Thursday ... is it good? On Friday ... it's not good; Saturday ... it's shit! On Sunday ... I've got to go back! This lasted a year. My problem was that I didn't have any visual strategy and I didn't know how to represent the place. But I did have a strong emotional experience there, because you could walk around for nearly an hour feeling you've never really moved because the place was so monotonous. I did give up the project two or three times, until one day I stumbled upon some architectural plans of the prison. You must keep in mind that at that point, everything was still there when I was photographing, as if the occupants had run away leaving everything behind; it was all still there, including documents. I studied the plan and asked the prison guard what these areas were in the prison that I couldn't get to because they were locked off. They had all these strange and funny names like "inertias" or "steriles". I then realized that the building was a man-made trap, architecturally designed to control and keep people in. This gave me the lead to photograph the building. For instance, the perimeter being divided into 36 spaces, I'd photograph all 36 spaces. The funny thing is to get to space 9 and to tell yourself, "Donovan [Laughs], it doesn't matter whether you like that picture or not!"

RC: Yes, what a terrible place. Too many people, 10 or 12 persons perhaps, who died of their hunger strike.

DW: Yes, but that's part of its history and I couldn't represent that. The only thing I could represent was the system in place, its architectural logic. The building being divided into 36 similar zones, I had to photograph every one of them. So, I had to create a process based on the system, its inherent logic. If I could pull that off, then I could create a piece where people could bring their own stories related to the place.

RC: Let's talk about what do you mean by "architecture of conflict".

DW: I mean architectural structures whose conception is based on the context. I'm interested in looking at those and understanding them. It's somewhat academic, but it's fascinating to me. *The Maze* became a model for me in photographic terms. I learned from that project to work on the logic of the architectural system, and at the same time on the logic of the use of the camera. I think of myself more as an operator than a photographer. So you learn a lot from looking at these places. You must understand that the Northern Ireland conflict began in the late 1960s right through the 1970s. These were the Cold War years, and the East/West divide was very clear. I grew up in this terrorist war. The architecture that was designed to deal with our conflict was actually super modern. Let me give you an example: during the Cold War, military structures were called military bases. But when you think of current conflicts, they're now called camps, right? ... The shift in terms shows the transient nature of today's conflicts. So much of the modern architecture that is built today is actually derived from the designs that the English made in Northern Ireland. This, to me, was absolutely fascinating, and it became my line of practice. I saw how structures conceived for the North Ireland conflict were reused in Afghanistan and Iraq. I remember arriving in Afghanistan and seeing the same military structures that I had grown up with on a day-to-day basis. When I'm photographing them, I'm not really photographing Iraq or Afghanistan, even if that's what I did; actually,

I'm photographing my own home and seeing how it's transmuted to somewhere else. And that brought me to exploring notions of history and memory, which in turn led me to the Arctic, because when they left Afghanistan the Canadians reinforced their presence in the Arctic, reproducing there the same structures. In many ways, my work is not political, it's about the notion of empire.
When I left the Arctic, I thought I was done with photography. I was in front of a blank page: either I dropped it or I tried something new. I thought to myself, thanks to a couple of friends, what other country has risen from a fallen world?

RC: And?

DW: That can only be America.

RC: One last thing about The Maze. *In the Steidl version, you've added a second volume in which you represent the destruction of the prison. And the title became:* Maze, *and no longer* The Maze.

DW: To be honest, I don't remember. It's a good question. I'm trying to remember. I think Gerhard wanted to get rid of the "The". Linguistically, it made more sense. "The" makes it a specific project. "Maze" carries the concept that covers the work, which can be extended to other situations. The Maze is a historical place that I represented as best I could. The work is a lived experience through an architectural system, and I think that it's more generic without "The".

RC: Sorry to insist on this point, but in the Steidl edition again, you added a second volume about the destruction. Do you see that as a will to erase, or on the contrary, to move forward?

DW: This is an important question. It is a way to move forward. It's an incredible story. I had no photographic strategy to represent the destruction of the Maze. I didn't know how to go about it. When you have no strategy for a subject that's there, it's no problem, you can put it aside for a while. But when something is about to disappear, you start to worry.

At the time, I was reading *Peeling the Onion* by Günter Grass, with his notions of "strata" and "crimes". I was looking at the destruction of the Maze, and that's exactly what was applied: the walls were falling one after the other, from the outside to the inside. I don't know if that makes sense, but I decided that I had to photograph it like that. Like peeling an onion as Günter Grass said. A large part of the site was still standing so I could work on that idea.
When you look at the book, you feel like the layers are slowly vanishing. And with each layer, I could see the mess that it was, and in which I was born. Every day a layer was erased, and I cried.
In the end, the entire onion got peeled and there was nothing left. And there were no answers. That made me think that you can never understand. Which is a form of acceptance, or liberation. But when the last wall fell, something remained ...

RC: In 2007 you published British Watchtowers. *I have a few questions. What is the meaning of the numbers and letters on the left pages?*

DW: They are the military names for each watchtower.
So if it says R12, that would be Romeo 12 – that would be the name of that site. And Romeo 12 might be looking at G40 – that would be Golf 40. So it's important to understand that the *Watchtowers* series is a matrix, like a digital matrix: everything that's looking at it can connect back to itself. The coverage is complete; it's a panopticon in a landscape.

RC: You were talking about Louise Purbrick earlier. In her essay she says that watchtowers are as old as the war, and she gives the example of the Great Wall of China, but it could also be compared with Hadrian's Wall in Great Britain.

DW: Yes, it could. That was one of the ideas behind the work. We're looking at modern structures, modern technology, modern surveillance, but actually the function, motivation and execution is as old as history. You take high ground and you observe. And that's why I went to Afghanistan: because when those structures were taken down and reused, it made me think about the need to talk about what history means and how our identities play out in time.

RC: You mean the same structures used on the Northern Ireland border were transferred to Afghanistan?

DW: Yes, elements of these structures were used and sent to Afghanistan, and Iraq too.

RC: About the watchtowers again, there are a few images in the book in which they are invisible. I was wondering if you ever photographed from one of these towers.

DW: No, I wasn't allowed to. But I was allowed to be in a helicopter, so I photographed it all from a helicopter. And the view that you see when there is no watchtower is the view that you would see from the watchtower. I wouldn't literally photograph that from the watchtower, because I wasn't allowed to, but from a helicopter. And I wasn't allowed to land on the sites either.

RC: There are three or four foldouts in the book, also double-page spreads. Was the purpose to show the reader how they are inscribed in the landscape?

DW: Yes, I found them fascinating structures, quite opposite to the extraordinarily pastoral nature of the landscape. I loved that tension between the object of the watchtower and the landscape it was set in. And I was also photographing very systematically: I would photograph the watchtower from four positions – east, west, north and south – and from two distances, and I would also photograph its view in the same way. I would photograph north, south, east, west and I would photograph it from the tower. Yes, there was an objective, and yes, these structures are extraordinary... in the same way the Bechers found industrial architecture fascinating. Because of what they reveal about the human condition, I find military structures fascinating. These structures completely reveal something of our own power and fragility and functionality.

RC: In 2009 you published Scrapbook, *a mix of your family photographs and various materials relating to the Troubles – press clippings, propaganda documents from both sides, etc. Was it a way to bring closure to your Irish work?*

DW: If I'm honest with you, the whole project was about coming home. It was trying to make sense of the place I'd left and to find a way back home. *Scrapbook* was very personal. The book itself was about scrapbooks and the nature of scrapbooks in Ireland and how the personal and the political coexist. In fact, that's how the book is designed: to fall apart to show memory and the fragility of memory. Conceptually that's what the book is about, but it's also personal, about me coming home. Every piece of work I make is personal … and you know, it should be. *Scrapbook* was about accepting the past, about coming home, and about vomiting up the history to start anew. I made it in collaboration with Timothy Prus, who was a great collaborator; it was an amazing collaboration with a brilliant brain. I couldn't have done it without him. It's our work. It wasn't necessarily putting an end to the Irish work; rather, it was a way to say, "I want to come back home." And I did. Once the book was published, I went home, I went back to Ireland.

RC: You mentioned Outposts: Kandahar Province *(2011) earlier. You photographed outposts, but were you able to see from their location, their view, as well?*

DW: I had no access, I had to be very careful …

RC: So, it was the same as …

DW: It was the exact same strategy as *British Watchtowers.*

RC: Right.

DW: Some of the pictures are taken from the helicopter, some of them are from the base. No, I didn't photograph from literally inside the watchtower, for security reasons. I couldn't do that. I did want to turn one of the watchtowers into a pinhole camera, but I wasn't allowed to do that either. However, I could stand by them and photograph the view from there. So, from fairly close. It was the same idea as for *British Watchtowers*, the idea of who's looking at who ... The idea of vision ... One thing that is central to all the work I made is how vision is about control.

RC: Yes, indeed.

DW: Not so much any more because I'm making different work now, but back then all that work was about vision as control. It goes back to photography and how I started photography, understanding how vision gave me control of myself. All those books were based on that notion of the power of vision. It was a united moment of personal history and photography and contemporary history.

RC: North Warning System *is supposed to be your last book on military surveillance. Do you consider yourself finished with this project?*

DW: I'm not finished with the notions of architecture and conflict. But I will close a chapter of it with this book. I grew up in a place where we had a lot of military infrastructure surrounding us. I photographed it; it's gone. I photographed the Maze; it's gone. And what's interesting is that through a colleague in architecture, through freedom of information, we learned that many parts of Belfast, the urban environment and the basic housing, what we grew up with, was completely designed by the military.[5] The military structures are all gone, but in fact it was involved all the way through to the domestic. You think of the military, you think of watchtowers and prisons, but actually it goes down to your local street [Laughs].

RC: In some ways, the book North Warning System *is like* The Maze*: a kind of zoom forward to an Arctic watchtower. You start from very far and come very close at the end of the book? Why?*

[5] *The subject of* Housing Plans for the Future, *the book that Donovan Wylie was printing when we were having this conversation.*

DW: It's a very hard place to photograph. It's on the northern tip of Labrador. And you have all the responsibility in terms of your own security and many other things. I did it that way because it's a radar. No one lives there. I wanted this idea of going around it, as if I were a radar, a pulse. It's looking at something, with no human being inside it. It's a machine, it's looking at something, but there's nothing there.

RC: There's no one?

DW: No, and that's what was exciting for me: why would they put that structure there if nothing is there? That can only mean two things: there has been something there or there will be something there. I wanted to end with that idea, using the system of a radar.

RC: About your recent work (we talked about this at Paris Photo) – you published A Good and Spacious Land *with Jim Goldberg, focusing on a new highway interchange in New Haven, Connecticut. After war-torn landscapes, could civil topography be a new focus of interest?*

DW: I've always worked on topography. America was a very interesting experience for me. Again, it felt that I was done with my practice after the Arctic. I felt like you should always finish with a white canvas and see what happens. I realized that America was a country that had that idea – of wanting to start again when it's all finished. It was a new world, a new idea. I had some friends there who invited me. I went with absolutely no idea of what I was going to photograph. Zero. But it was an opportunity with Jim Goldberg to try to start a new song, start a new understanding, and yet retain something of past experiences. So yes, I photographed the highway, the construction of the highway. I did it because I found it visually interesting. Then I did some research and I couldn't believe it: the American road system was called "interface" and "defence highway". This meant that I was looking at another architecture of conflict, and that enabled me to find myself in my own context in America and learn something new.

My book and Jim's book are fundamentally about mythology and myths. They're completely coming from our own context and stories. Jim's book is about a man who ran away from New Haven[6] and then came back. A man who ran out of petrol ... well, no [Laughs], not quite, but a man who was done with a practice and then found a new way to work in America.

RC: A few years ago I bought at Le Bal a small book entitled Donovan Wylie One Day Taking Photographs in Belfast. *At first glance, it looked like a fun story of a photographer being photographed. But if you look closely, you are in fact photographing walls and fences. Does it mean that the partition of Northern Ireland is still a reality?*

DW: OK, so two things ... That book was made by a truly great friend of mine, whom I love and share many ideas with, and who helps me with my ideas and gives me direction. We're close friends and in some way it's also a book about a funny photographer. Peter Mann, who made the book, sees me a bit in that way. So that's the context of the book.
Now, as I said, I'm from a mixed marriage, my mother was Catholic, my father was Protestant. Both care about things other than their religious status. I hope Brexit offers Northern Ireland a chance to have a special status within Europe, to be beneficial to everybody. I know it's hard for some to accept that, and it probably won't happen. We didn't vote for it; we didn't want to leave Europe.[7] Nearly half the population sees us as Irish and European.
And I love my Protestant friends and my Catholic friends. We are together. We've got to be smart about this. Northern Ireland, north of Ireland, we must do the best thing for us, for our people. I do think there are opportunities for Northern Ireland and opportunities for both sides.

RC: There we are back to the start of our talk. Ireland and its 32 counties ... It would be crazy to have a new border between Northern Ireland and Eire.

[6] *Jim Goldberg was born in New Haven in 1954.*

[7] *55.8% of the Northern Irish population voted to remain in the European Union.*

DW: Yes, that would absolutely not be beneficial. That's not what we want. That can't happen. No way there's going to be a border. We must be smart, we can't alienate our own friends… so we must be smart, figure it out economically, financially. If Northern Ireland had special status, it would be amazing. What's dangerous about Brexit for Northern Ireland is it makes us polarized, and that is a major problem, we don't need that. My parents came from two completely different backgrounds and the thing that united them was their love for each other and their artistic practice. They came from different backgrounds, but they never left their own families and they loved them both. That's Irish.

21 March 2018

INDEX

ACKNOWLEDGEMENTS

My gratitude, of course, goes to all those who have agreed to devote time to answering my questions.

I thank my friend and publisher, Vincent Marcilhacy, the team at *The Eyes* as well as Nathalie Amae, Irène Attinger, Jessica Backhaus, Simon Baker, Dirk Bakker, Pierre Bessard, Daniel Blaufuks, Yannick Bouillis, Patrizia Brandellero, Elina Brotherus, Olivier Cablat, Yseult Chehata, François Cheval, Federica Chiocchetti, Henri et Anne-Marie Coignet, Samantha Conlon, Pierre-Louis Denis, Jean-Marie Donat, Diane Dufour, Jean-Kenta Gauthier, Émilie Hanmer, Julie Héraut, Kevin Jones, Émilie Lauriola, Audrey Leclerc, Fanny Legros, Marie Lesbats, Charlotte Magné, Dieter Neubert, Tiffanie Pascal, Magali Peretti, Jérôme Poggi, Didier Quilain, Louise Réau, Patrick Rémy, Kurt Salchli, Cristina Sannini, Markus Schaden, Agnès Sire, Jérôme Sother, Sam Stourdzé, Christine Vidal, Françoise Vogt, Fabrice Wagner and Giulia Zorzi.

Very special thanks to Fannie Escoulen for her sensible advice, as well as to my precious friend Frédérique Destribats who has always been present.

Editorial conception: Rémi Coignet and The Eyes Publishing
Graphic design: Louise Réau, based on an original design by Magali Peretti
Typography: Garamond, Suisse Int'l, ArcherPro

English transcription: Samantha Conlon
French transcription: Rémi Coignet, Karin Crona, Julie Delabarre
Translation: Frédérique Destribats
Proofreading: Myriam Birch

www.theeeyes.eu – www.theeyespublishing.eu

Printed by Jelgavas Tipografija, Latvia, April 2020
Legal Deposit: April 2020

ISBN: 979-10-92727-36-4

With publishing support from cnap
Centre national des arts plastiques